Women Leading in Education

WOMEN LEADING IN EDUCATION

Diane M. Dunlap

AND

Patricia A. Schmuck, editors

State University of New York Press

Published by
State University of New York Press, Albany

© 1995 State University of New York

Printed in the United States of America

For information, address the State University of New York Press,
90 State Street, Suite 700, Albany, NY 12207

Production by Marilyn P. Semerad
Marketing by Dana E. Yanulavich

Library of Congress Cataloging-in-Publication Data

Women leading in education / Diane M. Dunlap and Patricia A. Schmuck,
    editors.
        p.   cm.
    Includes bibliographical references and index.
    ISBN 0-7914-2215-1 (acid-free paper).—0-7914-2216-X (pbk.
    : acid-free paper)
    1. Women school administrators.   2. Educational leadership.
3. Feminism and education.   4. School management and organization.
5. Women educators.   I. Dunlap, Diane M.   II. Schmuck, Patricia A.
LB2831.8.W66 1994
371.2'01—dc20   94-7301
                                                                   CIP

10 9 8 7 6 5 4 3 2

CONTENTS

We dedicate this book to all members past, present, and future of Research on Women in Education, a Special Interest Group of the American Educational Research Association.

Research on Women in Education is in its 20th year; much of the research on gender in education has been authored by past or current members. Members of this group have forged new pathways to change policies and practices in educational research and practice, have provided a safe haven to test new concepts, and have provided personal and professional support for many researchers who often found their work devalued by colleagues in their home universities.

FOREWORD

Charol Shakeshaft

We need this book. In a country where 71% of all K-12 teachers and 88% of elementary teachers are female, it is more than curious that by 1993, only 7.3% of superintendents, 24% of assistant superintendents, and 34% of principals are female (Montenegro, 1993). There is still much we do not know about sex discrimination, about female career patterns, about women leaders, and about inclusive conceptualizations of managerial and administrative theory. This book takes us farther down these roads toward a better understanding of women in leadership.

The chapters add to the body of knowledge about women leaders, filling in and illuminating the unknown categorized nearly a decade ago in Stages of Research on Women in Administration. These stages represent inquiry which seek to answer the following questions:

- How many women are school administrators and at what levels?
- What are the historical, demographic, career, psychological, and family characteristics of women who are school administrators?
- Why are there so few women school administrators?
- How do women administer and how do they describe their work as school administrators?
- Are the experiences of women explained or illuminated by managerial and administrative theory?
- What theories explain women's lives as leaders?

(Shakeshaft, 1987)

Surprisingly, after nearly two decades of attention to the underrepresentation of women in school administration, it is still difficult to systematically and accurately track the number of women in school administration. The most often used and available source is the periodic American Association of School Administrators (AASA) survey of chief state school officers. Although these are the best data available, even the AASA counts are not complete: "Forty-nine states and Washington, D.C., responded to the survey, although not all had information. Some states had partial data, a few had none, and some had complete information." (Montenegro, 1993, p. i) In addition to not being complete, state-by-state surveys are often not comparable, since states collect data using overlapping categories and job titles. Further, nowhere are we able to determine nationwide the number of women of color in school administration by position. This is not sloppy scholarship by researchers, but rather the lack of a reliable, uniform nationwide data base that lets us know just how many women are school administrators and at what levels. Tyack and Hansot (1982) point out that the absence of such a data base is no mistake and has historical precedent:

> Amid proliferation of other kinds of statistical reporting is an age enamored of numbers—reports so detailed that one could give the precise salary of staff in every community across the country and exact information in all sorts of other variables—data by sex became strangely inaccessible. A conspiracy of silence could hardly have been unintentional (p. 13)

This "conspiracy of silence" has political ramifications. If we don't have annual comparisons by sex and race, it is difficult to know whether things are improving, getting worse, or staying the same. Without such numbers, justification for action is difficult, and it becomes more difficult to identify and, thus, remedy the condition of the underutilization of women in schools.

There is much in this volume that explores the conditions that hinder or help women move into and then stay in school administration. We are learning more about which strategies for entry and advancement work as women confront the world in which time is a zero sum game. However, whether from a structural or a political analysis, we have moved away from understanding the subtleties of sex discrimination in the work world. We still don't know enough about how male gatekeepers function, nor have we made clear the complexities in female to female interactions.

As I travel around the country speaking with administrative groups, a common theme that emerges from my audiences is the belief that women are their own worst enemies. Despite considerable evidence to the contrary, the view that it is other women who keep women from advancing remains strong. Therefore, we need to examine why we cling to a "blame the woman" explanation, while ignoring or discarding what we know about female to female support systems and helping strategies.

Further, when representatives of schools negotiate with me to come and talk to their staffs, they almost always caution me that I must be careful not to upset the men in the audience. The result is that we have begun to act as if male behavior is "off limits" for research and discussion, a trend that will hinder any understanding of sex discrimination in the workplace.

Research on male behavior in school organizations might help us understand the link between organizational sexuality and organizational productivity, as well as identifying some reasons why doors are closed to women. Sexual transactions, some say, contain many of the same components of organizations—use of power, hierarchy, division of labor, and rewards for productivity. Despite case history, the two have traditionally been treated by scholars as unrelated—organizational transactions are public and sexual transactions are private sphere activities. Recently, however, theorists have begun to link the two, but little has been done within a school context. This silence in our organizational theoretical discussions about sexuality has meaning.

For instance, my studies of male superintendents found that one reason some men didn't hire women in key and close positions was that the men believed the sexual tension that they were sure would occur would be too great. For this same reason, male administrators explained that they preferred to work with men, rather than women, on committees and in small groups. Learning about organizational sexuality might identify additional barriers to women as well as linking workplace dynamics and productivity.

Examining productivity and style, this book extends our knowledge of women's leadership and the socialization which may result in gender specific management styles. While some studies document that women are likely to be more participatory than are men, other researchers point out that this style may be the style of newer managers, younger managers, or people who have been disinfranchised. Our understanding of the role of traditional female socialization and the part it plays in the development and refinement of communication and leadership styles that are inclusive and human is pushed farther by the research reported in this book.

The scholars who contributed to this book not only teach us, they move us to action. We learn once more from them what has always been true: research is a political and ideological act. These women have chosen their questions to help inform policy and practice in schools. Thus, this book not only expands our knowledge and data bases, it serves as a manual for action. The researchers in this volume are able to say, as the administrators studied by Bell were not, "Now that I'm a researcher, I can be radical."

Bibliography

Montenegro, X. (1993). *Women and racial minority representation in school administration.* American Association of School Administrators.

Shakeshaft, C. (1987). *Women in educational administration.* Beverly Hills, CA: Sage/Corwin.

Tyack, D., & Hansot, E. (1982). *Managers of virtue: Public school leadership in America, 1820–1980.* New York: Basic Books.

PREFACE

> When we cast our bread upon the waters,
> we can presume that someone down-
> stream whose face we will never know will
> benefit from our action, as we who are
> downstream from another will profit from
> that grantor's gift.
>
> —Maya Angelou, *Wouldn't Take Nothing
> for My Journey Now*

How a book emerges has its own story. This book was first conceived at the 1989 annual conference of the American Educational Research Association (AERA) Special Interest Group on Research on Women in Education (SIG-RWE). Sue Klein, a continuing inspiration for collaborative work, organized a session at that San Diego meeting to "move the sex equity agenda into the 1990s." We met and split the group into topics based on the 1985 *Handbook for Achieving Sex Equity Through Education* (Klein). Sue Klein, Pat Schmuck, Diane Dunlap, Mary Scherr, Colleen Bell, Michelle Collay, Joanne Cooper, Theresa McCormick, P. J. Ford Slack, and Lynn Wallich formed the group on women in the professions. We talked. We argued. We got excited about combining our work. We came up with many ideas and agreed to explore those ideas with our colleagues and to meet again at the next AERA meeting to further explore this new agenda.

The next meeting was held in a Washington, D.C. Hilton Hotel hallway because our group had outgrown the small room assigned to us. We found more new ideas and, although we didn't mean to block the hallway, our group continued to grow throughout that meeting as more and more women researchers were drawn into the conversation when a word captured their attention as they walked past, or a hand drew them into the group with a, "you're just the person we need—can you answer this question?" Subsequent conversations occurred the next years in Chicago, Milwaukee and San

Francisco—wherever our SIG or AERA met. In the tradition of artist Judy Chicago, we had conversations and dinners, and created a book.

It was that easy. Of course, someone had to take on the organizing role when it was time to turn those wonderful conversations into text. And we, Diane and Pat, took on that role. A publisher needed to be contacted and Lois Patton was the logical choice; SUNY Press under Lois' leadership was making a name in feminist education, and Lois and Pat had an excellent working relationship after the publication of one of SUNY's earliest books on women and education (Schmuck 1987). So this book came to be.

It was always an evolving book, like the evolving feminist theory and research agenda which surrounds it. We found the exchange of our research findings and ideas exciting, confusing, and frustrating. We challenged our notions of what constitutes schooling, what it means to be a female, what it means to be a leader, and how these concepts are interrelated. We agreed on some things, and argued about everything. We framed and reframed our conversation and the organization of the book. As each new chapter and new findings emerged, we found new questions and new excitement that drove us back to reexamine our assumptions once again and to reorganize the presentation of material more than once.

We learned some things about ourselves. First, we speak primarily as women working inside educational organizations and therefore, this is not a revolutionary book. We wanted this book to provide a challenge and a starting point for the feminist agenda of women in education in the next decade. Thus, it is a reformist book, based in the schools and universities of today. We assume, as given, that the hierarchical structure of society and schooling will continue to exist, that local boards of education will continue to operate, and that the positional authority of superintendents, deans, principals, faculty, and teachers will continue to exist.

Second, we assume that the *nature of relationships* between people in the hierarchy can and must be changed. We assume that superintendents, deans, principals, faculty, teachers, parents, and students can and will continue to find new ways of working together. We focus on continuing reform by and through women in education. For, we know that whether it is reform or revolution that emerges in the new century, women will be leaders within it.

We acknowledge the help of many people; Sue Klein's prodding moved us forward, and Lois Patton's support at SUNY was invaluable. Many people gave us useful feedback, but our special thanks to Richard Schmuck, Emily Brizendine, Kathleen Cohn, Nancy Evers, Muriel Mackett, Diana Pounder, and Christine Sleeter for their critical assistance.

Any work of this magnitude becomes personal. Richard Schmuck, Pat's husband, provided unflagging support, critical questions, dinner on many occasions, and editorial assistance. Dick holds a fierce red pen and believes standard English should suffice in presenting the most obtuse theory. We all appreciate his red pen, and the red pens of our colleagues and other chapter writers, and the work is better for it. David Rowe, Diane's husband, died suddenly in August 1991, just as we were in the beginning stages of text creation. This book has been etched out of Diane's grieving and has provided support in forging a new life. Other chapter authors had to step back from promised chapters to care for ailing family or an ailing school or campus; others then stepped forward to help carry the ever evolving manuscript to completion. Perhaps the greatest gift to us throughout this long process has been the four-year demonstration of women leading in education, in ways that preserve dignity, that support community, and that extend our shared knowledge and support of women's leadership in the future.

Bibliography

Angelou, M. (1993). *Wouldn't take nothing for my journey now.* New York: Random House.

Klein, S. (1985). *Handbook for achieving sex equity through education.* Baltimore: Johns Hopkins University Press.

Schmuck, P. (1987). *Women educators: Employees of schools in the Western world.* Albany: SUNY Press.

INTRODUCTION

Listening to the Voices of Women Leaders

Patricia A. Schmuck and Diane M. Dunlap

Listen to the women's voices. Listen to the silences, the unasked questions, the blanks. Listen to the small, soft voices, often courageously trying to speak up, voices of women taught early that tones of confidence, challenge, anger, or assertiveness are strident and unfeminine. . . . Listen to a woman groping for language in which to express what is on her mind. . . .

—Adrienne Rich

In describing their lives, women commonly talked about voice and silence: "speaking up," "speaking out," "being silenced," "not being heard," "really listening," "really talking," "words as weapons," "feeling deaf and dumb," "having no words," "saying what you mean," "listening to be heard," . . . We found that women repeatedly used the metaphor of voice to depict their intellectual and ethical development, and that the development of a sense of voice, mind, and self were intricately intertwined.

—Mary Belenky, Beth Clinchy, Nancy Goldberger, and Jill Tarule

The silences I speak of here are unnatural; the unnatural thwarting of what struggles to come into being, but cannot.

—Tillie Olsen

1

> The overarching theme of finding a voice
> to express a self-defined Black women's
> standpoint remains a core theme in Black
> feminist thought.
>
> —Patricia Hill Collins

A drienne Rich tells us of women's silence in the classroom, Belenky and her co-workers tell us of the development of self, Olsen tells us of literary history dark with silences that are "unnatural," and Collins tells us of the struggle of black women to find a self-defined voice. The concept of silence has become an important metaphor in feminist scholarship. Gerda Lerner documents women's silence in history (1979), Jessie Bernard in sociology (1973), Gilligan (1972) and Miller (1976) in psychology, and Tannen (1990) in language.

The twentieth-century struggle for women has been to find our individual and collective voice in order to proclaim our individual and collective significance. As the concept of "invisibility" was etched into our consciousness about African-Americans with Ralph Ellison's *The Invisible Man* (1963), the concept of silence has been etched into the feminist consciousness of the twentieth century. As feminist theory has developed over the past few decades, the silence of women has been the metaphor for women ignored, not listened to, and women not speaking. Women's voices have been silenced, or not heard, because of the presumption that women's lives and work consist of the mundane and the ordinary, thus their stories are inconsequential. Too often women, too, believe they have nothing important to say, so they become silent.

The silence of women is especially true in education where women have dominated by sheer numbers since the late nineteenth century, but never dominated in recognized positions of organizational authority. Women have been the historically unheralded force in the public schools of America. Excepting for a few public educational leaders such as Emma Flagg Young, Catherine Beecher, or Margaret Haley, women have been invisible and silent in the unfolding drama of public education in the United States, Canada, and Great Britain.

In the last few decades, women's invisibility and silence as educators have been abridged with a new feminist consciousness. In education we have gained a new understanding of women who were important as leaders and teachers in the nineteenth and early twentieth century thanks to the attention of scholars such as Pauly Kaufman who documented women teachers on the frontier (1984) and Hoffman who wrote of the mundane and ordinary lives of teachers in the early twentieth century (1981). Today Grumet

(1988), Acker (1989), Freedman (1983, 1990), Weiler (1988) and Biklen (1987) provide us a portrait of the modern-day teacher. Since about 1970 there has also been a growing literature on women in administration by Gross and Trask (1976), Shakeshaft (1987), Schmuck, Charters and Carlson (1981), and Ortiz (1982), as well as on women's place in the international sphere (Schmuck 1987; Kelly and Kelly 1989). These books have been written to document and understand women's experience in schools and to explain why women have been underrepresented in school leadership posts.

This book goes further. The chapters document the day-to-day drama of how women lead, how they envision their roles, how they are socialized, what inspires them to go forward—or not—, how they cope with multitudinous demands, and how women teachers exercise leadership. The purpose of this book is to make women leaders visible and to hear the voices of women who lead in education; to tell the stories of women who aspire to leadership positions, of those who are in leadership positions, and those who exercise leadership in their positions as teachers in public schools serving students from kindergarten and pre-school to grade twelve, and women in higher education institutions.

These chapters tell us about the mundane and ordinary; they are about careers, conflicts, leadership crises, and the day-to-day chores of running educational programs and organizations. Yet these women's stories are consequential; it is through the daily mundane and ordinary events that leadership is exercised.

The chapters are written by academics, who are often educational leaders themselves, and by practitioners from their own experiences or through a study of women leaders. The collection reflects various methods of study; case examples, personal stories, qualitative and quantitative reports, assessments of existing practice and attempts to devise theory on women leading. It is an eclectic book necessary at this stage in the formulation of our thinking about women leading in education.

The book is divided into four parts. Each part represents women at a different stage in career development.

Part I. Preparing Women for Leadership: Conditions and Critiques

Gosetti and Rusch open the book with a critique of the theories of leadership and organizations which dominate the thinking in educational administration. Through the lens of feminist theory they explain how privilege has been an underpinning of administration theory and how those on the margins can offer a new perspective. Edson provides a unique ten-year longitudinal portrait of 142 women in the United States who aspired to become school principals. She tells us of their successes and failures, of dreams realized, unrealized, and changed. In a case study, Acker shows how one woman primary-school principal in England served as a career broker to inspire women teachers to be leaders; she shows us the importance of one woman's leadership to inspire women teachers to exercise leadership themselves. Romero and Storrs focus on experiences of women students in a graduate program in sociology. This chapter shows how a traditional program can ignore, and even exacerbate, silence and invisibility among women and people of color. Chaillé reviews the knowledge and training in a field that is almost exclusively a woman's field: early childhood education. She shows how the theory and practice in early childhood, a field overwhelmingly populated by women teachers and practitioners, is dominated by male theorists. The field, which is seen as gender neutral, not only disadvantages the predominately women core of teachers but female and male students as well.

Part II. Socialization of Women into Educational Leadership: Conditions and Critiques

Hart reviews socialization theory. She explicates the ways people are inducted into the arena of school administration and how women, who have been marginal as school administrators, require a new formulation and understanding of theories in organizational socialization. She shows, by case example, how the concepts of organizational socialization are enacted in the reality of women who are new principals. Pence describes formal and informal patterns of socialization focusing on mentorship programs for school administrators, one that focuses primarily on women new to school administration. Collay and LaMar, as third-party narrators, craft a story of informal socialization in a small rural school and the norms of gendered relationships. They tell of a male superintendent and a female head teacher through the lens of the traditional gendered family relationships; of the instrumental role of the father and the expressive role of the mother. They play out the "mom and pop" of organizational life. Worrall tells us her story in her own voice; she tells us of how and why she rejected the attempts to socialize her into the prevailing culture of school administration, and she agrees she is not "suitable" for promotion. Finally, McCall reviews the socialization of seven student teachers, and shows how the culture of administrative bureaucratic domination thwarts student teachers' attempts to build an ethic of care and compassion in the classroom. All these chapters show us how the culture of schools socializes the entrants to the field—whether in teaching or administration.

Part III. Women Leading: Assimilation, Acceptance and Resistance

This section focuses on women who are in leadership positions. Schmuck opens the section describing the advocacy organizations for women in administration formed in the last few decades. She describes why they were formed, how they operate, what their agenda is and she includes a listing of state organizations for women administrators. Willi Coleman, an African-American woman, and Pat Harris, a white woman, tell their story in first person dialogue recounting their personal and professional struggles between ethnic studies and women's studies in a college. Their dialogue of conflict, miscommunication and distrust are representative of many stories of women and other minorities in higher education where multicultural interests turn into competition over scarce resources rather than into a story of cooperation and collaboration. It is perhaps all too familiar a story. Cooper analyzes the journal reflections of women administrators as they struggle with their identity as being female and administrators in traditionally male and hierarchical organizations. Through their journals we read how they resist male dominated bureaucratic procedures and find ways to be organizationally effective, yet remain true to themselves. Matthews, in a more traditional quantitative design, surveyed a state population of women superintendents, assistant superintendents, and high school principals. She investigates women administrators' commitment to gender equity issues in schools and classifies four orientations toward gender equity: isolationists, individuals, activists, and advocates. She tells us of women administrators who deny sex discrimination for themselves and for other females and who aspire to be "one of the boys," of women who identify themselves as feminists and actively work to support girls and women in schools. Matthews shows us that women administrators are not a monolithic ideological group; they have differing personal and political agendas and differing views about their responsibilities as women leaders to achieve equity. Schmuck and Schubert interviewed nineteen women principals, most of whom were not advocates for gender equity in their schools. The authors offer an explanatory framework for why women principals do not uphold a feminist agenda. Bell delves more deeply into the consciousness of women superintendents; she shows how women superintendents cope with their marginality in a male dominated field and how they reflect on their unique status. Scherr, also investigating the arena of the superintendency, interviewed women assistant superintendents and argues that the "glass ceiling" may be invoked by women's perceptions of the constrained roles of the superintendency. It is a rich description of women who have risen to the almost-top positions in the educational hierarchy but don't want to rise any higher; she describes how these women portray the superintendency as it currently exists and why they reject this picture. They do not want to play the superintendent role as currently envisioned but see no alternative ways to enact the role. The women in this section are all caught between their roles as "insiders" in educational bureaucracies who are marginalized while they work for change.

Part IV. Shaping Alternative Visions of Leadership: An Agenda for A New Century

All the chapters in this section provide alternative models of women leading in education. Ford Slack and Cornelius in the "Red Road" show how the conceptions of traditional administration run contrary to the values and assumptions of the Indian culture. Ford Slack, a white professor, and Cornelius, a superintendent who is Ojibwe in a primarily native school, confront the paradigm of school administration and offer an alternative picture. Valentine focuses on a nursing hospital and demonstrates a female "culture" in which the norms work to support women's role in the family, place high value upon children, and encourage collaboration among the teaching staff. Troen and Boles explicate examples of teachers in public schools who are leading important school changes. Their chapter addresses the recent movement to restructure schools by giving more power to teachers to influence school policy and practice. Hurty redefines the concept of power through a feminist lens; through her own experience as a principal she offers an alternative vision of power shared, rather than power as control. Regan, using the metaphor of the double helix, offers a feminist perspective on school leadership which confronts the traditional paradigm of administration. Dunlap summarizes many of the themes that emerge in the entire volume, and challenges us to develop a new research and practice agenda for the new century. This last chapter is a fitting end piece, giving promise to schools and colleges about women leading.

This is a beginning book, a collection of independent projects which should help us understand the wide range of leadership styles among women educators. It should inspire a more comprehensive approach to thinking about women leading in education. It is our hope that here are many ideas to encourage women leaders who, in Maya Angelou's word, look to "cut herself a brand-new path" when the old ways won't work.

Bibliography

Acker, S. (ed.) (1989). *Teachers, gender, and careers.* New York: The Falmer Press.

Biklen, S. (1987). Women elementary school teachers. In P. Schmuck (ed), *Women educators: Employees of schools in the Western world.* Albany: SUNY Press.

Belenky, M., Clinchy, B., Goldberger, N., Tarule, J. (1986). *Women's ways of knowing.* New York: Basic Books.

Bernard, J. (1973). My four revolutions: An autobiographical history of the American Sociological Society. *American Journal of Sociology,* 78, 773–91.

Collins, P. H. (1991). *Black feminist thought: Knowledge, consciousness, and the politics of empowerment.* New York: Routledge.

Ellison, R. (1963). *The invisible man.* New York: Random House.

Freedman, S., Erickson, J., and Boles, K. (1983). Teaching: An imperiled profession. In L. Shulman and G. Skyles (eds.), *Handbook of teaching policy.* New York: Longman.

Freedman, S. (1990). Weeding women out of "woman's true profession": The effects of reform on teaching and teachers. In J. Antler and S. Biklen (eds.), *Changing education: Women as radicals and conservators.* Albany: SUNY Press.

Gilligan, C. (1982). *In a different voice: Psychological theory and women's development.* Cambridge: Harvard University Press.

Gross, N., and Trask, A. (1976). *The sex factor in the management of schools.* New York: John Wiley & Sons.

Grumet, M. (1988). *Bitter milk: Women and teaching.* Amherst: University of Massachusetts Press.

Hoffman, N. (1981). *Women's true profession.* Old Westbury: Feminist Press.

Kaufman, P. (1984). *Women teachers on the frontier.* New Haven: Yale University Press.

Kelly, D., and Kelly, G. (1989). *Women's education in the Third World: An annotated bibliography.* New York: Garland Press.

Lerner, G. (1979). *The majority finds its past.* New York: Oxford University Press.

Miller, J. B. (1976). *Toward a new psychology of women.* Boston: Beacon Press.

Olsen, T. (1978). *Silences.* New York: Delacorte Press.

Ortiz, F. (1982). *Career patterns in education: Women, men, and minorities in public school administration.* New York: Praeger.

Rich, A. (1979). *On lies, secrets and silence: Selected prose 1966–1978.* New York: W.W. Norton.

Schmuck, P., Carlson, R., Charters, W. W. Jr. (1981). *Educational policy and management: Sex differentials.* New York: Academic Press.

Schmuck, P. (ed.) (1987). *Women educators: Employees of schools in the western world.* Albany: SUNY Press.

Shakeshaft, C. (1987). *Women in educational administration.* Los Angeles: Sage.

Tannen, D. (1990). *You just don't understand: Women and men in conversation.* New York: Ballantine Books.

Weiler, K. (1988). *Women teaching for change: Gender, class, and power.* South Hadley, Massachusetts: Bergen & Garvey Publishers.

I

Preparing Women for Leadership:
Conditions and Critiques

ONE

Reexamining Educational Leadership: Challenging Assumptions

Penny Poplin Gosetti and Edith Rusch

> What counts as knowledge is closely related to the interests and power of social groups. What counts as knowledge in differing groups is different but what counts as knowledge in schools and formal education systems is determined largely by the interests of the powerful.
>
> —Richard Bates

The narratives, research studies, and theoretical explorations in this book examine traditional notions of leadership and find them wanting. While many positive images of strong leaders emerge from these chapters, they coexist with equally strong, negative images of the heavy price paid by strong leaders. Invisibility. Silence. Inequality. Oppression. Missing viewpoints and perspectives. Contradictions. These words describe reality for educational leaders who struggle to integrate new perspectives of gender, race, and class in organizations. They describe reality for those who do not knowingly advance new ideas of leadership but, by their very presence, challenge traditionally accepted norms about leadership.

In this introductory chapter, we examine our traditional ideas of leadership in schools by looking at educational leadership through new lenses. Challenging ideas and assumptions about leadership is essential to developing new perspectives and to changing the social realities that foster continuing marginalization of women. This is a difficult task, however, because all of our individual and shared notions and ideas of leadership are not clearly visible to us. To achieve an enhanced clarity of vision, we must first develop new tools to help us see more clearly what is initially hidden.

This chapter is divided into two parts. First, we introduce concepts of embeddedness, multiple lenses, and privilege as tools to enhance our vision of leadership. Second, we apply these concepts to current educational leadership literature as one example of how difficult it can be to see issues unless we look at them from more than one perspective. The application of these concepts also highlights how easy it is to see bias when we modify our view with new perspectives.

Educational administration borrows its theories of leadership from many other disciplines such as business, management, organizational development, sociology, and social psychology. We examine the adoption of these theories as reflected in current writing in the field of educational administration. We argue that the texts, conversations, writings and professional activities that construct our knowing and understanding of leadership come from an embedded privileged perspective which largely ignores issues of status, gender, and race and insidiously perpetuates a view of leadership that discourages diversity and equity.[1]

We do not reject this canon, but call into question what it represents for tomorrow's leaders in tomorrow's schools. In his earliest writing on democracy and education, Dewey warned us that a society that does not want to fall victim to the inequities of stratification and separate classes

> must see to it that all its members are educated to personal initiative and adaptability. Otherwise, they will be overwhelmed by the changes in which they are caught and whose significance or connections they do not perceive. The results will be a confusion in which a few will appropriate to themselves the results of the blind and externally directed activities of others. (1916, 88)

He wrote about the interconnectedness of schooling and society, suggesting that, as a society, we are profoundly affected by how and what we learn and teach. Dewey proposed an educational system that openly addresses social relationships, one that fosters personal interest in issues of equity and diversity. He challenged educators to model "habits of mind" that teach openmindedness. We argue that many people in positions of leadership today lack the habits of mind that contribute to achieving the democratic society Dewey described. We also assert that the construction of leadership is so immersed in privileged truths that there is limited opportunity for multiple perspectives to emerge and change the social realities that foster marginalization and inequality.

Educational Theory: Uncovering New Perspectives

Challenging the ideas and assumptions about diversity and equity which exist in traditional educational theory is essential to developing new perspectives and to changing the social realities that foster marginalization. This becomes a difficult task, however, because not all ideas and assumptions are clearly visible. To achieve a clarity of vision which allows us to critically examine mainstream interpretations of traditional educational literature we must first understand the concept of embeddedness, a process which develops and perpetuates invisibilities.

Embedded Assumptions

Like a fossil captured in stone or a footprint indelibly left in wet cement, the conceptions and impressions of what we know, experience, and imagine become embedded in all facets of our lives. Theories, practices, rules, norms, and standards make up the foundations of societies and cultures. As foundations, they become the stone and the concrete into which we embed the fossils and footprints of our assumptions and values.

The footprint impression, which is clearly visible, becomes obscure over time as we accept it as a natural part of the concrete configuration. So too, do embedded notions become invisible. Like the footprint we unquestioningly pass everyday, the underlying values and beliefs of our societal framework become taken-for-granted and uncritically accepted. An example of assumptions and values that we traditionally accept as natural and normative, is the universal application of the male experience to our understanding of the world. Smith (1987, 19–20) explains this embedding process:

> the concerns, interests, and experiences forming 'our' culture are those of men in positions of dominance whose perspectives are built on the silence of women (and of others). As a result the perspectives, concerns, interests of only one sex and one class are represented as general . . . [and] a one-sided standpoint comes to be seen as natural [and] obvious.

While a footprint remains visible, the fossil is so deeply buried in the stone that unearthing it takes a concerted effort. Assumptions and values can likewise become so embedded that our usual way of looking at the world does not allow us to see them. We may suspect their existence, but the lenses that we use to view and interpret our life are framed by those very same assumptions and values. As a result, we cannot separate what is "natural" and "right" from that which is socially constructed. Until Gilligan (1982) showed us that our understanding of women's development is socially constructed

13

from the perspective of a male norm, we accepted the conclusions of Freud, Piaget, Kohlberg, and others as natural and obvious. Their perspectives, deeply embedded in our notions of good psychological research, actually limit our concept of the human condition and omit certain truths about life (Gilligan 1982).

As educators, our understanding of how to learn, teach, and practice leadership is determined by the assumptions and values embedded within the dominant leadership culture. The danger in allowing these embedded assumptions and values to remain buried and unexamined, however, is that they silently and powerfully continue to shape our reality (Sergiovanni cited in Beck and Murphy 1993). Their domination in our lives explains why we choose to include or exclude certain elements from stories and discussion, why we hold certain assumptions to be true despite the existence of evidence to the contrary, and why some beliefs seem obvious and natural (House 1983). Women, and other outsiders to the dominant leadership culture, usually do not become aware of hidden assumptions and values until they fail to follow the deeply embedded programs and agendas of the culture (Bowers 1984). With different lenses, however, these embedded notions can be unearthed and made visible.

Multiple Lenses

Recognizing that the clarity of an image depends on how a lens is "ground" helps us understand the importance of using multiple lenses. A lens that works well in reading, for instance, may provide a distorted image when looking at objects far away. Although we know that one pair of glasses does not fit all, as a culture, we are expected to use a common lens to view our world. This lens is a lens ground in the framework of the dominant culture. As a result, we come to know our world through images that reflect the deeply embedded values and beliefs derived from a dominant culture of white, middle-class heterosexual males. Other perspectives which do not reflect the norms and standards of this dominant culture become blurred or rendered invisible.

Despite what we have been taught by educational, religious, and other social institutions, we do not have to view our world solely through the lens of the dominant culture. Many lenses, ground from other perspectives, bring into focus some of the gaps and invisibilities embedded and fossilized into traditional ways of seeing, thinking, and knowing. These same lenses can also make the familiar footprint we pass each day, seem strange or new and in need of explanation.

Multiple lenses help us focus in more than one way on how we view a concept like leadership and increase our chances of bringing embedded notions into view. To expose the embedded assumptions and challenge the norms of educational leadership we explore the use of two powerful lenses: a lens of feminism and a lens of privilege.

A Feminist Lens

The power of a feminist lens is its ability to focus on the gaps and blank spaces of male-dominant culture, knowledge, and behavior. Through this lens we can locate in the spaces, women and other marginalized groups who have been excluded from the development of knowledge. If we step into these spaces with our lens, we begin to see more clearly that those characteristics of gender, which we are taught to accept as natural, are really constructed from the values, beliefs, and assumptions of the dominant culture. Although contemporary feminism is democratic in nature—seeking social change by confronting issues of oppression based on gender, race, class, sexuality, and economic status—the clarity of its lens comes from a focus on women and their experiences. By using a women-centered lens, contemporary feminism is able to move beyond the consideration of women as an "add-on" issue and, instead, look at society, culture, and the world from the standpoint of being female.

When we use the standpoint of women to view our world, we begin to uncover what Smith (1987) calls "fault lines": those discrepancies which exist between what traditional knowledge tells women they experience and what women actually experience in their everyday lives. Smith's fault line occurred when, as an academic researcher, she discovered that she had learned "to work inside a discourse that we did not have a part in making, that was not 'ours' as women. The discourse expresses, describes, and provides the working concepts and vocabulary for a landscape in which women are strangers" (p. 52).[2]

Despite its inherent uncomfortableness, the role of stranger, and the experience of the fault line, become part of a feminist lens that can give women a unique view of traditional ideologies and practices. As educational leaders, many women experience a landscape to which they are truly strangers; a landscape dominated by a culture of privileged, white, male leadership which sets the standards and norms of the education profession. Although they have achieved insider status, these women do not feel comfortable embracing many of the activities, values, and beliefs of the dominant leadership culture. In essence, these women have a foot in two worlds: the center and the margins. Collins (1991) describes people who have this uniquely distinct vision of social reality as "outsiders within." As outsiders within educational leadership, women can see the fault lines which exist between the dominant culture and their own experience as women leaders in the margins. They not only experience a different reality than the dominant group, but also provide a different interpretation of reality.

When we focus the feminist lens on traditional theories of education, psychology, and sociology, we discover that women are invisible in the development of theory. Women's invisibility, according to Thiele (1987), stems from the marginalizing practices of exclusion, pseudo-inclusion, and alienation. As an active process of disregard which overtly makes women invisible, exclusion takes place in the language we use, in the assumptions we make about what is natural, and in the practice of universally applying the male experience in all theory. Pseudo-inclusion is a more subtle form of marginalization that moves beyond disregard by incorporating women into theory. In this process, however, the male experience continues to be the norm and, as a result, women are considered from a "special case" or "add-on" perspective. Even as women become the subject of theory, alienation can occur. While the dominant culture points out that women are now the object of analysis in their own right, the feminist lens reveals a reality of using male categories to interpret women's experiences, thereby distorting the women's lives.

A feminist lens allows us not only to challenge the reality of the dominant culture, but also to propose new realities. Tetreault (1989), for instance, offers a five-phase curricular integration process that allows us to critically examine how we think about women in existing educational curricula, as well as envision a curriculum that "interweaves issues of gender with ethnicity, race and class" (p. 124). In general, our current educational systems are oriented to either a male defined curricula (exclusion) or one that adds to the curricula women who perform well within the masculine tradition (pseudo-inclusion). Presenting these orientations as phases one and two, Tetreault describes phase three as an examination of the differences between women's and men's lives using content, structure, and methods which are often more appropriate to the male experience (alienation). A far less common, but more desirable phase four uses a multidisciplinary approach to examine women's lives from the standpoint of women. This phase also analyzes women's experiences within their social, cultural, historical, political, and economic contexts. Phase five balances gender in the curriculum by recentering knowledge in a way that draws on the experiences and scholarship of men and women equally. It is this phase, according to Tetreault, that will transform our understanding of the social world.

The feminist lens challenges us to understand the realities of our social world in new and exciting ways. As outsiders within, we begin to see the fault lines and embedded assumptions which exist in the dominant leadership culture. The lens provided by this location helps us recognize that gender not only includes the embedded values and beliefs of a dominant patriarchal system but is embedded itself in how we view issues related to leadership theory and practice. With this understanding we can undertake the examination of the privileged assumptions about diversity and equity which are embedded in the learning and practice of leadership.

A Lens of Privilege

While the power of a feminist lens is its ability to locate groups who are excluded from the development of knowledge, the power of a privilege lens is its ability to focus on the subtle patterns of advantage and dominance used by the dominant culture to keep excluded groups marginalized. Through this lens we begin to see that privilege is not simply a benefit related to economic position or as Lenski (1966) defines it: "the possession or control of a portion of the surplus produced by a society" (p. 45). Privilege, from a broader perspective, exists as an invisible and frequently taken-for-granted collection of unearned advantages and assets which are conferred by virtue of our group membership. These advantages and assets not only give us choices, opportunities, and a degree of control over our own lives that others might not have, but they also grant us dominance and permission to control(MacIntosh 1988).

Although this lens can help us recognize unacknowledged forms of advantage and dominance, it is a difficult lens to focus because of the silences, denials, and invisibility surrounding the subject of privilege. In 1939, Mosca (cited in Lenski 1966) observed that a ruling class embeds its privileged status into the culture's value and belief systems by developing theories that justify social inequality. By shrouding privilege in this effective cloak of invisibility, those who are less privileged unknowingly accept their circumstances as natural and inevitable. More recently, McIntosh (1988) identified privilege as a colossal unseen dimension of social systems. She points out that "the silences and denials surrounding privilege . . . keep the thinking about equality or equity incomplete, protecting unearned advantage and conferred dominance by making these taboo subjects" (p. 9).

More insidious than the silences, the denials, and the taboo on privilege as a subject for conversation and contemplation, however, is the deeply embedded forms of privilege which members of the dominant group are taught not to see. Using as an example her dominant status as a member of the white culture, McIntosh (1988) explains that she was taught to think of her life as morally neutral, normative, average, and ideal. This way of thinking leads us to tolerate those who are not like us and to desire to have "them" become more like "us" (McIntosh 1988). Tolerance itself, however, can be an expression of privilege. Spelman (1988) describes this relationship between tolerance and privilege:

> If one is in a position to allow someone else to do something, one is also in a position to keep that person from doing it. To tolerate your speaking is to refrain

17

from exercising the power I have to keep you from speaking. In tolerating you I have done nothing to change the fact that I have more power and authority than you do. And of course, I don't have to listen to what you say. (p. 182)

When we take a lens of privilege and focus it on women who aspire to leadership positions, we see that they are tolerated by a dominant culture which embeds its privileged status in what these women read, learn, write, and practice. Women leaders often find themselves bombarded with advice from books such as *The Managerial Woman* (Hennig and Jardim 1977), *Games Mother Never Taught You* (Harragan 1977), and *Breaking the Glass Ceiling* (Morrison, White, and Velsor 1987) and seminars on dressing for success which describe how women must look and behave in order to succeed as a leader in a man's world. These books and seminars are examples of how embedded cultural values of privilege perpetuate our idea of a leader as the embodiment of all that is male, even among women authors.

The lens of privilege is equally illuminating when we focus it on our system of education. Through this lens we see the many ways in which schooling perpetuates the advantages and conferred dominance of privilege. Most simply, schools provide no training to see ourselves as privileged and unfairly advantaged (McIntosh 1988). In addition, patterns of privilege are perpetuated in a system which legitimizes inequality under the guise of meritocracy—an "equal" opportunity system of social and educational mobility based on merit rather than birthright (Bowles and Gintis 1977). Despite our belief in the democratic practices of public schools, there exists a dichotomy between those nonprivileged people existing in the margins who are struggling to achieve a voice and those people with privilege who are increasingly calling for an exclusive authoritative voice (Fine and Weis 1993).

Most alarming, perhaps, is the subtle and usually invisible way in which educational policy and practice embeds ideologies of power, privilege, and marginality into our schools. Although our privilege lens is an important tool, the difficulty in using it is made clear in Anderson's (1990) discussion of "meaning management." According to Anderson, the school administrator's primary role of managing the school's image becomes an administrative function which, by legitimizing the assumptions, values, and norms of the dominant culture, renders privilege, invisible. It is critical, therefore, that we begin to focus the lens of privilege on educational leadership so that we can understand how administrators manage their school's meaning and understand who benefits from the resulting social constructions.

Unless researchers in the field of educational administration find ways to study the invisible and unobtrusive forms of control that are exercised in schools and school districts, administrative theories that grow out of empirical research—

whether quantitative or qualitative—will continue to perpetuate a view of school effectiveness that is unable to address in any significant manner the problems of their underprivileged clients. (Anderson 1990, 39)

By using our lens of privilege to gain a clearer view of unearned advantage and conferred dominance, we may discover intersections which exist between gender, class, and race oppressions (Bohmer 1989). In the meantime, however, feelings of confusion and discomfort prevail when the subject of privilege is introduced as a discussion topic. Although conversations and interviews about privilege may be easily engaged in, we have observed that it is difficult for people to acknowledge their own privilege. The observation of this discomfort leads us to think that not only have we not asked all the questions about diversity and equity, but that the values, beliefs, and assumptions embedded in our current framework prevent us from seeing the ineffectiveness of our questions to address the fundamental values of diversity and equity.

Learning and Practicing Privileged Perspectives

The challenge we face when we confront the ramifications of privilege is highlighted by Cherryholmes (1988), who suggests that in order for marginalized people to have voice everyone needs to rethink what they say and do:

> Rethinking may rejuvenate commitment to conventional discourses-practices or it may lead to something quite different. To avail ourselves of possible choices, however, it is necessary to identify and criticize privileged themes in texts and discourses-practices as well as themes that are silenced. Textual themes and discourses-practices are privileged because, among other things, they're favored by power arrangements and supporting ideological orientations. The exercise of power that has no beginning produces texts and discourses and practices that have no authors. We deal with these by continually reading, interpreting, and criticizing them as we communicate about and evaluate them (p. 153).

To explore how privilege is embedded in the lives of educational administrators, we reflected upon our own experiences of learning about leadership during the thirty-five collective years we worked in public schools and higher education. This personal reflection was a critical exercise for understanding how we experience and perpetuate privilege because, as Grumet (1988) points out, if we focus only on the theoretical perspective of these issues, we literally overlook the privilege and the concomitant influence it has on our own practices as educators.

Educational administrators learn to see and respond to issues of equity and diversity, in large part, through their professional and academic learning experiences. In our own case we found that, despite the increasing number of women and minorities in school leadership positions, feminist theoretical perspectives, multi-ethnic viewpoints, and gendered standpoints were rarely included in our preparation and professional development as school administrators. Discussions of gender, race, and class, as applied to the act of leading, were seldom deliberately addressed in our formal education and certification as school leaders. Bates (1980) argued that these issues are ignored because what really counts as knowledge for educating school leaders is determined by powerful or privileged interests. Those interests, despite a decade of affirmative action laws and civil rights policies, remain predominantly focused on traditional, privileged, and predominantly male perspectives. These perspectives result in actions by school administrators that frequently overlook real social phenomena.

Two studies (Anderson 1990; Kempner 1991) illustrate the connection between the embedded privileges communicated in professional education and the resulting privileged viewpoints and practices of school administrators. Anderson (1990, 38–39) using the metaphor of the "construction of the inner eye," described how administrators learned to see or not to see stark inequities around them. In an ethnography of principals in a variety of socioeconomic settings, he found few administrators who were bothered by social inequities around them or who expressed any concerns for basic democratic attitudes like justice and fairness. Kempner (1991), who studied professionalism among school leaders, reported frequent responses of "no problem" when issues of diversity and equity were introduced. He also found that minority interviewees from the same settings did not agree with the "no problem" perspective about diversity and equity, pointing out how easy it is for privileged perspectives to create blinders about diversity and equity.[3]

These studies bring forward two key issues: first, a privileged perspective supports silences, the reproduction of silences and "no problem" as acceptable norms. Second, when we study behaviors through a lens of privilege, it highlights how difficult it is to modify views and actions. If one is in a privileged position in our society, such as a white-male, or if one attains a position that has privileged status, such as a white female principal, the status itself can perpetuate a "no problem" perspective. Also, education and training for school administrators rarely introduces the conversation about how to apply a democratic vision for the school. As Kempner pointed out, the myths that become standards for success as a school administrator are male models of discipline and power, business (also male) models of the administrative science, and anti-intellectual models of training that focus on mentoring by skilled and traditional veterans. He also concluded that university programs contribute to the problem, noting that

> administrators and university programs that accept uncritically the metaphors of business, the military, and athletic contests are subscribing to myths that are antithetical to the ideals of democracy. . . . We should question how well university certification programs are educating administrators to be democratic leaders who are aware of their moral responsibilities to the citizens they serve. (p. 120)

These studies bring forward the need for a deeper examination of the role privilege plays in the schooling of educational administrators. The studies also accentuate Dewey's (1916) call for leaders with habits of mind who recognize the role that privilege plays in accepting, empathizing with, and fostering societal interests in issues of equity and diversity.

Privilege in Transformational Leadership

A potent example of unexamined and embedded assumptions that promote privilege is found in the theory of transformational leadership. Typically credited to the seminal work of Burns (1978), transformational leadership is a relational concept that occurs when "persons engage with one another in such a way that leaders and followers raise one another to higher levels of motivation and morality" (p. 20). However, when this theory is examined using Thiele's (1987) methods for looking at women's invisibility, some very contradictory perspectives emerge.

The invisibility begins overtly with what Thiele calls the "pseudo-inclusion of women." Burns recognizes the gendered view about leading, stating:

> The male bias is reflected in the false conception of leadership as command or control. As leadership comes properly to be seen as a process of leaders engaging and mobilizing the human needs and aspirations of followers, women will be more readily recognized as leaders and men will change their own leadership styles. (p. 50)

Yet, despite his recognition that women may contribute something new to the study of leadership, the fact is that in his 462-page treatise, he makes only brief references to the leadership behaviors of three women. Burns also says transformational leaders are concerned with values such as liberty, justice, and equality, yet he concludes that discriminatory behavior by men is less disturbing to women than the women's personal sense of outsider status. This perspective reinforces the idea that equality is a woman's problem.

Burns only reinforces this outsider status in the consciousness of women and men by his descriptions of transformational leaders. Using terminology that accentuates dominance, he describes transformational leaders as men who are "more skillful," who take the "major role" in action, who "allow" links of communication. They are omniscient, they expose followers to broader values by refining their aspirations and gratifications; and they gratify followers' lower needs so that higher motivations will arise. Burns' text makes few references to equality for women and minorities or for attention to issues of gender, race, and class. These silences and exclusions in Burns' treatise are powerful examples of a privileged view of leadership.

Burns' ideas currently influence many scholars who use his male-dominated perspective to develop their version of a quality leader. However, we noticed that in his treatise on leadership (which won a Pulitzer Prize), Burns totally overlooks the contributions of Mary Parker Follett, who, in the 1920s, used almost identical terms to describe transforming leaders.[4] The female perspective, Follett's version of "leadership and followership," of "power with" instead of "power over," of "relational" concepts rather than "hierarchies" is never cited in Burns' text. Followers of Burns occasionally refer to Follett's perspectives in passing, but quickly move on to crediting traditional, white-male scholars for defining leadership concepts. The perpetuation of this privileged view about who has defined leadership continues to govern and define the views of women and men. To be silent about diverse perspectives in theory and practice is also a choice made by academics who write and teach texts.

Today, some writers depict transformational leadership as a "feminine" perspective that is emerging to play a revitalizing role in organizations of the 1990s (Rosener 1990; Torbert 1991). These writers suggest that transformational leadership encompasses many of the characteristics normally attributed to feminine leadership styles. In fact many authors, following Burns' prediction, suggest that the organizational movement towards transformational leadership opens doors of opportunity for women leaders to establish themselves as management insiders. We wonder if this is indeed the dawning of a golden age of opportunity for women, or if the rise of transformational leadership is, instead, an act of appropriation by the dominant leadership culture? Rosener (1991) notes that until recently, attributes traditionally associated with women (i.e., intuition, consensus building, encouraging participation) were seen as ineffective in traditional hierarchical organizations. Why would these attributes now become desirable? If we use a lens of feminism and take the position of the outsider looking in, we see that the literature on transformational leadership is still written primarily by men, for men. As leadership characteristics are described through the concepts and terms of this still predominantly male discourse, they become genderless and are merged into a universal and privileged perspective that, once again, renders women and marginalized people invisible.

Privileged Frames for Leadership

Another example of theory embedded with privileged perspectives is Bolman and Deal's *Reframing Organizations* (1991), a recently updated book on organizational theory. Describing the increasing importance of leadership behaviors for managers, they work from the premise that "we need leaders and managers who appreciate that management is a deeply moral and ethical undertaking" (p. xiv). Bolman and Deal use a wide array of organizational theories to develop "multiple lenses" (p. xv) or what they call "frames" that help leaders to see and understand more about their choices if they apply the logic of the frames. Unfortunately, the four frames still represent traditional perspectives of leading with examples drawn from a white-male, corporate, or sports world. Gendered examples for their frames frequently are stereotypes. Despite their value for moral and ethical perspectives, Bolman and Deal miss many opportunities in this leadership text to expand perspectives about diversity and equity.

One key example of this reinforcement of privileged viewpoints is found in a case study that details the interactions among a Hispanic female who is labeled by a new colleague as "the affirmative action candidate" (p. 132), an older male colleague described as "a good old boy," and a man described as their joint boss. Although Bolman and Deal acknowledge that the case demonstrates gender and sexual dynamics, they direct all their suggested behavior changes at the minority woman. No suggestions or examples are given for the offending "good old boy" or the man who supervises both employees, thereby reinforcing that the fundamental moral and ethical standards of the men in this organization are not at issue.

Bolman and Deal are respected researchers and educators whose work is frequently used to educate business managers and school administrators. They explicitly state their values about leadership, noting that, "Leaders need to be deeply reflective, actively thoughtful, and dramatically explicit about their core values and beliefs" (p. 449). Yet, their own core values and beliefs do not result in thoughtful attention to the dynamic issues of diversity that confront leaders in organizations.

Review of Current Literature in Educational Administration

Theories of leadership thread their way into practice through textbooks that introduce prospective school leaders to educational administration. To identify the embedded assumptions of privilege in the current literature, we reviewed (1) textbooks used in educational leadership programs; (2) texts for professors of educational leadership; (3) a leadership knowledge and skill base from the National Policy Board for Educational Administration; and (4) selected professional journals. The data not only support Kempner's (1991) "no problem" conclusions, they demonstrate the deafening silence of the discussion about diversity and equity throughout the education and professional development of school leaders.

Textbooks for Students of Educational Leadership

A review of educational divisions of major publishing houses found few texts on leadership, the principalship, the superintendency, the professoriate, or educational administration written by women or other marginalized groups. Those written by women tend to focus specifically on women. Those few texts that include content about women, equity, or diversity usually add a special chapter which highlights the inclusion of women and minorities as problematic.[5] Rarely is any attention given to balancing perspectives and voices of white males with perspectives and voices that have traditionally been silenced or marginalized. Occasionally, a credible discussion of the statistics and issues of workplace equity and diversity is included, citing the extensive research of Charol Shakeshaft (1989) on women in administration. These authors conclude that we need a variety of perspectives in a preparatory curriculum, yet the remaining content of their texts reflect a traditional privileged perspective of leading schools. The most recent example of this dichotomy is in a text for prospective school leaders by Kowalski and Reitzug (1993) which concludes with the following statement:

> American public schools remain a primary force for creating opportunity in a diverse society. As such, those who lead these institutions should be committed to fairness and equal opportunity. . . . This worthy objective is made more difficult when existing conditions indirectly tell minorities and females that equality is merely a myth. (p. 343)

Ironically, Kowalski and Reitzug limit their discussion of fairness and equal opportunity to previously published research and locate the discussion in one chapter at the end of the book. This approach to presenting issues of diversity and equity only perpetuates "that equality is merely a myth" by reinforcing a dominant and privileged view in all of the other chapters.

We located very few introductory texts which weave the research and experience of marginalized groups throughout the content. One introductory text for school administration (Sergiovanni, Burlingame, Coombs, and Thurston 1992) intermingles the work of several women, but makes no attempt to balance or recenter the total perspective of their text.[6] We found only one example of a recentered viewpoint in a text edited by Capper (1993); authors, content, and theories come from many perspectives, bringing forward a complex conversation about diversity and equity for school leaders. The opportunity for prospective school leaders to learn about and reflect on diverse and equitable perspectives about leading is almost nonexistent; the privileged perspective, for the most part, prevails.

Texts for Professors of Educational Leadership

Several current texts written for academics focus on methods, theories, and programs for educating school leaders that challenge privileged perspectives (Foster 1986; Murphy 1992; Shakeshaft 1989). For instance, according to Foster (1986) university teaching should promote praxis: a model of learning behavior that can transfer to action in schools. He promotes a collaborative debate about what leadership stands for as a way of giving ourselves a chance to see the myths, rituals, and symbols that lead to actions that foster inequity and injustice. Foster's viewpoint reflects Dewey's (1916) perspective on the relationship between democratic practices inside schools and democratic behaviors outside of schools. His viewpoint also supports our contention that academic scholars must become conscious of how their words and actions in classrooms translate to words and actions in schools. The scholars and practitioners must locate how the words and actions empower, oppress, or as we assert, sustain privilege.

Foster's work provides yet another insight about the difficulty educators face when challenging privileged viewpoints. Even as he presents an alternative view for the education of school leaders, Foster still draws exclusively from traditional and privileged male leadership theories to frame his discussion. It is one thing to promote a new lens, but as educators of leaders, if we refuse to accept the challenge of applying new lenses to our own work, the point is lost and the value diminished. As bell hooks reminds us, "It is necessary to remember that it is first the potential oppressor within that we must rescue—otherwise we cannot hope for an end to domination, for liberation" (1989, 21).

National Policy Board for Educational Administration: Knowledge Base

The selection and application of content is the responsibility and the privilege of academics who educate and certify school administrators. Following hooks' premise that challenging our own embedded assumptions is necessary to end forms of privilege or domination, we approached a new curriculum document published by the National Policy Board for Educational Administration with high hopes.

A curriculum document in a four-inch binder prepared by 102 participants across all educational agencies is hard to dismiss. The weight alone suggests status. This document entitled "Principals for Our Changing Schools" (1993), was a collaborative effort of scholars and practitioners who committed to "recast the preparation programs for the principalship into a more contemporary mold" (p. xii). The "essential knowledge and skills" (p. xiii) for learning about the principalship is presented in twenty-one domains which the authors point out, are overlapping and convergent when related to specific tasks. Stating at the outset that the current practice of educating school leaders with methods and concepts from a variety of other disciplines does not provide focus and meaning for practitioners, the participants in this design project attempted to create a new direction for professional preparation programs. The preface states:

> the preparation of school leaders should focus on the development of a broadly applicable knowledge and skills base that is timeless and that emphasizes knowledge and skills development rather that particular problems of practice. . . . One clear outcome of this process was the emergence of professional skills—in addition to content knowledge—as essential to a successful principalship. The professional repertoire of principals requires knowing how to act as well as simply knowing about concepts. (xi–xii)

Our critique of this three-year effort, based on the application of a feminist lens, is not positive. Because the document is introduced as a "new" knowledge and skill base "essential" for the education of successful leaders, we hoped to locate visible attention to emergent issues of equity, diversity, and justice in all twenty-one domains. Contradicting the premise of the project, the document is a traditional privileged perspective of the knowledge, skills, and values that have governed the practice of school administrators for fifty years. Only one domain, that dealing with philosophy and culture, deliberately incorporates multiple lenses for examining the role of education in a democratic society. We were struck, however, by the obvious lack of application of the multiple lenses to all the other strands in the proposed knowledge base.

Glaring examples of exclusion were found in several of the domains. For example, the leadership domain contains a suggested exercise to illustrate how "understanding one's beliefs and motivation, and receiving objective feedback are cornerstones of leadership development." (p. 1–13). The worksheet (p. 1–14) is a list of twenty-five values that trainers are encouraged to apply to "real-life leadership situations" (p. 1–13). The list uses predominantly male-oriented value-words such as: achievement, advancement, authority, autonomy, financial success, order, recognition, and winning. The list totally excludes the values of equity, diversity, tolerance, or respect. For women and men leaders, this list of values instructs acceptable, indeed prized, beliefs about leading.

The two domains that focus on communication contain flagrant examples of stereotyping. The domain of interpersonal sensitivity includes an exercise that pointedly identifies negative responses only toward women. Advice to principals for dealing with ethnic and cultural stereotypes reminds the principal that some cultures, such as Native Americans, do not value eye contact. There appears to be an assumption that the Native American would not be a principal. There is minimal attention to specific information on communication issues governed by gender, race, and class with only one short paragraph on "cultural and gender bias differences" (p. 16-13). Professional educators of school leaders are invited to note a three-page "add-on" reference list devoted specifically to cultural and gender issues. The list apparently is intended to alleviate challenging communication issues for school leaders. It was interesting to note that the well-known works of academic colleagues such as Carol Gilligan, Mary Belenky, James Banks, Carl Grant, and Christine Sleeter, who challenge assumptions about diversity and equity, were not included in this reference list. Based on the premise that these domains represent "essential" knowledge and skills, the silences and invisibilities are apparent.

Professional Journals

Practitioners in school administration, both in K-12 schools and higher education continue their education by participating in various professional organizations. Those organizations, via their publications, also contribute to the praxis of educational leadership. To gain insight into the social construction of ongoing praxis related to diversity and equity, we examined the professional discourse of eight major educational journals. The examined journals included *The School Administrator* published by the American Association of School Administrators, *Principal* published by the National Association of Elementary Principals, *The NASSP Journal* published by the National Association of Secondary School Principals, *Educational Leadership,* published by The Association for Supervision and Curriculum Development, *Kappan,* published by the Phi Delta Kappa honorary society, and *The Executive Educator* published by The National School Boards Association.

To locate evidence of privileged assumptions in the professional conversation, we conducted an ERIC search between 1983 and 1992 using the terms of "equity," "diversity," "gender," "multicultural," "women," "womens," "female," "females," "affirmative action," and "sex equity." The over-30,000 references identified were further limited by searching the specific

TABLE 1.1
Privileged Viewpoints in Ten Years of Professional Journals (1983–1992)

Journal	Articles identified by search	Challenge to privileged view	Limited challenge to privileged view	No challenge to privileged view
School Administrator	27	5	13	9
Executive Educator	31	8	8	15
Educational Leadership	56	16	18	22
Principal	18	1	7	10
NASSP Journal	37	8	15	14
Kappan	70	31	23	18

journal titles using the search terms. The resulting references were reviewed for classification by searching bound editions of each journal. The findings are devastating.

Drawing from perspectives of privilege discussed by Thiele (1987), McIntosh (1988), and Tetreault (1989), we categorized articles by the degree to which the content challenged traditional, universal, and essentialist viewpoints. In the data analyses shown in table 1.1, "total articles identified by the search" means major articles. We did not include editorials, commentaries, and essays in the analysis. Articles from all journals identified as "challenging a privileged view" contained a gender-balanced view, diverse voices and perspectives, and encouraged rethinking traditional and privileged views. An example of this type of article found in *The School Administrator* (Holmes 1991) dealt with sex equity. The author included interview data from administrators who openly discussed the "no problem" and "trivial issue" perspective they confront when trying to address equity issues in academics and athletics. In addition, the author garnered specific practical examples for changing behaviors, policies, and attitudes from school leaders who are committed to advancing equity issues.

Articles designated as a "limited challenge to privileged perspectives" typically included some attention to difference and diversity. Examples include articles with statistics on changing demographics in school administration with some notice of increasing numbers of women and minorities in the principalship. Frequently, the articles ascribed to this category addressed an issue related to diversity and equity but lacked an in-depth analysis of the issues, contained a one-sided analysis of the issue based on a privileged perspective, or included comments or titles that detracted from or changed perceptions of the issue. An example of this modified perspective was found in an article in *Principal* that examined gender differences among principals. The article is subtitled, "Recent studies seem to indicate that a woman's place is in the elementary principalship" (Andrews and Basom 1990). The authors noted that women in administration have the ability to be strong instructional leaders and, indeed, outdistance male colleagues in perceived success as an instructional leaders. However, the authors make no reference to the information in the subtitle—that a woman's place is in the elementary principalship. Yet within one brief subtitle, women were defined and confined to one position within the administrative structure.[7]

Articles designated as bringing "no challenge to the privileged perspective" avoided any discussion of gender, equity, diversity, and ethnicity, even when the content warranted this viewpoint. For instance, in the March 1987 issue of *Principal,* an article on situational leadership theory and its specific application to the tasks of the elementary principal avoided all discussion of gender differences and was accompanied by photos of men (Blanchard, Zagarmi and Zagarmi 1987, 13). The article that followed discussed the power of learning about leadership from corporate management texts and prominently featured a photo of a woman (Snyder and Anderson 1987, 22). The reader can conclude from these articles and photos that women who wish to become successful school leaders must learn expertise from white-male corporate models. Male school leaders, on the other hand, already have the knowledge and expertise to adapt their leadership to many situations. The silences and photos are subtle, but very powerful messages that embed privileged values, attitudes, and behaviors in the daily practice of school leaders.

The total number of articles for each journal during the ten-year period clearly illustrates the limited conversation about diversity and equity among practicing professionals. For instance, *Principal,* a journal directed at elementary principals, published only eighteen articles that addressed any issues about diversity and equity during the entire decade; only two of those articles focused on leadership access for women or minorities. With such a limited conversation, we can hardly be surprised that words and actions related to diversity and equity are equally limited.

The NASSP Journal, directed at secondary administrators, published thirty-seven articles during the decade. Even though access is a critical issue for women at this level of administration, no attention has been given to the subject since 1986. Between 1983 and 1986, six articles focused on race and gender issues in the secondary principalship, but since that time the journal is contributing to Kempner's (1991) conclusion of "no problem." Although the number of articles that focus on diversity appears to be increasing (six in 1992), all the content is directed to curriculum, students, or finance issues.

Again, it becomes very clear why school leaders respond to questions about diversity issues with "no problem." The call issued by Kowalski and Reitzug (1993) for leaders to be committed to fairness and equal opportunity is answered by a privileged silence in their professional journals.

Conclusion

Educators represent a unique point of access to the society. Through the process of education at all levels, we learn which values are accepted and held dear, which values are viewed as complex, and which values are not viewed at all. In order to foster values of a democratic society, scholars and educators of leaders must acknowledge that the organization of our current way of knowing about leadership is deeply fossilized in privilege. Most of the current discourse defines leadership characteristics and viewpoints in ways that silence rather than foster the discussion of diversity and equity. This discourse perpetuates societal behavior that is privileged, that lacks breadth and open-mindedness, that supports inequities and stratification.

We do not propose eradicating the current ideology, but to achieve a balanced education about leadership that recognizes the fossils and footprints of our embedded assumptions about leading, our rethinking must include the work of people from many perspectives. We echo hooks' (1989) call to document and share work that communicates how individuals confront differences constructively and successfully. The dialogue emerging from this type of learning experience has the potential to construct a different ideology of leadership, an ideology that includes all voices, an ideology that results in democratic, rather than privileged, leadership praxis.

Our review of theories of educational leadership through lenses of feminism and privilege has been intended as a context for the chapters that follow. However, our review is not complete without acknowledgment of the personal journey we made through our own embedded assumptions of privilege while writing this chapter and the papers that preceeded it. We experienced personally painful learning as we confronted our value structures (Rusch, Gosetti and Mohoric 1991). We also observed the painful learning experienced by others as they became aware of or struggled with their privilege. As a result, we conclude, along with hooks (1990), that confronting the socially constructed oppressor *within* is a critical key to achieving new levels of awareness about diversity and equity. The many voices of this book add to our understanding of women in leadership in education. The multiple voices and perspectives in the chapters that follow add diversity to our understanding of leadership concepts and challenge us to reconsider what leadership means for tomorrow's students, tomorrow's schools, and tomorrow's world.

Notes

1. Earlier versions of this perspective are found in Gosetti 1992; Rusch, Gosetti, and Mohoric 1991; and Rusch 1991.

2. During the writing of an earlier collaborative effort (Rusch, Gosetti, and Mohoric 1991), we paralleled Smith's fault line experience when we reflected on our own learning about leadership. We found that despite the similarities of our standpoints and our learning experiences, our fault lines were not the same. Our ways of seeing and of knowing were very divergent and our aptitudes for effective communication were frequently inadequate to the task. As we often questioned the strength of our habits of mind and habits of heart to continue, we surmised that for many men, relating to women's experience is frightening. For many women and men, hearing the experiences of people of color is too complex. Knowing in a different way is uncomfortable; for many of us it becomes a paradox. We want to expand our knowing, but in the struggle to communicate with empathy, we learn that our socially constructed being cannot and will not stay the same. At that point our habits of heart and mind fail us and the silence continues.

3. Like other researchers (Murphy and Hallinger 1987; Hoyle 1989; Murphy 1990; 1992), Kempner found that most school administrators expressed little value for university-based course work, particularly courses with theory or philosophy that might challenge value positions. When asked about their leadership education, most practitioners indicated that practical experiences and management tools helped them be better leaders. Noting that most administrators only want to reproduce what they learn from mentors in the field, Kempner concluded that administrators were not interested in reflecting on the values that govern actions they observe and replicate in the field. He reported that these actions were most frequently described using militaristic and athletic metaphors of power, control and domination.

4. Follett's earliest contributions were lectures delivered to businessmen between 1925 and 1932. These lectures were first published in an edited text by Metcalf and Urwick (1942). Her reference to transforming leadership is found in the lecture titled "The Essentials of Leadership" (1987, 52).

5. For examples see Kowalski and Reitzug 1992 and Lunenburg and Ornstein 1991.

6. Sergiovanni, Burlingame, Coombs, and Thurston (1992) achieves what Tetreault (1988) calls stage three or a "bifocal curriculum," intermingling the work of women like Mary Parker Follett, the perspectives of Ella Flagg Young, and the research of and about women in several chapters. The authors go far beyond just stating the importance of equity, but they still do not choose to address the gender balance or recenter the total perspective of their text.

7. Although *Kappan* and *Educational Leadership* have substantially more identified articles than the other journals we reviewed, the proportionate number of articles addressing issues of equity and diversity may be no different than that of the other journals. First, both of these journals generally contain more feature articles per issue than do the other journals. Second, both the *Kappan* and *Educational Leadership* use a thematic approach to their issues. While these issues offer many articles that focus at-

tention on ideas that may challenge privileged viewpoints, they do so on a special case basis. We found no journal that consistently gives attention to issues of equity and diversity, much less fosters discussions which challenge privileged perspectives.

Bibliography

Anderson, G. L. (1990). Toward a critical constructivist approach to school administration: Invisibility, legitimation, and the study of non-events. *Educational Administration Quarterly,* 6(1), 38–59.

Andrews, R., and Basom, M. (1990). Instructional leadership: Are women principals better? *Principal,* 70(2), 38–40.

Bates, R. (1980). Educational administration: The sociology of science and the management of knowledge. *Educational Administration Quarterly,* 16,(2), 1–20.

Beck, L., and Murphy, J. (1993). *Understanding the principalship: Metaphorical themes 1920s–1990s.* New York: Teachers College Press.

Blanchard, K., Zagarmi, D., and Zagarmi, P. (1987). Situational leadership. *Principal,* 66, (4), 13–16.

Bohmer, S. K. (1989). Resistance to generalizations in the classroom. *Feminist Teacher,* 4(2/3), 53–56.

Bolman, L., and Deal, T. (1991). *Reframing Organizations.* San Francisco: Jossey-Bass.

Bowers, C. A. (1984). *The promise of theory: Education and the politics of cultural change.* New York: Longman.

Bowles, S., and Gintis, H. (1977). *Schooling in capitalist America: Educational reform and the contradictions of economic life* (paperback ed.). New York: Basic Books.

Burns, J. (1978). *Leadership.* New York: Harper & Row.

Capper, C. A. (ed.) (1993). *Educational administration in a pluralistic society.* Albany: SUNY Press.

Cherryholmes, C. (1988). *Power and criticism.* New York: Teachers College Press.

Collins, P. H. (1991). Learning from the outsider within. In M. M. Fonow, and J. Cook (eds.), *Beyond methodology.* Bloomington: Indiana University Press.

Dewey, J. (1916). *Democracy and education*. New York: Macmillan.

Ferguson, K. (1984). *The feminist case against bureaucracy*. Philadelphia: Temple University Press.

Fine, M., and Weis, L. (1993). Introduction. In L. Weis and M. Fine (eds.), *Beyond silenced voices: Class, race, and gender in United States schools*. Albany: SUNY Press.

Follett, M. P. (1987). *Freedom and coordination*. New York: Garland. (Originally published in 1949.)

Foster, W. (1986). *Paradigms and promises*. Buffalo: Prometheus Books.

Gilligan, C. (1982). *In a different voice: Psychological theory and women's development*. Cambridge, MA: Harvard University Press.

Gosetti, P. P. (1992). Access to leadership: Looking at theory through new lenses. Unpublished manuscript, University of Oregon, Division of Educational Policy and Management.

Grumet, M. (1988). *Bitter milk*. Amherst: University of Massachusetts Press.

Harragan, B. L. (1977). *Games mother never taught you*. New York: Warner Books.

Hennig, M., and Jardim, A. (1977). *The managerial woman*. New York: Pocket Books.

Holmes, N. C. (1991). The road less traveled by girls. *School Administrator*, 48(10), 11–20.

hooks, b. (1989). *Talking back: Thinking feminist, thinking black*. Boston: South End Press.

———. (1990). *Yearning: Race, gender and cultural politics*. Boston: South End Press.

House, E. R. (1983). How we think about evaluation. In E. R. House (ed.), *Philosophy of education*. San Francisco: Jossey-Bass.

Hoyle, J. R. (1989). Preparing the 21st century superintendent. *Kappan*, 70(5), 376–79.

Kempner, K. (1991). Getting into the castle of educational administration. *Peabody Journal of Education*, 66(3),104–23.

Kowalski, T., and Reitzug, U. (1993). *Contemporary school administration*. New York: Longman.

Lenski, G. E. (1966). *Power and privilege: A theory of social stratification*. New York: McGraw-Hill.

Lunenburg, F., and Ornstein, A. (1991). *Educational administration: Concepts and practices.* Belmont, CA: Wadsworth.

McIntosh, P. (1988). *White privilege and male privilege: A personal account of coming to see correspondences through work in women's studies.* Working paper no. 189, Wellesley College, Center for Research on Women, Wellesley, MA.

Metcalf, H., and Urwick, L. (eds.). (1942). *Dynamic administration: The collected papers of Mary Parker Follett.* New York: Harper and Brothers.

Morrison, A. M., White, R. P., and Velsor, E. V. (1987). *Breaking the glass ceiling: Can women reach the top of America's largest corporations?* Menlo Park, CA: Addison-Wesley.

Murphy, J. (1990). Preparing school administrators for the twenty-first century: The reform agenda. In B. M. and L. Cunningham (eds.), *Educational leadership and changing contexts of families, communities, and schools: 89th yearbook of the national society for the study of education.* Chicago: University of Chicago Press.

Murphy, J. (1992). *The landscape of leadership preparation: Reframing the education of school administrators.* Newbury Park, CA: Corwin.

Murphy, J., and Hallinger, P. (eds.). (1987). *Approaches to administrative training in education.* Albany: SUNY Press.

National Policy Board for Educational Administration. (1992). *Principals for our changing schools: Knowledge and skills base.* Washington, DC.

Rosener, J. B. (1990). Ways women lead. *Harvard Business Review*, 68(6), 119–25.

———. (1991). Ways men and women lead—debate. *Harvard Business Review*, 69(1), 150–60.

Rusch, E. A. (1991). *The white spaces of leadership.* Unpublished manuscript, University of Oregon, Eugene.

Rusch, E. A., Gosetti, P. P., and Mohoric, M. (1991, November). *The social construction of leadership: Theory to praxis.* Paper presented at the *17th annual conference on Research on Women in Education, American Educational Research Association*, San Jose, CA.

Sergiovanni, T., Burlingame, M., Coombs, F., and Thurston, P. (1992). *Educational governance and administration.* Boston: Allyn & Bacon.

Shakeshaft, C. (1989). *Women in educational administration.* Newbury Park, CA: Corwin.

Smith, D. E. (1987). *The everyday world as problematic*. Boston: Northeastern University Press.

Snyder, K., and Anderson, R. (1987). What principals learn from corporate management. *Principal*, 66(4), 22–26.

Spelman, E. V. (1988). *Inessential woman: Problems of exclusion in feminist thought*. Boston: Beacon Press.

Tetreault, M. K. (1989). Integrating content about women and gender into the curriculum. In J. Banks and C. A. M. Banks (eds.), *Multicultural education: Issues and perspectives*. Boston: Allyn & Bacon.

Thiele, B. (1987). Vanishing acts in social and political thought: Tricks of the trade. In C. Pateman and E. Gross (eds.), *Feminist challenges: Social and political theory*. Boston: Northeastern University Press.

Torbert, W. R. (1991). *The power of balance: Transforming self, society, and scientific inquiry*. Newbury Park, CA: Sage.

TWO

Ten Years Later: Too Little, Too Late?

Sakre Kennington Edson

Introduction

This is the third phase of a ten-year longitudinal study begun in 1979–80. The first and second phases were reported in the book *Pushing the Limits: The Female Administrative Aspirant.*[1] This unique study of 142 female aspirants began because there was no published research focusing on women who actively sought principalships in public schools. The initial underlying question of the study was: Why would women persist in trying to attain public school principalships in the face of all the undeniable barriers outlined in the literature? To answer this question about female aspirants, this descriptive, longitudinal study was launched in 1979 with a grant from the Ford Foundation for the first phase of data collection. A total of 142 women in all major regions of the country (Northwest, West, South, Midwest, Southeast, and Northeast) filled out extensive questionnaires about their career backgrounds, experiences, and goals and were interviewed. These women were nominated by professors of educational administration, female superintendents, people in state professional administrators' organizations, and directors of state departments of education and sex-desegregation centers. To be included in the study, women had to be actively pursuing a principalship by working in or applying for an entry-level administrative positions, or by being enrolled in certification or doctoral programs in educational administration. All respondents remain anonymous throughout the study, identified only by their age, race, position, and geographical region (rural, city, suburban, or metropolitan area).

The first phase of the study in 1979 outlined the personal aspirations of the women and their perceived obstacles. Five years later, the second phase detailed the unfolding of the women's careers. In this final report ten years later, the women share life changes, their changing concepts of administrative work, and their hindsight reflections of their careers. In this chapter, the first two stages of the study are briefly outlined, followed by a more detailed description of the final phase.

Phase One: Research in 1979–80

A fifty-item questionnaire was sent to all 142 participants, covering the women's backgrounds, their perceptions of the field, and their plans for advancement. These questions were derived from the literature about perceived obstacles to women in administration, as well as their own aspirations. In addition, all 142 women were interviewed at their work sites or their homes. The typically one-hour, open-ended sessions began with the question: "How did you become interested in administration?" The interviews then were guided largely by the interviewees and what they wished to discuss about their careers. By using both questionnaires and interviews, assumptions in the existing literature were questioned and the voices of female aspirants, previously missing in administrative research, emerged.

Findings and Conclusions

In the first phase of the study, a distinct picture of female aspirants surfaced. First, these women were determined to "push the limits" of administration to allow women leadership roles in public schools. Second, they were quite realistic about the obstacles facing them as female aspirants, and they did not see their goals as easily attainable. Third, they felt so strongly they had the necessary skills, credentials, experiences, and the desire to serve children, that they could overcome the obstacles and make a difference in schools. They knew many of the older male administrators would retire, and they expected to be candidates for those positions. While guardedly optimistic about local affirmative action efforts in the 1970s, they seemed relatively unaware of how few women succeeded nationally in gaining the very goal they set for themselves. Phase one underscored the persistence of these 142 women who were not only pushing the limits of educational administration, but their own visions of what they, as individual women, could achieve.

Phase Two: Career Update in 1984–85

Five years later, a brief career update questionnaire was sent to all 142 women, funded by Northwest Women in Educational Administration: 139 women responded, two were deceased and one was reported to have left education. Participants responded to questions about their progress to date, their current opinions about administration, and what, if any, advice they had for other women trying to advance in school leadership.

Findings and Conclusions

At this five-year mark, one-third of the women had become principals, one-third were in positions advancing their careers from their first interview (though not yet principals), and one-third were still in their same positions.

Among the women advancing in their careers, several issues had become apparent in the first five years of the study. First, women aspiring to be principals at the elementary level were more likely to succeed than those at the secondary level. Second, a quarter of those moving to new positions held doctorates—underscoring the importance of advanced degrees for some female aspirants in traditionally male-dominated professions. (The caution of "some" is used because six of the eight women who held doctorates at the beginning of the study—including four minority women—still had not reached a principalship at the five-year update.) Third, minority women advanced at the same pace as nonminority women, despite envisioning positions beyond principalships and higher graduate degrees than most nonminority women in the study saw for themselves, and despite experiences of both gender and race discrimination. Among the women who did not advance, the explanations varied. Younger aspirants mentioned deferring their careers while raising young children. Several older women cited frustration with discrimination, while others noted that economic conditions reduced the number of anticipated administrated openings. Several aspirants in rural areas expressed concerns about the lack of opportunities they faced in their small districts, where few mentors existed, limited kinds of experiences were available, and gender discrimination persisted. Finally, nearly a quarter of the original respondents were considering leaving education or completely abandoning their administrative goals at the five-year update. Many women felt undervalued in education and were hopeful that other professions, such as business, might offer them better opportunities. At the beginning of the study, none of the women mentioned other fields of interest other than education.

At this stage, a distinctly different picture of female aspirants emerged. Clearly, instances of discrimination and immediate family concerns were more apparent at the five-year update, tempering the optimism noted in earlier stages. For example, the idea that women could "have it all" in combining families and careers was proving problematic. Many in the study found the juggling of all these roles increasingly difficult as they tried to move up the career ladder. Some questioned whether they were as willing to pursue a career geared to helping other people's children at the expense of their own. This was a perspective few had considered when first interviewed.

Some of the negative attitudes emerging in this phase of the study may well have stemmed from the political climate in the United States. When the study began, there was a national emphasis on women's issues backed up by legal mandates. Since then, the courts and the executive branch have eroded away much of the legislative gains of the 1970s.

The field of administration was changing as well. As older, nonminority males retired, many of those positions were not filled with women as the informants had expected at the onset of the study. Fiscal cutbacks plagued many of the regions of the country, resulting in hiring freezes that affected their career progress. Further, as women moved up the career ladder in education (as in other professions), many were confronted with what came to be described as the "glass ceiling"; they could advance to a certain level, but the next steps—though visible—were beyond their reach. Some questioned the value of affirmative action to assist women, even though others admitted some minority candidates benefited from the programs.

Despite these guarded concerns, most remained optimistic that they would succeed in some field of leadership, if not in education. They still displayed the need for professional stimulation and growth so evident at the onset of the study. Although they were more apprised of the difficulties facing women in education, they still encouraged dedicated women to pursue administrative careers. They believed that women had much to offer education in a time when the profession clearly needed help. The call for restructured schools and increased teacher empowerment were the very issues these aspirants felt qualified to address. Clearly, more time was needed to assess whether their optimism would be upheld.

Phase Three: Final Career Update in 1989–90

As might be expected at the ten-year mark, contacting all of the subjects in this final stage of the study was more difficult than in previous updates. A brief career update questionnaire was sent to their last address, and some of the women had not only changed jobs, but had changed regions as well. Of the final questionnaires sent, 86 (or 61 percent) were returned. Follow-up telephone calls verified employment of another forty-one subjects, making a total of 92 percent traced. After a decade, the last positions held by 131 of the original 142 women were documented, including the four who died over the course of the study.

Findings

In the decade of this research, many changes in the women's aspirations, life situations, and careers are evident. The goal of these women to achieve a principalship is reflected in the national trends which show an increase of female school administrators, especially elementary school principals (Figure 2.1).

While women nationally made only small gains in leadership roles other than at the elementary level, these 142 respondents did quite well. Twenty-three percent hold positions that are pre-principalship (i.e., teachers, counselors, librarians, or assistant principals); 34% attained principalships during the ten-year span of the study; and 21% reached levels beyond the principalship (i.e., superintendencies, district or state level positions, or professorships). Small percentages of the women are retired (4%), left education (4%), or are currently at home and not employed (3%) at the update (11% either died or contact has been lost). In ten years, a total of 58% of the women reached their initial goal of a principalship or beyond. Of the thirty-seven minority women, 65% advanced to a principalship or beyond.

Because only 61% of the questionnaires were returned, this concluding phase of the research paints a more limited, and therefore cautious, portrait of the aspirants. However, because this is still the only longitudinal research of its kind, generalizations based on those who responded to the final questionnaire may provide some insight for future research agendas.

Aspirations: Of the 86 respondents (61% of the original study), 42 women no longer considered themselves active aspirants in administration. Reasons cited for this change were: (1) they were satisfied with their current administrative positions (some of these were now principals); (2) they had retired; (3) they had not been able to succeed in gaining a principalship; or (4) they had put their careers on hold largely due to family or health reasons. Of the remaining women, thirty-seven still considered themselves active aspirants in educational administration, while seven were uncertain.

At the beginning of the study, these aspirants held high expectations. These 142 women believed they could make a difference to students and to schools if they succeeded in gaining principalships or beyond. However, when surveyed a decade later about whether they believed they had reached their potential, only thirty-eight of the women contacted believed they had. Nearly as many felt they had not, and a handful were undecided. Certainly in the eyes of the women in this study, female aspirants in educational administration have more to give to education.

Figure. 2.1   Distribution of U.S. Public School Administrators

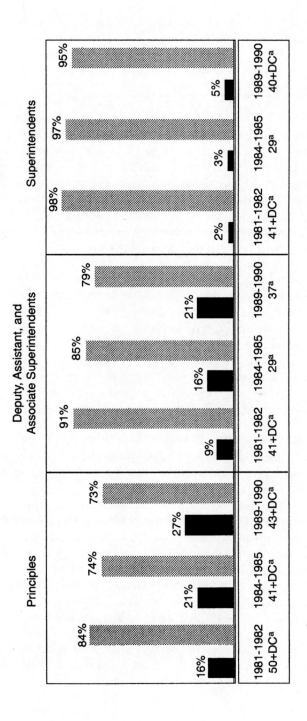

Source: E. Jones and X. Montenegro, *Women and Minorities in School Administration* (Arlington, VA: The American Association of School Administrators)

[a]Only this number of states (and Washington, D.C. where indicated) responded with information broken down by sex.

For many, however, their personal aspirations have changed due to their experiences in administration or because their attitudes about the profession have changed. Many women wished they had started aspiring in administration ten years earlier, thereby putting themselves in a better position for advancement. Indeed, many commented that they were ready for a principalship in 1979–80 when they first interviewed, but they did not have support to advance at that time. Displaying the same eagerness as shown at the beginning of the study, the aspirants expressed a strong desire to have more responsibilities than their present position allowed. A state program manager (Midwestern metropolitan area) states: "There is still so much I want to do and experience. And I know I can help cause positive change in schools. This job is one way to do that, but I do not want to do this the rest of my life." A current assistant superintendent (Northeastern suburb) writes: "What I envisioned in 1979–80 was a principalship. I did not aspire to central administration then, but now my next step is a superintendency."

Since this study followed women who aspired to the principalship, there is no data to know whether these aspirants are the same or different than those women seeking positions today. While the barriers may have lessened over the decade, women still face a dampening of their expectations. Those who overcome the barriers often do so only by their own personal determination and persistence. One has to wonder if the dampening of expectations for the women in this study is systematic of a "cooling out" phenomenon operating for all female candidates in educational administration.

Doctorates. At the ten-year mark, 32 of the women responding to the questionnaire held doctorates. This represents 23% of the total 142, an increase from 8% in 1979–80 and 17% in 1984–85. Two others were completing their dissertations. Of those holding their Ph.D.s, 18% of the total 142 women (or 26) had achieved a principalship or beyond. Four of the five minorities holding doctorates had principalships or beyond.

When asked what they might wish to change about their careers, many of these women specifically mentioned the doctorate. An elementary principal (Northeastern town) assesses: "I should have realized I had a career about ten years sooner, and pursued my doctorate rather than just a credential." An older state administrator (Midwestern metro) reflects: If I could wave a magic wand, I would have gotten my Ph.D. before starting in administration. I am not going to do that now." Regret over delay and a choice of degrees also bothered an assistant principal (Southern metro). If she could change anything about her career, she notes: "I would have continued to work on my doctorate immediately after completing my specialist degree." She is still hoping to attain a principalship and then reassess whether she has any further goals in administration.

Those who did obtain their doctorates expressed concern over the length of time devoted to the effort. A director (Northwestern town) acknowledges, "I should have finished my dissertation years ago. Much of my educational career I have been underemployed while in the doctoral program." The general consensus, however, is that having a doctorate *would* make a difference in a women's administrative career. One superintendent (Midwestern rural) underscores the need to seriously consider graduate degrees earlier: "I wish I hadn't enrolled in the doctoral program so late. If I had enrolled ten years earlier, I would have been further down the 'pike' by now."

Mentors. Mentors are often acknowledged as essential to those aspiring in educational administration. In 1979, 68% of the women acknowledged having mentors, typically a male principal. There is some evidence that mentors have, indeed, assisted the women in this study. Of those who identified mentors in 1979–80, 42% (or 59 women) became principals or beyond by the end of ten years, whereas only 17% (or 24 women) who did not have mentors were able to advance.

In the ten-year update, a high school principal (Southern suburb) notes it was a male mentor who "gave me a chance as his assistant. This happened in 1980 when many women did not get the chance." An assistant superintendent (Southern metro) also credits mentors with helping her succeed in administration. "Having mentors who believed in me and trusted me to move into areas where I could make a difference helped my career." Perhaps this kind of support is why 26 percent of those responding to the final inquiry still consider themselves active aspirants in educational administration ten years into this research project.

Goals. For women who advanced beyond the goals they originally envisioned for themselves, the added responsibilities of their new positions caused growth and enthusiasm. However, only 16 percent (or 23) of those in the study actually reached the highest goals they set for themselves in 1979–80. While a small number (11) had risen higher than they envisioned, over half (82) did not attain the original goals they set out to fulfill. Minority aspirants, who noted higher goals than nonminority women at the onset of the study, were somewhat more likely to advance beyond their highest goals. Some respondents found their experiences as administrators spurred them on to higher goals.

Other respondents, whose goals changed away from being a principal over the decade, cite various reasons for their altering their career aspirations. One educator (Southern suburb), who taught and then took a coordinator's position, is now back teaching. She explains why she no longer wants the elementary principalship: "You could run a school without a principal, or a cook, or a bus driver" she argues, "but you couldn't run it without a teacher. That's why I decided to stay in teaching." Some women changed their goals after internships or experiences in lower-level administrative positions which taught them they that they liked being closer to students than administrative work might allow. Others, however, were forced to abandon earlier goals due to ill health, often citing cancer as a motivation for the change.

Motherhood. For women who had no children at the onset of the study, motherhood brought changes they did not anticipate. One woman (Southeastern town), who now stays home with her four children and writes freelance, acknowledges: "I wanted desperately to be a middle school principal when this study first began. I came incredibly close: second out of 176 applicants. But now I have lost all interest in this goal. My five-year goal is to raise my kids and perhaps in ten years try for an elementary principalship." Others are now finding a temporary answer to the dilemma of juggling careers and families by taking part-time administrative positions. Working three-fourths of a day in the district (Western suburb) as a program administrator while raising her children, another respondent mentions: "I was surprised that this level of position was open to someone like myself who will not work full time."

Women who are administrators and who have children at home straddle the dual worlds of parenting and working. While the world of teaching more easily accommodates the dual world for many women, the demands of administration still often presumes one has a "wife" at home.

Discrimination. Women aspiring to be principals face overt and subtle forms of discrimination. Initially, many in this study were reluctant to recognize the impact of sex discrimination on their careers, believing they had the experiences and skills to overcome such prejudice. Over time, however, more and more of the aspirants noted the instances of discrimination they faced. Several minority and older aspirants wrote about their frustrations. In a Western metro, an assistant principal in a high school who did not reach a principalship despite over twenty years of work and aspirations simply says: "I've been thwarted by my district." At this point, she is just hoping to hang on until she reaches retirement age. A district specialist (Southeastern city) writes if she could "remove the frustration of politics and sexual prejudice that would, in fact, take care of 5 or 10 years" she believes she lost.

Still others seemed genuinely puzzled that their careers stalled. A teacher (Southern metro) poignantly wrote: "I thought I would probably be a curriculum coordinator or something of that sort by now." Though hopeful she will someday advance, she seems uncertain as to why she has not succeeded to date. As in earlier phases of this research, there is a personal reluctance to believe that discrimination exists. They look only to their own skills and credentials, believing these will be sufficient to achieve a position.

Administrative Work. Aspirants were asked to note any changes in administrative work over the decade. Only a few reported little change. More described the increased demands, stress, paperwork and discipline needed, coupled with declining funds and weakened public support for education. A teacher (Northwestern town) sums up the complexity of administration today: "Administrators need to be more than educators; they must also be business managers, salesmen (sic) and negotiators. . . . Budgetary restraints and negotiation laws have added burdens and taken time away from direct contact with children." An elementary principal (Northwestern metro) quips: "If you like a neat and tidy job, this is not for you."

On a more positive note, respondents saw increased efforts toward more school-based governance and more emphasis on instructional leadership and team work. Many also indicated that more women are in administration than ten years ago, although in some cases "just a few more." High school principalships and superintendencies were two areas cited that still had few, if any, women.

Advice. Although they saw the increased difficulties of school management, respondents were encouraging to women who might be considering a career in administration in the 1990s. When asked what advice they offer, a majority of the women said either "go for it!" or "do it!" Although several women stated upcoming aspirants should "push for advancement when younger," many emphasized the positive aspects of the work while acknowledging the challenges. An assistant superintendent (Southern suburb) suggests: "If you are willing to sacrifice your time, are a people-person, are organized and consider yourself on a mission, you are ready for administration. If any of these are lacking, administration may not make you happy." An elementary principal (Southern city) reflects: "Remember what you really liked about school and build on those attributes. Remember what you didn't like about administrators and extinguish those behaviors in yourself. Smile and laugh often; it does wonders for your mental health!"

Respondents offered practical advice about getting mentors, attending the "best" schools to get doctorate degrees and shaping internships to expand skills and experiences. A secondary principal (Northeastern rural) urges: "Be yourself. Be ethical and hard working. Keep reading, thinking and collaborating. . . . Befriend men as well as women . . . and never, never get too far away from your students." In a more cautious approach, an elementary principal (Southern metro) writes: "Be prepared to work hard, accept knocks as challenges and know how to give and take. Success is possible, but you still operate in a man's world with an 'old boy network' of advancement."

A few women noted that fields such as business, law, medicine, or government are now more open to female aspirants than ten years ago and that many of these professions are more lucrative than education. But by and large, these aspirants consistently urge other female aspirants to persist. Acknowledging "many other fields are open to competent women at greater salaries," an assistant superintendent (Southeastern town) concludes: "This job is exciting, rewarding and critically important. Good people are needed to administer our schools and to improve the plight of children." Clearly these women believe female administrators can, and should, be a part of improving schools.

Conclusions

The joys of a qualitative, longitudinal study become evident with each passing stage. In each phase, there is a richness of the descriptive detail to be captured, and over time the sense of personal change and development is exciting to note. This study of 142 women over a decade, with repeated glimpses into their lives and careers, has been rewarding and enlightening.

Concluding ten years of research is no easy task. Many questions remain unanswered; perhaps as many as were answered. It is unclear, for example, whether or not the expectations of many of these women will ever be fulfilled. Many changes have occurred in administration and in the lives of these 142 women over the decade, some of which were never anticipated in 1979–80. For those who attained their goals or who perhaps reached beyond even what they envisioned, there is understandably great satisfaction. For those who did not advance, there is equally understandable disappointment. Even though a majority of these aspirants share frustration at the ten-year delay they so often experienced in their educational careers, they remain philosophical and focused about their careers in education.

What accounts for the success of these 142 women? First, these particular aspirants were initially nominated for the study because someone in education—besides themselves—believed they would succeed. Perhaps these aspirants possess something not all female candidates to leadership positions hold: the benefit of knowing someone else successful in administration believed in them early on in their careers. This would underscore, once again, the significance of mentors and role models for female aspirants.

A second reason many of these aspirants experienced career success may simply be the "Hawthorne Effect" of being monitored in a research project. From their own accounts, participating in a longitudinal study was a positive experience for these women. When the final update questionnaire was sent to them, many spontaneously responded with grateful and excited comments. One assistant principal (Northeastern rural) wrote: "Thank you for your concern and continued interest in the 142 aspirants and in all other women seeking a goal sometimes temporarily beyond reach." In a Midwestern suburb, a secondary principal noted: "Sorry about the messiness of the questionnaire, but I was so excited to answer. I did not want to wait to go to the typewriter!" A retired former elementary principal (Northwestern city) simply said, "Thank you for asking about my career." Another secondary assistant principal (Western metro) shares: "Thank you for your continued interest in us and our careers. You, too, have a special place in my heart. I enjoy telling some people that I am in a book." An assistant superintendent (Southern metro) writes: "I was thinking of you recently. I knew it was time to hear from you. I have enjoyed being a part of your study." A woman in the Northeast (city) who currently holds an elementary principalship responds: "Thank you for calling to remind me about returning the questionnaire. . . . It was nice to hear your voice. Somehow I felt encouraged to charge on—after speaking with you." Only two women expressed less than positive reactions to the study: one asked not to be questioned further and the other could not even remember being involved in the study.

Yet, if one looks closely, these grateful comments come from fairly minimal contact throughout the study. There was one initial visit in person, followed by a postcard when the book was published and two other questionnaires answered via mail or telephone. Perhaps this is a sad commentary on the loneliness of administrative roles in general, where even minimal contact takes on great importance. Hopefully, a mentor would have more continuous and significant contact with an aspirant than this research project afforded.

In the end, whether it is having someone believe in your career goals or taking part in a research project, one begins to sense how little is needed to encourage women in administration. Despite all the obstacles for women trying to advance in a largely male arena, these female educators continue to be committed, resilient, and, for the most part, successful. As one elementary principal (Northwestern metro) humorously concludes, "Go for it! And don't buy a dumpy gray suit!" Given the large numbers of female educators in schools who would like the opportunity to "go for it," it would appear the field of education has a great deal to learn about encouraging and supporting its own professionals.

Afterword

Recently I did a presentation to my son's fifth grade class about conducting research and publishing a book. During the questions, one student asked me, "Did writing this book change your life?" I was taken aback at the depth of that simple question, one I could not answer on the spot.

I know that studying this topic has changed my life. When I began this study, I was not a feminist. Studying the struggle of women to become school administrators changed that. I also found myself abandoning my earlier plans to become a school administrator, because I, myself, did not want go through what many of these women were willing to do. I clearly did not share their commitment to education and to students in public schools, one I believe is necessary to sustain women in a long struggle of this nature. I have gone on to become an administrator, but in the field of social services, not education.

And, finally, I birthed this research out of a basic interest in people and how they view their work. Many of my colleagues in the 1970s will perhaps remember my whimsical fantasy was to become the "female Studs Terkel" of educational administration! That deep interest in people and their work continues to this day. The women in this study became individuals I cared about, not just subjects for a research study. When they wrote of successes, I cheered with them; when they told me about failed marriages or lost opportunities, I shared their sadness. And when they became ill or died, I wept. They had an impact on my life, just as perhaps I had on theirs.

This project took on an importance I never envisioned when I first dreamed of doing a national study. In a sense, my cause became that of the women I followed, with the resulting book, articles, and chapters becoming the expression of that cause. In a sense, the work took on a life of its own, leaving me little choice. I felt compelled to tell their stories—for my sake, for their sake, and for the sake of all the other women striving to be school administrators.

Note

1. S. Edson, *Pushing the limits: The female administrative aspirant* (Albany: SUNY Press, 1988).

THREE

The Head Teacher as Career Broker: Stories from An English Primary School

Sandra Acker

From 1987 to 1990, I investigated teachers' workplace cultures in primary [elementary] schools in England. [1] This chapter describes one of those schools and the ways in which its head teacher [principal], Liz Clarke, influenced the careers and lives of her staff.

Although leadership behavior of principals has been studied extensively, it is only recently that feminist perspectives have begun to make inroads into this body of research. Noddings (1990, 410) laments the "separation of female administrative aspirants from feminist thought" due to the absence of feminist scholarship from educational administration as a field of study. How might feminist theories influence our understanding of school administration?

There have been many attempts to categorize feminist theories (e.g., Eisenstein 1984) and a few efforts to link different feminist theories to educational issues (Acker 1987; Stromquist 1990). Types of feminism are frequently distinguished from one another by their basic assumptions about the nature of women's oppression and the strategies required to alleviate it. Thus, a liberal feminist position is identified by its emphasis on increasing women's access to better life chances, through improving motivation, altering socialization, or abolishing discrimination. Socialist and radical femi-

49

nisms concentrate on exposing and developing countermeasures against the untoward effects on women of capitalism and patriarchy, respectively.

However, recent feminist theoretical analyses have moved away from such classifications, almost as if retreating to a prior consideration, the conundrum of what it means to speak of "women." Are women to be defined in opposition to men, stressing differences; or by their similarity to men, stressing equality (Scott 1990)? If they are the same as men, the need for feminism itself would evaporate once the effects of past socialization and discrimination are removed. If they are different, we are asking for special treatment. Moreover, we have the additional difficulty of defending sameness among women who patently differ among themselves in many ways—social class, race, age, sexual orientation, nation—such differences often making them appear closer to men from the same category than to women from another. Are the qualities of women to be construed as biological or socially constructed? Are they to be celebrated as true womanhood or abhorred as learned behavior under patriarchy?

Feminist writing about educational administration began largely in the liberal feminist mode, pointing to the under–representation of women in the management of education and identifying barriers to their progress up the ranks. Such an approach was hardly surprising, given the scarcity of women in such positions. According to Sadker and colleagues (1991), some of the barriers and gender differences identified in early studies began to disappear in the mid-eighties in the United States. The theorists shifted away from questions of equality (are women administrators as good as men? have they as many opportunities?) to those of difference (what is a female administrative style?). Feminist writers went on the offensive, and theories of administration that took insufficient account of female experience were attacked (Intriligator 1982; Ferguson 1984; Blackmore 1989). The existence of a female organizational culture was proposed (Shakeshaft 1989).

There were also claims that women's typical leadership styles are superior to those of men and better suited to running effective schools. Sadker and colleagues (1991, 284), for example, portray women administrators as typically possessing valued traits such as "concern for others; a greater focus on teaching and learning; a more democratic, participative style; greater effectiveness in representing the school and working with the community; more emphasis on using outside resources to apply new ideas to improve instruction; and increased attention to monitoring student participation and evaluating student learning."

The attempt to depict a quintessentially female style of administration is paralleled by similar efforts in other fields. Feminist scholars try to identify women's ways of knowing (Belenky et al. 1986), women's approach to moral decision-making (Gilligan 1982), women's preferred pedagogies in higher education (Gray 1989), and so forth.

But the sameness/difference conundrum remains with us. If women administrators do work differently than men do, what is the origin of the difference? If it is social rather than biological, "values that are structured into women's experience" (Ferguson 1984, 25), can we be sure that such values are structured into the experience of all, or even most, women? If the observed differences are a tendency rather than an absolute (Shakeshaft 1989, 190), under what conditions will the tendency become expressed in a school that does, in fact, work differently?

To answer the latter question requires accounts that go beyond surveys and interviews to give actual portraits of schools in operation. In the remainder of the chapter, I draw upon my ethnographic research to describe the ways in which one woman head teacher [principal] influenced the opportunities, images, and self-perceptions of the teachers in her school. In the conclusion, I return to the theoretical issues raised above.

The Study

My original decision to study the work of primary school teachers grew out of a suspicion that generalizations about teachers based on the situation in the United States were being uncritically imported into the received wisdom of educational researchers in Britain. What contact I had so far with British primary schools failed to convince me that teachers were fiercely individualistic and isolated from other adults (Acker 1991). I hoped that firsthand observation might resolve my doubts one way or the other. In March 1987, I approached the head teacher of Hillview School, whom I knew but not well, and asked if I could come into the school and find out something about how primary school teachers worked, both to increase my own knowledge and to separate myths from reality.

At that time, I had no clear notion that I would be engaging in a study of gender issues, nor did I represent my purpose as such. It was only some time later that I realized my research was about "gender" as much as it was about "teachers." Teaching, in many countries and especially at elementary school level, is a "world of women" (Acker 1983). This observation is frequently made in service of apologies for its semiprofessional status, but from a feminist perspective, teaching provides a wealth of possibilities for rethinking organizational cultures and careers (Biklen 1985; Acker 1989; 1992a).

Observations on occasional days in that first term convinced me there was much of interest in the school; moreover, I was strongly attracted to its vitality and energy as well as its caring ethos. I continued visits into the following year.[2] Hillview was an inner-city school, although not in an area of great deprivation. It served the entire primary age range from four or five to eleven. It was headed by a woman, with a male deputy head teacher and eight other teachers, three of whom were part-time. All but one of the teachers were white. Hillview's two hundred children were very mixed in social class and ethnic terms. Some came from working-class white areas; some from upwardly mobile minority ethnic groups located several miles from the school; others from "countercultural" families living in the inner city and attracted by Hillview's tolerance of diversity. Others were middle-class children whose parents wanted them to experience a cross-section of society. The school was busy, crowded, and lively. The teachers had to be very flexible and tolerant of ambiguity and disruption of plans.

The most intensive period of my fieldwork took place in the 1987–88 and 1988–89 school years, adding up to about 880 hours. In the 1987–88 year, I concentrated on the "Middle Juniors Unit," a school-based innovation that involved one full-time and three part-time teachers in cooperative teaching of a group of about sixty children. The unit also integrated the children formerly part of the "special class" into the mainstream. Intensive observations of those four teachers were extended by blocks of time spent with the head teacher and occasional observations of other teachers. I took part in school activities and informal and formal meetings of staff. I took field notes during observations and supplemented these with perusal of documents. I taped interviews with all of the teachers. I continued occasional visits and regular staff meeting attendance at Hillview until December 1990 when I moved to Canada. I kept in touch and visited the school four times between 1991 and 1994.

Among themes that emerged in the data was "lives and careers." In reviewing my notes and interview tapes with this theme in mind, I was surprised by how much relevant data I had collected. My approach enabled me to draw not only upon views and ideas expressed in response to specific questions in interviews, but to add to these sources of information notes on what actually happened to the teachers over a number of years. Similarly, I could chart changes in the teachers' workplace culture over years when government interventions were significantly changing the nature of the work teachers did (Acker 1990b; 1992c).

A related area of interest, and the one particularly germane to this chapter, is the work of the head teacher. In "Managing the Drama" (Acker 1990a) I tried to convey the complexity and simultaneity of Liz Clarke's routines; the variety of "events" (interruptions to the routine); the challenge of the "stories" and "sagas," matters that were ongoing or that resurfaced sporadically and required skill and sensitivity for their resolution. In that article, however, I paid less attention to Mrs. Clarke's relationships with her staff than to other aspects of her role. But when sifting the data looking for insights into career patterns and plans of the teachers, the head teacher appeared repeatedly as a central character.

Lives and Careers

I found that teachers planned careers, but that plans were provisional (Acker 1992a). Even those who were ambitious in conventional terms expressed some doubts and reservations. Others had altered their ambitions in response to circumstances or perceived lack of encouragement for their aspirations. Most striking was what I dubbed "accidents": births, bereavements, miscarriages, illnesses. A "rational career planner" model, such as found in some of the literature, would have been *irrational* in the face of so many unpredictable fluctuations.

In the stories teachers told, luck often played a greater role than planning. Marjorie Howard got one job when she ran into a head teacher in the village store. Others told similar tales. It was generally believed that men had the advantage in primary school career climbing, although some teachers thought this was less pronounced than in the past. Although regarded as unfair, it was more a fact of life than a deeply resented inequity.

Most of the older women teachers had interrupted their careers either for childbearing or for other reasons such as travel or work outside teaching. The younger teachers had only short times out, in some cases returning directly after maternity leave. Some of the teachers' careers included spells in fixed-term contract or part-time work.

Most of the women had domestic commitments of the traditional sort. A few were single or divorced, but most were currently married and nearly all of these had children. Teachers with young children made complicated arrangements with nannies, childminders, relatives, playgroups, or nurseries. They had to have plenty of stamina and good time-management skills.

There were a number of career moves during my fieldwork. Hillview's deputy head left for a headship in another school near the start of my research. Later on, two other teachers left the school for deputy headships elsewhere. One teacher left teaching. A part-timer moved to a full-time position in another school and then to a deputy headship in a third school. New teachers entered as each of these left. Another part-timer at Hillview moved to full-time status there.

Behind these "moves" were complex stories; moreover, these moves were only the most visible face of "career." Changing from one age group to another; taking on new responsibilities within the school; attending inservice courses; innovating in the classroom; rethinking one's personal goals and ideas about teaching were all part of "career," seen in a broader sense. I came to understand careers as featuring individual choices, stances, and life events, taking place in the wider context of fluctuating rewards and pressures and pleasures to be found in teaching. Perceptions were formed and decisions were taken in the context of the workplace. Teachers advised each other, and watched and analyzed each other's experiences with job interviews or new responsibilities. They shaped their views of what was feasible, likely, or preferable through participating in the workplace culture of the school. The head teacher's role in influencing these perceptions was substantial.

The Head Teacher's Influence

Like the head teachers I encountered in other schools, Liz Clarke saw encouragement and support for teachers as a major part of her role. Her efforts extended beyond advice and encouragement, however, to more subtle maneuvers. Below I discuss the ways in which Mrs. Clarke influenced working experiences and career prospects for her staff.

Support

My field notes contain many expressions of encouragement and praise for the teachers from the head, often spoken at staff meetings. There were also tokens of gratitude such as chocolates or a bottle of sherry at the end of the term. Support was also evident for teachers' efforts to add to their qualifications or advance their careers. When teachers were about to be interviewed for posts elsewhere, the head teacher provided advice about interview techniques and sometimes mock interviews. Liz suggested to one teacher that she write down the questions after an interview for a deputy headship, both for her own future use and to be shared with the other teachers. In two cases where teachers had unsuccessful interviews for positions in other schools, she arranged for county advisors to come in and "debrief" the teacher concerned.

At Hillview, career advice carried extra weight because Mrs. Clarke could also be a role model for the women teachers. Debbie Stevens, one of the teachers, commented, "Liz is a woman, and I feel that if I wanted advice about career development I could get it from her." Both Debbie and another teacher, Rosalind Phillips, were encouraged by Liz to enroll in an M.Ed. program in management education [educational administration] at a nearby university. At the time, it was possible to receive "day release" from the Local Education Authority (LEA) to attend courses for master's degrees. The teacher would have a half-day "off" each week, usually for two years, with money provided to the school for a replacement. It was thought that management courses had greater prospects of such support than some of the others.

At the start of my study, Rosalind was working part-time in each of two schools. She worried about whether her part-time status would make her ineligible for day release. In a telephone conversation with me, she commented that Liz would support her, "she's so good, she'd probably let me go even if I weren't released." In an interview, she gave a fuller account of Liz's advice:

> She said to me all along that she didn't think I ought to do this two school job for much longer for my own career prospects. . . . I had to put down my roots. . . . She has mentioned it on a couple of occasions. She's never said what she thinks I ought to be doing, but she's always said she feels I ought to make a commitment. She has said that she didn't think I ought to pursue the special needs role anymore . . . like Martin [the primary education management tutor at the university], he says the same thing.

She contrasted this kind of support from Mrs. Clarke with its absence from another head she has worked for:

> Tony Grant doesn't really go in for that kind of talk . . . in the very first place, he didn't think I'd even get my place on the M.Ed. degree because I was only part-time in his school. He's probably done the most to discourage me. .

There were many other examples of career-related comments by teachers in my field notes. For example, when a deputy headship was advertised in a less than ideal school, Helen Davies said to me "Liz thinks I should apply, I could turn it round." To me, Liz mused that she might telephone the head teacher at another school with a good reputation for special needs to arrange a visit for the teacher who had that responsibility at Hillview: "It would be good for her to visit somewhere else." Liz took more subtle steps, too. At a staff meeting shortly after one teacher had an unsuccessful interview for a deputy headship elsewhere, Liz asked her to explain some of her classroom procedures to the other staff. My notes say, "I suspect the intention is to bolster her self-esteem."

At Hillview, the head teacher's role in influencing teacher careers went beyond the relatively common manifestations described above. Mrs. Clarke took care to hire teachers who would share her vision for the school. She put a great deal of energy and thought into their deployment within the school. When the time came for them to move on, she went to great lengths to help them. Many of her efforts took place behind the scenes. Her actions might be seen as a kind of sponsorship or monitoring, a point to which I shall return.

Selection

Head teachers I spoke with during the study explained to me that it took a long time to stamp one's own influence on a school staff; one estimated that it could be as much as ten years. Mrs. Clarke had been at the school for four years at the start of my study and was then just beginning to see hoped-for changes materialize. Such estimates are based on the time taken for teachers with divergent views or practices to leave the school for one reason or another, to be replaced with those more in the image of the new head. Another parallel process involved longer-serving teachers modifying their practices or views to be more in line with those of the head. Changes might also occur in the communities that provide pupils for the school, or the extent of support forthcoming from the Local Education Authority (LEA). These stories tended to have a ring of heroism about them: the new head "turning round" the school, remaking it in his or her own image. Reflecting on this point, Liz said to me in an interview (with slight tongue in cheek): "I identified the true nature of the school and intensified it."

During the major part of my study, head teachers had considerable control over hiring; later on, government policies diluted this power as the school governing body[3] came to hold formal responsibility. There were two particularly interesting features of Liz's hiring practices. One, which is commented on by Evetts (1989, 1990) in her study of primary school head teachers' careers, is reliance upon personal networks to find appropriate individuals. Vacant posts had to be advertised, at least in the LEA circulars, and often in national newspapers. In several cases, advertisements brought in teachers from outside the city, or whose past experience had been elsewhere although they were now living locally. In the first year of my research, new appointments of Dennis Bryan, Debbie Stevens, and Kristen King added a cosmopolitan touch to the school, complementing the depth of experience and local knowledge teachers already in the school possessed.

In addition to major appointments, there were part-time and temporary positions in the school that became vacant more frequently. Here the head had considerable control over staffing. Many of the teachers working in such a capacity were known to Liz prior to appointment. Rosalind Phillips, when she was previously working in secondary education, had taught Liz's own children. A supply [substitute] teacher in the school lived in Liz's village and had taught at a school where Liz had worked in the past. A retired teacher who did volunteer teaching one day a week in the school had also taught with Liz in earlier days. The wife of the deputy head did some supply teaching for the school. Amanda Prentice, who joined the school in 1989, previously taught at a nearby school and was a friend of one of the Hillview teachers. Marjorie Howard, who was part-time at Hillview before Mrs. Clarke arrived, had found her way to the school though having taught with a friend of the previous head teacher.

Other part-time, temporary, or substitute teachers came in with no previous connection. But once a teacher was known in the school, she was on a kind of mental register. When a position opened up, first recourse would be for "people we know and trust." Hillview's children could be very difficult for teachers unused to inner-city teaching. It helped if a teacher was known to be able to cope with, and relate to, "our children." Experience in the city schools elsewhere, such as less advantaged parts of London, might substitute for being "known." In several cases when a vacancy occurred, efforts were made to give the edge to someone already connected with the school; for example, a job specification could be written to match the person's particular talents and experiences.

The other notable feature of Liz's hiring efforts was her support for teachers with young children. Debbie Stevens, Rosalind Phillips, Kristen King, Sheila Jones, and Dennis Bryan all had small children. The other full-time teachers were either childless or had older children. Liz herself had three children, now grown up, and she could empathize with teacher parents.

There were a number of examples of Liz's concern. When scheduling parent interviews after school and in the evenings, Liz tried to adjust the timetable so that teachers with small children could go home in between if they wished. On another occasion, when a staff meeting after school overran its normal time, she suddenly looked at Debbie and said "Don't you have to be back for Marilyn [the nanny]?" Debbie said in an interview "I'd never worry [about the head teacher's reaction] if I had a problem at home, say if things got bad with Katy." On another occasion she repeated the point: "I think she is very understanding of the family situation and doesn't expect anyone to be at school till 6:00 every night, doesn't judge people by the amount of hours they're up in the classroom."

It seemed that such an outlook was relatively rare among head teachers. In an interview, Dennis Bryan, the deputy head, commented that "Liz cares about everything" and it makes things more difficult for her. In "everything" he included "teachers' children, their husbands." Debbie also reported that she and Dennis has discussed this way of working:

> Dennis made a remark the other day—about how kind and considerate she was in taking into account everyone's timetabling problems, whereas his previous head, and mine, would have said you've got to do this, that's your hours. Whereas Liz thinks, oh, so-and-so can only get child arrangements then; this

would interfere with so-and-so's other job elsewhere; that would interfere with another commitment. And we spoke to her about that then, and she said that was the way she liked to work, and it made her feel better; if she thought it was harming the children in any way, then she would change it.

When a teacher was away for a number of weeks due to complications of an ectopic pregnancy, Liz commented to me that some people ask her why she hires women of childbearing age. She said, "you have to expect this, that they will have children. But they do work extra hard." My observations suggested these teachers were indeed grateful and tried to repay Liz's trust in them by hard work and strong commitments to the school.

Staff Deployment

I have already indicated that there was room for maneuver in hiring staff. Other opportunities existed for Liz to take an active role vis-à-vis staff deployment and development. This role was only partly visible to the staff.

Nancy Green probably owed her move to a deputy headship in another school to Liz's strategic answers to a phone call from the head of the prospective school. This head teacher had not been especially impressed by Nancy when Nancy had visited her school, but had then read Liz's highly enthusiastic reference, so telephoned for some less formal elaboration. I was in the office "shadowing" Liz at the time. Liz stressed that although Nancy was shy and might not make an immediately electric impression, she had "so many talents, energy, a preparedness to work . . . " Naturally, the other head asked what Liz called the "crunch question," whether Mrs. Clarke would want Nancy as her own deputy head. Liz had to explain why Nancy would not be right for her—Nancy's preferences for organizational order and clarity often clashed with Liz's more flexible style—yet she would be "right with the right person."

Helen Davies and Marjorie Howard both enjoyed timely sabbatical terms Liz arranged for them at the university when some danger of burnout loomed. When Liz herself went on sabbatical, she made sure Dennis would be appointed acting head teacher and Helen as acting deputy. Later, when Dennis spent a year away on a teacher exchange, Debbie Stevens became acting deputy. Helen explained how Liz gave teachers useful experiences through delegation:

> She creates a good atmosphere . . . and she does appreciate what people do . . . she is willing to delegate, and not to delegate for the sake of it, but to delegate for people to have responsibility and she will accept the decisions they make. . . . Liz looks at the people, the personality, she looks and seeks

what they're good at, and she will delegate those jobs to those who are good at doing it. She boosts your ego and your confidence through that. She'll only give you the jobs she knows you can handle.

Teachers were not expected to spend their careers with one age group, or with one curricular responsibility; there were frequent changes. Sometimes a change was contemplated because the teacher would benefit from the variety, overlooked talents might surface, or the experience would help career prospects; sometimes there were gaps in staffing because someone left or was away for a time due to maternity leave, secondment, sabbatical, illness, or a teacher exchange. These openings increased scope for flexibility, although they also threatened stability, as they were not always predictable. When Liz thought about who might go where for the following year, she always kept in mind the possibility of any such plans having to be altered and altered again.

An additional element entered the calculations in 1990–91. The 1988 Education Reform Act introduced "Local Management of Schools" (LMS), a scheme whereby the major responsibility for school budgets would be transferred from the LEA to individual school governing bodies. A school the size of Hillview would have several years before fully operating LMS, but some of the effects were being felt by 1990–91. School funding was based on a formula that took insufficient account of the proportion of experienced, and thus more highly paid, teachers in a school. Liz had to think hard about saving money and making sure no teacher lost her job. For the time being, Debbie's and Amanda's maternity leaves were saving the day, as those teachers could be temporarily replaced with cheaper substitutes.

The good of the children was a particularly important consideration in staffing decisions. When a class of children had been disrupted because of staffing changes, Liz made attempts to give them more continuity, either by allocating a particularly strong teacher or arranging for the class to stay for two years with one teacher. Another consideration was fostering innovation in the school. In several cases, moves were made to enable teachers to work together in efforts to develop cooperative teaching.

Staff deployment, to Liz, was like a puzzle or a game, complicated but enthralling. She agreed with my analysis: "That is the bit of the job that I probably enjoy as much as anything, you know, solving it in the shower. It's usually in the shower that I think of something like, hey—this is the moment to move so-and-so."

At another time, she explained to me that she tried to balance everyone's needs, taking into account personalities, wishes, childcare, career plans, and so forth, at the same time putting the "good of the school" first.

She told teachers this, too. At a staff meeting in April 1989 she explained that she was working on staffing arrangements for the following year: "The good of the children in the school is what I must think of first. A very close second is your preferences. I may not be able to give you all your preferences." As Liz had just returned from her term away on sabbatical, she added: "I'm now in a position to take a global view. Thank you all very much for keeping the school so well. There's a lovely feeling. The children seem very calm, very motivated, and very happy."

Staffing moves could have mixed consequences. Moving Marjorie Howard to reception teaching [four- and five-year-olds] was a stroke of genius as she was brilliant with the little ones. I was mesmerized as I watched her make everything into a drama or a game, keeping up a fast-paced performance. Teachers knew that contrary to popular belief, reception teaching could be the most demanding job in the school. Some children came in without sufficient cultural or language resources to make the transition to school easy. Moving play equipment and repeatedly bending down to the tiny children was physically exhausting, and as was generally true throughout the school, classes were large and resources insufficient.

Marjorie initially approached the move with great trepidation. She had originally been a secondary school teacher, switching (as was common) into primary school teaching when she returned after some time away with her own children. Mrs. Clarke had already persuaded her to change to full-time teaching. The idea of her teaching reception stemmed from an offer she had made to Nancy Green, who was having a difficult time with certain children in the reception class that year. Marjorie told me in an interview that one day after school, she had found Nancy in tears: "I said now look, Nancy, if it's that bad, for God's sake, tell me in the morning and I'll go straight to Mrs. Clarke, and we'll swap classes. I said I'll go down there, to give you a break. I didn't care about the work, I was thinking of her, really." Although the swap never happened, Mrs. Clarke heard about the offer and "the next thing I knew, Mrs. Clarke said, 'I'll take you up on that offer.'"

Although Marjorie was inclined to refuse, it became too difficult for her to do so and she eventually agreed, not without considerable anxiety:

> I lost half a stone in weight, and I didn't sleep for a fortnight, when she said about going into reception. I was so worried about it, and had terrible nightmares of her pushing me, pushing the car into the dock with the handbrake off [laughs]. I really was very worried. It's a monumental jump, to me, starting off with comprehensive [high school] age children.

Her anxieties proved unfounded but the story serves to emphasize the stakes involved. Moves within the school for teachers had consequences and were not always taken in their stride. Rosalind Phillips reacted unhappily to the suggestion that she might share a particular class when her preference was to be a floater and work with small groups of children while she pursued her M.Ed.; her worries about it probably contributed to her decision to leave her part-time post at the school and work full-time elsewhere. Teachers often found it hard to "say no." I suspect this was partly because they were women trying to be helpful and kind. Marjorie said: "I don't like to ever say no to people, because it doesn't seem helpful. You try to please people and do what they want, to keep the peace."

I found the situation made an interesting contrast with my work in an university department where individuals had more autonomy over their situations. In another case I asked a teacher why she couldn't just refuse to have a particular child in her class. He was seriously disturbed and causing havoc in the school (see Acker 1990a for more details). She explained that she simply couldn't refuse; that the consequences for her in career terms might be too severe. Put more positively, teachers who coped well with particularly difficult situations gained a great deal of credit in the head's eyes, as well as credibility in the school generally.

Sponsorship: Labels and Triggers

After several years in the school, I could see that some teachers had gradually risen in the esteem of the head. I don't mean to suggest that anyone actually sank, but some teachers seemed able to display special qualities that triggered Liz's strongest sponsorship efforts. A subtle labeling process appeared to be at work. In the schools I studied or visited, heads, including Liz, rarely did any systematic observation of teachers actually teaching classes, although they would pass by or through the classrooms frequently. Judgments about teaching competence were not necessarily arrived at by direct empirical evidence derived from the classroom.

On the other hand, the role the teacher took in the wider life of the school was more visible; for example, taking responsibility for writing a policy in a particular curriculum area, giving a talk to parents, organizing a school concert or fair, general participation at staff meetings, or working with the head or other teachers to plan some other aspect of school work. Mrs. Clarke had clear ideas about who was "like a rock" or "a good, average teacher" or "a brilliant teacher." Evetts (1989) argues that sponsorship has to be triggered by appropriate behavior. Somehow a teacher has to show that she is able and willing to benefit from special efforts on her behalf.

Debbie Stevens's progress through the school illustrates the labeling process working successfully for a teacher. Right from their first meeting, she and Liz got on well. Hillview was Debbie's second teaching job. She had spent several years in an inner-city London primary school. She moved to the Wesley area when her husband changed jobs and their first child was only a few months old.

In her second term at Hillview, Debbie became the only full-time teacher involved in the experimental team-teaching effort mentioned earlier. Thus she found herself in a leadership role, which she handled ably. Liz sung her praises to me on several occasions. She admired her gentle style, her competence and commitment, her grace under pressure. In her early months at the school, Debbie had problems getting her child care sorted out and arranging a house move. Her child woke frequently in the night, and her husband gave relatively little support with housework and childcare. Debbie's ability to cope with these multiple pressures probably increased her value in the eyes of the head teacher.

Generally she was amenable to the head's ideas. When Liz suggested it would be good for her to get experience taking a class of younger children, she said she "wouldn't mind." Despite the complications of her domestic arrangements, she managed to put time into the school well beyond the minimum, staying late when necessary, coming into school before and after the term to sort out materials, going on short inservice courses as well as working on a master's degree. During the time of my research, Debbie had two more children. While on her maternity leaves, she kept in touch with the school and attended weekly staff meetings.

In January 1990, Liz mentioned that she might try to get her an acting deputy headship if Dennis's foreign exchange materialized. By September 1990, Debbie was teaching the oldest children (a traditional position for deputy head, especially when male) and acting as deputy head, after only three years and a term at the school. Two years later, after Dennis became head teacher of a different school, Debbie was deputy head at Hillview.

In contrast, Sheila Jones was less successful in triggering sponsorship efforts. At the start of my research in 1987, she was a part-time teacher in the school. Sheila said she had been ambitious in the past and would have liked to have become a head teacher. She was becoming less certain of this goal, but was edging closer to full-time work. Sheila had been "secondary trained." Generally this seems to be thought (by other teachers) to be a disadvantage in English primary education, as it is assumed to be synonymous with being less flexible, more didactic, and less child-centered. Some of the other teachers had "overcome" their training to become adept at acceptable primary school pedagogies. But Sheila, who had also held several jobs outside teaching, and spent ten years teaching at a very rigid primary school, felt uncertain about her ability to produce the type of primary practice favored in the school. In the following year, she shared a class with another teacher and it was evident that she found the children difficult, especially at the start of her term. My suspicion is that she failed to manipulate her image sufficiently to be regarded as a strong teacher, although she was respected for her many talents, and was actually able to cope with this class in the end.

Sheila hoped for an "incentive allowance"[4] but did not manage to achieve one. She embarked upon a course in library management and got recognition from the head and others for her efforts to reorganize the school library, as she did for her successful running of the school fair for several years. But then she had a second child and her hopes of moving into full-time teaching suffered a further setback. Coming back after maternity leave, she "took groups." For a teacher to take groups means that rather than have her own class, or a shared one, she works with small groups of children who need extra help, or, alternatively, takes another teacher's class to permit that teacher to do some other work. After a year, she decided to leave teaching entirely. Mrs. Clarke told me how sorry she was that Sheila was leaving:

> She has not enjoyed the last twelve months. Being a relief teacher is not an enjoyable experience in a primary school, because you get all of the hassle and none of the satisfaction. . . . We've not developed Sheila. That is partly because of having the children, and her family situation. She's given up on her career now. Maybe when the little one is in school . . . she could still do it, although she'll be that bit older. She is someone who could easily be in a position of authority within a school, and she is not going to move on. So I'm sad about that.[5]

It is important to realize that the images head teachers have of their teachers are not fixed. The teacher's behavior—and indeed other factors such as her family phase—can alter the "label." Liz noted that the "old stagers" in the school—herself included in the description—had found their intellectual capacities developing alongside the newly appointed younger teachers who "are intellectual about what they are doing."

Betty Chapman provides an example. At the start of my research, she was clearly a committed classroom teacher but without any strong career ambitions. Her family responsibilities were dominant. Four years later, her children were older and she had more time and energy. I wrote in my field notes that Betty looked younger every time I saw her. Some other teachers had left and Betty had taken on more responsibilities; she now held a temporary incentive allowance (see note 4). The age group she taught was the one that went through the first national testing following the 1988 Educational Reform Act and she was able to explain what was happening to meetings of parents, school governors, and colleagues. Liz spoke to me of Betty's contributions in highly complimentary terms.

Conclusion

Few discussions of the relevance of gender to the principal's role have specifically addressed the question of women principals' influence on careers of women teachers in their schools. What evidence there is suggests that female principals are not necessarily initiators of equity measures (Sadker et al. 1991, 288). The ethnographic approach of my study, which combines interviews with participant observation, provides an unusual and longitudinal view of events and relationships in a school. The aspects of Liz Clarke's work discussed in this chapter are not single acts but processes that occur over time.

Over time I was able to document how Mrs. Clarke gave teachers a great deal of moral and practical support, encouraging them to attend relevant courses, preparing them for interviews, sometimes making direct efforts to help them secure deputy headships in other schools. She made sure that teachers joining the school shared its sense of mission and she gave opportunities to teachers with small children. She arranged for staff to move around the school, teaching different age groups and getting a variety of experiences in curriculum areas and leadership roles. In deploying staff, she took into account the needs of the teacher, including any family responsibilities, as well as the needs of the children in the school. The teachers were active agents, too; those who were able to construct an image that projected ability and motivation might get an extra boost of sponsorship, although all teachers benefited from support. It might be said that Mrs. Clarke engaged in a process of *teacher development,* rather than simply helping teachers with careers in a narrow sense.

Clearly, Liz Clarke's approach to her teachers matched what one might expect from a female principal on the basis of some of the feminist theories discussed earlier. Her support for her staff makes a marked contrast with its absence in other chapters in this volume (e.g., McCall; Troen and Boles). Her style exemplified the values of "caretaking, nurturance, empathy, [and] connectedness" Ferguson (1984, 25) identifies as women's preferences. As I have shown elsewhere (Acker 1990b; 1991; 1992a; 1992b), the school was run on democratic, collegial, and participatory lines. It is very similar to the "female world" Valentine describes in this volume. However, Mrs. Clarke was still clearly the leader. It was "her school," as Nias and co-workers (1989) found for head teachers in their study. As Kanter suggests, power can be conceptualized as the ability to get things done and can be based on relationships rather than threats: "empowering more people through generating more autonomy, more participation in decisions, and more access to resources increases the total capacity for effective action rather than increases domination" (1977, 116).

Similarly, when Statham and colleagues look comparatively at women in a range of occupations, they comment that maintaining relationships was a key concern throughout. Yet maintaining relationships was not to be seen as opposed to task accomplishment: "women may be blending task and person involvement in unique and effective ways not previously recognized in the workplace" (1988, 26).

Nevertheless, we must beware of taking the difference model to its logical extreme. Mrs. Clarke manages her school in a way likely to be more characteristic of women, but this does not mean all women principals will be like Mrs. Clarke, or that Mrs. Clarke works the way she does solely because she is female. For example, a previous head of Hillview was also female, but teachers with longer service at the school described her in very different terms. She "liked everything to look nice, and to be quiet and orderly." Many times I was told the story of the lights on the office door, intended for teachers as well as pupils: green for enter, yellow for wait, red for no entry. When I asked one teacher in an interview whether anyone had ever been particularly encouraging or discouraging about her career, she replied: "Liz has been the most encouraging. [The former head] was the one who discouraged, not me in particular but I think she was discouraging to everyone. She wasn't interested, she didn't want to know."

Not only are there individual differences among women principals, but there are likely to be features of the environment which make it easier or more difficult to manage in the style described. Marshall and Mitchell (1989), in a study of assistant principals in the United States, found that both men and women, but especially women, displayed "connection" and "caring" orientations. However, pre-administrative and on-site socialization were so strongly prescriptive that actual behavior did not correspond to the preferences. Some women found creative alternatives, but only within a context of strong pressures towards a "formal, authoritarian, detachment orientation." Cultural and structural factors may be extremely important in determining whether a particular leadership style is enabled to emerge.

It may be significant that Hillview is a fairly small school, with a physical layout that permits frequent interactions among teachers. Shared experience of the stress of teaching seemed to bind the staff together, not against a common enemy but in support of one another and in search of solutions to common problems (Acker 1992b).

It may be significant that Hillview is in England, and in a particular Local Education Authority [school board]. Many English primary schools are fairly small, and some are "infant schools" for children aged five to seven. Although men, who are a minority of primary teachers overall, are greatly over-represented in headships and deputy headships, women are nevertheless 47.1% of primary school head teachers in England and Wales (97.6%

for infant schools) (Acker 1992a). Moreover, the career structure for the classroom teachers is not as flat as in some American schools, for the "incentive allowance" scheme (see note 4) and the tradition of deputy head teachers carrying a full teaching load mean that a teacher may achieve a certain status and improved salary within the school without leaving the classroom. Head teachers in primary schools also frequently do some teaching, especially in very small schools. Thus, there are opportunity structures in place that allow women teachers to imagine they might have a career in the traditional sense of moving up a ladder.

Collegiality may also be more typical of English primary schools than those in the United States (Acker 1991). Nias and co-workers (1989) found a number of primary schools in England where teachers worked in "collaborative cultures." Mrs. Clarke suggested that advisors in the LEA had encouraged collegiality throughout the county. Hiring practices in LEAs, or school boards, vary. Some school boards in north America move principals around regularly, for example every five years. Teacher hiring may also be at board level rather than under some control by the individual school. Both of those practices could work against the formation of a close, collegial culture such as the one found at Hillview, a culture where the staff and the head teacher share a vision of what the school should be like.

In today's Britain, however, there are forces working against the style of leadership Liz Clarke displayed at Hillview. The 1988 Education Reform Act introduced a number of changes into the ways schools are run and the requirements placed upon them. The introduction of "Local Management of Schools" (devolved budgets) and open enrollment means many head teachers are becoming more preoccupied with finances and projecting a winning image for the school than with relationships. The onslaught of changes produced by the government's "reforms" has encouraged a model of leadership removed from the symbolism of "head teacher" and better described as "new managerialism" (Al-Khalifa 1989).

Al-Khalifa argues that a mythology about leadership elevates stereotypical male traits such as analytical detachment and toughness. Management is rationalistic, technocratic, hierarchical, and often generic—that is, it calls upon similar skills whatever the context. Marshall and Mitchell (1989) make a similar argument in the United States about the "professional culture of school administration," as does Ferguson (1984), who attacks "bureaucratic rationality" and the gendered and hierarchical separation of administration from teaching. Al-Khalifa suggests that the new managerialism stems from a desire for rationality and certainty in times of turbulence and change. Women, she believes, become uneasy about being "new managers"; it is alien to their concept of self.

A conversation with Rosalind Phillips, one of the Hillview teachers, after she had attended a lecture for her M.Ed. in Management Education, captures the tension between the opposing trends of new managerialism and women's perhaps superior styles. She was perplexed that "everyone likes Liz, and before I came on the course I'd have said she was the better head hands down, but Tony [the other head she worked for] fits the theories so much better." The leadership theories she was studying were presumably the same ones criticized by Blackmore (1989) and others (including Schmuck and Dunlap, this volume) as being based on the experiences of men. Perhaps, in time, the influence of feminist perspectives upon educational administration will mean that a head teacher or principal who cares about her teachers and helps them to develop their careers and capacities will, after all, "fit the theories."

Notes

1. I have retained British terminology and idioms in quotations and other places where using the American word or phrase might detract from the authenticity of the description. I have added the American equivalent in brackets where this practice aided clarity, e.g., head teacher [principal].

2. In April 1988, I started going regularly into a second school, which also provided a welcoming atmosphere, but contrasted in a number of ways with Hillview. It enabled me to view Hillview in a comparative, and sharper, perspective. Material from both schools on teacher careers appears in Acker 1992a.

3. Schools have governing bodies, made up of appointees of the Local Education Authority who reflect the political composition of local government, as well as representatives of parents and teachers. The head teacher may either be a governor or attend ex-officio. If a school is affiliated with a church, as many are, the church also appoint governors. Schools not so affiliated will make up numbers by bringing in individuals from the community such as local businessmen. Hillview had eleven governors. Governors have been given increased responsibilities by the Conservative government, including staffing and finance.

4. During my fieldwork, each school had a certain number of such allowances. Primary schools usually had "A" and "B" allowances (worth £ 1,206 and £ 1,905 respectively as of January 1992) and about one-third to one-half of the teachers held them. Allowances could be awarded for good teaching, for shortage subjects or difficult to fill posts, or for extra responsibilities (the most common use); school governors (see note 3) were involved in their allocation, although the head teacher had considerable influence. In 1993, the allowances were replaced by a new system where certain qualifications and responsibilities could mean extra points

on a salary scale. Many teachers hold extra responsibilities without formal reward.

5. By 1993, Sheila had returned to supply [substitute] teaching in the school. See my earlier discussion of the irrationality of the rational career planner model when applied to the teachers.

Bibliography

Acker, S. (1983). Women and teaching: A semi-detached sociology of a semi-profession. In S. Walker and L. Barton (eds.), *Gender, class and education*. Lewes: Falmer Press.

————. (1987). Feminist theory and the study of gender and education. *International Review of Education*, 33, 419–35.

————. (1989). Rethinking teachers' careers. In S. Acker (ed.), *Teachers, gender and careers*. Lewes: Falmer Press.

————. (1990a). Managing the drama: The head teacher's work in an urban primary school. *Sociological Review*, 38(2), 247–71.

————. (1990b). Teachers' culture in an English primary school: Continuity and change. *British Journal of Sociology of Education*, 11(3), 257–73.

————. (1991). Teacher relationships and educational reform in England and Wales. *The Curriculum Journal*, 2(3), 301–16.

————. (1992a). Creating careers: Women teachers at work. *Curriculum Inquiry*, 22(2), 141–63.

————. (1992b). Gender, collegiality and teachers' workplace culture in Britain. Paper presented at the annual meetings of the American Educational Research Association, San Francisco, April.

————. (1992c). Responding to reform: Teachers' work in an English primary school. Paper presented at the annual meetings of the Canadian Society for the Study of Education, Charlottetown, June.

Al-Khalifa, E. (1989). Management by halves: Women teachers and school management. In H. DeLyon and F. Migniuolo (eds.), *Women teachers: Issues and experiences*. Milton Keynes: Open University Press.

Belenky, M. F., Clinchy, B. M., Goldberger, N. R., and Tarule, J. M. (1986). *Women's ways of knowing*. New York: Basic Books.

Biklen, S. K. (1985). Can elementary schoolteaching be a career?: A search for new ways of understanding women's work. *Issues in Education* 3, 215–31.

Blackmore, J. (1989). Educational leadership: A feminist critique and reconstruction. In J. Smyth (ed.), *Critical perspectives on educational leadership*. London: Falmer Press.

Eisenstein, H. (1984). *Contemporary feminist thought*. London: Unwin.

Evetts, J. (1989). The internal labour market for primary teachers. In S. Acker (ed.), *Teachers, gender and careers*. Lewes: Falmer Press.

———. (1990). *Women in primary teaching: Career contexts and strategies*. London: Unwin Hyman.

Ferguson, K. (1984). *The feminist case against bureaucracy*. Philadelphia: Temple University Press.

Gilligan, C. (1982). *In a different voice*. Cambridge, MA: Harvard University Press.

Gray, E. (1989). The culture of separated desks. In C. Pearson, D. Shavlik, and J. Touchton (eds.), *Educating the majority: Women challenge tradition in higher education*. New York: Macmillan.

Intriligator, B. (1983). Leadership theory revisited. *Journal of Educational Equity and Leadership*, 3(1), 5–17.

Kanter, R. M. (1977). *Men and women of the corporation*. New York: Basic Books.

Marshall, C. and Mitchell, B. (1989). Women's careers as a critique of the administrative culture. Paper presented at the annual meetings of the American Educational Research Association, San Francisco, March.

Nias, J., Southworth, G., and Yeomans, R. (1989). *Staff relationships in the primary school*. London: Cassell.

Noddings, N. (1990). Feminist critiques in the professions. In C. Cazden (ed.), *Review of Research in Education*, 16. Washington, DC: American Educational Research Association.

Sadker, M., Sadker, D., and Klein, S. (1991). The issue of gender in elementary and secondary education. In G. Grant (ed.), *Review of Research in Education*, 17. Washington, DC: American Educational Research Association.

Scott, J. (1990). Deconstructing equality-versus-difference: Or, the uses of poststructuralist theory for feminism. In M. Hirsch and E. Fox Keller (eds.), *Conflicts in feminism*. New York: Routledge.

Shakeshaft, C. (1989) *Women in educational administration*. Newbury Park: Sage

Statham, A., Miller, E., and Mauksch, S. (eds.) (1988). *The worth of women's work: A qualitative synthesis*. Albany: SUNY Press.

Stromquist, N. (1990). Gender inequality in education: Accounting for women's subordination. *British Journal of Sociology of Education*, 11(2), 137–53.

FOUR

"Is That Sociology?": The Accounts of Women of Color Graduate Students in Ph.D. Programs[1]

Mary Romero and Debbie Storrs

Introduction

Challenges presented by the increasing presence of women and persons of color in education have placed the issue of diversity high on the education agenda for the twenty-first century. Unlike previous generations of students, the current higher education student body is no longer culturally homogeneous nor is it predominately male. Moreover, unlike past decades where higher education was reserved primarily for the white, predominantly male elite, our society can no longer afford to keep women at home and all minority people in manual labor positions. The United States needs a literate and well trained labor force to meet the demands of an increasingly technological, internationalized, competitive world society. The country is more likely to meet these needs by fostering policies which promote ability and interest as the criteria for inclusion rather than gender or color.

Past history in higher education would not seem to make this a likely scenario. Tensions in the traditional educational system increased after WWII as working-class males took advantage of the GI Bill and entered higher education in record numbers. Later, white women and women and men of color took advantage of affirmative action and desegregation programs and also entered higher education in steadily increasing numbers. Criticisms of "irrelevant" and "overly narrow" curricula grew. However, there was no over-throw of the predominant Euro-American perspective nor termination of male dominance in academic decision-making; there was no educational revolution. Instead, a few concessions to criticisms slowly appeared: under-funded ethnic studies and women's studies programs were created, a book or a lecture on the minority experience was added here and there to the tra-ditional curriculum, and a few (very few) faculty and staff of color were hired. The faculty of color were scattered throughout the university but were pri-marily located in marginalized departments in untenured, temporary posi-tions. Worse yet, demands for an inclusive approach to all aspects of higher education have yielded high levels of emotional rhetoric on all sides of the argument making it very difficult to know what is actually happening in the "ivory towers" of this country.

The Method of Study

A fresh perspective to long-standing problems of equity in higher edu-cation can often be the stimulus for identifying both the issues and solutions to change. We began our investigation into the status of women of color graduate students in sociology in response to concerns voiced by minority women at various regional and national sociological association meetings. As members of the Social Issues Committee of the Sociologists for Women in Society (SWS) we became concerned by the feelings of isolation that women of color in graduate school were voicing within the association. We wanted to place women of color at the center of our analysis in order to doc-ument their experiences and to see if understanding those experiences yield new insights into how the higher education community can construc-tively respond to issues of diversity. We believe that setting the agenda for the turn of the century involves clarification of the current status of diver-sity on campus and the identification of barriers restricting the develop-ment of a truly inclusive learning environment.

We interviewed twenty-six women of color who were in sociology grad-uate programs about their graduate experiences. These women varied in age, ethnicity, geographical area, and stage of their graduate programs. Of the women we interviewed, 7.9% identified themselves as Native American, 42.3% as African American, 19.2% as Asian American, and 30.8% as Latina. They ranged in age from 25 to 65 with 46% concentrated between 25 and 35 years of age. These women were enrolled in graduate programs across the United States with 38.5% from the West Coast, 38.5% from the East

Coast, 15.4% from the South, and 7.6% from the Midwest. The sample included women in various stages of their graduate career. For example, 11.5% reported they were engaged in course work, 26.9% were completing comprehensive exams, 53.8% were in the dissertation process, and 7.7% had recently graduated.

Open-ended questions were asked so that the women were free to identify the issues they faced in graduate sociology programs, rather than simply select responses from a set of fixed responses. Women were asked about financial aid, mentoring support, their relationships with faculty and other graduate students, research, teaching and publishing opportunities, and programmatic recommendations for the discipline or their department.

The responses reveal deep structural barriers within graduate education that current strategies do not address. A major theme in the interview responses was that both the formal and informal structure in graduate programs create barriers and obstacles to success. In fact, these stories illustrate how existing affirmative action programs have not generated the conditions for full diversity and equity in higher education. Responses are summarized in the following paragraphs under the general categories of curriculum and allocation of resources.

Formation of Knowledge and Ideology: The Absence of Inclusive Curriculum

Curriculum becomes a question of equity since success in higher education is often conditioned by one's relationship to knowledge and forms of thought (Collins 1990; Smith 1987). The dominant epistemology in higher education has been defined from an Eurocentric, masculinist tradition (Collins 1990). Sociology graduate programs are representative of this larger dominant epistemology. The power to define sociological knowledge, what knowledge is and the methods to obtain it, has been held predominantly by white, upper-class males. The closer one is to the dominant ideology of knowledge and culture in higher education, the more successful one is. The closer the students' fit with the culture of higher education, the easier they maneuver through the system because the rules, norms and culture are familiar and similar to their own. Furthermore, the rules of the game of higher education are not always readily accessible to others and it often takes time to learn such rules. As a result, women of color are at an immediate disadvantage.

The majority of the women interviewed revealed that courses in race, ethnicity and gender may be listed in a course catalog, but were seldom regularly available. The women frequently questioned the legitimacy of departmental claims that these seldom offered courses were among the department's "specialties". For example, Vickie (like many other women we interviewed) made the mistake of assuming that courses on race relations listed in the catalog were actually being taught: "They (the department) have some courses listed in the catalog but they just don't offer them. So when you look at it (course catalog) you're sort of deceived. You have to actually look at what they are offering."

Although not all these women of color graduate students were developing race, class, and gender as their major areas of interest, all of the interviewees expressed disappointment in their department's treatment of race and ethnicity as subject matter. In addition, a surprising number of departments had a very limited selection of courses on gender. The following were typical of the descriptions of the curriculum provided:

> They (the department) require you to take these courses in various aspects with specialties like family, but they never had a course on race and ethnicity or culture, basic culture, or something like that. So I think that would be a really good addition. Maybe not as a mandatory course but certainly as an option for graduate students to take. Because I think there is some interest there but there just hasn't been any initiative by the department to sort of deal with the issue.

> There are no courses (on gender). There's one course in the family that a woman professor has taught. After that, the courses have not been offered since she left which was about a year and a half ago. Courses for women in particular as far as either family, women in society or women and work, there has been no courses on that. So I would say for women there has been no courses particularly geared to them. For minorities on the other hand, there have been a few courses on minorities, ethnic minorities, and social stratification . . . but there are really no courses that particularly deal with minority women.

> The department needs to be more receptive of other areas of interest besides mainstream sociology. We're still pretty conservative and mainstream. The department does not pay much attention to race and ethnicity and I was very frustrated in terms of their curriculum. In order to take a course on race and ethnicity I had to go outside the department to study those things. It was always a residual category or a category that didn't have any critical place (in sociology).

Without exception, these women discovered that race and frequently gender were not treated as serious areas of study by sociology faculty. They reported that a majority of faculty in sociology departments still adhere to a traditional and narrow definition of sociology, resulting in the exclusion or at least the devaluation of race and gender. This was often made obvious by faculty remarks. For example, Rosa described a faculty member's response after hearing about her interest in the area of race and gender:

We were all going around introducing ourselves and saying what we were do-ing. So when my turn came I said my name is such and such and my disserta-tion is going to be on the labor force participation of Latinas in (X) city. And the same professor just cracked up. He said "What? Latinas? Is that sociology?"

Numerous accounts were given about the ways in which the study of race and ethnicity were devalued in the program, and women of color risked not being treated as serious students by pursuing research in the area. One of the strongest messages given to a student about appropriate areas to study was reported by Josie. At the beginning of a meeting with her comprehen-sive committee, one professor turned to Josie and said:

"You know, I finally figured out what's wrong with you, Josie." And I was kind of stunned. And I said, "Oh, well what?" And he said, "You act too much like a (Josie's ethnicity) and not enough like a sociologist." And he went on to say "and if you don't straighten up you know what's going to happen? You'll be put down in Ethnic Studies and (Josie's ethnic group) Studies or something like that for the rest of your life."

The experience served the function of socializing Josie to view race and ethnicity as illegitimate areas of study in sociology, particularly if the per-spective was not European. In addition, such statements reveal the value hi-erarchy of programs and departments in academe, where ethnic studies and women's studies are seen as less valuable than "discipline-based studies" and peripheral to the "core" missions of higher education.

Another woman received similar messages from her department. When a white male student pursued research on gender and/or race, it suddenly became a legitimate area of study. The student, Diana, drew an analogy with international students to make a similar point:

They (faculty) were telling me that it (the study of her ethnic group) was too subjective and I should learn and do more things, be more objective and cover a broader area, and write about other people in other groups rather than just my own. But I never once have heard one of the foreign students who were doing their own country ever told that. They were doing the same thing I was doing. So it was okay for them to do it. And I really felt a little prejudice there.

While faculty were observed mentoring international students who pur-sued research topics addressing such areas as occupational stratification, mi-gration patterns or family studies in their country of origin, minority women students addressing similar topics in their communities in the United States reported disparaging comments from faculty and graduate students.

Not only was the subject matter of race and ethnicity not treated seriously, but non-white scholars were systematically ignored and berated. Women reported that faculty were often reluctant to use books or articles written by African American, Chicanos and other nonwhite sociologists. Another problem many women discussed was the ethnocentric perspectives embedded in required textbooks and readings and the lack of alternative perspectives. For example, Angie, an African American woman, recalled her discomfort and difficulty in accepting ethnocentric assumptions she encountered in an urban sociology course. The following account illustrates Angie's unsuccessful attempt to convince the instructor of the seriousness of omitting the perspectives of people of color and the implications for interpreting data and developing theoretical frameworks based on false assumptions.

> There was an article we were assigned to read which was about residential patterns of blacks. It was talking about white flight and so on. Well, there was one line in this article that said middle-class and working-class whites know that blacks who have money want to live with them. And here this statement was, in black and white. As I read it . . . I disagreed. It's not because they want to live where white people are. If they had enough money and really wanted to live with white people and in upper-class neighborhoods then that's where they would move . . . because it's still close to their schools and to their churches. So . . . he asked me why I was so quiet about this particular article. I said "because the article is false." He said "what do you mean?" I said "this one line in this article is totally insane." He said "you can't discredit the whole article because of that." I said, "Yeah, I can because if this is what the person thinks then the whole article is based on a faulty premise." He said, "I don't think you should discredit this man's work because he made one mistake." That's the difference between he and I. He's white and accustomed to reading things like this that white people write about black people all the time and he buys into these mythologies. Well, I don't buy that. Because as an African American I've decided I'm going to define myself and not going to be confined by white people's definitions any more. I said, "you don't have to take this article out but at least put a disclaimer on this." He tried to say he didn't know enough about urban sociology to say that was false. I said, "I don't know enough about urban sociology to disclaim the rest of the article, but I know enough about black people to say that the premise is false."

While methodological and theoretical debates are essential in training graduate students, the absence of literature from outside mainstream sociology creates a monocultural nature of sociology. Under these conditions women of color reported receiving little if any support for developing analytical skills that included a critique of false assumptions about their communities and "blaming the victim" theories and concepts.

Since race was not considered important or central in sociology departments, these students took a risk in their career by expressing an interest in the area. They encountered problems with finding faculty to support their research and also ran the risk of not being viewed as "serious scholars". As Donna noted, "If you're interested in communities or ethnic studies then you're going to be ghettoized and you're going to be perceived in a certain way." Cleo recalled similar advice from a sociology faculty member. However, she did not yield to the warning:

> One of the things that they (faculty) said was, don't go into that (Chicano topics) because you're going to ghettoize yourself. And actually that's what helped me to get a job is the fact that I specialized in the area. . . . I told other graduate students as well that you can't always listen to everything the department says. Because one of the areas that's really very hot right now is the issue of race, class and gender and feminist theory. And so I suggest to the students that they should know more than mainstream sociology because in fact there are other areas of interest that are opening up.

Women of color interested in developing expertise in the area of race and gender turned to women's studies, ethnic studies, and international studies programs. These interdisciplinary programs were more likely to provide the training required to conduct research in racial ethnic communities and other diverse communities in the world. But this knowledge was gained at a substantial cost. This cost entailed being perceived as less scholarly and less ambitious than students interested in mainstream sociology. These women also experienced fewer opportunities to develop relationships with sociology faculty because they were spending time outside the department.

Many of the departments had the illusion of diversity and multicultural curriculum by claiming race/ethnicity and gender studies as one of their specialties and by listing course offerings in these areas in department catalogs. However, the reality is quite different. Because of the narrow focus and limited perspectives accepted in sociology and because advertised courses were not actually offered, graduate programs did not reflect higher education's supposedly broad support for a multicultural curriculum. Thus, unlike the recent onslaught of neoconservative arguments that indicate that Western literary thought and scholarship are being replaced by multicultural curriculum (Bloom 1988; D'Souza 1991), women of color graduate students reveal the resistance to change within the canon in sociology and resulting inequities because of this resistance.

Allocation of Department Resources: Breaking through Traditional Networks

Departmental resources, such as research and teaching assistantships, distribution of funding, and the assignment of mentors serve as primary facilitators for success or failure for graduate students. Consequently, access to and distribution of resources are fundamental issues of equity in higher education. Accounts given by these graduate students indicate that the criteria for distribution and access to resources and policy determination is not an open system accessible for all graduate students. Rather, access to resources was a closed system accessible only through academic networks and social relationships with faculty. For example, Denise reported:

> That's the kind of thing (application process for an RA position) where it depends on who you know. Who you hook up with. What's around. I mean there's no formal way to do it at all. And it's been a problem. I constantly hear, "Oh so and so is working on this project and that project," and I think, "God, that's really interesting. I would love to do that but how did they find out about it?" And that's part of the informal process.

Funding was used to attract and retain women of color to their programs, usually in the form of teaching or research assistantships. The criteria for such positions were often unclear to these women and were not likely to be formalized in terms of widely publicized rules or regulations. For example, Christine reported how she accidentally discovered a teaching assistantship was available in her department by seeking out information:

> I don't think at that particular time it was even in the handbook (how to apply for a teaching assistantship). You know, what the general procedures were about the assistantships. So really it just so happened that I asked at more or less the right time about how do I apply for an assistantship?

Jean described a similar system operating in her department:

> Their (the department) way of funding students is so secretive. . . . Sometimes they do it based on extra money that they have. They'll just award a student. Or it just depends. I have no idea how it's done or if it's been done since they gave me this large sum of money. I'm not sure. I know that they fund entering grad students on a two year basis. And I think the money that I got was excess money that they were able to give me for one year rather than for two. I'm not sure. I think it varies depending on how much money they have at the beginning of the year.

Another student, Angie, gave a similar account about the vagueness surrounding department resources: "There's the feeling that the assistantships are not being handed out on an equitable or fair basis. In fact no one is really sure what the criteria are for awarding them and so that's a source of discontent among graduate students."

Many other respondents, including students in the final stage of the program, were unable to describe the criteria their department used in funding students. The majority of these women reported information about teaching and research assistantships tied to social networks rather than to the position being publicly posted and allowing open competition for positions. Consequently, personal relationships with faculty were essential for success in acquiring teaching and research opportunities.

Department support in the form of research or teaching assistantships is very important because it provides much more than pure financial assistance (Nigg and Axelrod, 1981). These assistantships provide students with a variety of experiences and opportunities that aid in their completion of and success in graduate programs. For example, the women we interviewed revealed how research assistantships socialized graduate students to the research process as well as provided publishing opportunities while still in graduate school. Teaching assistantships also provided important but different opportunities and experiences such as proctoring, grading exams and, in some cases, lecturing. Both research and teaching assistantships provided students with opportunities to interact individually with faculty and other graduate students and undergraduates.

Women's experiences illustrate the depth of structural inequities that make it difficult for certain groups to gain access to networks necessary for success. Affirmative action also does not dictate the quality of faculty-student interaction, which is a very important factor in the success of students in graduate programs. A major source of information about the quality and quantity of faculty-student interaction was obtained through questions on the topic of mentoring.

While half of the women we interviewed claimed to be mentored, there was a broad range of definitions of what mentoring relationships entailed. Some faculty offered students advice about the program, others shared experiences and information about the profession and others had valuable resources to offer such as research assistantship positions. Fewer relationships were described in terms of the traditional professorial mentoring of guiding students through their studies and working closely on research. However, since student recognized that mentor relationships were particularly important in maneuvering in a system that allocated departmental resources through personal networks and relationships with faculty, they were willing to take whatever form was available. Graduate students gave numerous accounts illustrating the relationship between the allocation of department resources and mentors.

> When I applied to TA for any of those courses I never got chosen to do that. . . .
> It's like applying for a job. The professors let the graduate advisor know who they
> want. The only way to get into the department is somebody says I want that person. That's how you get in. That's how it works. I mean that's not how it officially
> works but that's how we decided it works. And that's also how you get funded. If
> someone doesn't want you, then you're kind of left on your own.

Some sociology departments attempted to aid the mentoring process by assigning students to advisors upon entering the program. However, in many cases the assignment did not coincide with the student's interest. In the case of first year students who had not identified an area of interest, their relationship with advisors were less likely to develop into a mentoring relationship. Jean experienced such a situation and described the difficulty she had: "It was stressful my first year. Just because I wasn't sure what I was doing. What my interests were. Who I could work with. And most of all I was not confident in myself."

Jean's comment addresses a problem that many entering students, regardless of race, had in developing a useful mentor relationship. Because they lacked a research focus and were not sure about areas of interest, students did not appear interesting enough to faculty. Therefore, faculty did not spend extra time with those students who may, in fact, have needed that extra time more than the focused student. Thus, these students were defined as "not serious students," unworthy of faculty time and effort. This attitude persisted at least until students identified a research interest. If the identified research interest centered on race or gender, the perception of lesser status usually continued to interfere with faculty support of students.

Many of the students we interviewed reflected back on the process and recognized the need for student initiation in developing a mentor relationship. For example, Katie explained that mentoring does not happen automatically but rather students must: "go and talk to these professors and establish a relationship with them. And then work with them and then they get to know you. So it's something that you have to kind of like nurture. And some of the students I think what happens is they come in and they think that okay here I am, what are you gonna do for me. But it doesn't work that way."

The most structured mechanism for developing mentoring relationships was through research and teaching assistantships. Working closely with faculty on their funded research projects and assisting in large undergraduate courses provided graduate students with the opportunity to learn more about the faculty's interests and to demonstrate their own skills, creativity, and sociological knowledge. Students recognized that assistantships also provided the means for maintaining the mentor relationship. Several students expressed concern over the lack of continuation of faculty support during the dissertation stage when they were unlikely to be working directly with faculty.

Many women described the difficulty of establishing a mentoring relationship because there were so few available faculty like themselves to mentor them and few faculty with similar research interests. Kim explained the difficulty women of color have in finding mentors in a male and white dominated department: "First, I think the professors kind of feel that we are different to them. It's true. I have different ideas. I have a different language. I was involved in political things and they were not. You know I mean we are totally different. I am a woman. I have an accent. It's totally different."

Although faculty of color in sociology departments were over represented as mentors to women of color graduate students, the women we interviewed said they were often forced to look elsewhere for support because of the limited numbers of minority faculty to chose from. Faculty of color in ethnic studies and women's studies often filled this void by mentoring graduate students; however, mentoring outside the department further limited their access to resources in sociology departments. Mentoring by minority faculty was important to graduate students of color because they tended to be less paternalistic than white mentors, were more supportive of graduate student's interests in race and gender, and were able to offer important resources and emotional support.

In addition, positive mentoring led to additional resources and opportunities such as presenting at professional meetings, publishing opportunities in journals, and job placements after the dissertation. Marilyn summarized the relationship between mentoring and graduate students experiences in sociology: "It's just that there are people who have made very good connections with faculty and work with them and seem to get the benefits of having that connection."

Students generally agreed that obtaining departmental support was important because it: (1) often provided important research skills and/or teaching opportunities; (2) connected graduate students to the informal network which provided access to information not formally structured in the program; and (3) assisted in developing and maintaining faculty and graduate student relationships. For example, Nancy, one of the women who had not been funded reported: "One of the problems that I had is that the year I did my residency I didn't get an assistantship. So that it meant that although I was going to class with folks I didn't have any work assignment. So that I was not in the group of folks who learned the ropes by being there."

Clearly, maneuvering through graduate school was a process made easier with information via teaching or research assistantships because information was often tied to such positions.

When distribution of resources are structured through personal networks, inequities are likely to follow. Women of color graduate students are likely to have less access to such resources due to their estrangement from such networks, the absence of faculty of color or faculty with similar research interests, racial and gender stereotypes as well as the monocultural nature of sociology programs.

Conclusion

The voices of women of color graduate students in sociology counter the recent claims by institutions of higher education that purport to adhere to a multicultural perspective. The reality for the women we interviewed in these sociology departments is that traditional mainstream sociology continues to hold precedence over other perspectives. A result of this tradition is the devaluation and marginalization of women of color whose areas of interest are in race, ethnicity or gender. Based on the cultural curriculum described by women of color graduate students, it becomes questionable as to whether graduate programs in sociology are preparing future faculty to teach contemporary sociology in the manner that our society should demand. At the university level, multicultural education has become viewed as an important goal. Graduate education programs that fail to train their students to effectively teach about issues of race, gender, and class undermine this goal. Women's accounts of their experiences in graduate school also reveal the nature of department resources as one based on personal relationships with faculty and access to academic networks. These privileges are often denied to women of color. Their perspectives of these inequities provide us with alternative solutions for change.

Popular reactions against affirmative action, multicultural education, ethnic studies and women's studies, falsely assume that Euro-American males would be erased from the pages of history, literature, sociology and political science. Programs aimed at eliminating institutionalized inequality through the inclusion of other cultures and women into the curriculum and educational systems has "elicited so much fear, hostility, antagonism, and virulent rhetoric from the otherwise complacent and condescending concerned dominant white group."[2]

The notoriety that Allan Bloom (1988), Dinesh D'Souza (1991), and the National Academy of Scholars have received over the last few years has led many to believe that the university is in the midst of a revolution and that major shifts have already occurred. However, the truth could not be further from the reality described by Bloom, D'Souza, and others. Playing on the insecurities of an aging white male faculty threatened by budget cuts and unprepared to address the challenges of an inclusive university, anecdotes and misappropriated terms and concepts have been used to create distorted images of educational programs and policies introduced into higher education over the last two decades.

Traditional strategies for achieving equity in higher education have been affirmative action or equal access programs. However, it is clear from women of color's experiences that affirmative action has not been successful in achieving equity. Affirmative action as a solution to achieving equity in higher education fails primarily because of its limited scope and inability to impact the structure and systems of exclusion that exist in academia.

The agenda for the future needs to address academic culture and structure, particularly as they influence curriculum formation and departmental resource distribution. Preparing women of color to become competent sociologists who can fulfill the demands of a multicultural education requires the placing of race and gender at the center of analysis rather than at the periphery or margin as is now the case. To this end, courses must be redeveloped to incorporate race, class, and gender issues. As new courses are developed and added to the curriculum list, they need to be taught on a regular basis and required of all students in the program. An important element of this intervention is to increase the numbers of minority faculty, particularly women of color, so that this perspective is represented effectively. Equity in terms of resources also demands a radical revision of the way graduate programs are structured. The systems of exclusion that limit access to information, mentoring and funding are more difficult to eradicate as they often hinge on the good will of others to share such resources. However, many of these resources can also be structured in ways to ensure greater equity. For example, to achieve a more equitable distribution of funding, departments need to make the criteria for teaching and research positions clear and distribute positions according to established criteria. In addition, structural mechanisms for distributing resources through mentoring need to include the assignment of students to mentors based on similar research interests, providing compensation and incentives for faculty to engage in mentoring, and opening access to networks of information by open posting of positions and regular sharing of knowledge about pertinent research opportunities. Aggressive recruitment and retention for faculty of color are also necessary steps to foster mentoring relationships for students of color.

Affirmative action programs have yet to take an aggressive step towards creating a learning environment promoting diversity. Women's stories about graduate school underline the enormous efforts made by individual students to create opportunities and eliminate barriers. Clearly the networks women of color have established outside their department and across campuses have been key to their success. Providing funding for a range of network activities is the logical next step. Based on the comments made by women we interviewed, the activities to explore include ready access to computer E-mail systems, travel money, women of color lecture series or visiting scholar programs, and annual conferences and meetings addressing concerns of women of color in sociology

Many of the proposed changes are likely to fuel the rhetoric and debates within higher education as equity continues to be perceived as attainable through existing federally legislated access programs such as affirmative action. In addition, neoconservative arguments against a multicultural curriculum are supported by the increasing financial pressures faced by many colleges and universities. However, these obstacles to change are in serious conflict with the failure of traditional equity solutions to make substantial changes, the increasing diversity of the United States, and the need for an educated and literate work force.

The accounts of women of color enrolled in Ph.D. programs in sociology point to the necessary changes in sociology graduate programs to prepare sociologists for the twenty-first century. The patterns of exclusion and inequity in higher education cannot simply be addressed by affirmative action or equal access programs. Until we recognize and implement strategies that create an inclusive curriculum and make resources available to all students, equity in higher education will remain a goal and not a reality.

Notes

1. This research was partially funded by the Sociologists for Women in Society (SWS), Center for Research on Women at Memphis State University and a grant from the Center for the Study on Women in Society at the University of Oregon. We want to thank Rose Brewer and Athena Theodore for their comments on the questionnaire and Diane M. Dunlap and Patricia A. Schmuck for their insightful suggestions.

2. Although written about affirmative action, Nijole V. Benokraitis and Joe P. Feagin's comment holds true for the wide range of program developed in higher education to address issues of diversity. Affirmative Action and Equal Opportunity: Action, Inaction, Reaction (Boulder, CO: West View Press, 1978), p. 211.

Bibliography

Benokraitis, N. V. and Feagin, J. P. (1978). *Affirmative action and equal opportunity: Action, inaction, reaction.* Boulder, CO: Westview Press.

Bloom, A. (1988). *The closing of the American mind.* New York: Simon & Schuster.

Collins, P. H. (1990). *Black feminist thought: Knowledge, consciousness and the politics of empowerment.* Boston: Unwin Hyman.

D'Souza, D. (1991). *Illiberal education: The politics of race and sex on campus.* New York: The Free Press.

Nigg, J. and Axelrod, M. (1981). Women and minorities in the PSA region: Results of the 1979 survey. *Pacific Sociological Review,* 24(1), 107–28.

Smith, D. E. (1987). *The everyday world as problematic: A feminist sociology.* Boston: Northeastern University Press.

FIVE

Gender Awareness and Contradictions in the Education of Early Childhood Teachers

Christine Chaillé

Early childhood education is at the heart of gender role construction. It is during the early childhood years that our children construct notions of their possibilities and limitations based on their sex. Moreover, those who give care to young children (as professionals or nonprofessionals) usually are women who struggle to juggle or integrate home, family, career, child care, preschool programs, family support programs, parent education, and early public schooling. Early childhood education is an important part of any family's daily life and children's experiences.

Who are early childhood educators? What is early childhood education? I use the definition of "early childhood education" from the National Association for the Education of Young Children to refer to programs and professionals that work with children and their families from birth through age eight, thus encompassing day-care and preschool programs as well as the early primary grades of school. For those not familiar with the field of early childhood education, it is important to note the variety of the field with differing career paths, differing years of training, training in different disciplines, and the lack of coherent local, national, or international professional standards and practices. The teacher in Head Start who began as a parent volunteer and has obtained training on the job is considered an early childhood professional. Considered similarly an early childhood professional is a teacher with a liberal arts degree who obtains a fifth year and master's degree in elementary education with a focus on early childhood education. So, too, is the family day care provider who participated in a community-college training program in small business procedures and health and safety training.

The field of early childhood education has complex historical roots, emerging from an interactive blend of the social welfare and philanthropic, the women's labor movement and child care, the kindergarten and public education movement, and the behaviorist "hothousing" emphasis on accelerating children's learning through early education, many seemingly disparate historical influences. It is important to keep these complexities of history and of people currently in the field in mind as we think about issues relating to gender, for, in many regards, it is this diversity and lack of a common identity that accounts for the contradictions I will describe.

It is fitting, and necessary, to examine the issues of gender that face leaders—teachers, caregivers, teacher educators, and adult students—in early childhood education today. In this chapter, I will raise these issues with a broad stroke in order to generate further thought, purposely glossing over complexities of theory and previous thoughtful work in the field. This chapter will begin by raising what I see as a conflict or contradiction in our thinking about the field of early childhood education in regard to gender. I will then consider some of the curriculum conflicts that can be viewed from a gender-focused lens. Finally, I will look at some of the political issues bearing on gender that are current and that have implications for women leaders.

Points of Conflict in Early Childhood Education

As we look broadly at the historical and current work in early childhood education, two strands relevent to gender characterize the field. These two strands are, in some regards, in conflict.

On the one hand, social gender roles define the professionals and nonprofessionals in early childhood education. Early childhood education has always been predominantly a female field. Child-care workers, preschool teachers, parent educators, kindergarten and primary teachers are, for the most part, women. Professional programs at the university level in early childhood teacher education include some men, but the profession remains largely female. Early childhood education and care has always been a socially sanctioned field in which women could take charge even when women were not permitted to engage in other professionals, as evidenced by the pioneering work of women in the early kindergarten movement such as Elizabeth Peabody, Susan Blow, Patty Smith Hill, and Alice Temple. The profession has also provided a nurturing environment for many of the leaders in the field today, old and young, including Lilian Katz and Barbara Bowman, who have championed developmentally appropriate practices in early childhood education; political leaders advocating for children and families such as Marian Wright Edelman, Ellin Galinsky, Hillary Rodham Clinton, and Sharon Lyn Kagan; and leaders of curriculum change based on our understanding of child development such as Constance Kamii and Louise Derman-Sparks.

In addition to being a field that is predominantly female, early childhood educators, probably more than in other arenas of education, foster the nurturing role of the teacher. The master early childhood teacher is supportive, forms relationships with her students, anticipating and fulfilling many of the child's needs, social, emotional, and cognitive. Most explicitly with infants and toddlers, but also with preschool and kindergarten children, being "maternal" is highly valued by the profession, and by the public who interacts with the profession. The "good caregiver" in many ways embodies the "caring" teacher described as the model for all education by Noddings (1992). Among early childhood educators, the issue of blending and adequately representing the child "care" and childhood "education" elements led Bettye Caldwell, a leading early childhood educator and former President of the National Association for the Education of Young Children, to call for a new term describing this blending that could refer both to child care and education without separating them—"educare." Perhaps because of the awkwardness of the term, or perhaps because of the substantive difficulty in blending the two into one professional identity, the term "educare" has never caught on. Nonetheless, it points to the fact that early childhood professionals perceive the need to represent caring in the terminology used to describe the profession.

On the other hand, there is a "selective tradition" in early childhood theory and research which encourages certain theoretical positions and research paradigms to dominate the field. This selective tradition has, as in many other disciplines (see Jipson and Paley 1991), favored men and male models. The three theoretical traditions that are commonly covered in child development courses, for example, are behaviorism, psychoanalytic theory, and cognitive developmental theory, each represented in the literature and citations by male theorists: B. F. Skinner, Sigmund Freud, and Jean Piaget. Other theorists that come to mind whose work has significantly informed early childhood education include Lev Vygotsky, Erik Erikson, Lawrence Kohlberg, Albert Bandura; and currently Howard Gardner, Robert Stern-berg, Jonathan Kozol, and David Elkind. Evelyn Weber's (1984) widely used text, for example, entitled "Ideas Influencing Early Childhood Education: A Theoretical Analysis" covers the following theorists as primary: Friedrich Froebel, G. Stanley Hall, Arnold Gesell, Edward Thorndike, John Dewey, Sigmund Freud, Lawrence K. Frank, Erik Erikson, and Jean Piaget. One is hard pressed to come up with any women theorists whose influence parallels the above list. Research in early childhood education has been predominantly informed and influenced by psychology and sociology, both fields traditionally male dominated. Furthermore, the primary professional organization, the National Association for the Education of Young Children, has, in its recent history, had 28 presidents, and 8 of them have been male. According to NAEYC, census figures estimate that men make up around 3–5% of childcare and preschool workers, and NAEYC's membership is probably representative of those proportions. A quick survey of Bredekamp's (1987) guidelines for supporting developmentally appropriate practices reveals that close to forty percent of the articles cited appear to be written by men (using first names as the key). Thus, despite the predominance of women working in the field, and despite the affinity of the field to what has been socially considered as women's issues, men have been featured as the public figures, researchers, and theorists. Regardless of the reasons, explanations, and causes of this disproportionate representation of males in positions of influence and power, there has been little acknowledgement, discussion, or awareness of the facts of such a selective tradition.

In addition to this "selective tradition" in the field of early childhood education, there appears to be a selective focus on some issues relating to gender and not others. (Please note that here I am putting forth my "take" on the field, and I would welcome being challenged by those reading this article.) For example, there is a visible focus on young children's sex-role stereotyped behavior, on how young children play with sex stereotyped toys (e.g., dolls and trucks) or by activities (e.g., boys take leadership roles). Yet there is little consideration given as to *how* boys and girls develop such consciousness at an early age about what a sex-appropriate toy or activity is, the processes of socialization. Early childhood theorists and researchers, primarily psychologists, tend to ignore the social context or gender constructed roles, and remain at a psychological rather than a sociological level of understanding about the deeply embedded gender constructs in our society. As a result of that shallow analysis of sex-role socialization, the early childhood literature tends to focus on ways teachers can promote non sex-role stereotyped behaviors, through toys, activities, and their own interactions (cf. Edwards 1986; Sprung, Froschle, and Campbell 1985). With some notable exceptions (Polakow 1992; Lubeck, 1985) the pervasive and insti-

CHRISTINE CHAILLÉ

tutionalized sexism that could lead towards an explanation and context for the sex-role stereotyped socialization is not addressed. Thus we are left with the feeling, as we read the literature for practicing professionals, that the "problem"—of stereotyping according to gender, and of children learning sex-role stereotypes—is the teacher's responsibility. (This is not to say that teachers do not have responsibility for the promotion of sexism in their classrooms through choice of materials, curriculum orientation, and their own differential treatment of boys and girls.)

Second, the need for men as teachers in early childhood settings has been discussed and promoted (Robinson 1988), with arguments for more male teachers focusing on their positive influence on children. Robinson (1988) particularly argues that more men teachers in early childhood education would "enhance the professional self-image of early childhood education." The argument for more male teachers has been used also in discussing families without fathers present, and on the need for male role models for young children, especially young black boys. Beyond that, there has also been an attempt to shed a more positive light on rough and tumble play, normally viewed as "aggressive" play more common of young boys (Pellegrini 1989; Pellegrini and Perlmutter 1988). Traditional early childhood approaches to aggressive play tend to view it as something to be changed, teaching children to play peacefully, to solve their own problems, and to learn to resolve conflicts with words and not violence (cf. Carlsson-Paige and Levin 1992; Oken-Wright 1992). Others argue that we should learn to value some forms of aggressive play as a way of reaffirming masculine behavior (Pellegrini 1989). What's usually ignored in the idea of accepting or facilitating more "boyish" behavior is that girls could perhaps also benefit from being less passive and well-behaved.

Another concern of many in the field relates to the issue of parental involvement in early childhood programs (Parke 1981). A good deal of attention is given to bemoaning the lack of participation of fathers, when dealing with two-parent families, and of designing ways of involving fathers in their children's education (McBride 1989). For example, introductory texts on parent education sometimes describe formats such as breakfasts, work parties on the weekends, aimed at fathers who work. It is interesting (and disturbing in the assumptions it reflects) that while token reference is made to working women, there are not the same major concerns raised. This could be the result of one of three assumptions. First, it could be that there is, despite statistics, still an assumption of "traditional" family composition, with mother at home. Second, fathers' contributions could be seen as more valuable, while mothers' contributions are taken for granted. Or, third, it could be that this occurs because working women are more likely often find the time or make it a priority to be involved in their children's

90

education. This latter assumption is consistent with the idea that mothers are the psychological parents despite working arrangements.

Absent from the visible early childhood literature are more overt, activist feminist arguments regarding early childhood education. Could it be that these silences reflect the deep reluctance of women in the field to confront an essential conservativism grounded in precisely the nurturance that we in the profession profess to model and promote? I will discuss this issue by turning to an examination of those values that are promoted through the "early childhood" curriculum, as well as those that are not.

Curriculum Issues

In considering the curriculum as a way to examine the silence in the field of early childhood education on issues that bear on gender, I will consider two aspects: the role of the teacher, particularly the contrast between the teacher as controller and the teacher as nurturing caretaker, and the focus on subjective knowledge in early childhood education.

The Role of The Teacher

One critical curriculum issue that has implications for early childhood education is the role of the teacher. Historically, many movements in curricular reform have run counter to the emphasis on connection and relationship that has been at the core of early childhood education. Some of these movements have "trickled down" from elementary education and have had an impact on how we deal with younger children, both in public schools and preschool settings. A case in point is the example of assertive discipline, an approach to classroom management that is widely used.

Assertive discipline incorporates certain techniques which permit the teacher to note disruptions without rewarding them by paying direct attention to them. Let's say a child is talking to a neighbor while the teacher is trying to demonstrate something to the whole group. The teacher would write the child's name on the board. A second disruption would lead to a check by that child's name. Depending on the system set up, a third disruption might mean the child has to go to the principal's office, or stay in for recess. Because a system has been set up, the teacher need never interact, need never pass judgment, need never even talk to the child about her misbehavior or about the reasons for her punishment. The child is learning to behave herself in an impersonal system where sanctions are predetermined and there is no room for argument, dissuasion, forgiveness, grudges, bias, or caring. Assertive discipline purposefully takes personal relationships out of consideration.

Underlying these predominantly behaviorist movements is an assumption that the teacher needs to be pulled out of the educational equation. Skinner describes this assumption in his classic book, *The Technology of Teaching* (1968), in which he defines teaching as "an arrangement of contingencies of reinforcement under which behavior changes" (p. 113). He goes on to describe how notoriously difficult it is for teachers to do a good job of that, and how much better the "teaching machine" is at teaching. The Direct Instruction program, an extreme behaviorist-grounded method promoted by Engelmann (1980) and others at the University of Oregon, for example, is touted as "teacher-proof," in the sense that the teacher (even an otherwise incompetent one) delivers the already prepared and scripted program. Engelmann and his colleagues are currently involved in the production of videodisk technology that even better teacher-proof the context in which learning occurs.

In early childhood education, in contrast, the teacher's relationship with the child is of primary importance, and the teacher is expected to be actively involved in the classroom, albeit in a different way that that conceptualized within a behaviorist framework. From the perspective of early childhood educators, children are constructors of knowledge in an environment orchestrated by an adult or adults who are knowledgeable, caring, and responsive to their individual and developmental needs.

> The developmental appropriateness of an early childhood program is most apparent in the interactions between adults and children. Developmentally appropriate interactions are based on adults' knowledge and expectations of age-appropriate behavior in children balanced by adults' awareness of individual differences among children. (Bredekamp 1987, 9)

From this "developmentally appropriate" position, the lines are blurred between the teacher's role, the child's contribution to the learning situation, and the curriculum, resulting in an artful orchestration that puts much "power" into the teacher's hands, rather than in the curriculum, and with full consideration of the child. The resulting emergent curriculum is not, and cannot be, prescribed, standardized, or easily assessed.

This tension between those who argue for the acknowledgement of the valuable role of sensitive teacher observation and application of her knowledge of children versus those who feel the educational "system" must be behaviorally and mechanistically "operated" is reflected today in many policies and tensions in the field of educational administration. One of the arenas where this debate is carried out is in accountability and testing. Arthur Combs (1973), in a dated but still relevant critique of behavioral objectives, argues that we need to put more, not less, emphasis on the teacher's judgment. Movements today against achievement testing (Kamii 1990) and toward the development of portfolios, which require teachers to exercise judgment, are consistent with Combs' arguments.

The Early Childhood Focus on Subjective Knowledge

Another way of looking at the curricular issues that can shed some light on the contradictions in early childhood education is in terms of the Belenky, Clinchy, Goldberger, and Tarule (1986) notions of women's ways of knowing. They make a distinction between separate and connected knowledge, and between procedural and constructed knowledge. Procedural and separate knowledge is based on the belief that science is an accumulation of objective facts, and that absolute truth exists. In contrast, constructed knowledge is grounded in human, but perhaps especially women's, attempts to understand a "core self that remains responsive to situation and context" (p. 138). In an oversimplistic application of their analysis, it could be argued that in early childhood education we have put more emphasis on subjective, connected, and constructed knowledge and less on separate, procedural knowledge that have those who work with older children. In the early childhood profession, there is an underlying assumption that the teaching of procedural knowledge is developmentally inappropriate for young children (Bredekamp 1987). Let's look at one example of this from Bredekamp's *Developmentally Appropriate Practice,* widely accepted as the "bible" of professional practice in early childhood education. In the first statement about curriculum goals (p. 67), appropriate practice includes the following assumption:

> Curriculum is designed to develop children's knowledge and skills in all developmental areas—physical, social, emotional, and intellectual—and to help children learn how to learn—to establish a foundation for lifelong learning.

In inappropriate practice:

> Curriculum is narrowly focused on the intellectual domain with intellectual development narrowly defined as acquisition of discrete, technical academic skills, without recognition that all areas of children's development are interrelated.

One reflection of this is the emphasis on process as opposed to product in the preschool and early grades (see Chaillé, in preparation, for a discussion of this issue in relation to science education). Thus, for example, the goal of mathematics education is not the memorization of algorithms, but the ability to reason using mathematics as a powerful tool; the goals in the area of reading and writing are not merely the acquisition of skills but include

93

children learning that literacy is purposeful, meaningful, and necessary in their daily lives. In other words, for the early childhood educator seeking to be developmentally appropriate, "skills" in any curricular domain are not decontextualized but deeply contextualized. Decisions about the goals in a particular curricular area as well as the teaching methods that are appropriate are dictated by this deep contextualization. Children learn to read in an environment rich with print and opportunities and motivation to read it; this is, by my definition, what is meant by "whole language." And the same arguments apply to any other curriculum area. Children learn mathematics best in an environment in which number and mathematical reasoning is common and visible to them. Children learn science best when scientific thinking, experimentation, and problem-solving are facilitated, valued, and modeled.

Aside from the early childhood positions within particular curricular domains—language, mathematics, science—described above, the broader notion of curricular integration which has been advocated for years by early childhood educators, particularly at the preschool level, puts the emphasis on *connection*, by the learner and from the learner's perspective. Forman and Kuschner (1977) contend that the aim of education is the "general adaptation of the individual" meaning "the ability to invent procedures for establishing the continuity across experience" (p. 27). They go on to describe the implications for teaching:

> The process of teaching, then, is one that strives to maintain continuity across experiences. The best way to achieve this goal is to structure a curriculum that allows a maximum amount of freedom for children to ask their own questions, to set their own problems, and to generate their own confusion. (p. 45)

Children at work on a project (see Katz and Chard 1989) are, in an important sense, creating the curriculum to fit their needs and interests, and the complex interconnections between science, literature, language, mathematics, social studies, are difficult to see, much less "track," as the proponents of a more mechanistic model would have us believe.

This perspective on curricular integration changes as children continue through elementary school, where, increasingly, time, space, and teacher instruction segments by curriculum area and works to actively hinder curricular integration. Howard Gardner (1991) contends that what we do in schools is inconsistent with how children learn; he finds early childhood educators to be avidly agreeing with what he has to say about how educational structures need to change to be more open to other "ways of knowing"—for him, different intelligences. Valuing spatial intelligence, for example, both through the activities and materials available to children and through how we assess what children learn, is rarely found in our schools today, but is being recommended in movements of school and curricular reform that are consistent with what Gardner recommends.

And there are those that say that the voices that force the change away from curricular integration in later elementary years are *male* voices. Listen to Madeleine Grumet (1988, p. 25):

> It is the female elementary schoolteacher who is charged with the responsibility to lead the great escape. At the sound of the bell, she brings the child from the concrete to the abstract, from the fluid time of the domestic day to the segmented schedule of the school day, from the physical work, comfort, and sensuality of home to the mentalistic, passive, sedentary, pretended asexuality of the school—in short, from the woman's world to the man's. She is a traitor, and the low status of the teaching profession may be derived from the contempt her betrayal draws from both sexes. Mothers relinquish their children to her, and she hands them over to men who respect the gift but not the giver.

From Grumet's perspective, in the early childhood years, we are transitioning children from the female world of the home to the male world of the workplace, at least the workplace as it has been. And that workplace has, at least historically and in theory, been one in which mechanistic models predominate and connection is not as valued as separation. There has been little acknowledgment of, or even discussion of, the possible gender implications of the transitions that occur as we consider the different paradigms of teaching and learning in early childhood education and in elementary education. Yet I think that gender implications can be drawn.

We can also see this "female-orientation" of early childhood education, and an emphasis on subjective knowledge, almost on a continuum depending on the age of children served. Thus, for example, it is legitimate and sanctioned for teachers of infants and toddlers to emphasize, more explicitly, traditionally female, so-called "feminine" values of nurturing, personal relationship, physical contact. It is *not* legitimate for teachers in the primary grades to do so. Carl Bereiter (1972) for example, in an article titled "Schools without Education" bemoans the fact that teachers are expected to do so much more than teach skills and to "care" for children, a position I hear echoed in many concerns of the public regarding the funding of education. He makes sharp distinctions between child care, which is "simply providing a suitable place for children to be kept," training in the basic skills of literacy and calculation, and education. These distinctions fly in the face of the early childhood tradition of addressing the needs of the "whole child." In addressing children's complex and integrated needs, teachers of young children, particularly preschoolers, are expected to blend subjective and procedural goals, and the functions of care, training and education are purposefully and explicitly integrated. It is also worth noting that there are those (Bereiter included) who argue that the "teachers" of infants and toddlers in particular, and preschool children generally, require no specialized training. Bereiter says, for example:

> I don't wish to imply that child care and skill training are jobs that require no talent. Clearly a good child care worker needs to be strong on human qualities, needs to relate well to children, needs tact, patience, imagination, etc. On the other hand, it is doubtful if a child care worker needs any special knowledge other than what may be acquired readily from those who already know the ropes. (1972, 408)

As then-President Ronald Reagan said in explaining his opposition to comprehensive national child care, "Mothers and grandmothers have been taking care of children for years." He implied that since mothers and grandmothers have been doing it without specialized training, early childhood professionals needed no training either.

To former President Reagan I respond, yes, many mothers and grandmothers did prepare their children to learn the lessons of school. Family has always been the first good teacher. But let's not mythologize the family of the past. As Stephanie Koontz (1992) has argued, Donna Reed was not representative of the majority of families. Even in the past, when children did not have the good counseling of their mothers or grandmothers, they did not achieve in school. Now, more children do not have the wise counsel of mothers and grandmothers, and the feminization of poverty (i.e., impoverishment of women) places children in increasingly vulnerable positions (Polakow 1993).

Thus, curriculum and training issues have political aspects that are only tangentially acknowledged by early childhood educators. Political realities are about status, pay, and professionalism, and primarily women's unacknowledged and undervalued work in caring for young children. Political realities are also about child care in our society. How will it be achieved? Who will pay for it? Who is responsible for children's well-being? Who is to blame when children are marginalized and subjected to tedious, low quality education, more so when they are poor (Kozol 1991; Polakow 1993)?

Political Issues in The Field of Early Childhood Education

Curricular issues can be seen as political issues. Early childhood education is not valued, and the political agenda that early childhood educators have adopted includes: (1) making early childhood education and care an honored profession and improving salaries and benefits for people who work with children; and (2) making children's issues a national priority. I will deal with the first issue here, and will conclude this chapter with reference to the second.

The first political issue concerns the drive toward higher status and better compensation for early childhood educators and the professional stance toward aggressively pursuing a political campaign to improve wages. A current public information and political action drive being promoted by childcare workers and by the National Association for the Education of Young Children is the Worthy Wages campaign. Information has been issued that talks about the "true cost" of quality child care, calculating and publicizing what wages *should* be in an attempt to promote both high quality and adequate compensation. A number of people involved in the Worthy Wages campaign have been advocating for day-long "strikes" in child care centers, in which parents would be enlisted to help publicize the need for better compensation and its connection to quality child care. The call for strikes, whatever form they would take, has been met with controversy and concern by many in the early childhood community, and with the exception of a few large cities has not been widely implemented. Why this apparent aversion to public and political activity advocating higher status and better pay for early childhood educators? I contend that it is because, for many teachers of young children, the denial of care and abandoning of support, even for a "worthy" cause, is unthinkable. Teachers who view themselves as supports for children and their families have a difficult time advocating for their own needs and rights, particularly at a temporary "cost" to the ones they support and serve.

There is probably also deep-seated ambivalence about the issue of whether or not early childhood education is a "true profession." One definition of a profession incorporates the need for clear career paths, professional development, and training criteria. Yet the National Association for the Education of Young Children has been struggling for many years—unsuccessfully at this point—to arrive at consensus on a model for professional development that can address the diversity in the field. Without clear professional identity and supportive professional development career paths, it is difficult for individual child-care workers and teachers of young children to either have self-identity that supports their personal efforts or broader organizational support to mount a political campaign that has clout. There are interesting historical parallels here to be made with labor movements among the also largely woman-dominated field of nursing, where strikes have been highly controversial, albeit effective, and probably for many of the same reasons.

In presenting these seemingly disparate strands of issues—curricular and political—I am hoping to generate more discussion and self-reflection on the part of educators around the gender issues that either are implicated by these issues or lie at their core. There are two arenas in which this reflection and action is already occuring: in the anti-bias movement and in the field of work and family.

Promising Developments

The anti-bias movement, spearheaded by Louise Derman-Sparks (1989), is an effort to raise the consciousness of early childhood educators about racism, sexism, and ageism, and to create a climate of activism in the field. The premise of the anti-bias movement, as stated by Derman-Sparks, is stated in her preface:

> Anti-bias curriculum embraces an educational philosophy as well as specific techniques and content. It is value based: Differences are good; oppressive ideas and behaviors are not. . . .
> Through anti-bias curriculum, teachers enable every child to achieve the ultimate goal of early childhood education: the development of each child to her or his fullest potential. (1989, x)

Anti-bias curriculum, in theory, goes beyond "awareness" of stereotypes. Through modeling, curriculum, teacher interactions with children and with each other, and group discussions the purpose of the curriculum is activism: to work against stereotyping that oppresses any individual in any way. The focus of the anti-bias movement is broad, and has been directed at any kind of "ism": race, class, gender, sexual preference, religion.

Working toward an anti-bias curriculum requires ongoing self-reflection, collaboration with others engaged in similar efforts, and is, as Derman-Sparks states, not achieved through any kind of "recipe." Over time, the anti-bias movement will, I believe, have a positive effect on what I consider a "naivete" of the early childhood profession with regard to gender issues. However, the most visible effects of the movement thus far have been in the arenas of race and ethnicity; and the primary audience for anti-bias materials and workshops have been at the preschool level. Even in model preschools attempting to implement anti-bias curriculum, less attention has been given to issues of gender than to issues of culture and ethnicity. Gender issues need to be brought to the forefront by those advocating anti-bias curriculum.

The second promising development, which has been emerging for some time, is the increasing body of research and advocacy coming out of the discipline known as "work and family," led by Ellin Galinsky of the Work and Family Institute (cf. Galinsky 1991). Connecting economic development and labor issues to early childhood education is a promising way to bring to national consciousness the need for quality child care and for political and economic solutions to address the needs of young children. With the political climate changing and one of the early champions of children's rights in the White House (Rodham 1973), we can anticipate increasing attention to child care and early education as it impacts working women and families. Curricular issues must be closely linked to the issues of "provision of care" to promote professional goals in a political context, and the work and family arena is one where those issues can come together.

Implications for Early Childhood Teacher Education

The well-trained early childhood teacher, focused as she is on children, well versed in understanding child development, centering curriculum around children's needs and interests, and educated to respond flexibly and with enthusiasm to individual needs and differences, is remarkably naive when it comes to awareness of how she treats boys and girls differently, even while she may have some awareness of how society treats boys and girls differently. Her role in promoting differential treatment needs to be explicitly addressed, with all the dilemmas we are faced with in understanding the different ways women know the world and what our response as educators should be. She also needs to reexamine her own role in raising consciousness about the very issue of the profession and ways of knowing that have been discussed. Understanding the deeper curricular issues that are gender related, and understanding the political context of such stances, needs to be addressed explicitly and implicitly in how professionals are trained and in what. Coursework and practice should incorporate reflection on gender issues.

The schizophrenia regarding the selective tradition at least needs to be made apparent: reading about the male-domination in the field, and the possible relationship between the particular theoretical perspectives and gender issues; understanding the sources and bias of many of our theoretical and research perspectives, and critically evaluating them in that light; and bringing to the forefront women researchers and theorists where appropriate; all of these actions can help promote the critical reflection that we need in a field that is in the process of redefining itself, and in which women are finding voice.

Implications for Leaders in Early Childhood Education: Newfound Power and Possibility

Historically we can see some interesting cycles relating to gender issues in early childhood education. We see an ebb and flow of curricular emphases, and what earlier in this chapter was described as "early childhood values"—emphasis on the whole child, curricular integration, blending of caring with education—can also be seen as underlying some of the largely unsuccessful curricular and institutional movements of the sixties and early seventies. Reemerging as "developmentally appropriate practices," though now grounded in more widely accepted developmental theory—constructivism—and, presumably, supported by empirical research, it is important to reexamine the gender issues that frame our paradigms. And in a time of political possibility, it is increasingly important to think about what leaders in early childhood education are doing to bring attention to issues relating to gender, issues that impact not only young children's experiences and development but the well-being of early childhood professionals themselves. In the Clinton administration, children have become a part of the national rhetoric, even in economic planning and health care, holding out a promise that children will be on the national agenda in the years to come.

Bibliography

Belenky, M. F., Clinchy, B. M., Goldberger, N. R., and Tarule, J. M. (1986). *Women's ways of knowing: The development of self, voice, and mind.* New York: Basic Books.

Bredekamp, S. (ed.) (1987). *Developmentally appropriate practice in early childhood programs serving children from birth through age 8.* Washington DC: National Association for the Education of Young Children.

Carlsson-Paige, N., and Levin, D. E. (1992). Making peace in violent times: A constructivist approach to conflict resolution. *Young Children,* 48(1), 4–13.

Chaillé, C. (in preparation). Process vs. product: The dilemma for teaching science to young children.

Chaillé, C. and Britain, L. (1991). *The young child as scientist: A constructivist approach to early childhood science education.* New York: HarperCollins.

Chodorow, N. (1978). *The reproduction of mothering.* Berkeley: University of California Press.

Derman-Sparks, L. (1989). *Anti-bias curriculum: Tools for empowering young children.* Washington, DC: National Association for the Education of Young Children.

Edwards, C. P. (1986) *Promoting social and moral development in young children: Creative approaches for the classroom.* New York: Teachers College Press.

Engelmann, S. (1980). *Direct instruction*. Englewood Cliffs, NJ: Educational Technology Publications.

Galinsky, E. (1991). The private sector as a partner in early care and education. In S. L. Kagan (ed.), *The care and education of America's young children: Obstacles and opportunities*, Ninetieth Yearbook of the National Society for the Study of Education, part I. Chicago: University of Chicago Press.

Gardner, H. (1991). *The unschooled mind: How children think and how schools should teach*. New York: HarperCollins.

Jipson, J. and Paley, N. (1991). The selective tradition in teacher's choice of children's literature: Does it exist in the elementary classroom? *English Education*, 20.

Katz, L. and Chard, S. (1989). *Engaging children's minds: The project approach*. Norwood, NJ: Ablex Publishing Corporation.

Lubeck, S. (1985). *The sand box society: Early education in black and white America*. Philadelphia: Falmer Press.

McBride, B. A. (1989). Interaction, accessibility, and responsibility: A view of father involvement and how to encourage it. *Young Children*, 44(5), 13–19.

Noddings, N. (1992). *The challenge to care in schools: An alternative approach to education*. New York: Teachers College Press.

Oken-Wright, P. (1992). From tug of war to "Let's make a deal": The teacher's role. *Young Children*, 48(1), 15–20.

Parke, R. (1981). *Fathers*. Cambridge, MA: Harvard University Press.

Pellegrini, A. D. (1989). Children's rough-and-tumble play: Issues in categorization. *Educational Policy*, 3, 389–400.

Pellegrini, A. D. and Perlmutter, J. C. (1988). Rough and tumble play on the elementary school playground. *Young Children*, 43(2), 14–17.

Polakow, V. (1992). *The erosion of childhood*. Chicago: University of Chicago Press, 1982; new ed., 1992.

Polakow, V. (1993). *Lives on the edge: Single mothers and their children in the other America*. Chicago: University of Chicago Press.

Robinson, B. E. (1988). Vanishing breed: Men in child care programs. *Young Children*, 43(6), 54–58.

Rodham, H. (1973). Children under the law. *Harvard Educational Review*, 43, 487–514.

Skinner, B. F. (1968). *The technology of teaching.* New York: Appleton-Century-Crofts.

Sprung, B., Froschle, M., and Campbell, P. B. (1985). *What will happen if. . . : Young children and the scientific method.* New York: Educational Equity Concepts, Inc.

II

Socialization of Women into Educational Leadership: Conditions and Critiques

SIX

Women Ascending to Leadership: The Organizational Socialization of Principals

Ann Weaver Hart

When women are appointed to leadership positions, they enter existing social groups with established norms, beliefs, and assumptions that guide interactions and relationships. School principals, superintendents, and other educational administrators must take charge and become functioning, integrated group members at the same time that they try to understand and accommodate the unwritten norms of the new group. This process is complex for all newly appointed leaders, but it is particularly difficult for those who are different—in ethnicity, race, or gender—from traditional incumbents in leadership roles. A number of organizational dynamics exert influence in this process; understanding these dynamics empowers new leaders (Hart 1991).

Organizational socialization theory identifies specific features of the taking-charge process likely to result in the personal development of the new leader; changes in the knowledge, skills, and professional practices used in the enactment of the leadership role; and the evolution of fundamental assumptions and conceptualizations of the role itself held by the group (Wanous 1980). This chapter applies organizational socialization theory to the analysis of case studies of leadership ascension by women as school

105

leaders—specifically as school principals. While this process poses greater challenges for socially incongruent leaders (ethnic and racial minorities and women), an increased understanding of organizational socialization can lead to successful transitions to leadership and improved outcomes in educational organizations for all those interested in improving leadership in schools. I take a noncritical approach in the chapter in the sense that I ground the analysis in established traditions of research and theory on school organizations rather than in traditions of critical theory.

Background

The school principal consistently emerges in research and tales of practice as an important factor in the success of schools. Principals create conditions for success by shaping the coherence of instructional programs, providing clear instructional goals, setting high and attainable academic standards, sharing information about policies and teachers' problems, making frequent classroom visits, providing incentives for learning, and maintaining student discipline (Bossert, Rowan, Dwyer, and Lee 1982). These effects are described by Edmonds (1979, 32), who argued that "one of the most tangible and indispensable characteristics of effective schools is strong administrative leadership, without which the disparate elements of good schooling can neither be brought together nor kept together." Recent reviews have found over fifty empirical articles published since the middle 1970s asserting that principals substantially influence schools (Leithwood et al., in press).

The demands of practice often pressure new school leaders to abandon the skills and knowledge they acquired in their formal education and conform to existing norms. Compelling descriptions of the results of this process of professional socialization exist (Duke 1982; Greenfield 1985b). The most frequent result: the replication of existing practice and patterns of school leadership. The dynamics through which these effects emerge remain poorly understood, primarily because the individual leader remains the main focus of leader succession studies. This focus on the new leader leaves the highly social nature of the succession experience largely unexamined.

The social character of leader succession becomes especially apparent in case studies (Ogawa 1991). Research on female school leaders confirms this conclusion, revealing the effects of different kinds of sites on women's leader succession experiences. Schmuck (this volume), for example, found important variations in the socialization experienced by principals in rural schools. Gender-based differences emerge in other studies as well. Collay (this volume) moreover found that gender stereotypic roles flourish in some rural settings where the "mom and pop" model of leadership remains strong. Others find similar socialization experiences that mold a female leader to a perception of appropriate woman's place while benefitting from women's abilities to effectively use less hierarchical authority structures and collaborative decision making.

Alternative views of leadership provide insight into gaps in knowledge a leader-centered approach to succession leaves. One powerful theoretical perspective—organizational socialization—illustrates how a "collectivity of subordinates" (Blau 1964, 23) fundamentally shapes a person's ascension to leadership. This view draws insight from the leader and the organization simultaneously. It demonstrates how socialization—adjustments and adaptations on the part of individuals to the expectations of the group—and leader influence on the group combine to create the organizational outcomes of leader succession. Firestone (1990) described the effects of the process in educational organizations when he studied the "cultural politics of executive succession" of superintendents. Others observe similar processes among principals (Leithwood, Begley, and Cousins, in press; Ogawa 1991; Parkay et al. 1993; Roberts 1989a; Wright 1993).

An organizational socialization framework helps fill these gaps by showing how organizational socialization processes affect all the members of a group, including formal leaders such as principals. Leader successors are newcomers who must be integrated into existing groups, validated by social processes, and granted legitimacy by subordinates and superiors before they can have significant impacts on the actions of others. Even if they are currently members of the organization filling other roles, their newness in the leader role dominates their experience. This need for validation by the group referred to as endorsed leadership by Scott (1987) places particular pressure on people who differ substantially from conventional preconceptions about leaders. Women are included in this category in almost all situations in which they rise to leadership positions. Yet Blau argues that, without socially validated authority, there is no leadership:

It may be suggested that the distinctive feature of authority is that social norms accepted and enforced by the collectivity of subordinates constrain its individual members to comply with directives of a superior. Compliance is voluntary for the collectivity, but social constraints make it compelling for the individual. In contrast to other forms of influence and power, the pressure to follow suggestions and orders does not come from the superior who gives them but from the collectivity of subordinates. These normative constraints may be institutionalized and pervade the entire society, or they may emerge *in a group in social interaction* [emphasis added]. The latter emergent norms define leadership. (Blau 1964, 200)

Given that all new leaders require this endorsement for full effectiveness, and given that women by nature of their sex alone deviate from many people's preconceived ideas about leadership, women stand to benefit greatly from a thorough understanding of the validation process and skill in promoting it. Women draw strength from the groups they lead as these groups develop their own particular character and social commitments. I emphasize that this is not exclusively a women's view. As Schein (1985, 197) pointed out: "leadership [is] a shared set of activities rather than a single person's trait, and a sense of ownership of group outcomes arises." In the sections that follow, I discuss some primary features of the organizational socialization process and then use women's experiences in schools to illustrate the utility of a socially empowered view of leadership ascension by women in educational organizations.

An Organizational Socialization View of Women's Experiences

The traditional leadership literature, with its emphasis on traits, situations, behavior, and contingencies (Hoy and Miskel 1991; Stogdill 1980), provides little insight into the process of taking charge for educational leaders falling outside conventional conceptions of "school leader." Correlational and multivariate studies systematically demonstrate that women and men from diverse ethnic and racial backgrounds falter when associated as "leaders," because their best traits, skills, and knowledge fall outside prevailing preconceptions and expectations of leadership. Yet the case study literature abounds with stories of remarkable effects attributable to the leadership of people who are members of these under-represented groups.

Often when women ascend to leadership positions in schools, those whom they are assigned to lead immediately form negative expectations on the basis of a past, less than satisfactory, experience with one woman in a position of power or on the basis of cultural stereotypes about women leaders. Researchers report incidents when teachers, upon hearing that a principal succession is eminent, express the unexplained hope that "they won't appoint a woman" (Fauske and Ogawa 1987). Some admit their surprise when things turn out all right.

> I worked for a woman principal . . . and it was not a good experience. But I couldn't let you think that we . . . feel that way. You helped me realize that it's a personal thing. It's been a pleasant surprise. (Hart, 1993, 216).

This response can be explained in part by the "incongruence" of women and members of minority groups with the cultural assumptions and expectations people hold. As these newly appointed leaders interact with the social and organizational culture, these assumptions and expectations may be confirmed or disconfirmed. For this reason, the organizational socialization literature provides insight in three important ways: (*a*) it helps researchers understand the social nature of the experience, interpret events, and develop new models for the leadership succession experience for those outside major cultural assumptions about leaders; (*b*) it helps the newly appointed and culturally incongruent leaders experiencing the ascent to leadership diagnose and analyze their experience and take action to shape the process; and (*c*) it provides guidance for the superiors of these new leaders as they design deliberate organizational experience and support structures that enhance the likelihood that diverse new leaders will be successful and contribute new talent and insight into the improvement of educational organizations.

In this section of the chapter, I *briefly* outline the succession experiences of three women and use research reports of their experiences to illustrate the importance of considering leadership as a socially interactive process. Incongruent new leaders like women and minorities must be even more acutely aware and more able to influence this process than are those who fit cultural expectations of the way a "leader" looks, sounds, and acts.

Leigh

The new principal of Chesterfield High School felt immediately at home as soon as she was appointed. Although this was her first position as principal (having served as an assistant principal for several years following a long career as a teacher and librarian), she found the school familiar, its students and problems similar, and the challenges facing its educators much like those she had faced in other large comprehensive high schools. Leigh was meticulous in her appearance and personal habits, often wearing crisp, professional gray houndstooth suits or a black and white dress with a red jacket. The students compared her to Nancy Reagan when they first met her, associating her appearance with the cold, perfectionist, patrician personality of Mrs. Reagan. Her career experiences were much affected by her sex. Leigh had been denied one appointment in favor of a male counselor because her principal wanted to keep her and felt he could not do without her. In one confrontation, a student blurted a common, early belief about her, "If they'd hired a man to be principal, they wouldn't have someone so incompetent" (Lamoreaux 1990, 12). Leigh found herself joking about herself, consciously applying the language of support and cooperation, and apologizing to the faculty for decisions that were criticized (asking for help avoiding future "goofs"), all tactics common to women in leadership roles (Shakeshaft 1989).

Despite these difficulties, Leigh emerged as a well-liked and admired leader at Chesterfield barely three months after taking charge. This outcome was attributed by Lamoreaux (1990) to her ability to communicate a clear vision and affect the way in which people in the school viewed themselves. By communicating this vision, demonstrating her commitment to the high school and to the young people who came to learn there, she created a vision of "caring, of sharing, and of relationships."

Diane

Diane brought experience as a social worker and supervisor of a behavioral intervention team to her work as an elementary principal (Oliver 1992). Diane had a strong self-image and was confident that she could "do a good job" as a principal. She believed that her social work experience was essential, making it possible for her to "understand people and [help] them perform. I can recognize both the strengths and weaknesses in people. I can help people in getting along with others. The crisis training has made me capable of dealing with parents." While she hired six new teachers, the majority were seasoned, experienced staff, leading her to conclude that "I'll have to use participatory management using team leaders."

Like Leigh, Diane was given no significant formal induction to her role. The district's orientation for new administrators was a "good overview" but left her feeling isolated and on her own. Early meetings with the PTA and faculty seemed to her to go very well: "The cooperation has been great."

By October, Diane began to have conflicts with parents, often over student discipline. She just "couldn't understand how some parents could be so unreasonable . . . it's just plain rudeness . . . they really overreact." While she "used to get a lot of feedback from the district office, because I know those people," she found herself having some difficulty deciding what advice to take. The "good ole' boys" often gave advice she felt conflicted with district policy. She felt isolated, in need of "more communication," yet her confidence level remained high: "This is a great job and I'm going to be good because I love it."

This sense of isolation and confrontation grew with time. December found Diane more and more concerned about parental complaints to the district office about her and more convinced that a good principal is one who is good at "PR." High conflict and poor public relations "give the perception that I'm not doing a good job." At the same time, she saw herself as "more humanistic," a "lot softer than in the past. As I build relationships, I'll probably have to become more formal." She also found that it was "not as easy as I thought to really have an impact on a school. . . . There's a perception that you'll be here for a while" but the teachers "will be here longer." Relationships with teachers were difficult for her: "I find it hard to confront teachers without giving them the impression that they aren't doing a good job. I want to instill in teachers a feeling that we're peers."

As these feelings grew, so did Diane's performance anxiety. By January she felt "more frustration . . . less confident" yet did not know why. "I wonder, do I fit, do I measure up? There has been nothing to dispel that." Her district supervisor told her that she needed to "clean up and make this a better organization."

Isolation was a major problem for Diane. She had no network of professional colleagues and felt somewhat removed from other principals. While "little groups of principals" existed in the district, she was not one of them. This isolation caused her distress. In March, she remarked, "When you're not invited to breakfast, it's a hard message your first year. I feel like there is a lot of politicking. I don't know who to identify with." While she had praised the PTA at the beginning of the year, relationships quickly soured. "I've been in a big power struggle with them . . . they still don't trust. me." She reiterated in March that "the district needs to make provisions for more training." Diane retreated, interacting primarily with the fifth/sixth grade team, excluding other teachers, who then "felt decisions were being made during lunch." Because she hadn't "felt a kinship with other principals," she turned to a small group of teachers. Reflecting back, Diane felt she needed "to keep thoughts to myself until decisions are made, and then talk with everyone at once."

June brought little change in Diane's principalship. While she continued to identify her social work background and her "people skills" as her greatest advantage, she had ongoing problems with parents and supervisors, and parent complaints continued. The district, she felt, defined success as "no parent calls or complaints" and "if your reports are on time." The most important rewards of the job: "Feeling like your faculty likes you, hugs from the kids . . . feeling accepted by other administrators." Her final assessment of her experience: "If reports are not in on time, or if you are 95 cents off on your books, you will hear about it within three days."

Ellen

Ellen came to the principalship from twenty years as an elementary school teacher, the last three of which were spent as a teacher leader coordinating reading curriculum and instruction from the district office (Oliver 1992). Like Diane, Ellen approached her new assignment with great confidence. "I have a lot of experience in so many facets of the curriculum and in curriculum leadership. I have knowledge that others just don't have. I feel like I can always fall back on some prior experience." Ellen's role models "developed from different personality styles meshing with my own. I did have an outstanding principal that saw strengths in me . . . he let me be a leader."

The challenges of a new assignment and a new year excited Ellen. She saw her major goal as "letting the staff catch the same vision that I have for a strong educational program for the kids," but complained that they "aren't all as dedicated as they need to be." By October, she complained about "administrative tasks, organizing the staff, parents concerns. . . . " More important work called her: "Getting into the classroom, serving as a model for teachers . . . I was catching so many errors . . . I've also had to model classroom management skills . . . " and "conferencing with teachers talking about problems." She found it frustrating "not being able to change people." She was pleased that some people had complimented her and that she had been able to take "more of a leadership role" from the "unit leaders . . . to lighten their load."

By late fall, Ellen described herself as "more patient . . . accepting failure in others better . . . trying to accept people in their own station in life. . . . I used to make (almost, but not quite) snap judgments." She felt that she held different values from those prevalent in the community. "The things they hold dear are different from mine." At the same time, she "had some problems with teachers who just don't understand community values."

Feedback on her progress was hard for Ellen to obtain. She felt the quick orientation meetings early in the year had not provided sufficient preparation for her work, and, as the year progressed, she didn't "get much feedback from the district. . . . The meetings we did have were too overwhelming." When problems arose, she would call on her own strengths and on friends for support and then "just try to survive." While she began to find daily routine easier, "personalities and idiosyncrasies" continued to be a challenge.

Despite these difficulties, Ellen believed that she had "softened, tempered" as the year went on. She said she was a "better listener" and was "trying to be more clear-headed, less emotional." As a leader, Ellen described herself with confidence: "I'm clear thinking. I have a lot of knowledge. I'm able to make decisions. I'm not frightened of decision making. I assume a direction in making decisions. I take responsibility for good and bad decisions that I've made." She said her "basic ideas remain intact." At the same time, Ellen wanted to be "less sensitive, more unemotional." She felt she had a "tendency to feel sorry for people, when" she "should be looking at performance." She said she tried "to be supportive and not be an authority figure."

These themes developed over the course of the year. March came with Ellen still "working with staff who are in the wrong profession . . . in the process of putting a person on probation. . . . I have to be so careful. I feel like I have to be a lawyer. . . . It's hard for me to watch really weak teachers."

Late in April, the parents still saw Ellen as "the new kid on the block." She, on the other had, did not feel like a "rookie." "I think I'm really sensitive to problems of parents, teachers, and students. I can smell problems. After I have identified them, I go through systematically to solve them. I start at the individual level to work things through. I'm really aware of affect." Responsiveness, decisiveness, and the ability to meet individual needs characterized Ellen's idea of a successful principal, but she felt the district saw success as "one that can take care of every problem so no one ever calls them."

By June, this feeling became very strong for Ellen. A conflict involving parents, the police, and a child resulted in a court appearance for her and a perception that she was isolated, that the district was "distant . . . you basically stand alone. You need to play the game (the political game) to get help. . . . I didn't realize how little you feel that support. . . . I felt alone . . . like you're dangling over crocodiles with their mouths open." Ellen expressed disappointment that she was "encumbered with tasks that take away from what we're supposed to be doing. . . . We should be with kids mastering things they should be learning. . . . It's hard to get people to change, to get them to realize they're not doing the job they are paid to do." Ellen also felt that "some people are deceitful. . . . I guess it's called politicking—it's hard for me. This staff is hard that way. I wasn't ready to see deceit. Parents are the same about teachers." While she felt that "mentors, advisors, listeners" had helped her, she alone could go through the experience and only friends who were principals could understand how it felt with "teachers bitching when you've been a support to them." She felt some bitterness toward the district for a lack of feedback and support: "There are no rewards. You only hear from them when there are problems. There are no positives if you are a good curriculum leader. . . . If they want a manager they should hire someone who can take care of those things. Even the superintendent's goals don't focus on education."

Organizational Socialization

The research on organizational socialization returns consistently to four key themes. These are: (1) tactics employed in the socialization process; (2) the personal and social contexts which shape the entire process; (3) socialization stages through which new members pass; and (4) the outcomes or effects of socialization practices likely to result from these factors (Hart 1991).

Organizational Socialization Tactics. Organizations apply deliberate and unconscious tactics to the socialization of new members or of members new to particular organizational roles. These tactics can be used in a context that is collective or individual. Each has advantages. Collective socialization promotes commitment and job satisfaction. Individual tactics may result in increased role conflict and ambiguity, but they also enhance innovation, creativity, and change (Van Maanen 1978; Little 1990). Contexts may be more or less formal. Mentors often play a large part in these socialization tactics. An assigned mentor possessing specific traits and knowledge, deliberately assigned to a specific novice, and carefully structuring activities provides a formal exposure to organizational values and norms. But mentors also constrain innovation; entrusting the socialization of newcomers to established old timers can guarantee the preservation of conventional practice (Van Maanen 1978). Highly formalized socialization procedures can create an orientation that promotes this recreation of the past— a custodial orientation toward the role (Van Maanen and Schein 1979).

Tactics also may address the content of the socialization—specific knowledge that the new principal must master. This tactic—the sequencing and control of knowledge content to be mastered—is not commonly used in educational organizations (Hart 1993), yet it holds powerful potential for shaping the future leadership of schools.

A third feature of socialization tactics refers to its social or isolated nature—its sociality. Socialization may be serial—following in someone's footsteps—or disjunctive—building a whole new role in the absence of role models. In the absence of role models, new principals often must create their own roles as they go along, leaving them unsettled but freer. If leaders differ substantially in the personal characteristics from those who commonly fill their role—women, for example—they experience significant stress, must negotiate more ambiguity, and receive less support than others (Ortiz and Marshall 1988; Valverde 1980). Sociality also may demand that a new principal abandon an existing professional self-image or that women and minorities recruited for leadership roles possess desired skills and values absent among sitting leaders. This tactic may cause more individual discomfort while infusing a school environment with instructional leadership, school achievement, or social goals absent in the conventional administrator.

Leigh, Diane, and Ellen experienced socialization to their new assignments as an individual, idiosyncratic process. The quality of their experiences depended on the relationships they had with established members of the organization and formal or informal mentors. While this pattern commonly dominates school administration succession, it presents particular challenges for women, because they often have fewer personal contacts and lack role models with whom they regularly interact. At the same time, this situation can be to their advantage. When healthy interactions can be shaped, they are freer to innovate and nurture innovation than are principals who feel constrained to replicate the past, custodians of the conventional role. Two features of organizational socialization—investiture or divestiture required by the process and the presence, absence, or nature of role models—shaped initial outcomes for these women.

Investiture/Divestiture. While Leigh worked as an assistant principal and sought the principalship for some time before becoming a principal, Diane and Ellen came directly to the assignment from very different roles. Leigh felt at home, fit into the school, and quickly took on responsibilities in a way that teachers and students found supportive and affirming. Albeit informally, her work invested or reinforced her professional self-concept. While scholars find that investiture often minimizes change, it reduces anxiety, ambiguity, and conflict. Ellen and Diane experienced major personal conflicts over a divestiture of self. Diane saw herself as sensitive, responsive, and good with people. Her expertise lay in social work. Yet her major difficulties arose as a result of interpersonal relationships, often over student discipline, even though she previously supervised a behavioral interventions team. Ellen felt herself a curriculum and instruction expert and complained bitterly about others' failings as teachers and about conflicts with supervisors and parents.

With the exception of a very short orientation meeting, none of these women received any formal socialization to their roles. In Ellen's and Diane's cases, the lack of deliberate organizational tactics by the district left them feeling at loose ends, unsure what the district wanted from them except no complaints from parents and reports on time. Both fell back on old patterns and self-concepts that, by their own accounts, left them dissatisfied with their first year as principals.

Role Models. Significant role models were absent for all these women. Leigh leaned on women friends, sometimes teachers, and hid her performance anxiety. She was much younger than most women in similar positions. Diane and Ellen felt their area directors were available to them if they needed help, but problems that developed left Diane defensive about criticism over her lack of organization and parent complaints and Ellen resentful about her isolation from other administrators in the district, even though both worked in districts where "mentors" are routinely assigned to new principals. Like Leigh, they expressed serious anxiety about their performance, the lack of feedback they received, and a need to be nice and be liked.

Personal and Social Context of Socialization. A firmly established social world greets all newcomers. Yet, even if this world prescribes behavior very tightly, it "does not exert an irresistible hold" over the new leader (Wentworth 1980, 58). The personal and social context thus exerts powerful influence over the leadership succession experience. Entry requires that the new leader learn the nature of the existing culture while striving to affect some changes within it (Crouch and Yetton 1988). The personal context—the talents, preferences, characteristics, thinking, and experiences of the new member—provides a setting for the ascension to leadership. It includes the situational or professional self-concept, the core self-concept (divorced from a setting), intellectual functioning, sense of self-direction, and changes that occur with experience (Brousseau 1983; Kohn and Schooler 1983).

The social context is more diverse and more complex. It is the human system into which a new leader seeks integration. A new leader must come to understand and use fundamental values, beliefs, and assumptions about worth to drive and energize those already in the group. Three strong influences shape the social context—the similarity of group members, the frequency of interaction or contact, and the tendency of people to interact with others who are like themselves (Gecas 1981). Positive outcomes depend on the *legitimacy* of interactions in the perception of those involved, not on their frequency (Monane 1967). Contact between men and women in some professional contexts such as travel or frequent consultation, for example, is limited by negative perceptions of its legitimacy (Shakeshaft 1989). The tendency people demonstrate to limit contact with people who are "different" in a social context severely handicaps women moving into leadership positions. If a new leader does not fit preconceptions, people tend to isolate her, protecting the system from her influence and shortcomings. Women also may unintentionally draw attention to differences when they are unaware how they are perceived; or they may deliberately manipulate the social context by seeking opportunities to draw attention to their skills and knowledge congruent with the values and needs of the schools (Hart 1988).

Personal Context. From the first contact, everyone focused on Leigh's personal characteristics—her appearances and dress, her meticulous habits, her two divorces. She felt that women administrators suffered more scrutiny than men, that the slightest mistake on her part would have been characterized as "just like a woman." Her ability to understand and respond to individuals around her, however, was one of Leigh's strengths. At first labeled a "Nancy Reagan," she won the respect of others through her continual responsiveness.

Neither Ellen nor Diane mentioned their sex as a factor in their leadership experiences, yet both continually emphasized that they were at times too emotional, too sensitive to others' opinions, too eager to be nice and to be liked. Both expressed great confidence in their talents, knowledge, and abilities at the first of the year; both experienced major disappointments in interpersonal relationships with teachers, parents, and supervisors.

Social Context. When the personal characteristics of these three women interacted with their social contexts as new leaders, the resulting dynamics yielded very different outcomes than they might have predicted. Leigh, the outsider, approached the school analytically and with guarded optimism, looking for areas where she might use her best talents. Diane and Ellen were more glib, more willing to announce in the fall that they had the school pegged and were ready to have an impact, change the school, convert the teachers to their vision. Both gave lip service to their collegial relationships based on peer status with teachers; both acted as hierarchical and authoritarian leaders by their own accounts.

School culture receives much attention in the leadership literature. Diane and Ellen treated the cultures they described as deficiencies to be moderated by their leadership and influence rather than as environments to be understood. Their impact at the end of one year appears to have been minimal, while Leigh's impact at the end of three months was noticeable to those around her.

Socialization Stages. All newcomers pass through a series of stages during organizational socialization. By understanding the features of these stages, women can draw on research and theory to help them shape a more constructive leadership ascension experience.

During the first stage—encounter or anticipation—learning needs are intense. Learning includes cognitive and affective content. During this stage, newcomers must make sense of the new environment and deal with the surprises that continually confront them (Louis 1980a; 1980b). Researchers report that women feel significantly higher levels of anxiety about performance and the value of their potential contributions at this stage of leadership succession than do men (Nicholson and West 1988). During the second stage—adjustment or accommodation—the new leader confronts the task of fitting-in. Women confront skepticism about their mastery of the skills and their possession of the traits needed to lead. The final stage is a period of stabilization or role management and location. The new leader begins to master the new job, is initiated into a group of comrades and interpersonal relationships, and demonstrates to the group how she fits in and provides needed knowledge and skills. This stage presents a "social contracting" of relationships (Fulk and Cummings 1984).

Encounter. Diane and Ellen appear to have experienced an unjustified euphoria at the outset of their principalships. They interpreted their responsibility in heroic terms, seeking to change the school, anticipating no accommodation, no adjustment on their parts. First impressions suggest that Leigh, more diagnostic and exploratory, might have been seen by some as initially tentative. The first interviews conducted with Ellen and Diane suggest two very talented, confident, and assertive leaders with strong understandings of their best talents (people skills and curriculum).

Adjustment or Accommodation. This perceived strength and unreflective assurance and a lack of attention to social context as a *neutral* but critical factor, left Ellen and Diane vulnerable. They pursued change from others while seeking little change in themselves except to be better listeners or more organized. Consequently, while Lamoreaux reports a pervasive belief that Leigh was firmly established as the acknowledged leader at Chesterfield in a matter of months, June found Diane and Ellen in turmoil. For them, *stabilization* had not taken place by the end of a year. The parents still resisted them, all but a core few teachers remained part of the camp of "others," and supervisors were a source of anxiety or anger. Ellen even talked about whether or not she might want to return to teaching. It can be said that neither had moved beyond the first stage in the course of a year.

Outcomes of Socialization. Outcomes emerging from the interaction of new school leaders and an established school context can be organizational and personal. A custodial response—when the newcomer is reshaped to become the custodian of preexisting practices and values—is most likely when succession is dominated by role models and reshapes the professional identity of the successor. Research identifies this as the overwhelmingly prevalent outcome of principal succession and professional socialization (Duke 1987; Greenfield 1985a; 1985b).

While a lack of role models often poses a barrier and challenge to women seeking leadership roles (Ortiz and Marshall 1988), this lack also leaves women who ascend to leadership more free to innovate and create. Innovation occurs in different domains—content and role. Content innovation is more likely without role models. It occurs with changes in the way a new leader performs her role through the ideas and processes she encourages people to adopt. While she accepts traditional norms and goals, the new leader adopts new tactical alternatives and tasks and draws on a new knowledge base for support.

Role innovation is the most dramatic outcome of leader succession. It redefines the mission, goals, and content of leadership. When a strong professional identity is affirmed and individuality supported, this outcome is promoted. Under role innovation, the new leader makes a genuine attempt to redefine ends as well as means (Schein 1971b). This outcome also is more likely to result in personal growth and change for the new leader. "High role innovators are more likely than low innovators to report having experienced personal change." (Nicholson and West 1988, 110). Leaders who attempt content and role innovation experience the most jarring as well as the most potentially creative succession experiences.

While isolation is mentioned by many new principals as a surprise and shock (Duke 1987; Greenfield, 1985b; 1985), the intense isolation experienced by all three women described earlier (regardless of their emerging successes and difficulties) strikes the reader. When that isolation accompanied a growing failure of existing professional skills and interventions to accomplish desired goals, problems were exacerbated. That appears to have been the case for both Ellen and Diane.

Conclusion

This chapter provides a glimpse of the power of organizational socialization to affect the outcomes of leadership succession for women. If nothing else, it highlights the critical importance of contextual diagnosis and deliberate actions on the part of women to secure the validation of members of the school social group while they seek to find the best avenues through which they can contribute to the achievement and development of the school.

Contrary to conventional wisdom, the two women principals who appeared at the first of the year to be most likely to become integrated and effective leaders experienced the most difficulty. They both were insiders, possessed or seemed to posses critical instructional and interpersonal skills, and already knew a number of people within their districts. It is possible that their single-minded pursuit of "instructional leadership," "change," and observable "impacts" handicapped their ability to understand the social context in which this all important work must occur.

Organizational socialization research predicts the outcomes suggested by these three brief cases. The two women least concerned about their interaction with their new social groups and most concerned about their impacts on them were both disillusioned and weary at the end of their first year. They experienced conflict with and criticism from important subgroups with the school and district. Perhaps more painfully than most, they learned that leaders and those they lead interact and produce outcomes as a result of that interaction.

The application of organizational socialization literature to these three cases also provides insights into specific interventions women and other nontraditional leaders (and those who appoint them in leadership positions) can take to improve their success. First, formal, carefully planned socialization experiences for first-time leaders and for transition appointments provide a forum in which to set the stage for the complex social process of leader succession, convey information about the process, and give guidance and practice applying the skills and knowledge related specifically to the taking-charge process. None of these women were given any formal preparation; the mentors assigned to them gave hit-and-miss assistance. By contrast, planned formal mentor assignments can be used as a strategy to provide desired role models and break the cycle of undesirable role models that are observed in school leader succession traditions (Pence, this vol-

119

ume). Needs for affiliation and peer relationships can be better filled by this kind of intervention, as well. All three women reported feelings of isolation and turned to teachers and old friends rather than face the complex challenges of the principalship alone. While these friends and colleagues gave welcome solace, the support of a group of peers simultaneously going through the same experience would be much more useful.

Second, explicit in a formalized socialization experience, district leaders should state their goals and hopes for the new leader. The three women whose successions were discussed in this chapter experienced little or no formal socialization. They never met with other new principals; they never discussed with their superiors how their leadership might be very different from that of their mentors. Very little opportunity for brainstorming or dreaming occurs on its own, and school districts seldom bring new principals together except to train or enculturate them in existing practices. Ellen exemplified the frustration new principals can feel when they see their superiors as political enemies against whom they must "play the game." Scholars report that high role innovators also experience personal growth. A school district can "kill two birds with one stone." By encouraging role and content innovation, superiors also encourage personal growth and invest in their district's own human resource pool. But successors need help understanding what role and content innovation might include and how they might be a resource for new ideas.

Third, during the taking-charge process, supervisors can help successors analyze the expectations and preconceptions about leaders that members of the school social group (including communities) hold. The new principal then can devise an explicit strategy for emphasizing her own best talents and skills that specifically address these expectations and beliefs. She also can find ways to deemphasize obviously incongruent features (like race and sex). Over time, when she comes to meet the professional and personal needs of those she serves, congruities will become less important.

A potential fourth intervention relates to this notion of diagnosis and response to incongruities. Supervisors and new leaders should attend to their own progress through the organizational socialization stages and watch for the development of accommodation, adjustment, and instantiation into a contributing place in the organization. Periodic meetings and discussions about progress toward integration can go a long way in drawing attention to the actions needed to facilitate this process.

Finally, the nontraditional successor must take some responsibility for her own success. The barriers remain high and the challenges many. More skills diagnosing and intervening to promote her success will be required of her than of other new leaders. Being attentive to her own incongruities and drawing attention to the talents and skills that made her a promising school leader in the first place can go far toward promoting her own success. The preconceptions people hold about leaders and leadership exert powerful influence over their judgments and behaviors, even when they are subconscious. Schein (1985), examining organizational culture and leadership, asserted that these imbedded assumptions and beliefs are preconscious. While the physical and behavioral artifacts and the values of school culture are visible to the new leader, the cultural elements that pass from person to person, through organizational generations are so deeply imbedded that group members have difficulty describing them. They are not questioned, but assumed. Under these conditions, members of the school social group can act on the best of motives, feeling supportive of the nontraditional leader, and still adversely affect her experience. The need for self and organizational analysis increases for the new leader.

As part 2 of this volume vividly illustrates, enlightened attitudes toward incongruent leaders have failed to achieve over the last twenty-five years what many seeking greater equity of opportunity had hoped. The "glass ceiling" appears to function in part because women choose not to apply for the highest leadership positions (Scherr, this volume). Other studies lead to the conclusion that special advocacy groups also are insufficient to change traditional stereotypes. More assertive means to provide social and leadership skills that undermine remaining barriers are called for. Specific interventions by new leaders and their superiors offer additional resources for supporting the successes of women and ethnic minority leaders in schools. These skills can enhance the likelihood of appointment and improve success following those hard-won appointments.

Bibliography

Blau, P. M. (1964). *Exchange and power in social life.* New York: John Wiley.

Bossert, S. T., Dwyer, D. C., Rowan, B., and Lee, G. V. (1982). The instructional management role of the principal. *Educational Administration Quarterly,* 18, 34–64.

Brousseau, K. R. (1983). Toward a dynamic model of job-person relationships: Findings, research questions, and implications for work system design. *Academy of Management Review,* 8, 33–45.

Collay, M. (1995). The community of the school in rural settings: The "Mom and Pop" model of school administration. In D. M. Dunlap and P. A. Schmuck (eds.), *Women leading in education.* Albany, NY: SUNY Press.

Crouch, A., and Yetton, P. W. (1988). The management team: An equilibrium model of manager and subordinate performance. In J. G. Hunt, B. R. Baliga, H. P. Dachler, and C. A. Schriesheim (eds.), *Emerging leadership vistas.* Boston: Lexington.

Duke, D. L. (1987). *School leadership and instructional improvement.* New York: Random House.

Edmonds, R. (1979). Some schools work and more can. *Social Policy,* 9, 32–36.

Fauske, J. R., and Ogawa, R. T. (1987). Detachment, fear, and expectation: A faculty's response to the impending succession of its principal. *Educational Administration Quarterly,* 23, 23–44.

Firestone, W. A. (1990). Succession and bureaucracy: Gouldner revisited. *Educational Administration Quarterly,* 26(4), 345–75.

Fulk, J., and Cummings, T. G. (1984). Refocusing leadership: A modest proposal. In J. C. Hunt, D. M. Hosking, C. A. Schriescheim, and R. Stewart (eds.), *Leaders and managers: International perspectives on managerial behavior and leadership.* Oxford: Pergamon.

Gecas, V. (1981). Contexts of socialization. In M. Rosenberg and R. Turner (eds.), *Social psychology: Sociological perspectives.* New York: Basic Books.

Greenfield, W. D., Jr. (1985a). Being and becoming a principal: Responses to work contexts and socialization processes. Paper presented at the annual meetings of the American Educational Research Association, Chicago.

———. (1985b). The moral socialization of school administrators: Informal role learning outcomes. *Educational Administration Quarterly,* 21, 99–119.

Hart, A. W. (1988). Attribution as effect: An outsider principal's succession. *Journal of Educational Administration,* 26(3), 331–52.

———. (1991). Leader succession and socialization: An synthesis. *Review of Education Research,* 61, 451–74.

———. (1995). *Principal succession: Establishing leadership in schools* in D. M. Dunlap and P. A. Schmuck (eds.), *Women leading in education.* Albany: SUNY Press.

Hoy, W. K., and Miskel, C. G. (1991). *Educational administration: Theory, research, and practice,* 4th ed. New York: McGraw-Hill.

Kohn, M. L., and Schooler, C. (1983). *Work and personality.* Norwood, NJ: Ablex.

Lamoreaux, D. (1990). New shoes: An educational criticism of a new principal's first quarter. Paper presented at the annual meetings of the American Educational Research Association, Boston.

Leithwood, K. A., Begley, P., and Cousins, B. (in press). *Developing expert leadership for future schools.* New York: Falmer Press.

Leithwood, K. A., Steinbach, R., and Begley, P. (1992). The nature and contribution of socialization experiences to becoming a principal in Canada. In F. W. Parkay and G. E. Hall (eds.), *Becoming a principal: The challenges of beginning leadership.* Boston: Allyn and Bacon.

Little, J. W. (1990). The mentor phenomenon and the social organization of teaching. In C. Casden (ed.), *Review of research in education,* 16, 297–352. Washington, DC: American Educational Research Association.

Monane, J. H. (1967). *A sociology of human systems.* New York: Appleton. Century. Crofts.

Nicholson, N., and West, M. A. (1988). *Managerial job change: Men and women in transition.* Cambridge: Cambridge University Press.

Ogawa, R. O. (1991). Enchantment, disenchantment, and accommodation: How a faculty made sense of the succession of its principal. *Educational Administration Quarterly,* 27, 30–60.

Oliver, J. (1992). The professional socialization of principals. Unpublished dissertation, Department of Educational Administration, University of Utah.

Ortiz, F. I., and Marshall, C. (1988). Women in educational administration. In N. J. Boyan (ed.), *Handbook of research on educational administration.* New York: Longman.

Parkay, F. W., and Hall, G. E. (eds.). (1992). *Becoming a principal: The challenges of beginning leadership.* Boston: Allyn and Bacon.

Pence, L. J. (1995). Learning leadership through mentorships. In D. Dunlap and P. A. Schmuck (eds.), *Women leading in education:* Albany, NY: SUNY Press.

Roberts, J. (1989a). *Cultural orientations of first-time high school principals during selection and entry.* Paper presented at the annual meetings of the American Educational Research Association, San Francisco.

Schein, E. H. (1971b). Occupational socialization in the professions: The case of the role innovator. *Journal of Psychiatric Research,* 8, 521–30.

————. (1985). *Organizational culture and leadership.* San Francisco: Jossey-Bass.

Schmuck, P., and Schmuck, R. (1990). Democratic participation in small town schools. *Educational Researcher,* 19(8), 14–20.

Scott, W. R. (1987). *Organizations: Rational, natural, and open systems,* 2nd ed. Englewood Cliffs, NJ: Prentice-Hall.

Shakeshaft, C. (1989). *Women in educational administration,* 2nd ed. Newbury Park, CA: Sage.

Stogdill, R. M. (1980). Traits of leadership: A follow-up to 1970. In B. M. Bass (ed.), *Stogdill's handbook of leadership.* New York: Free Press.

Valverde, L. A. (1980). Promotion socialization: The informal process in large urban districts and its adverse effects on non-whites and women. *Journal of Educational Equity and Leadership,* 1, 36–46.

Van Maanen, J. (1978). People processing. *Organizational Dynamics,* 7, 18–36.

Van Maanen, J., and Schein, E. H. (1979). Toward a theory of organization socialization. In B. Staw (ed.), *Research in organizational behavior,* 1, 209–264. Greenwich, CT: JAI Press.

Wanous, J. P. (1980). *Organizational entry: Recruitment, selection, and socialization of newcomers.* Reading, MA: Addison-Wesley Publishing Company.

Wentworth, W. M. (1980). *Context and understanding: An inquiry into socialization theory.* New York: Elsevier.

Wright, L. V. (1992). A study of supervisory priorities of first-time high school principals. In F. W. Parkay and G. E. Hall (eds.), *Becoming a principal: The challenges of beginning leadership.* Boston: Allyn and Bacon.

SEVEN

Learning Leadership Through Mentorships

L. Jean Pence

School administrators often feel isolated even though they are constantly interacting with others. The image of an administrator is one who is "in charge" or "leads," yet many administrators are cautious about sharing their concerns and mistakes. This is particularly true for new administrators who want to show their competence, but are faced with many new demands and challenges. Neophyte administrators can become frustrated and confused trying to learn complex educational administrative roles. They are striving to link administrative theory with practice in the field.

Women administrators have additional difficulty learning their administrative role because there are conflicting attitudes about the stereotypes of what it means to be female and what it means to be an administrator. Developing relationship with veteran practicing administrators provides a link for neophytes and proteges that are important for learning the tasks and challenges of a new position. These relationships can especially be important to a woman or minority who is "different" from the stereotyped image of an administrator who is white and male.

Sally, a protege in an Oregon Mentorship Program, shared her view of the importance of mentorships. "You can know about something—I mean you can read about leadership until you're blue in the face [but] to try to go out and do it is another thing. I mean, you've got to have that transfer. I don't think it happens naturally. I think just because you know something in a book doesn't mean you have the skills to go out and make it happen."

This chapter is a report of two recent studies of mentorships and programs in educational administration in Oregon public schools (Pence and Nolf). Pence analyzed formal and informal mentorships to discover relational, operational, and demographic characteristics common to both groups and what interactions and activities contributed to the perceived success of mentorships. The characteristics of successful formalized mentorships were compared with the characteristics of mentorships that naturally evolved. Data were analyzed to determine what was important to successful mentorship experiences from the perspective of the mentor and the protege.

Nolf described the characteristics of the Oregon Mentorship Program, a formal program, and described successful or deleterious experiences as perceived by the mentors and the proteges. She compared the mentor responses to the protege responses to see where they were concurrence and divergence. Since both studies used the same formal mentorship program, their findings can provide guidance for providing assistance in preparing new school administrators.

Mentorships Defined

Mentorship is an ancient concept originally traced to Homer's epic, *The Odyssey*, when Ulysses chose his wise and trusted old friend, Mentor, to guard and guide his son, Telemachus. Informal mentorships, as the one described in Greek mythology, were considered an integral part of an individual's growth and development. While the concept of mentorship is ancient, it received very little attention, except in connection to men in the "old boys" network, until the 1970s. Efforts were then made to actively recruit and promote women and minorities into administrative positions. Organizations began using mentorships to help guide the way of under-represented groups to executive ranks.

Formal and informal mentorships provide mentors and proteges an opportunity to discuss and reflect on situations and solutions. Sally, a protégé, stated:

I think the mentorship program teaches and gives you some idea what you can expect from a working relationship with somebody else. I . . . read a lot of books on leadership. I was real interested in how people did visioning and being able to talk to people around the state who had a handle on that. So having a concept and understanding it intellectually and getting a chance to see people actually doing it even though they may not have been in school for a couple of years because they didn't know that was the thing, but they were doing it. It was also what I found Linda doing. I found her practicing the things I was learning about—the things I was interested in abstractly.

In 1978 Levinson and his colleagues reported mentors were an important force in the development of successful men; that study lead to greater attention to the mentoring concept, particularly, for helping under represented groups. Formal mentorship programs appeared to be a way to provide guidance and support for the entrance and promotion of women and minorities in administration. Mentorships are an excellent way to provide guided field experiences that help protégés and neophytes learn operational facets and assist in the socialization process. Some organizations, including schools, have begun formal mentor programs; those programs range from being voluntary to being mandated at the state level. Even though the results of those formally organized mentorship programs have mixed reviews as to their success, the literature suggests that the advantages outweigh the disadvantages (Klauss 1981; Price 1981; Daresh 1987; Daresh and Playko 1992; Kram 1985; and Vertz 1985).

A "mentor" is usually a designated, more experienced person who influences the career development and socialization of a less experienced individual in an organization. A "protégé" is a person who is less experienced in a particular job; one who develops expertise under the guidance of a more experienced practicing administrator. The "mentorship" is a relationship between two people in which the person with greater experience and/or expertise teaches counsels, guides, and helps the other to develop both professionally and personally (Alleman 1987). These definitions served as the foundation for the studies completed by Pence and Nolf.

Informal Mentorships

Pence (1989a) selected a stratified random sample of a representative population of 417 administrators to survey. The sample represents approximately 20 percent of the total Confederation of Oregon School Administrators (COSA) membership of 2,286. Approximately 95 percent of school administrators in Oregon are members of COSA. Data were collected about naturally evolving mentorship relationships from the COSA membership which included superintendents, principals, and central office administrators. The sample corresponded to the different administrative positions and was stratified by gender and district size; women were over-sampled to ensure responses for validity. Of the 237 respondents from the COSA membership to the written questionnaire, 83 (39.2 percent) were women and 129 (60.8 percent) were men.

All subjects were surveyed to collect operational, relational and historical characteristics of mentorships. The questionnaire also contained questions about demographics of the respondents including information about the respondents' career development and association with a mentor or protégé. Pence interviewed three dyads who had maintained informal mentorships between five and ten years. Data collected from the interviews and from the questionnaires were combined to identify what characteristics the respondents perceived made the relationship successful.

Formal Mentorships

In an effort to assist states in formulating pre-service and in service activities to assist school administrators, the U.S. Department of Education in 1986 allocated 7 million dollars. LEAD Centers were formed in many states to bring together practitioners of school administration, colleges and universities, and state education agencies. Grants were awarded to innovative programs for training school administrators. In 1986, the Oregon Mentorship Program was founded when Northwest Women in Education Administration (NWEA) teamed with the Confederation of Oregon School Administrators (COSA), the Department of Education (ODE), and the Northwest Regional Educational Laboratory (NWREL). A small grant provided the seed money for this program. Each year, twenty practicing administrators were "appointed" to act as mentors to the twenty aspiring administrators (protégés). The mentors assisted the aspirants in their exploration of educational administration. This program costs very little to operate since the proteges pay $100 for the dinner meetings.

Pence and Nolf questioned participants in the Oregon Mentorship Program mentorship program. There are two distinctive aspects of this program; first is the attempt to provide opportunities for women and minorities to pursue pre-service administrative experiences through this program. Second, the program designated mentors and protégés from different school districts. A steering committee matched mentors and protégés and developed plans for four statewide dinner presentation meetings. During the school year, mentors and protégés discussed important educational issues and shared their plans with other participants. These four dinner meetings served as the major activity to help mentors and aspirants clarify their work together and learn new ways to work together.

Between fall 1986, and spring 1988, forty aspirants (protégés) and forty mentors had participated in the program. Those forty pairs were the population for the formal mentorships in Pence's study. Data were collected from the dyads through written questionnaires and semi-structured interviews. Of the 48 respondents from the formal mentorship program, 19 (82.6 percent) were women and 4 (17.4 percent) were men. Three dyads from the participants of each the two years of the formal program were interviewed.

The questions for the semi-structured interviews for both the formal and informal pairs were designed to: (1) elicit additional descriptive comments about the individual's mentor or protégé; (2) the mentorship experience; (3) whether the experience was satisfying or rewarding; (4) what the negative aspects of the relationship were; and (5) what effects having an appointed partner had on the relationship. Results of the data from the COSA sample and the Oregon Mentorship Program sample were very similar. Data from the interviews very closely paralleled data from the questionnaires.

Nolf focused on the aspects of the formal program from its inception in the fall of 1986 through the spring of 1990. She stated that university educational administration programs concentrate on theory and provide only limited opportunities for extensive field experiences, internships, or mentorships. Nolf (1991, 5) stated, "Many educational leaders recognize the value of mentorships in furthering the development of future principals' knowledge, positive leadership qualities, communication skills, clarity of vision, problem-solving skills, and sensitive and caring attitudes through collaboration with practicing school administrators." This study described those activities and characteristics of a formal mentorship program that were useful as perceived by the mentors and the protégés. She compared the mentor responses to the protégé responses to see where they agreed and disagreed. The data were presented to provide guidance for individuals responsible for educational administration programs.

Nolf's study provided insights into another view of the Oregon Mentorship Program. The population was comprised of all the available mentors and protégés who had participated in the program from 1986 to 1990. The subject group consisted of 77 mentors and 79 protégés; 2 mentors were deceased before the start of the research. The gender balance of the mentors was almost equal with 39 males and 40 females. Since the mentorship program was designed to assist women and minorities, the gender balance reflected that goal with 21 males and 58 females as protégés.

All subjects in the group were asked to complete a self-administered questionnaire designed to gather descriptive data. The response rate was 71.4 percent (55) of the mentors and 73 percent (57) of the protégés. Three of the mentors had served as mentors in the program twice; they completed a questionnaire for each mentorship experience. The questionnaire dealt with status of the respondent in relationship to the mentorship program; the programmatic structure and support of mentors or protégés; and the professional status profile of the respondents. Practicing administrators who served as mentors to aspiring administrators were one group. Aspirants who were protégés to assigned mentors were the other group. Comparisons within and between groups were made. Analysis or responses within the two groups and response similarities and differences between the two groups were made.

Relationships

Pence and Nolf reported that the relationship aspects of mentors and protégés are most important. Data from both the self-administered questionnaires and the interviews showed the most vital factors to informal and formal mentorships are trust, mutual respect, friendship, commitment, and communication. The level of those factors determines the level of success that members of dyads experience and under gird everything else that occurs in a mentorship.

Trust

Protégés and mentors believed taking time to get to know each other and developing a trust relationship were the first steps in establishing a relationship beneficial to aspirants and protégés. David, who has been a mentor to several protégés, said;

> The most crucial thing in my estimation is you've got to build a trust relationship to the point where you can say something critical to the individual and they don't come unraveled, or if they do, you never leave them. You know it's a little like a marriage. You never leave it there but you put it back together. You eventually get that relationship to the point where you can say something to them that is critical and they say okay how do we work our way through this. And if you never get that openness and that honesty between you, it's really tough to know whether they got the stuff or not to do what they want to do. (p. 94)

Shawn, a protégé, believed "there's a special relationship about trust. And you can bet that word trust and all the elements of trust is [important] and it sure was there with my relationship to Stan." Stan, Shawn's mentor, agreed that their relationship was built on trust in each other. One secondary principal said "being in the 'foxhole' together—coming through for each other" was important. Sharing and discussing experiences in the same school helped mentors and protégés develop a foundation for their trust relationship. The level of trust determined the openness and strength of the mentorship relationship.

Mutual Respect

Mutual respect is another critical aspect of successful mentorship. Eighteen percent of the COSA respondents stated that mutual respect contributed the most to their relationship's success. Trust and mutual respect appear to go hand-in-hand. One respondent shared they had "genuine concern and respect for each other as professionals." One principal commented that their mentorship relationship was successful because they had "mutual respect—[we] made each other look good." Another said, "We like and respect each other" (p. 103).

Linda served as Sally's mentor in the formal program; Linda was a middle school principal and Sally, a teacher, aspired to become a high school principal. Their relationship flourished during that first year and continued to be strong. Linda believed one reason their relationship was successful was that it had mutual respect.

> She, by choosing to be a high school principal, and preparing herself in a kind of nontraditional way, I felt I could help her a lot. As it happened the year that I mentored her, she mentored me. Sally was my outlet. I could tell Sally all the things that were going on. Since she is very bright and she's very trustworthy and she's not in my district, I had someone to talk to. So, you see it was a reciprocal kind of a thing. That's why we became such good friends because I needed her as much as she needed my advice or all of my salty kinds of insights. I think the reason it worked out was because it was a mutual thing, she served a need while I met with her. (p. 104)

Mutual respect resulted in mutual support and mutual benefit. One protege said of her mentor,

> You're going to continue to discuss things that are important to you and lean on each other when you're in need. All women, particularly these women in administration, have lots of need for support. It's lonely. I know it's real important for her because there are very few other women friends. Women on her staff can be friends with her, but she is still their boss. And she can't really share everything and cry and all the things you need to feel really comforted in trying times. (p. 106)

Friendship

Mentors and protégés' definition of a successful relationship varied from pair to pair, but friendship was one of the most frequently mentioned factors in both samples. Over 67 percent of the respondents described their mentor-protégé relationship as a friendship. Even though the duration of their relationship may have been short, they felt they benefited from the relationship. Many respondents said they developed strong friendships with their partner. For some, continued contact was infrequent, but they still considered their partner as a friend and they could "pick up where they left off" very quickly. Betty, who participated in both formal and informal mentorships, described a mentor-protégé relationship in terms of a friendship; "You can have lots of acquaintances and you enjoy good relationships with your acquaintances. But with a real friend you could talk about just anything. I guess that's what the mentorship relationship is for me" (Pence 1989a, 98).

Commitment

Respondents commented that commitment of the mentor to assist the protégé was also a determinant for a successful mentorship relationship. Several mentors said they were committed to help their protégés achieve their professional development goals. David, an informal mentor, believed he had a certain responsibility to teach people how to become good leaders. "Leaders," he said, "aren't just born or magically appear on the scene." He believed good mentors can help people develop into good leaders. He also recognized that a mentor's commitment of time and effort is the key to working with protégés. "Every one of those people that you sponsor and work with takes a piece of your life. And it requires a great deal of time" (Pence 1989a, 100).

The commitment of time and effort was also apparent in formal mentorships. Respondents felt time was a critical factor to the success of the relationship. "Unfortunately, I was matched with someone who had very little time and energy for this program." "It was often hard to synchronize schedules." "Obviously, if one is committed to something, one spends time on it." "Time is imperative" (Nolf 1991, 116).

Availability of time for mentor/protégé contacts was an important attribute. The most essential activities were spending time either through self-scheduled meetings or informal contacts. Establishing goals for the year-long program and receiving support from an employer helped make the mentorships successful. Dyads that achieved a successful mentorship relationship scheduled time for meeting, shadowing, and talking. Two dyads even exercised together so they could meet more frequently. As one mentor commented.

> When you have two children, and a husband, and a house, and a 60 hour a week job and you take on a mentor thing, you kind of have to incorporate it into something else. So, we exercised together because I simply didn't have an hour two or three times a week to sit down and just deal with Sally. The reason it [the mentorship] was successful, was because we both devoted time to it. We met at least twice a week for a full year. (Pence 1989a, 100)

Nolf and Pence reported if either of the pair lacks commitment, the mentorship is weakened or the relationship fails; strong commitment on the part of the mentor or protege resulted in more satisfactory mentorships.

Communication

Participants in more successful mentorship relationship appeared to be more willing and open to share ideas, thoughts, failures and successes with each other. Melody, a mentor, said it well, "I think what you get into with the mentorship program depends on the protégé, and it depends on your willingness to give them your time and effort." One respondent commented, "His willingness to listen. His willingness to share" contributed to the success of their relationship. A superintendent said, "Her willingness to reach out and help me. My willingness to reach out and take the help." "Our willingness on both parts to let it evolve as we saw fit and not model it after someone else's experiences," contributed to another dyad's successful relationship (Pence 1989a, 102).

Matching Mentors and Protégés

There were other factors that affected mentorship relationships. Mentors and protégés reported that educational philosophy, physical proximity, gender matching, and goals could positively or negatively influence the success of the mentorship. Care must be taken in formal mentorship programs to consider the philosophy and interests of the mentor and protégé when developing the match. Mentors and protégés in the informal mentorship relationships generally developed satisfactory relationships. Participants in the formal mentorship relationships were more dependent upon the ability of the individual matching them. Their relationships were more artificial in the beginning, but with commitment and some common beliefs about education their mentorship relationship could be as satisfactory as the informal ones. The shorter length of time that the formal mentorship dyads had worked together affected the relationships. Those who developed strong ties maintained their friendship after they completed their year in the program.

Educational Philosophy

Several mentors Pence interviewed indicated a firm educational philosophy must be the basis for operational decisions. Most mentors felt sharing common beliefs or educational philosophy with the protégés was important. They believed the most essential activity protégés can engage in is developing and articulating their own educational philosophy. Melody, a mentor, stated:

> I think that is one of the most important things because if you have a real firm understanding of what you believe, then all your decisions will radiate from

that central theme. And that you can answer people's questions about why you did that and that and the other thing if you have a real understanding of what you believe. I think it not only bodes you well in the position, but it's what makes you answer questions in interviews, and stand up to parents, and that kind of thing.

David, a mentor, also believed helping proteges determine their values is very important.

When you are faced with tough times, tough decisions, tough things that you have to take action on, what gets you through those is what you believe. You need to know that ahead of time. And then you take those other things like policies and regulations, laws and procedures and all that rote kind of thing—you hook that on to your belief system. But if you don't have anything to hook that to, boy, you're in trouble. Because you'll flounder and you'll look like a fool— you're the person who in the midst of chaos is adding to the chaos [and] is supposed to be leading the troops.

Physical Proximity

Proximity of the mentor and protégé was also an important factor, close proximity enabled them to get together more frequently. One protégé looked forward to the "magic hour" when he and his mentor would sit down and talk about what happened each day. Participants in informal mentorships generally were working in the same school districts and had more frequent opportunities to talk and work together. Participants in the formal mentorship program were in different school districts and became very creative about getting together to discuss leadership and administration. Although protégés tended to visit their mentors more frequently than vice versa, both the mentors and protégé rated site visitations as valuable. Increased opportunities to share experiences strengthens the mentorship. The geographic distance between mentors and protégés was a negative factor for several participants in the formal mentorship program. The distance inhibited frequent contacts and interactions that could strengthen the mentorship. Protégés benefited when mentors could observe them in action. Mentor observations could help improve the protégés' self-esteem.

Gender Issues

Nolf (p. 114) reported that respondents' comments on gender affecting the relationship included: "*Quality* of the candidate, not the gender is the important factor for me." "I do not strongly identify gender issues related to current issues of administrative leaders: I don't think that our professional sharing and trust building was based on gender." Although most respondents felt that having a mentor of the same gender was irrelevant, more women than men felt having a mentor of the same gender was help-ful. There was no indication, however, that the women had a male mentor with whom to compare the relationship. Age of the mentor and protege seemed to make little difference. Respondents in both studies reported that experience of the mentor was more important than similar age.

Formal Program Selection

Nolf reported mentors and protégés perceived the formal program's structure the same and most of the participants were satisfied with the struc-ture. Some mentors and protégés expressed the need for a more formalized and rigorous selection and matching process. Comments such as: "the pair-ing of the mentor and protégé should be the most important element in the project. Without compatibility, the poor protégé is doomed to failure." "It just depends on the match." "Really depends on the person you get. I was very lucky. We hit it off and decided to do our own thing . . . but it was very difficult if you did not have a good match" (p. 115). Some mentorship rela-tionships were successful even though their personalities, ages, and interests were different. For example, Melody and Todd developed a strong friend-ship even though they had very different styles and interests. Todd said, "I guess it doesn't have to be a buddy, buddy—things going great . . . [for] the relationship to work" (Pence 1989a, 99). Most successful formal mentorship relationships, however, are based on some similarity of basic philosophy and interests. The more closely the mentors and protégés agreed on their values and beliefs the stronger the relationships were.

Setting Goals

The formal program was designed to be flexible to allow mentors and protégés to establish their own goals and experiences. A high priority for proteges was setting year-long goals. Some protégés reported not setting a single goal while others did establish goals. One respondent stated "we did talk to each other about what each hoped to achieve as a result of the pro-gram." Many aspirants set a goal of obtaining an administrative position and the mentors wrote letters of recommendation and helped with their job searches. Other aspirants knew exactly what they wanted to learn. Todd, as-piring to be an elementary principal, developed an extensive set of objec-tives when he incorporated his mentorship into his practicum for administrative certification. In those cases where protégés knew what they wanted from their formal experience, mentors followed the lead of the pro-tégés and helped them toward their learning objectives. Bob, a mentor, felt it was important the "we deal with the things that Matt felt were important not things that I necessarily felt were important" (Pence 1989a, 101).

Occasionally mentors were not clear about what protégés expectations were and vice versa. They preferred additional structure with more clearly defined goals for the program. Comments that supported that view were: "Expectations should be clearer." "This was an unusual situation for me, one that was confusing for me and really still is: What was my responsibility, as an individual, a mentor, a professional?" (Nolf 1991, 116).

Conclusions

Both Pence and Nolf found that mentorships can be very valuable to aspiring and neophyte administrators. With the alarming rate of retirees from school administration we need veterans to pass along their craft. One way these administrators can transfer their knowledge is to establish a relationship with a protégé. Informal mentorships among administrators have existed for years; but because they generally were male to male relationships, women received minimal opportunities to interact in these relationships. School organizations can use formal mentorship programs similar to the Oregon Mentorship Program to assist women's entree.

The statistics indicate that numbers of women in administrative positions are still low. Among superintendents there are only 7.5 percent females and among high school principals there are only 7.6 percent females. Having individuals familiar with the complex role of public school administration who are willing to establish mentorships with women, will aid in increasing the numbers of women superintendents, principals, and other administrative positions. There is, however, a danger that veterans pass down "business as usual" rather than encouraging neophytes to lead education in a new way. With a good foundation in theory and practice protégés will have the confidence to take risks and try innovative practices. Satisfactory mentorship relationships are one way to help develop that foundation in educational leadership.

Pence's and Nolf's studies in Oregon can help school districts and professional organizations design formal mentorship programs. Both studies support the following similar key features of mentorships.

Program Features

* *Type of mentorship*. In public schools formal or informal mentoring relationships can increase the number of women and minorities in administration. Since there are more women in tenured teaching positions compared to men, that may reduce gender barriers. Formal mentorships frequently are not as intense a relationship as informal mentorships; however, the length of time spent in the mentorship can positively affect the intensity.

- *Matching mentors and protégés.* Sharing common values, belief and educational philosophy is important for successful mentorships. Sharing similar beliefs and philosophy can offset personality, age, or gender differences between mentors and protégés.
- *Effects of demographics.* Demographic characteristics, age, sex, racial/ethnic, position, and level of position, have the least effect on the mentorships in Pence's and Nolf's studies. The ability, knowledge, and openness of mentors had more effect on whether the relationship was successful.
- *First steps.* Relational characteristics must be established before mentors and protégés can discuss operational activities of school administration. A program must be designed to provide activities that will assist the mentors and protégés in establishing their initial relationship. Traits of trust, mutual respect, commitment, communication and friendship are the most critical relational factors in successful mentorships and are common to informal and formal mentorships. The degree to which those characteristics are present determines what other activities and interactions of mentorships can take place.
- *Professional interaction.* Mentors and protégés focused their relationships on professional aspects rather than social aspects. Some informal mentorship relationships developed deep personal friendships; those mentorships went beyond the professional level to the social level. Formal mentorships primarily operate on the professional level because proximity limits opportunities for those dyads to interact socially.
- *Learning about the job.* Learning from mentors about operational activities and interactions is important for protégés' transition into administrative positions. Exposure to a wide variety of experiences gives protégés a better sense of decision-making processes, what processes work well, and what pitfalls to avoid. Mentorship experiences link theory and practice.
- *School district support.* For mentorships, particularly in formal programs to succeed there needs to be strong support at the state, regional and or district level. Lack of district support was more evident for participants in the formal program. Lack of support for "release time" for protégés to shadow their mentors in another district severely limited the benefits of the experience.

Mentor and Protégé Features

- *Commitment of the relationship.* Successful mentorships required a strong commitment to the relationship from both mentor and protégé. Individuals in successful dyads take their relationship seriously almost like a marriage or family relationship. They make sure they schedule time to discuss philosophical education issues and day-to-day situations.

- *Time factors.* Protégés in the formal program indicated that lack of time coupled with distance from the mentor negatively affected their mentorships. They felt they were infringing upon the schedule of the mentors who were successful, busy people. Busy mentors who were committed to promote the mentorship relationship schedule time in their calendars for their proteges. Mentorships that commit the needed time are rich with experiences and opportunities to share.
- *Building self-confidence.* Protégés believe being at ease with mentors increases their self-confidence. The ability to discuss any issue or concern and ask questions without fear of repercussion strengthens and increases the value of the relationship and helps protégés develop self-confidence. Self-confidence increases when mentors demonstrate trust and confidence in protégés' opinions.
- *Career planning.* Career planning and exposure to other practicing administrators are the major goals of aspirants in both formal and informal mentorships. Neophyte administrators are more concerned with operational activities such as budget, personnel, and student issues. After they become comfortable in their administrative roles, they seek advice on career advancement from their mentors.
- *Encouragement from mentors.* Mentors encourage protégés to accept additional responsibilities in administration and to seek administrative positions. Mentors provide opportunities for protégés to become more visible to other administrators and school board members, thus enhancing the protégé's employability.
- *Physical proximity.* Closer physical proximity of the mentor to protégé cemented the mentorship relationship. Frequent discussions and observations increases the protégé's confidence. Protégés in the formal program believed that lack of proximity reduced the spontaneity of their relationship. Mentors and protégés working in different districts, however, experienced increased confidentiality; protégés and mentors felt freer to share confidential information. Women and minorities received broader contacts when they worked with administrators from different districts.
- *Benefit to mentors.* Mentors as well as protégé benefit in successful relationships. Practicing school administrators frequently feel isolated and seldom have anyone with whom to discuss ideas; protégés can fill that void. Mentors receive satisfaction by sharing their experiences and knowledge with protégés and by helping protégés achieve success.
- *Negative aspects.* Formal and informal mentorship relationships can have negative experiences. Lack of direction, jealousies from other

staff members, different styles, and too many responsibilities are problems for protégés in either mentoring situation.

- *Experienced mentors.* Success promotes success. Mentors and protégés who had a prior successful mentorship will mentor aspirants. They have a clearer idea of what should occur throughout the relationship and know how to help protégés. They also recognize the importance of continuing the mentorship for a longer period of time.

Consideration for Formal Programs

Formal mentorships can operate within a variety of structures; program design can vary depending on the needs of aspiring or practicing administrators. The following are considerations when initiating a formal mentor program:

- *Establish a plan for the program.* Who are the organizations that should be involved? Mentorship programs can be developed at a state level (using universities, colleges, and professional associations) or at a district level. We think there is some benefit to programs at a state or regional basis which involve all or several districts. The following advice, however, is given to help establish plans at a state, regional, or district level. Time spent planning and organizing the formal program before implementing it is important. The purpose of the program should be decided and articulated to participants before the program begins. For the program to be more successful, support from the districts, especially superintendents and school boards is critical. For practicing administrators the mentorship program should be separate from administrative evaluation; proteges should not feel threatened by confiding problems and concerns to their mentors.
- *Develop goals and objectives.* What are the goals of the mentorship program and what are the goals of the individuals? Mentorship programs are more successful if there are some structured guidelines; these may be loosely guided. District officials need to communicate whether the program is for exposing aspirants to administrative positions and responsibilities, for promoting underrepresented employee groups, for orienting newly hired administrators, for providing professional development, or some combination of those goals. To help mentors and protégés plan their time together, include information about the length of commitment and suggested amount and or length of meeting times in the guidelines. Encourage the pairs to continue their relationship for two years if possible. Structure suggested activities

loosely enough to enable mentors and proteges to develop their own set of activities and interactions.

- *Identify mentors and protégés.* How will you select and match protégés and mentors? Who will make the selections? Establish criteria for selecting and matching the mentors and protégés. Voluntary participation is highly recommended to ensure a successful relationship. A program that is coordinated at the state or regional level gives districts the option to use in-district veteran administrators, practicing administrators in neighboring districts, or retired administrators. If formal programs are developed at the local level, two districts could exchange mentors and protégés to provide a richer experience. Provide options to change partners in the even the mentor and protégé finds their match is unsuitable.
- *Conduct an orientation for mentors and protégés.* What do protégés and mentors need to know? An orientation session for both protégés and mentors should be held to review the goals and objectives of the program along with the responsibilities and expectations of the mentors and protégés. When possible negative aspects of the relationship are discussed before the protégé and mentor begin, they will have developed possible solutions to deal with those problems. Cultivating an environment that builds trust will help ensure a more successful relationship.
- *Provide resources for the program.* What are your resources? With limited resources, districts may need to be creative in how, or if, they will compensate participants. Take care to not add to already busy administrators' schedules without some benefit to them. A mentorship is an excellent way to use retired administrators who owe a district some time. Shadowing a veteran administrator gives an aspirant some first-hand knowledge of what school administration is about.
- *Develop a system for monitoring the program.* How will you monitor the program? This is not to be confused with evaluating individuals, but some type of reporting back to the district can assure the mentorships will be successful. Complete a mid-year report or check to make sure the mentor and protégé are meeting, and that their relationship has not encountered major problems. Discuss their successes and concerns to help them move their relationship forward. Establish periodic group meetings to allow participants to share ideas and concerns. This activity often helps other dyads broaden their experience.
- *Develop an evaluation process.* How will you evaluate this program? Determine the outcomes of the mentorships in relation to the goals and objectives of the program and develop criteria to measure those outcomes. Since mentorship relationships are personal and professional,

decide if anecdotal data is adequate to measure the program's success or whether you will need quantitative data. Interviews with mentors and protégés can provide a good view of each mentorship relationship. Other factors to examine could include career development of aspirants, skill level of aspirants, more women and minorities in administrative positions, cross-gender mentorship relationships, and amount of risk-taking by neophytes. This is not an inclusive list, but some ideas to consider.

Recommendations for Further Study

This research raised additional questions that are potential areas for further study. Formal mentorship programs for school administrators are in nascent stages of development and further research needs to be conducted to ensure they are being implemented for the right reasons.

A formative study about the perceptions of dyads participating in formal programs including operational and relationship activities and interactions is one area to consider. Most studies are summative and based on the memory of past events and perceptions of mentors and protégés. An ethnographic study of dyads as they develop their relationship might shed insights into how those relationships are formed and progress through stages. Future research could examine whether females tend to go through the mentoring stages or are mentored differently than males. Are more women and minorities having opportunities to connect with mentors? What affect do those groups have on veteran administrators? Do veterans adopt new leadership techniques as a result the mentorship relationship? What is the level of risk taking by aspirants and neophytes? Do they take more or fewer risks if they have a mentor? How does cross-gender mentoring affect the relationship? Is it easier now for men and women to mentor each other than it was in the 1970s?

Identifying and researching characteristics and outcomes of additional formal mentorship programs, operated by professional organizations and school districts, will shed additional light on how best to design programs to optimally benefit mentors and protégés. Comparative studies of different formal program designs and perceptions of the participants will provide additional information about organizational structure in school settings.

Studying unsuccessful mentorships and comparing that data with research done on successful mentorships might uncover additional characteristics that affect mentorships. Additional studies should be conducted on episodic and multiple mentor relationships to determine if they have similar or different characteristics than single mentor relationships.

Further study needs to be done on whether new instructional leader-ship concepts are transmitted through mentorships, whether mentorships only promote the status quo in administration, or whether protégés sift and choose information. Do mentorships stifle creativity and innovation or do they provide a foundation for creativity to flourish?

Summary

Formal mentorships are important to most participants in learning com-plex educational administrative roles. That type of program is a springboard for and supplemental to other mentor-protégé relationships. Trust, mutual respect, commitment, communication, and friendship are vital relational factors for successful formal and informal mentorships. Similar educational values serve as a basis for determining what operational activities the dyad experience together. Operational activities are important to protégés, but are dependent upon the relational factors. Mentors as well as protégés ben-efit from the relationships. Mentorships can provide a link between theory and practice for aspirants and neophytes. They can also serve as a good or-ganizational pre-socialization for aspirants and socialization for newly hired administrators. Formal mentorships are complementary to other adminis-trative preparation. Incorporating a formal mentorship component into a university preparation program or district induction program can enhance a beginning experience for aspirants and neophytes. Formal programs also provide a framework to actively seek, support, and promote under-represented groups into administration. As with any type of program, there are some inherent negative aspects, but the positive aspects outweigh those negative aspects. Using this research and additional research on mentor-ships for public school administrators will result in developing more effec-tive and successful formal mentorship programs.

Two mentors, David and Linda, talked about how their relationships have changed as their protégés have developed. David said,

> There was a stage of getting her convinced that she can do it. And then there's the always inevitable stage of vice principalship and convincing them they don't know everything and they quit trying to act like they do. Then there's the pe-riod of frustrations—am I ever going to get one of those jobs? And you have to sort of take them through that. And that's a real tough one. You really have to hold some hands during that time because by that time they have got a vision and a dream and it doesn't look like it's going to happen. You have to counsel some patience and wait till the right thing comes along. Don't get too excited about this—your time will come. It will happen to you. So you go through that with them. Then, of course, there's the euphoria of when they get the job. Then

there's the tears, or anger, or scared, actually it's fear after they have gotten it and they are faced with their first two or three big ones. I've really got to make this decision. Is it going to turn out all right? Is everyone going to hate me when I do it? Am I capable of doing a job this difficult? There's lots of stages through the whole thing. (Pence 1989a, 130)

Linda also recognized how her relationship with Sally changed:

I still felt like I can help her. And as a matter of fact, I look at the next step to get her out of . . . and get her into a larger district. I feel like I can help her with the next step. After the next step I feel like we will be totally equal, in terms of, she will have learned everything that I know about getting in places . . . I think in small ways it's beginning to [change]. . . . I find that we are sharing more. (Pence 1989a, 131)

Throughout the different stages a mentor must serve a lot of different roles. They must be sensitive to the needs of the protégé and determine when to step in and when to let go of the reins.

Bibliography

Alleman, E. (1987). Managing mentoring relationships. Mentor, OH: Leadership Development Consultants, Inc. Unpublished manuscript.

Daloz, L. A. (1986). *Effective teaching and mentoring.* San Francisco: Jossey-Bass.

Daresh, J. C. (1987c). Mentoring: A key feature of the Danforth Program for the preparation of principals. Paper presented at the thirtieth anniversary convention of the University Council for Educational Administration, Charlottesville, VA, October.

Daresh, J. and Playko, M. (1992). *The professional development of school administrators.* Boston, MA: Allyn and Bacon.

Klauss, R. (1981). Formalized mentor relationships for management and executive development programs in the federal government. *Public Administration Review,* (19), 489–96.

Kram, K. E. (1980). Mentoring processes at work: Developmental relationships in managerial careers. Ph.D. Dissertation, Yale University. *Dissertation Abstracts International,* 41(5), 1960B.

———. (1985a). Improving the mentoring process. *Training and Development Journal,* 39(4), 40–43.

————. (1985b). *Mentoring at work: Developmental relationship in organizational life.* Glenview, IL: Scott, Foresman and Company.

Kram, K. E. and Isabella, L. A. (1985). Mentoring alternatives: The role of peer relationships in career development. *Academy of Management Journal,* 28(1), 110–32.

Levinson, D. J. (1978). Seasons 1: As they developed in the life of James Tracy, executive. *Across the Board,* November, 1978, 52–60.

————. (1978). Seasons 2: The life of James Tracy. *Across the Board,* December 1978, 72–78.

Levinson, D. J., Darrow, C. N., Klein, E. B., Levinson, M. H., and McKee, B. (1978). *The season's of a man's life.* New York: Knopf.

Missirian, A. K. (1980). The process of mentoring in the career development of female managers. Ph.D. dissertation, University of Massachusetts. *Dissertation Abstracts International,* 41(8), 3654A.

Nolf, G. L. (1991). A descriptive study of the Oregon mentorship program. Ph.D. dissertation, Portland State University, Portland, Oregon.

Pence, L. J. (1989a). Formal and informal mentorships for aspiring and practicing administrators. Ph.D. dissertation, University of Oregon, Eugene, Oregon.

————. (1989b). Mentorship programs for aspiring and new school administrators. Oregon School Study Council, University of Oregon. *OSSC Bulletin,* 32(7).

Price, M. (1981). Corporate godfathers: By appointment only. *Industry Week,* 29 June, 71–74.

Schmuck, P. (1986). Networking: A new word, a different game. *Educational Leadership,* 43(5), 60–61.

Vertz, L. L. (1985). Women, occupational advancement, and mentoring: An analysis of one public organization. *Public Management Forum,* 45(3), 415–23.

Webster's new universal unabridged dictionary, deluxe 2nd ed. (1983). New York: New World Dictionaries/Simon & Schuster.

Women finally get mentors of their own. (1978). *Business Week,* October 23, 74–80.

EIGHT

The Mom and Pop Model of School Administration: A Case Study

Michelle Collay and Helen LaMar

> At the end of the year, people are seeing the value of the grant support. This is what we hoped. Get involved and come down and see what's going on!
>
> —Lorna Krohn, elementary principal

In urban settings, schools are often viewed as tax-supported bureaucracies where other people's children are housed. In small, rural communities, however, school staff and the families they serve are members of the community. In this chapter, two rural school administrators offer their perceptions of the roles of men and women as teachers and as administrators. We draw parallels between societal expectations of women and men and the ensuing gender-related behaviors and issues of leadership evident in the administration of rural schools. The different roles men and women played in those schools recalled images of "mom and pop shops," or the corner groceries of yesteryear. Male superintendents and high school principals served as patriarchs responsible for site management and organizational matters, where female principals and lead teachers served as advocates for teachers' professional needs. The participants of our study have provided insightful lessons about leadership in all schools.

We believe our collaborative research is useful in two ways: first, studying teachers and administrators in rural schools provides a bare bones context in which societal expectations are unfettered and openly expressed.

145

The parallels between societal expectations about gender and administrative practice are illustrated in this case study. Second, historical assumptions about the need to control or diminish "feminine" characteristics of school leadership in favor of "masculine" ways are faulty. We believe "traditional" feminine values, especially those of respect for the social context of the family, can contribute directly to the quality of schooling.

We examine living dynamics of school administration through the actual family metaphors which emerged in this case study. First, we provide the context of our involvement with rural schools; second, we introduce the story of two key leaders in one school which illuminates parallels between gender roles in society, and therefore in schools; and third, we review social and historical precedents which have characterized those gender roles. We close with a discussion of how a deeper understanding of social interactions between men and women leaders might change our thinking about schooling. In our quest for "gender equity," we must continue to acknowledge and value the "feminine" perspective in leadership. Let us not equate "leadership" only with contemporary masculine forms of behavior. Multiple perspectives emanating from both the masculine and the feminine sides of life are necessary in the restructuring of schools.

Background

The Bush Foundation of St. Paul, Minnesota granted funds to address the high rate of attrition of first-year teachers in eight rural prairie schools. A pilot study pinpointed several organizational factors which were associated with new teacher turnover, among them: size of school (9–16 teachers), a teaching principal, lack of staff development opportunities, and the teacher being new to the community (Harris 1988). In addition to these findings, the facilitators were themselves rural educators. The team of eight were four education faculty and four graduate students. Almost all had taught in rural schools and were currently supervising student teachers and presenting workshops in the same settings. Many years of experience as teachers and supervisors in rural schools of several states led our team of eight university-based facilitators to observe that rural school administration is often conducted family-style. Each facilitator worked with the superintendent at each site to plan and implement the two-year project. Within several weeks, however, a lead teacher or teaching principal emerged as the key project player at each site. In six of the eight project schools, the person working "behind the scenes" to implement teacher professional development was a woman. The quality and depth of our interviews at Ruckhert School led us to use it as a case study on the metaphors of family present in all eight schools. The two administrators Helen interviewed were the superintendent and secondary principal of the school, Greg Tunn, and the elementary principal, Lorna Krohn. The two authors are the grant director (Michelle) and a local university-based facilitator (Helen). Pseudonyms are used to protect the anonymity of the school-based participants.

The charge to the facilitators was as follows: as an outsider, introduce discussion, opportunities, and possibilities to a school staff. Use outsider status to disrupt return to the status quo. The grant called for an advisory council or faculty development committees to create or further develop a stronger professional culture at the school site, thus improving retention of the new teacher. Facilitators participated in organizational development training and collectively developed a plan for intervention at each site. Facilitators worked with full staffs to support teachers and administrators in the development of individual professional goals. As a committee, they developed schoolwide curriculum goals based on individual and collective needs. Facilitators then encouraged teachers to identify what skills each might bring to their newest member and therefore, to the full staff. The new teacher was the catalyst which attracted grant support, but university-based facilitators focused on professional growth opportunities for the entire school staff, thus addressing the research which demonstrates the powerful influence of colleagues on new teachers (Harris and Collay 1990). The following case study represents common patterns observed by all facilitators.

Ruckhert School is a long, narrow cinderblock building typical of the early 1960s: no-frills and efficient construction. As we drove toward the school which sits perpendicular to the end of a Main Street wide enough to turn around a four-horse team, we passed the post office, corner bar, church, small grocery store, and a few houses. Ruckhert felt at once welcoming and isolated, a few buildings surrounded by open prairie. The school playground has one set of swings in the middle of a part gravel, part grass yard. The wind blew leaves easily across this openness, bumping swing against swing.

At our first meeting, Greg Tunn described his position as, "Superintendent, business education, also principal, direct plays and speech!" Lorna, the elementary school principal with whom Michelle had arranged the meeting, was nowhere in sight. Greg figured she'd be along soon and we began. Lorna was engaged down the hall with teachers and children and joined us later. She said little during this initial meeting, and we took an opportunity on the way to lunch to introduce ourselves. Over the course of this first meeting and several, subsequent phone conversations, Greg, the superintendent and high school principal, made it clear that administering a grant for teacher staff development would tax his time and resources. Greg had expressed concern to Michelle that, given all the hats he was already wearing, he would like monetary compensation for his efforts. He told us the community would not support the idea of teacher release time, citing an example of board members critical of teachers taking "time off." He recounted some examples of board members "finding fault with the school"; that concern was present throughout our conversations. We explained that the grant would pay for teacher release time and cost the district nothing. While the grant money would be a welcome boost for staff development activities, Greg harbored additional frustration with the whole notion of a grant to support new teacher professional development: like many rural schools, Ruckhert had become a training ground for new teachers who subsequently leave for better paying jobs. He has been left therefore with the task of restaffing each year.

Meanwhile, a subplot was unfolding. Helen, as the local university-based facilitator, had been spending time with Lorna at the school. Michelle joined them one afternoon early in the school year, and the three sat on tiny chairs in her first-grade classroom to review Lorna's efforts to bring the project into her school and Greg's concerns about its administration. Lorna reassured us that the elementary teachers were interested in participating, but wasn't convinced that she could persuade the high school teachers to join the project. Just one, the English teacher, the only woman on the secondary staff, had indicated interest in our project. We agreed to begin with the elementary teachers and one secondary teacher, perhaps engaging the others later. During that visit, Lorna also described a more immediate concern for her and other rural educators: the depopulation of the prairie. As we sat in her classroom, Lorna informed us that, across the hall in the superintendent's office, Greg was negotiating with board members for tax money to pay the next month's salaries. Amid pressure to consolidate, the very survival of the school was at stake. We planned with Lorna about the role the project might play in getting the teachers ready for possible reassignment the next year.

Life in Schools

Different societal expectations of men and women and their parallels in administrative practice were a powerful theme in these interviews. Gender differentiation in the workplace has been studied by sociologists and their language of role differentiation, segregation, and stratification is useful in understanding gendered roles in schools (Blackmore and Kenway 1993; Morgan 1988; Parsons and Bales 1955; Stockard 1980). Currently, two-thirds of all teachers are women, yet leadership positions are male-dominated. Nationally, over 95 percent of superintendents of K–12 districts are men (Bell and Chase 1990). In particular, gender stratification in rural schools is extreme. In the state of North Dakota, for instance, 98 percent of K–12 superintendencies were filled by men. Sixty percent of the schools had a male secondary principal and a male elementary principal, 32 percent had a male secondary principal and a female elementary principal. In the eight schools of this project, all the superintendents were male. In three of the eight schools, female elementary principals played the key role, however, in implementing the project; in three others, female teachers did so. In the final two, a male elementary teaching principal and a male superintendent were the primary project leaders.

Teaching

The first theme of gender differentiation for teachers is evident in the assignment of teachers. Primary teachers were almost all women and secondary teachers were almost all men. Gender differentiation is presented first in the participants' description of social activities and responsibilities. In the following quotation, Greg's description of the different responsibilities of elementary and secondary teachers provided a backdrop for understanding the place of gender in rural schools. Recalling a recent social gathering, he said, "That's a typical elementary approach, they're more sympathetic and they have more time." During an interview with Greg, Helen asked him about this historic segregation of elementary and secondary teachers in his school:

> I think we no longer have that stigma that the high school faculty think they're better than the elementary teachers. That's long gone here. Because we bring secondary people down into the elementary for the musics, for the phy eds, art, library, there are four or five teachers involved coming down to the elementary. They know what those elementary teachers really go through and all they have to do, so they respect the work they put into the school. Under their breath they say, "Those gals are doing a wonderful job down there and we didn't really appreciate it before."

Greg was clear that male secondary faculty and female elementary teachers had very different professional responsibilities.

> I've really been struck since I've been here, I let the high school teachers know that the elementary jobs are probably tougher, a lot more difficult than the high school positions. They have to cover so many positions, they have to do so much more paperwork. And I also let them know that they should go down and see what those gals are really doing.

149

The segregated women and men of Ruckhert School indeed had very different teaching days. The three women elementary teachers and Lorna were responsible for six grades of school and the support programs. Lorna said of her job description, "I have Chapter One, third and fourth grade math, and elementary principal. That's about all for this year!" All four women were mothers, were employed full-time, and except for Lorna, commuted from other communities. Their contact with children included parenting (like all primary teachers), watching them before and after school, and sitting with the children in the lunch room. With the exception of the social studies teacher, the men were part-time secondary teachers. They had specific disciplines to teach, were only at school for those few classes, and were not around for as much "noninstructional" time. The pay scale was such that one young man was supporting a wife and two children on full-time wages of $14,000 after several years teaching. The others farmed or had part-time businesses.

Our efforts to engage the men in professional staff development in the project were stymied by their lack of time and commitment. The male high school teachers were employed elsewhere or were coaching after school. Greg was very aware of this difference and remarked, "I treat them equally because I think they both have a profession. They both need to deal with their situations, and they need to respect each other for what they're doing." The differences in teachers' status seemed linked to whether teaching was their sole profession, or part-time; to the age of the children they taught; and to the ways women and men perceived their roles as caretakers or instructors. In this community, teaching was not considered a profession in the way farming was. Those beliefs were evident in Greg's concerns about community opinion of teachers "taking time off" for staff development.

Leadership

School leadership is another context where gender differentiation is associated with gender segregation and stratification. After male rural teachers become superintendents or secondary principals, they merely add new duties while retaining the teaching responsibilities spelled out above. Administrators are first socialized as teachers, an experience which powerfully shapes beliefs about what men and women do in schools. At another project school, the male high school principal was also the shop teacher. His assumptions about the gendered nature of teacher roles changed little with the addition of greater responsibility, and he in fact reified the cycle by maintaining traditional hiring patterns in his school. Even after Lorna became a principal, her reference group remained the other elementary teachers and the one female high school teacher with whom she had been peer. Greg's responsibilities as high school principal, on the other hand, kept him in closer contact with the men at the secondary level. Different styles of leadership between men and women were evident in every project school.

The differences in role responsibilities of male and female administrators were made explicit when Helen asked Greg about improving interactions between the elementary and secondary teachers. "In order to keep that mix between secondary and elementary happening, you have a joint faculty meeting. Do you have other kinds of things?"

> Socially we don't. We do have a get-together in the fall for in-service, a little dinner. It seems when someone has a birthday here, we do have a couple of gals who bring cakes, and everybody shares in it. If somebody has a baby, we have our showers and the men and the women all turn out. In the Spring we have a get-together, we invite the school board for that. And I have to credit Lorna, a lot of times, she's the one that organizes, if someone has a death in the family, everyone's involved. . . . That's a typical elementary approach, they're more sympathetic and have more time. They take the time to do something like that. That little something special for someone. It might not be a big thing, but it means a lot to that person.

Greg initially downplayed the presence of social activities in his school. But as he elaborated on the school's social routines, it became evident that in fact, frequent social obligations were dealt with in his school, but not by him. The elementary principal, Lorna, was primarily responsible for addressing social-emotional needs in the community of the school, including the social integration as well as professional induction of new teachers. Helen asked Greg about the induction of new teachers, which was the primary focus of project activity. "What sort of things does the school do to try to induct new teachers into both the more formal parts of the school, but also so they feel more comfortable and can ask questions?"

> In the fall, we have that get-together and board members are invited. Teachers usually have been told about things at interviews. Here the board members are involved with the new teacher and know the new teacher. Because we're a rural community, we try and find local people. Because of the economics of the state, because of the farming, we try to pick up these people who have raised a family, are ready to come back to work.

Greg's primary concern about new teachers was finding them and keeping them. He was well aware that farmers' wives made the best long-term teachers. They provided a second income, worked hard, and were unlikely to depart for higher salaries because of their marriage to a farmer. Ironically, the purpose of our project was to help retain new teachers in rural schools, so

151

his frustration was losing teachers to larger districts might have been addressed by support from the grant. From the perspective of an administrator, the retention of new teachers was critical to the smooth running of a school. Retaining them with meager salaries and convincing the school board to raise salaries was a major stumbling block for him and other superintendents in the same situation.

Greg was proud of what the school was able to accomplish even with its small size. Small school administrators, like Greg, value the direct involvement of students in activities, often citing it as a reason to keep their schools open. Greg's words also reflected the attitude of a caring parent, committed to providing the best possible education for local children. His own children as well as the children of the other teachers attended Ruckhert School or a small school in neighboring towns, so their beliefs about schools were from both parent and educator perspectives.

> A larger school may have twenty-one students in a play, but they're talking 300 students. Twenty-one students in a play here out of thirty-three students. They're poised on stage, and we're proud of them. We're proud of what every kid does here. Totally proud, even if they participate in sports in the neighboring town, we're happy about it. They're our kids.

Although he valued the benefits of small schools, Greg also expressed his frustration with changing economic times and the challenges of maintaining the status quo of sports teams and elective courses. As "head of household," he had his work cut out for him. "We can't afford teacher release time." The task of defending decisions fall above the "fault line" described by Helen Regan (1990). The leader or headmaster is operating in a competitive public sphere. There is a right and wrong answer. The administrator with the greatest public visibility will receive the greatest criticism for inappropriate spending or poor fiscal management. Teacher staff development is low on the list of priorities in any tight fiscal situation, and Ruckhert School was no exception. A superintendent struggling to keep the school doors open has little energy or incentive for teacher professional development, which is invisible and not easily defended at a local school board meeting. As in many of our other schools, the administration of grant funds was assigned to the teaching principal, Lorna. Assigning this fiscal authority to someone accustomed to working collaboratively behind the scenes caused confusion in the mind of the superintendent. Regan (1990, 568) describes that stratification of tasks with these words: "Above the fault is the world that operates competitively in an either/or mode . . . below the fault line lies organization which is horizontal and collaborative . . . this is where caring and nurturing, relationship and community building happen. It is a both/and world." While neither administrator had much extra time, Lorna had made the initial contact about the grant, she felt the board would support her, and she was primarily responsible for the two new elementary teachers who were the most immediate recipients of grant support. Greg continued to present concerns about board member objections, time involved in project administration, and questioned whether the benefits of the project would contribute to the long term survival of the school. Lorna's attempts to bring secondary teachers into the project remained futile.

Authority

Assumptions about authority for specific leadership duties related to the project were tested and roles redefined throughout the school year. Conflict between teaching and leadership roles arose in winter, however, when Greg was invited to a regional project meeting and Lorna was invited to a national conference of educators to present her experiences in the project. Greg saw a discrepancy in the status of the conferences and expressed this concern: he felt he was not representing his school directly, and as superintendent, felt responsible to make fiscal decisions about disbursal of the grant the community's perceptions of "unnecessary travel." The public authority which rested on his shoulders was as much determined by societal expectations of men as it was by the superintendency. Clark describes the "separation of male/female and economic/domestic spheres" (1990, 81) of men and women in rural schools. This separation of spheres and related issues were present throughout these interviews as differences in societal roles of men and women. We believe the conflicts which continued to emerge were directly related to unspoken assumptions about public authority. How would it look if a woman held the purse strings? Would Greg still have the respect of the board? Would Lorna still be considered a teacher colleague?

We knew that taking the lead in implementing the project would present a political challenge for Lorna. As the elementary principal, a woman, and practically a full-time teacher, she seemed more comfortable being viewed as a colleague of the other teachers. Her own story indicated the long road traveled in becoming visible as a leader in her school. Lorna's interview began much the way Greg's did, with a description of her many duties. Helen asked Lorna specifically about staff development activities for new teachers:

> For me, being the principal, I like to have a really good meeting in the fall. I relied on the one teacher who came back this year for suggestions. Anything that I might have forgotten, she would add. I thought it was a really complete list. I

wanted to make sure if they had a question, before they charged on, to ask. It's important to leave the lines of communication open. I hope they feel they can come and ask.

Helen had heard evidence of that reassurance in her conversations with the teachers and responded: "The new teachers felt they could go and ask anybody anything on the elementary staff." Lorna described her role as one of nurturing and supporting new teachers.

One of them had gotten behind on the reading assignments and I guess I did do some follow-up. And I know this teacher was real upset thinking, oh dear, she had done something wrong . . . after I sat down with her and helped her plan, she felt a lot better. And that's the type of thing I guess I like to have open, so we can work through it and just keep going.

Lorna's idea about the purpose of staff meetings followed the same logic. She intended to provide a place for problem solving, not just to dispense information. "We're a lot more consistent in the elementary about having weekly meetings and more information type things. Not just where administration is going or doing, but input on how to work out things."

Lorna experienced frustration in her attempts to bring the secondary staff into the project. The history of detachment from staff development because of external obligations of secondary teachers and the gender split presented her with a challenge. Still, she was optimistic. "And that's something that we have really overcome in the last years, because in most schools, it's high school, elementary. I think we've really tried to work with that. I think we're really more together." Responding to another question about shared socials, she remarked, "We do have our Christmas party together." She noted, though, "Other than that, we don't have social activities." Lorna's comfort level with the community and her belief that it would support the project was based on her close ties with school families. She was quite visible in the community and had adopted a "management by chats in the yard" style which she described in the following passage:

I guess I've made it a point of interest for myself to try and visit with people in the community and go out more than some of the other teachers have. I can go around town and almost name everybody who lives there, where the other staff couldn't do that. I think you have a better rapport with the people. And through the years, that's something that's been lacking.

Helen asked Lorna to reflect further on why the rapport that Lorna mentioned had been absent, and Lorna said:

> I think some of it has to do with the type of community—that the teacher is there to work, and they're the ones getting the big salary in the community (remember a recent starting salary was less than $14,000!) The farm economy is really poor, then they look at you like you're taking their money. I come to basketball games, and we have some teachers who don't. I usually try to make myself visible. And in a small town, I think you have to do that. In a larger system, people don't look at it the same way.

Lorna's attitude toward her role is evident. She referred to herself as a teacher, and describes a commitment to improving public relations. Yet her sense of the larger economic picture is an attribute most often associated with men in the public sphere of administration. While Lorna's style of leadership could hardly be called authoritarian, she did hold legitimate power, and thus "authority" in her credibility with the community. Was it her status as teacher and woman that allowed her access to people in a culture where teachers are often held in tighter status because of their greater level of schooling? As she recalled another superintendent for whom she had worked, Lorna demonstrated that she still saw herself as a teacher who valued direction from leadership. This man had insisted teachers attend workshops and left materials for reading in their boxes. "Some of the teachers didn't care for him, but I did. He made you feel more like a professional."

We were continually impressed with Lorna's ability to negotiate the dual role of principal and teacher. Helen asked her to reflect on the inherent conflict of the role of teaching principal with this statement: "You teach and you're the principal. You must find yourself at times between the teachers and the superintendent."

> Especially at evaluation time. When it comes time to evaluate some of the teachers. I feel maybe there could be more as far as creativity, learning centers, fun things for the kids to do in their spare time, and they just really don't take the suggestions. Yet it's hard to be stern because maybe I'm not doing anything spectacular sometimes either, so then it's kind of hard that way. And when I sit at the school board meetings, I sit there as an administrator. Yet when it comes to the teachers, especially negotiating salaries, they wanted me to negotiate for the teachers. I just refused. I've sat at every board meeting as the elementary principal, and to sit on the other side of the table with teachers would have left bad relationships between the board and me.

Helen recalled other stories Lorna had shared. After being appointed elementary principal, she had come to a board meeting and not been immediately welcomed up front. She recounted: "I just pulled my chair up to the table!" Helen asked: "Can you talk about how you've seen your role evolve as the principal, both with the board and here at the school?"

> Well, I think it was something that just came gradually. Once they knew that I had something to add or to keep them better informed about what's happening in elementary, they were more receptive of my opinion. Or even now, the last major issue was kindergarten, whether it was going to be here or a nearby town. And they asked me what I felt, even after talking to Mr. Tunn and hearing the others, what I thought. And I felt that was a step up, rather than not asking my opinion at all, I mean I really don't have any right to give my opinion, but they asked it. But that's through seven years of sitting there, too.

Lorna's lengthy teaching experience before becoming a principal was not unusual. It mirrors national statistics on the experience and preparation of female school administrators. (Bell and Chase 1990, Ortiz 1982; Schmuck 1982) Schuster and Foote report the differences between men and women in teaching experience previous to the superintendency: "More than three-fourths of the women superintendents, compared to nearly two-thirds of the male superintendents, had more than five years of teaching experience" (1990, 18). As a principal and a teacher, Lorna was sometimes expected to behave like a teacher, yet she would also be asked for expert advise as a principal when it was needed. Helen related her own observations about Lorna's evolving role as the teaching principal: "It's been interesting for me to watch you over the year in relation to this project. You talked with people and you had responsibility for getting things together. Has it been hard working with the project business, in relation to you and the rest of the staff?"

> I feel that it's such a good thing and provides so many opportunities, yet people aren't taking advantage of it. At the end here, people are seeing benefits. And this is what we tried to tell them all the time. Get involved and come down and see what's going on! At the last meeting with the ones that usually come, they had a better feeling. They're finding out that it isn't a lot of extra work on their part, but more for their benefit. And even when I had first started, I was scared to sign up, thinking it's going to be loads and loads of forms to fill out. And that always turns the teachers off, because they have enough to do without that.

Lorna's last remark highlights again her sensitivity to the daily grind of her teachers. As an administrator, she was dedicated to providing opportunities for her teachers to grow professionally, yet she remained protective about their use of time and energy. She had described earlier the conflicts created by her mentorship in both teaching and administrative roles, but this example demonstrates the value of her leadership having emerged from the ranks. Helen asked Lorna about her hopes for the future. Lorna responded:

Can I say what I'd like to see? I would like to see the two administrators in a school say, "This is the plan, this is what we're going to work toward." They can work together toward that end, getting everybody together, to see what is the best plan, what's good for the school. We do it in the elementary, but I think in the high school, that's really something they're missing. What is the plan of attack, what should we be doing? So that all teachers are doing it, not just some. And that's the way we felt about the grant. Why should it just be elementary, why are we doing it? Now all of a sudden then, everybody is bringing their ideas and requests.

Lorna's persistence in the project created opportunities for elementary teachers that they fully appreciated. Stories about their adventures in staff development got back to the hold-outs, those who had no time for such participation. By the end of the year, some of the secondary teachers expressed interest in the project, and joined in the discussion of ideas for the next year. The success the elementary teachers expressed even won over the superintendent, as he admitted at the end of the year:

I guess first of all I thought it would be kind of a hassle with time, because in a small school you wear many hats and you have to cover many areas. Teachers have felt that they have benefited more than been hassled. Finding subs and so on, even if you have to go someplace, we are reimbursed, so it hasn't really affected the budget. The kids, the basic fact is that it's helping, indirectly, those kids' needs. Those teachers are willing to take that time to go off to a workshop, go into another class, improve themselves. The time is coming when schools are going to be restructured. For those teachers who are willing to take advantage, they may be willing to retrain in some areas and be fit for another school system so they don't have to leave the state.

Interpretation

The Expression of Gender in Schools

This pattern of gender differentiation in teacher staff development was evident in all eight of our project schools. In the role of teacher, women and men had different teaching responsibilities and social tasks. The female teaching principal or lead teacher frequently had the greatest personal stake in improving professional development opportunities for teachers, while the male superintendent continued to represent outside interests, suffer under community pressure, and talk about budget concerns. The responsibilities of male superintendents have been reviewed by Schmuck and Schmuck (1992, 18) in the small schools study:

We saw superintendents not only developing budgets, hiring and firing personnel, working on curriculum, conferring with attorneys, meeting with the

157

board, and attending Rotary, but also driving a bus, attending out of town sports events, and directing traffic.

Men's roles appear to be quite public, proactive and everpresent in the formal decision-making. This particular sex-stratification of roles is described by Zelditch (1955, 317) as the male being "instrumental" and the female "expressive."

> [The instrumental role has] the authority required to make binding managerial decisions, and associated with this managerial complex the primary responsibility for discipline and training of children. . . . [The "expressive" role has] responsibility for maintenance, of solidarity and management of tensions, for the skills prerequisite to this role, primarily the responsibility for care and emotional support of children.

The societally dictated roles of women, all of whom were teachers, made them responsible for maintaining the social-emotional aspects of the community. The metaphors of family interactions became evident as women in lead teacher roles became the advocates for supporting teachers' growth and development. We observed that Greg spoke frequently about the students and their welfare, taking pride in his roles as provider. Lorna's remarks were more about providing opportunities for teachers.

In many of the preceding passages, however, both superintendent and teaching principal express similar concerns. They described the personal and professional needs of teachers, the school's relationship to the community, and their hopes and concerns for students. The difference in their attitudes toward the task, however, seems to have been affected by social constructs of gender. What is appropriate behavior for a man and a woman in our society? How would the teaching staff regard a male superintendent who taught first-grade children and planned baby showers? The polarity evident in Greg's and Lorna's practice of administration strongly reflects cultural norms expressed in the metaphors of family. The powerful influence of community traditions on contemporary roles educators play cannot be underestimated. Such norms and traditions create and perhaps dictate masculine and feminine ways of leadership, as exemplified in these two remarks. Greg recalled: "The teachers have usually been told about things at interviews." As superintendent, Greg was responsible for protocol and dispensing information. Lorna's approach was more nurturing: "I wanted to make sure if they had a question . . . they would ask." These two concepts of leadership must be examined in the context of the community's expectations of men and women.

Some insight into the parallels between administrative practice and traditional family roles may be gained by reviewing the organizational evolution of schools. An historical perspective on the evolution of women's and men's roles in rural schools is presented by Strober and Tyack (1980, 498):

> Typically, women teachers found their way into rural classrooms during the summer session, when the younger children attended and males were needed on the farm. For the winter term, trustees often preferred men as instructors, since they were presumed to be more capable of disciplining the older children who attended then. Teachers were young men and women who regarded schoolkeeping not as a full-time job, but as a temporary way to make money when they were not attending college or working on the farm or helping out with housekeeping.

Teaching still provides "off season" work for men and women alike. Many teachers who live in rural communities work on farms, in the trades, or in retail. Clark (1990, 81) provided further interpretation of how roles of men and women evolved in rural schools:

> The young female schoolteacher was often identified with the sentimental heroine who appears in so many romances—the female figure who maintains the virtues of a lost preindustrial order, a pastoral time when (as it seems in the creations of nostalgia) women stood for warmth and human caring while men sternly governed a family-style organization.

The teachers at Ruckhert school were behaving in concert with the community's expectations. Lorna's idea about new teacher induction and school administration was based primarily on accepted roles for women in her community. She knew her neighbors in the community, created a safe place for teachers to solve problems and improve their practice, and contributed to the family atmosphere of the school by planning social activities for the staff. She brought teachers into decision-making and attempted to engage those teachers whose other responsibilities removed them from frequent collegial interaction. In the changing context of school consolidation, Lorna focused on empowering her teachers to move more easily to a different school or position. Her style could be described as characteristic of "facilitative leadership," as defined by Dunlap and Goldman (1991, 13): "Facilitative power reflects a process that, by creating or sustaining favorable conditions, allows subordinates to enhance their individual and collective performance." Her values could also have grown out of community expectations that rural women must be flexible and marketable in a single region. Regan (1990) discussed her study of feminist administration and relates it to teaching. She wrote:

> [Feminist administration] is symbolized by the double helix with its intertwining strands and connecting bridges, is an inclusive mode of leadership in

schools practiced by people who understand the necessity of the both/and as well as the either/or ways of being in their work. It requires that both teachers and administrators participate in the decision making in schools, and thus it conceptually overlaps with several thrusts of the current reform movement: teacher empowerment, shared decision making, school restructuring. (p. 576)

Greg, on the other hand, was also working within the norms of the rural community. As superintendent, citizens expected him to behave as "head of the household," making sure the bills were paid, convincing the board to keep the school open, trying to retain staff and keep his own head above water. In a study of teachers' perspectives of school principals, Blase (1990, 735) described how "protective tactics were perceived to be used primly to reduce the vulnerability of principals to various forms of pressure (e.g., criticism, demands) from others, especially administrative superiors, community members, parents, and to a lesser extent, influential teachers." In rural schools, constituents' pressure is directed primarily toward the superintendent. His role as a "in loco parentis" father figure was demonstrated by his pride in the students, "We're proud of what every kid does here."

There is strong historical precedent for the importance of both paternal and maternal roles in running the school. Strober and Lanford (1986) described the creation of graded schools and the role of women and men within them. "Proponents of these schools argued that women were not only cheaper than men, but also better teachers of young children. Moreover, they noted, any disciplinary problems that women teachers might have could be solved easily: the teachers would simply send difficult children to resident male principals" (p. 218). Strober and Lanford's historical description reminds us that both men and women have been assigned and enacted gender-based tasks by the community since the beginning of the frontier school.

Bureaucratic Organization of Gender

In addition to the historical roots of "gender-appropriate" behaviors in teaching, the nature of the teaching principalship adds another dimension to our understanding of school leadership. From an organizational perspective, K–12 school districts in North Dakota are required to have a superintendent, a secondary principal, and an elementary principal. Elementary teachers are most often women, so conferring the title of "principal" on one of them (to meet state requirements) changes little in how that person interacts with female colleagues. The state bureaucracy requires that an elementary principal be named, but in practice, most teaching principals continue to affiliate with other teachers. An example of the lack of socialization into an authority role is described by Lee (1987) in her study of elementary teaching principals. One fourth of her subjects were not provided with an office, a secretary, a telephone, or an aide. They were still primarily head teachers only with added administrative responsibilities. The lack of a shift in hierarchical status, upon taking the principalship, may have contributed to the inner conflict expressed by Lorna, as she recalled, "It's hard to be stern because maybe I'm not doing anything spectacular sometimes, either."

Studies of the full-time teaching principal (Chance and Lingren 1989; Lee 1987) also have concurred that teaching principals, even when they value instructional leadership, find little time to step out of their collegial role. Another role attributed to the teaching principal by Lee is the "go-between." In her words, "They see themselves as facilitating communication between the superintendent and the faculty. Working very closely with the superintendent, they are required to keep the faculty informed; make announcements, and prepare noon duty schedules" (p. 3). Lorna's discussion of her ambivalent interactions with the school board illustrated the dilemmas she faced in being both a female colleague and an administrator.

Conclusions

In this case study of Ruckhert school, we have described two competent and caring administrators who are carrying out socially-constructed gender-appropriate roles and argue that both have been culturally socialized to take them. The superintendent acts as paternal head of household and the teaching principal played a more nurturing and maternal support role. Whether viewed through an historical, philosophical, or organizational lens, the norms of behavior seem closely related to the community's gender expectations. What's appropriate for women versus men to do in teaching and administering is quite different one from the other in the eyes of the Ruckhert community. Indeed, how school leadership is executed at Ruckhert exposes the inadequacy of explaining it with a simple, hierarchical leadership model. Our analysis is that non-hierarchical teaching and shared leadership are realities at Ruckhert because the female principal has retained her affiliation with female teachers. The faculty activities of collegial support and collaborative decision-making are today often labeled as "feminist," and although such democratic practices may not be viewed as "strong leadership" by more traditional bureaucratic and hierarchical criteria, they are heralded activities in contemporary discussions of school reform. The advantage of this perspective from an organizational standpoint is that it focuses our attention on the human condition of the school. The "collaborative leader" facilitates the growth of others, while ignoring the trappings of authority.

Regarding the role of teacher as nurturer of children rather than teacher as certified professional gives rise to another interpretation of the power of women as teachers. Laird (1988) wrote about teaching school in a critique of the patriarchal assumptions in national school reform reports. "The implication is clear in both these reports that 'professional' values traditionally defined by men rather than so-called 'feminine' values associated with childrearing must become sovereign in schoolteaching." She admonishes creators of reform policy to acknowledge that "schoolteaching is a form of childrearing" (p. 459). To acknowledge that traditional "feminine" characteristics are good for schools may cause some men to feel defensive about their taking initiative to reform our schools. Traditionally feminine roles are not in and of themselves and only avenue for childrearing; men and women can learn to work cooperatively for school improvement.

In our eight schools, the teaching principal or lead teacher emerged as a key player in efforts to establish a professional climate for teachers. In the pilot study which led to project funds being granted, schools too small for formal leadership and funds for staff development were most vulnerable to new teacher attrition. This parallel points to the need to redefine "leadership" in rural schools. There is a need for a public head to educate community members and school boards. There is also a need for nurturance in the private sphere. Both roles are required for success in school reform. By equalizing the masculine and feminine roles in both authority and social regard, without substantially altering their content, these roles may become separated from the social restrictions of their gender origins, and become instead, integral administrative roles for the school itself.

The actual change agents in this project were most often those with little status as leaders—the female teaching principals in the elementary schools. Because they institutionalized the feminine leadership qualities of cooperation and encouragement, they influenced not only the children they taught, but parents, community members, and other teachers. They seemed more effective that did the male superintendents who held community-recognized, top-down authority. Also, the female teaching principles proved themselves more flexible and adaptable to new structures and processes for their staff. These have become critical traits for leadership as school reform grows more complex.

Lessons from rural schools might then inform all schooling. We must reexamine our efforts to reject gender-based behaviors as women move into the ranks of male administration, and not lose sight of a more "feminine" style of facilitating change. Bell (1990) indicated that while two-thirds of all teachers are women, formal educational leadership continues to be dominated by men. The person with the greatest potential to influence restructuring, therefore, may be the last person invited to the table. The irony of this dilemma is that true authority may lie within this "invisible" role. Authors in this book question the assumption that real power necessarily lies in the formal leadership of a school. The small, rural "mom and pop shops" of the Great Plains may be the last holdout of resistance to what Bell and Chase (1990, 27) described as "the norms and language of educational administration [which] work against nonhierarchical, nonbureaucratic leadership."

Rural women teachers have restructured schools in their own way—in these more intimate settings where feminine roles and feminist beliefs can be negotiated, expressed and valued. Rural schools may be "undemocratic," but they are places where women in traditional feminine roles are providing leadership in schools. In their positions as teachers, mothers, and farm wives, their power lies in supporting new possibilities for others. In their hands, shared leadership has taken form. From small patches of fertile ground in rural communities, a model of leadership has emerged which is both historic and instructive. We encourage women entering formal roles of leadership to remember the one-room school teachers who preceded them as they seek equity with men.

Bibliography

Bell, C. and Chase, S. (1990). Women as educational leaders: Resistance and conformity. Paper presented at the annual meetings of the American Educational Research Association, Boston, April.

Blackmore, J., and Kenway, J. (1993). *Gender matters in educational administration*. London: Falmer.

Blase, J. (1990). Some negative effects of principals' control-oriented and protective behavior. *American Educational Research Journal*, 27(4), 727–53.

Chance, E. and Lingren, C. (1989). The great plains rural secondary principal: Aspirations and reality. *Research in Rural Education*, 6(1), 7–11.

Clark, S. (1990). A woman's place in the rural school in the United States. *Genders*, 8 (Summer 1990), 78–90.

Dunlap, D. M. and Goldman, P. (1991). Rethinking power in schools. *Education Administration Quarterly*, 27(8), 5–29.

Harris, M. (1988). New teachers in North Dakota. Paper presented at the National Rural Education Association, Bismarck, ND.

Harris, M. and Collay, M. (1990). Teacher induction in rural schools. *Journal of Staff Development*, 11(4), 44–48.

Laird, S. (1988). Reforming "women's true profession": A case for "feminist pedagogy" in teacher education? *Harvard Educational Review*, 58(4), 449–63.

Lee, G. and Lemon, D. (1987). Administrative proficiencies and the full-time teaching principal. *North Dakota Elementary Principal*, 32(4), 7–9.

Morgan, G. (1986). *Images of organization*. Beverly Hills: Sage.

Ortiz, F. (1982). *Career patterns in educational administration: Women, men and minorities in educational administration*. New York: Praeger.

Parsons, T. and Bales, R. (1955). *Family, socialization and interaction process*. New York: The Free Press.

Regan, H. (1990). Not for women only: School administration as a feminist activity. *Teachers College Record*, 91(4), 565–77.

Schmuck, P. (1982). *Sex equity in educational leadership: The Oregon story*, Newton, MA: Educational Development Corporation.

Schmuck, P. and Schmuck, R. (1990). Democratic participation in small-town schools. *Educational Researcher*, 19(8), 14–20.

Schuster, D. and Foote, T. (1990). Differences abound between male and female superintendents. *The School Administrator*, 47(2), 14–16, 18–19.

Stockard, J. (1980). Why sex inequities exist in the profession of education. In J. Stockard et al. (eds.), *Sex equity in education*. New York: Academic Press.

Strober, M. and Lanford, A. (1986). The feminization of public school teaching: Cross-sectional analysis, 1850–1880. *Signs: Journal of Women in Culture and Society*, 11(21), 212–35.

Strober, M. and Tyack, D. (1980). Why do women teach and men manage? A report on research on schools. *Signs: Journal of Women in Culture and Society*, 5(3), 494–503.

Zelditch, M. (1955). Role differentiation in the nuclear family: A comparative study. In T. Parsons and R. Bales (eds.), *Family, socialization and interaction process*. New York: The Free Press

NINE

Suit-able for Promotion: A Game of Educational Snakes and Ladders

Alyson M. Worrall

Before I applied for a vice-principalship, a female superintendent[1] suggested I start dressing as though I wanted the job. Although I was always neatly dressed, she pointed out that my couture was too casual for a potential VP. She stressed the importance of image. Although I found it hard to believe that my image would play such an important role, I went out and bought a new wardrobe.

In this chapter I examine my board's selection procedure for vice-principals. As a woman who has just been subjected to it and who is currently awaiting placement as a vice-principal in a secondary school, I feel my experience with the process is different from that of my male counterparts. Only by participating in the selection procedure have I become aware that the process is geared towards men; it is solidly based on male principles of competition and career advancement, despite the board's insistence to the contrary. Using my own experience as a guide, I will comment on what I perceive to be its effect on women.

My examination is not motivated by failure, for, to all outward appearances, I am successful. I am eligible for what is considered a promotion. This eligibility, however, immediately calls into question the definition of success. To call my potential move into administration a success and a promotion means accepting the classroom teacher as the least important member of the educational community. It also means accepting a hierarchical organizational structure as being equally applicable to the lives of both women and men.

By creating a text for research (Aitken and Mildon 1991) based on my experiences and then analyzing it for themes, I hope to discover what effects the process has had on me and what my future options are. I have divided the text into sections which correspond to the stages in the procedure, beginning with a background of my working career prior to my decision to apply for a vice-principalship.

Upward Mobility without Really Trying

My working life has been a series of steps, each one leading to a more responsible position. At sixteen, I started my first summer job as a lifeguard. Two summers later, I was managing the pool and its staff of seven. I never saw the fierce competition for those few management positions. I knew just when I turned eighteen one of them would be mine. It was. According to the aquatics director, my leadership qualities were obvious. From these first experiences in the working world, I assumed that talent and ability would be the only criteria necessary for advancement.

When I applied for my first position as a mathematics teacher I was the tenth person to be interviewed out of ten applicants. Yet, when I left the interview, I was sure the job was mine because I had never failed to be hired before. Why should it be any different this time? Although I had been promised quick notification of a decision, it was two days before I received the call offering me the job. During that time, I alternated between disbelief that I may have failed to get the job and anger at the thought that a man may have been hired by the all-male interview panel. Once appointed, however, I forgot my anger and doubts.

Eight years later, a vice-principal, who believed in my potential for leadership, advised me to "advance" my career by applying for a Position of Added Responsibility (PAR)[2]. Until then, I never saw myself as anything but a classroom teacher. Like many women, a career plan was not something I had developed (Grant 1989). When asked at my first PAR interview where I envisioned my career five years hence, I made something up.

Once again, I got the job. I attributed my immediate success partly to the fact that I never applied for a job I would feel uncomfortable accepting. I was very selective which echoes the experiences of other women in teaching (Grant 1989). Thus, the level of confidence I brought to the few interviews I attended conveyed an image of strength and sureness in my abilities that was not unlike some of the males with whom I was in direct competition. This persona made it easier for interviewers who needed to show some progress in advancing women in male-dominated mathematics departments. If they could give a PAR to a female and not upset the department's ethos, so much the better.

After one year as an assistant department head I returned to the school where I began my career. The head of mathematics and I got along well, and I enjoyed my position as his assistant head. Although a number of headships in mathematics were available and my vice-principal encouraged me to apply, I was not interested because I still had no career plan and was quite happy in my job. However, I did have the vague idea that it was good to keep my options open. So, despite my misgivings, I interviewed for department headships at four different schools. My ambivalence about advancement must have been obvious to the interviewers because I was unsuccessful in every case. I experienced anxiety at the prospect of having to accept a job I did not really want and I assumed saying no would be prejudicial to future chances of promotion.

During the next year my department head began to complain that I had changed and was becoming difficult to work with. I examined my behaviours and found that I had changed. As I tried to introduce minor modifications in department policies, I was offering my own ideas rather than accepting his unquestioningly. I needed power. He saw this and was unwilling to hand over any of his. In his view, I had become different and difficult.

I was uncomfortable with the notion of being seen as "power hungry," for I did not see myself in those terms. I now realize, however, that it depends which definition of power one uses. The definition which I find most acceptable is "Power . . . is the capacity to have an impact on one's environment, to be able to make a difference through one's actions" (Lips 1987, 403). As long as I worked for someone who could ignore my ideas and veto anything I put in place, I would always lack power. I wanted to be able to influence my environment, and the only way to do so was to apply for a department headship. When my department head showed me such a posting and suggested I apply for it, I did not feel he was doing so for the good of my career. We both recognized a way out of our predicament.

The previous year I was unsuccessful in my bid for this particular position. It went to another woman who was now a vice-principal. This time I was hired. Part of my success was the result of applying for a position I really wanted. I was not motivated by the politics of being seen to be actively working on a career but by the sincere desire for power. I was now a department head only three years after making my first application for a PAR. The journey to this position seemed natural, and I still believed that talent and ability were all that I needed. It took the application procedure for vice-principal to convince me otherwise.

The Paper Chase

During my first year as an assistant head I began taking education courses to satisfy prerequisites for certification in school administration.[3] Although I was not planning to become a vice-principal, I thought I would complete the certification process in the event I changed my mind. By having qualifications to teach any grade from kindergarten to high school graduation and with ten years teaching experience, one could start studying for the administration papers. I had the teaching experience and was qualified to teach both junior and senior high school, but I had to return to school part-time for two courses to become accredited to teach kindergarten to grade six. The courses turned out to be far more interesting than I could ever have hoped, but after completing them I had no desire to continue into the principal's course. With no career plan, certification as principal could wait. I now had the prerequisites for admission, and there was no need to rush into anything further.

It was almost six years before I applied for the principal's course. My own principal urged me to get my qualifications because he felt my strengths could be well used in school administration. I resisted until I came to the conclusion that if the paperwork were out of the way I could apply for a vice-principalship when I really felt ready. Consequently, I applied for admission, was accepted, and began two academic years of driving to a nearby university campus one evening a week. The class enrollment was nearly four hundred at this campus alone. There were other off-campus settings with similar numbers. Most of those taking the course were women. Most of those teaching the course were men.

I spent much of my time in these two courses wondering about the basic qualifications of my instructors. One had to be either a principal or supervisory officer, but, other than that, there did not seem to be any reason why some had been chosen to prepare the next wave of school administrators. The class was organized into manageable groups of twelve to fourteen candidates, each assigned to a single instructor. We were told the quality of the course depended on the candidate: we would get out of it what we put in. There was no mention of the quality of the instruction. Depending on the group leader, one could find oneself doing an inordinate amount of work or none at all. One could receive excellent, practical advice while learning the theory and regulations, or one could be the recipient of inept instruction disguised as collegiality. I got the former for the first course and the latter for the second.

I found it interesting that many of the men expected an immediate appointment to vice-principal after completing the courses quickly followed by principalship. They also foresaw promotion to superintendent after acquiring qualifications. No man I met in the course intended to be a vice-principal very long. Moreover, not one man lacked a career plan. Many of my classmates were amazed that I was taking the course when I had no immediate desire to enter administration. In answer to the question of why was I bothering, I could only reply that it did not hurt to have the qualifications in case I changed my mind. Unlike the men, and some of the women in the course, I was much like the women studied by Rosemary Grant (1989): promotion for its own sake was not at the top of my career agenda. In fact, my career moves were, like theirs in part, motivated by lack of job satisfaction. When the job I was doing no longer fulfilled my need for power, I would look around for something which would allow me to control my own life and destiny.

Once I had the appropriate qualifications I continued to ignore my principal's encouragement to apply for a vice-principalship. He found my reticence difficult to understand and interpreted it as a lack of self-confidence. What he could not comprehend, and what I was unable to communicate to him, were the differences between my male counterparts and me. I questioned the status quo because I saw the typical promotion track mirroring a male journey. Also, I did not see myself as being able to adopt the same attitude as other vice-principals with whom I worked who had conformed to the system's expectations to achieve their promotion. Lips (1987) noted this is not an atypical response for successful business women who commented that in order to achieve success they felt they had to give up their social life, hobbies, and recreation, and found relationships with friends and family difficult to maintain.

Because I sought promotion for my own needs rather than for its own sake, I had not served on committees I had no enthusiasm for, had not feigned interest in issues that bored me, or taken on extra responsibility so my résumé would contain a list of accomplishments. I was not willing to devote my time and energy at the expense of my friends and my own psyche in order to participate in that game. I did my job well and my extra-professional activities were those which provided me with personal satisfaction. I pointed out to my principal that I lacked a highly visible profile with the board which would make the selection team unlikely to take my application seriously. He countered that such profiles were not necessary and, if gained at the expense of doing a good job in the current position, were of little value. I continued to doubt his advice.

It took a combination of many factors to change my mind. Before I would apply for a vice-principalship, I had to believe that I had the capacity to withstand the stresses of working as a school administrator. I looked into myself and found that I possessed an inner strength that had been absent earlier in my career. I looked into my future and could not imagine myself in the position of department head for the next nineteen years. Finally, my major supporter, my principal, was due to retire at the end of the next academic year. I needed to apply immediately if I wished to take advantage of the esteem in which he was held by senior board officials. I felt as ready as I would ever be, so I applied.

The Paper Cut

After submitting a formal letter of application in May, I was asked to supply the interview panel with my curriculum vitae, a list of my leadership responsibilities beyond my position as department head, and the text of a speech written from the perspective of a vice-principal who has been invited by the school's parents' group to address the issue of evaluation standards and the erosion of "the basics" in education. I worked feverishly on the speech, for I understood that my continuation in the process depended as much on my ability to write a politically correct text as it did on my professional accomplishments. While I constructed this bit of fiction, I monitored it for evidence that I was being untrue to my personal beliefs. I was determined not to play games that meant compromising my own values. When I finished, I was pleased with the result. It would be September before I would find out if the superintendents were impressed with my application. Meanwhile I continued to do my job, but I found that the application process caused my attention to be diverted, and focussing on my immediate obligations became difficult.

A Casual Affair

In the confusion of the first day of school, I received a telephone call from a board official congratulating me on my success in round one and inviting me to an informal interview the following Saturday. As part of the interview, all candidates would be given thirty minutes to write a response to another scenario. Dress, I was told, was casual. I knew I was ready for the interview and I groaned at the thought of another scenario to solve, but what did casual dress mean, especially when I had already been told that I dressed too casually for work? Easy enough for a man, I thought. Just take off the tie, forget the jacket, and wear a pullover.

I spent most of the week trying to answer the question of dress. It seemed ridiculous to me, and to anyone else I chose to consult, that it could be so important. If I got it wrong would there be no formal interview? When I arrived at the board offices on the Saturday morning, I noted I had been right about the male "slacks and pullover" solution to the problem. Although my usual notion of casual dress does not include a denim skirt, cotton pullover, and pumps, my attire seemed to be in line with the tone of the assembly. Being able to determine what casual dress meant was another exercise in problem solving.

The interview was anything but informal. The atmosphere of the timed scenario was one of a formal examination. All sixteen candidates were gathered into one room, given the day's agenda, and then told to sit in every second seat around the large, conference table while the scenario was handed out. At the superintendent's command, we began writing. I felt the exercise was really intended to gauge my reaction under pressure. This hidden agenda was only the first in a series of occurrences which made me question the process.

After completing the written component, there was a one-on-one interview with a selection committee member. While this was supposed to be an informal discussion about my résumé, I was asked a series of questions about why I wanted to become a VP, what I thought the job entailed, why I thought I should be selected over the candidate in the next room, and how I managed to do my current job while my mind was engaged on being promoted. My résumé never came up. Perhaps the "informal interview" was to determine my mental agility given that I expected a different format.

Home Game

At the end of September I was informed of my success in stage two and told I would be interviewed in my school by one of the selection committee who would give me thirty minutes to describe three leadership initiatives I was responsible for within the school, the board, or beyond. My interviewer was a high school principal who had previously interviewed me in an unsuccessful bid for a PAR at her school. She had a reputation for being "one of the boys," a woman who enjoyed people's perception of her as being as hard-nosed as any of the men in her position.

The interview began with her explanation of how I would be timed, how notes would be kept, and how she would verify the information I provided with my principal. She then bent her head to her notebook and indicated I should begin. The only time she spoke was to ask me to pause while she turned the page of her book. She wrote, and I spoke to the top of her head for the entire time. At the end of thirty minutes, she called time, closed her book, wished me farewell, and left for my principal's office. I had no indication of how well or how poorly I had done. The whole experience left me exhausted, angry, and depressed. I waited anxiously for her to leave so I could consult with my principal who said they talked about me briefly then spent time comparing notes on school opening in September. After a three-week wait, I was relieved when I received an invitation to a final interview.

Trick or Treat

On 31 October, six months after my initial application, I presented myself at the board offices for the "formal" interview. Originally there were sixteen applicants employed by the board and forty-seven employed in other jurisdictions. Now there were a dozen of us.

Once again I spent time carefully selecting clothes for the interview. The advice given me about dressing as a VP was still ringing in my ears. Again, the men had an easy decision. Just put the jacket and tie back on. When I arrived at work most of the staff was dressed for Hallowe'en. Someone asked what I was dressed as. "A VP," I replied as I left the staff room.

The interview room was set up with the candidate facing the four-person selection team. For my interview, the female principal took notes leaving me free to concentrate on the three superintendents. The chairwoman explained that all candidates would be asked the same questions in the same order. At the completion of the formal questions there would be a round of "Trivial Pursuit." I would have ten seconds or less to respond to a two- or three-word phrase with everything I knew about that topic.

I prepared for the interview by meeting with a female candidate whom I had known for years. A few days before the interview, we gathered all the material we thought relevant and spent an evening exchanging information and quizzing each other on important points. Since May, we had remained in close contact and tried to keep each other's spirits up when news seemed slow in coming.

The interview itself was less imposing than I expected. My initial nervousness dissipated, and I felt I answered the questions appropriately. The chairwoman said notification of success or failure would be by letter, and the interview ended. I returned to my school to wait. A few weeks later, I was at home ill when my principal telephoned to congratulate me on my success. I was almost too sick and too tired to care. I thanked him for telephoning and went back to bed.

Hard Times at Bleak House

I have been eligible for promotion for almost a year now. Originally, there were eight on the list; four females and four males. There were four appointments and now the four females remain. I was asked by a superintendent whether I was disappointed at being passed over. His question came when I was yet again in charge of the school in the absence of my principal and vice-principal. He heard a description not of my disappointment but of my anger. I was angry because I was passed over even though I frequently acted as a VP without title and authority, and because all the appointments went to males. As he justified the latter to me and I nodded my understanding, I became angrier with myself. I was in a position I swore I would never occupy. I felt I could not speak freely for fear of not being promoted. If I am not appointed to a vice-principalship by the end of my second year on the list, I will have to reapply. I am considering not doing so.

Meanwhile, I wait, do my job, and try to maintain visibility with the superintendents who have the authority to appoint me. Many of my colleagues have drawn away from me because they expect I will leave and because they see me more as an administrator than as a teacher. Although they have not quite stopped talking when I enter a room, I no longer feel one with them. Neither do I feel one with the administration. I am still a member of the teaching staff and a teachers' federation member bound by professional ethics. I cannot be included in all administrative discussions and often must leave the room to maintain the integrity of my position. I am truly in limbo.

Analysis

All Dressed Up and Nowhere to Go

Dress is a major theme within my text. My public self was challenged by the female superintendent who advised me to change my appearance. I did so but after a few days of the "new me," during which I fended off comments, disguised as humour, from my colleagues, a department head bluntly asked me about my sudden transformation. I explained my attire was the visible result of being told the female equivalent of the advice to men seeking promotion to "wear a tie." As time passed, the joking stopped, and the image was accepted.

Creating a new image of myself is consistent with messages directed at women through the media. We are told the way we look is an underlying cause of our mistreatment, as in the case of the rape victim who dresses "too provocatively," or a reason why we can lose our jobs, as in the case of Christine Craft whose age was cited as contributing to her "unsuitable" television image (Faludi 1991). When I applied for a vice-principalship, I promised myself I would not compromise my principles in order to get the position. I tried to become what the board wanted by changing how I dressed for work. It was, I rationalized, a trivial issue that did not count as a compromise. Now I realize that I have not been as true to my promise as I have led myself to believe. If clothes are an expression of the inner person, then who have I become?

The Sound of Silence

It is evident in my text that, as I moved from one phase of the process to the next, I was silenced. When I am asked by the superintendent whether I am upset at not being appointed he is allowed a glimpse of my true feelings before I murmur agreement with the decision to appoint all the males. While I nodded my understanding, I worried that I spoke too freely. I recognized my outburst as a political act which could provoke a negative response from those who decreed my silence (Lewis and Simon 1991). In addition, I became cautious with my colleagues, weighing my words against the negative impact they might have on my chances of promotion. I felt unable to speak my mind lest I be seen as uncooperative and unwilling to uphold the board's priorities and mission statement. I have tried to believe that this situation is only temporary and that once I have the job in hand I will be able to speak again. If, however, this is true then who am I in the interim? If, on the other hand, it is false, will I ever regain my voice?

Following The Leader

As a result of my experience, I am convinced the board is not interested in challenges to the masculine establishment. Elisabeth Al-Khalifa (1989) points out that much of the new emphasis on management in schools results from the influence of business and its impact on effective schools research. Although she describes the trend in general management literature toward a more collaborative organizational culture, she writes "little of this has been translated into practical action and the possible contribution of women in building this new culture is ignored" (p. 93). J. Rothschild notes "women's socialization prepares them better to develop and lead such [collaborative] organizations."(see Fullan and Hargreaves 1991, 61) However, Fullan and Hargreaves add:

As more women move into senior positions, our models and understanding of effective leadership may undergo significant transformations. It will be important to seek, appreciate and foster new forms of collaboration. We must also learn from and integrate more stereotypically masculine qualities of task orientation and analysis if we are to move collaborative work into the domain of rigorous inquiry and improvement. (p. 61)

While they acknowledge the role of the feminine in management and point to a need for change, they believe collaborative, feminine practices will only be valid once they are overlaid with masculine "virtues." This was evident in the selection procedure where the emphasis was on competition and making it through to the next round. The co-operative approach that another female candidate and I used in preparing for the interview was not the norm. The expectation that candidates would not share information concerning the final interview served to reinforce the win/lose approach to selection. After all, as a superintendent pointed out, it would only be to my disadvantage if another candidate were better prepared because I talked about my experience.

Part of the reason for the intense competition for appointment to administration is the scarcity of positions. In a system which employs nearly 1,500 teachers at the secondary school level, there are only twenty-one principalships and approximately thirty-five vice-principalships. Openings are created only when an incumbent retires or is promoted to the next level in the hierarchy. Until this pattern is broken, I can see no future change in the way in which selection is carried out. One suggestion for change comes from Gaskell, Mclaren, and Novogrodsky (1989), who write:

the hierarchical structure of teaching, and the procedures that assign more value to positions of management than to teaching must be examined and questioned. Teachers need to ask why teaching is not as well remunerated and respected as administrative work, and decide whether the arguments for that difference make sense. . . . The ways that administrative work is organized must also be held up to scrutiny. Administrative posts might be made temporary ones, so that many teachers had an opportunity to be administrators. (p. 77)

Before this can happen, however, the current education system will have to be reorganized. I doubt that the attendant loss of male power will be seen as acceptable to those who have the most to lose.

Power Play

My text is a chronology of a loss of power as I have defined it previously in this chapter. By the end of the selection process I am powerless.

Throughout the experience I was unable to direct what happened to me. I could only wait patiently while others decided my fate. Withdrawal was the only choice I was free to make. If my goal was to influence my environment then I have not achieved it for my career is in the hands of the board. If I am appointed I will have little to say about my placement. Although I have been told that I may refuse a posting without prejudice, it is likely professional suicide to do so. If I am unwilling, I know the board will find someone who is willing. I have never had so little control over my career as I do now. It is analogous to joining the army and pledging to serve the state loyally wherever it sends me.

A War of Words

Although it is not immediately apparent in my narrative, language is also a strong theme. Much of the language associated with the training and selection of VP's within our board is very militaristic. I am now enrolled in a series of induction workshops designed to prepare the shortlisted candidates for their roles as school leaders. Monographs we have been encouraged to read include Fullan's *What's Worth Fighting for in the Principalship*. I did not realize that school administration was a battle zone.

Language has become more for me than trying to convince my principal I am not a guy and have never been one. In writing this chapter, I worked to match my words with my beliefs. During my quest for a vice-principalship, I was frequently reminded by feminist friends that moving into administration was not better than classroom teaching and those who did not choose this path were just as worthy. After expressing shock that they thought I believed such things, I realized I was unaware that the language I was using was indicative of such attitudes. Like the men, I saw myself as on the way up, rather than just out of the classroom.

Conclusions

In the beginning of this chapter I noted that I believed the process to be solidly based on male principles of competition and career advancement. How else can one describe a regimen that is designed to foster an atmosphere of winners and losers? Making it through to shortlisting makes one a winner. Anything less makes on a loser. I was congratulated, through gritted teeth, by a male peer who made it to the final interview but was not selected even though he expected to be one of those chosen. He felt like a loser. I did not feel like a winner. I have already decided not to reapply if I am not appointed before my "enlistment" runs out. If I am not good enough now, then I have no desire to work at making myself more acceptable in the future. In a way I am already less acceptable to the board because I am unwilling to advance without question.

Initially I felt elation at being chosen, but the glow has faded as I tally the personal cost during the last year. In addition to my own classroom teaching and supervising the members of my department, I was involved in administrative duties which far exceeded my timetable allotment, and in extra-professional activities I felt would enhance my chances for promotion. I spent much of my time worrying about what I needed to do to be seen as a good VP candidate. All the while I believed I was taking care of myself and my relationships by saying "no" often enough. Although a career plan was, and is still not, evident, my principal stated that if I were serious about becoming a VP I had better be sure I was over whatever self-doubts had plagued me in the past. I replied that once I made up my mind to do something I became totally committed to it with no doubts or ambivalence. What a truly male attitude! The selection process honed it to a fine point.

It came as a shock to realize I had become everything I said I would not. I had changed my appearance, monitored my thoughts so they remained politically in tune with my board's stated objectives, and become capable of convincing myself I had done none of this. From the board's point of view, I had become a promotable female—one who could be appointed at some future date to help satisfy the Ontario government directive of fifty per cent representation by females in administration by the year 2000 while at the same time not causing any loss of male power.

What finally awoke me to an understanding of what I had become in the process of being shortlisted was the heart attack and subsequent hospitalization of a principal in the system. When I learned what had happened, my first reaction was one of sympathy that recent events in her professional life had led to this. The second was to speculate whether this would create an opening in the principals' ranks which would have a domino effect among the vice-principals. The third, and most horrifying, reaction was to wonder what sort of monster I had become that I could view the severe illness and possible death of another as an opportunity for myself. Since then, she has recovered and will take up her duties in a new school.

As a new school year approaches, I will continue as a department head and classroom teacher. I have administrative responsibilities built into my timetable once again. What the process has taught me about myself has been quite sobering. All the men who were shortlisted with me are now vice-principals. I doubt any have stopped to think what the cost has been. Perhaps this is the major effect of the process on me. As people are added to the shortlist in November, the competition and jealous eyeing of one another will begin anew. By then, I may already have been appointed or perhaps not. Either way, I do not think I will ever be the same again.

Epilogue

After completing this chapter, I returned to work and found that I was unable to ignore the effects of the selection process on me. It became increasingly difficult to censor myself and remain silenced. At one of the induction workshops I told a superintendent one of the scenarios we were asked to work on was sexist and needed to be rewritten. He did not appreciate my suggestion. I grew tired of alternating between hope and despair as rumours of possible positions waxed and waned. The sense of powerlessness became unbearable. I exercised my only option. With one year of eligibility remaining, I asked the board to remove my name from the shortlist.

My decision brought no response from the board initially. However, it has had a major effect on me. For the first time in two years I feel free to speak my mind, dress as I please, and refuse responsibility which exceeds my job. In addition, colleagues have noticed that I have regained my sense of humour. I smile more now. I has been a relief to take back control of my destiny.

This chapter began with a female superintendent's advice. It has now come full circle. I have received a letter from this same superintendent to inform me that the board has accepted my decision at this time. It would appear that I have not committed professional suicide for the letter contains encouragement for the future. I do not know what I will do with the next nineteen years of my career but I know what I will not be doing. I will not be sacrificing my beliefs and freedom for a position which no longer is "suitable" for me.

Notes

1. In Ontario, a superintendent is not the chief executive officer of a board of education but rather a member of the board's administration. Some superintendents are in charge of families of schools within the board's jurisdiction while others have responsibility for running divisions at the central offices.

2. A Position of Added Responsibility (PAR) is the term given to any job for which a teacher receives additional salary for additional duties. At the secondary school level, these positions are typically department headships and assistant headships. Such teachers, however, are not considered to be administrators and are still full-time classroom teachers. Depending on the collective agreement with the board, the teaching load for a department head may be lessened to allow time to carry out the additional duties.

3. Those wishing to become a vice-principal or principal in Ontario must complete a two-part course which is offered by faculties of education on

behalf of the Ministry of Education. The first half of the course covers program and implementation of curriculum while the second looks at supervision and assessment of teachers.

Bibliography

Aitken, J.L. and Mildon, D. (1991). The dynamics of personal knowledge and teacher education. *Curriculum Inquiry*, 21(2), 141–62.

Al-Khalifa, E. (1989). Management by halves: Women teachers and school management. In H. de Lyon and F.W. Migniuolo (eds.), *Women teachers: Issues and experiences*. Milton Keynes: Open University Press.

Faludi, S. (1991). *Backlash: The undeclared war against American women*. New York: Doubleday.

Fullan, M.G. (1988). *What's worth fighting for in the principalship? Strategies for taking charge in the elementary school principalship*. Toronto: OPSTF.

Fullan, M.G. and Hargreaves, A. (1991). *What's worth fighting for? Working together for your school*. Toronto: OPSTF.

Gaskell, J., McLaren, A. and Novogrodsky, M. (1989). *Claiming an education: Feminism and Canadian schools*. Toronto: Our Schools/Our Selves Education Foundation.

Grant, R. (1989). Heading for the top—the career experiences of a group of women deputies in one LEA. *Gender and Education*, 1(2), 113–25.

Lewis, M. and Simon, R. (1991). A discourse not intended for her: Learning and teaching within patriarchy. In J. Gaskell and A. McLaren (eds.), *Women and education*. Calgary: Detselig Enterprises.

Lips, H.M. (1987). Women and power in the workplace. In G.H. Nemiroff (ed)., *Women and men: Interdisciplinary readings on gender*. Fitzhenry and Whiteside.

TEN

The Bureaucratic Restraints to Caring in Schools

Ava L. McCall

My cooperating teacher, another first-grade teacher, and I took Mike and Billy [two first-grade students] out for pizza last week because they sold the most seeds in the seed-selling contest the school had. It was a lot of fun because I got to know Mike a lot better as a little kid instead of always trying to get him to learn something. It seems like I'm always pushing him since he's kind of "low." So I had a lot of fun with him. I like to show them [her students] that I care and not just in saying "Good work" on papers and stuff. I think they need it, especially in first grade. They need to know their teachers are caring and they're not just there for work, work, work.

—Linda, a student teacher

I really care. I see children as people with valuable thoughts and young minds that really want to learn. They need guidance, but don't need to be pushed one way or another. They just need to be nourished.

—Nancy, a student teacher

For Nancy and Linda, two women who participated in my study of caring in student teaching, developing caring relationships with students was an important aspect of learning to teach, especially when students seemed to have limited experiences with giving and receiving care. Their efforts to care for their students illustrate what Nel Noddings (1984) calls the ethic of care. Noddings has encouraged teachers to receive, "feel with," and hold dialogue with students in order to develop deeper relationships with them. Through these deeper relationships, teachers can more effectively and sensitively guide students as they learn academic content and skills. As students receive care from their teachers, they also learn to care about themselves. As they learn to care for themselves, they learn to care for others, even those who are different from themselves.

Many children enter schools today without knowing how to care for themselves or others and fail to recognize their connection to the community in which they live. Often the family does not teach children, like Mike described above, about their importance and worth, nor does the family model care and concern for others. If children do not learn this within the family, schools must deal with the emotional and social needs of each child in order to foster intellectual and academic development. How are teachers able to show caring for students in their teaching? What factors encourage caring and what discourages it? Through studying the student teaching experiences of seven women, I document how caring for children occurs, and what factors discourage caring behaviors. The purpose of my study is to (1) show examples of the ethic of care as demonstrated by student teachers in their classrooms, (2) argue that care is gender based, and (3) to illustrate how administration and bureaucratic obstacles restrain student teachers' efforts to make their classrooms more caring places.

Methodology

In conducting the study, a variety of data gathering methods were used to provide an intimate view of the teaching experiences of preservice teachers (Bogdan and Biklen 1982; Dobbert 1982; Emerson 1983; Lincoln and Guba 1985; Spradley 1979). The seven women student teachers of this study taught me about themselves as I endeavored to understand their actions and thoughts.

Sample Selection

Seven female elementary education majors were selected to serve the semester prior to their student teaching as informants through "purposeful sampling" to learn about select cases without needing to generalize to all cases (Patton 1980). I chose the pre-service teachers based on attitudes encouraging students to influence what occurs in classrooms, a desire to engage students actively in learning, and an ability to develop curriculum based on the teacher's and students' backgrounds and interests. I interviewed nineteen potential informants, received ratings from the professor of the curriculum development/methods course in which all were enrolled, and held interviews with the field experience supervisors who observed the preservice teachers teach. From this field of potential informants, I chose six in addition to Nancy (all proper names are pseudonyms) who served as the key informant for my pilot study.

All informants were white women, of lower-class and middle-class midwestern backgrounds, and about age twenty-two. The university student teaching department placed five student teachers within the local school district, Charlotte, Andrea, Karen, and Bonnie together in one elementary school, Nancy in two different elementary schools. Robin and Linda student taught in two different school districts, Robin in a nearby small town, and Linda in an adjacent rural area. Six of the cooperating teachers were women, one was male, and all were white. With the exception of one white woman who served as a temporary administrator, all principals of these schools were white men.

Methods of Data Collection

The primary methods of data collection were participant observation (Gold 1969; Schwartz and Schwartz 1969) and informant interviewing. During the fifteen-week semester, I observed each informant for half a day every week or every other week and interviewed her at the conclusion of each observation. I observed the curriculum and teaching methods, their interactions with children and cooperating teachers, and modifications they made in the standard curriculum and routine. Interviews enabled me to discover the meanings the informants attributed to the events in their classrooms, the factors that influenced their curricular and pedagogical choices, and their interactions with children and cooperating teachers. These data were triangulated with the student teachers' journals and lesson plans and interviews with the cooperating teachers and university supervisors. Charlotte, Andrea, and Linda in particular furnished data through interviews and journals on their interactions with and impressions of their principals. Their cooperating teachers as well as Bonnie's cooperating teacher furnished additional data on these principals through interviews. Finally, I used "member checks" (Lincoln and Guba 1985) to give my informants opportunities to react verbally to my ongoing analysis and interpretations of their experiences and provided occasions for them to react more formally to my written descriptions and analysis of these teaching experiences.

Analysis and Interpretation of Data

I followed Glaser and Strauss' (1967) constant comparative guidelines in analyzing the data. As data were collected and reviewed, they were coded into preliminary conceptual categories of examples of caring in teaching. With the collection of additional data, the initial categories were modified, refined, or crystallized. For example, I searched for instances in which the student teachers modified the adopted texts or developed units of study to address the needs and interests of their students and engage them more personally in learning. Additionally, I examined the data for factors that encouraged and/or inhibited the student teachers' efforts to make the curriculum more interesting and relevant to the students. This analysis of data occurred during the period of the study and subsequent to it.

Efforts to Make Classrooms More Caring Places

> I do think the kids knew that I care for them and that I somehow made a difference. I made them feel like they are human beings. I take time to listen. I hear what they have to say. I believe I have made an impact. One boy, Jim [one of her students], I feel I have been able to make an impact on him as far as his temper goes. I think he is trying not to get so angry. I have also shown them that there are fun ways to learn. They are learning when they didn't know they were learning. (Interview with Nancy)

All of the student teachers wanted to make their classrooms places where children felt important and affirmed especially by making the curriculum interesting, challenging, relevant, and equitable. While the amount of concern for students communicated through personal interactions, teaching methods, and the curriculum they taught varied among the women in this study, each strived to address children's needs and interests in her teaching. Their efforts to make classrooms more caring places were supported by their personal commitment, strategies and skills they developed in the teacher education program, and encouragement and opportunities provided by their cooperating teachers. The student teachers provided examples of caring in teaching by building connections between their students and curriculum, promoting children's active involvement in learning, and fostering care and respect among the students within their classrooms.

Building Connections between Students and Curriculum

Each student teacher developed and taught at least one original unit of study in science and social studies. Whereas textbooks contained curriculum prepared by authors outside of the classroom for a general population of students, the curriculum these women created was designed for their particular students. They consulted their cooperating teachers who often encouraged their curriculum development and then selected topics which related to their students' interests, backgrounds, and needs. Their preparation in curriculum development in the teacher education program assisted them in their search for diverse resources, materials, and teaching strategies. Because of their students' interest in dinosaurs, space, and endangered animals, for example, Charlotte and Karen prepared units of study on these topics. Nancy developed a unit on Taiwan so that other children in this classroom could learn more about the country from which one of the children came. Still another effort by Linda, Charlotte, Robin, and Nancy to connect the curriculum to *all* of the students was to include women's contributions. Rather than focus on the achievements of men only in the development of transportation, space exploration, and the period of the Civil War that might have been of interest to the boys in the classroom but not necessarily to the girls, these preservice teachers strived to broaden the curriculum to interest all students. For example, when Nancy noticed that the girls were indifferent during discussions about soldiers' activities during the Civil War, she introduced them to women's contributions as peace activists, as nurses, and as those who maintained their homes and families while men were away fighting. People of color were also included through the work of Harriet Tubman and the underground railroad. This curriculum development effort helped communicate to children that caring classrooms are places they can influence the curriculum and study topics of interest and relevance to them.

Promoting Children's Active Involvement in Learning

When most of the preservice teachers began their student teaching, they discovered that the prevalent instructional strategy was children reading from textbooks and completing workbooks and worksheets requiring little thought. Too often, students were passive and bored as they searched for the "right" answers to fill in the blanks of their worksheets. Nancy expressed her frustrations about this approach in her journal: "I know that the children must also be frustrated. They are never given any time to do anything. They are constantly given assignments to keep them busy."

Nancy and Charlotte encouraged children's active and meaningful involvement in learning through the use of cooperative research in conjunction with an original unit each had developed. Students were divided into small groups, and each group selected an aspect of the topic they were studying to research. They devised ways to represent what they had learned and shared their learning with the rest of the class. The teacher and students learned together with the teacher providing guidance and encouragement as the children needed it. After finding information on Taiwan, the children in Nancy's classroom concluded their cooperative research with one group preparing a filmstrip illustrating transportation, another group making models showing housing, still another creating a story about children's education, and a fourth group preparing an illustrated report on animals.

Andrea relied heavily on group discussion as a strategy to involve students in learning by encouraging them to share what they knew, thought, felt, and experienced. This teaching method was supported by Andrea's cooperating teacher and her frequent use of large group discussions to keep students involved in her teaching. During these discussions Andrea and the children raised questions, expressed opinions, shared experiences, challenged each other's thinking, and considered ethical issues. By inviting her children's comments about the topic they were studying, she affirmed the importance of these contributions.

> A lot of time in classes what the teacher says is right and what the kids say is fine, but not usually as important. It doesn't have as much weight. I want to change that. I know that I am not always right. I tell them I was wrong, I tell them that I don't know something when I don't know something. I don't want school to be belittling to them . (Interview with Andrea)

Fostering Care and Respect among Children

> When Ann [a student] said today they should respect the teachers, don't break their property, listen to what they say and obey them, that is so terrible. Obey the teacher, respect the teacher. Everything is the teacher. That's the image they have. They don't think it applies to everybody. (Interview with Nancy)

Nancy and Linda in particular exuded a great deal of warmth, empathy, concern, and respect for their students and strived to help them reveal this same concern and respect for one another. They emphasized cooperation over competition to enable more children to learn. During spelling games, Linda divided her first-grade children into teams, reviewed the rules of working together and being nice to each other, and emphasized the importance of including all children. As they worked, she gave specific suggestions for involving two boys less skilled in spelling who were being ignored by others in their groups.

When children became loud, argued with one another, or mistreated materials or each other, these women usually talked with the children and reasoned with them as to why an action was wrong. They explored ways of encouraging students to understand how their actions affected others while demonstrating this same understanding of their students. "I try to explain to them why I'm upset if I do get upset and why that action that they did was wrong in my eyes. But I don't think it does anything to snap at them and yell at them," said Linda. Nancy also explained that students learn how to interact with others by the way she behaves toward them, "You're not reasoning if you're ordering the kids around so why should they reason? And they start ordering other kids around." Linda's cooperating teacher described Linda's empathic approach in dealing with conflicts among students by asking them, " 'Well, how would you feel if that person did that to you?' She'll try different techniques that make them realize by themselves that this isn't the right way to behave or this isn't the right thing to do because I wouldn't like it being done to me." These two women were concerned that children learn to meet their needs without infringing on the teacher's rights or other students' rights. As Nancy and Linda dealt with children in caring, respectful, yet instructive ways when they encountered difficulties in interacting with one another, these preservice teachers strived to teach care and respect on the cognitive as well as experiential levels.

Patriarchal and Bureaucratic Barriers to Caring

> If I play "dumb" female, they [male principal and custodian who are good friends] love me! If I play knowledgeable, competent person, they get uneasy. It is very obvious. Others chat about it a lot. (Linda's journal)

> I think the principal treats the teachers as if they are elementary students themselves. He has sorta "I'm the man" attitude. The main reason I wouldn't want to teach here is because of him. He doesn't make me comfortable. I really couldn't recommend working at this building. You never know if the principal is going to be nice or if he is going to look over your head or if he is going to be sarcastic. The first few weeks it bothered me about Mr. _____, now I really don't care. I really don't feel comfortable with him as a person. And I really don't think he knows what kind of a teacher that I am. (Interview with Charlotte)

The caring the student teachers revealed to their students was often not part of their relationship with their principals. Linda, Charlotte, and Andrea not only became aware of their principals' discouragement in their efforts to care for their students, but also these men's use of various forms of oppressive treatment in dealing with them as teachers and as women.

Encouraging Uniform Curriculum and Pedagogy

The standardization and uniformity characteristic of bureaucratic organizations (Darling-Hammond 1984, 1988; Ferguson 1984; Helsel and Krchniak 1972) seem to discourage caring in teaching. The school system in which most of the student teachers taught was beginning to emphasize uniformity in the curriculum by mandating the use of adopted textbooks. Although this bureaucratic emphasis on uniformity was intended to enable students to move smoothly from one school within the school system to another, it did not consider teachers' professional judgments about what materials were most appropriate to use with the specific students in their classrooms. As Bonnie's cooperating teacher explained,

> Several years a reading book might have been adopted and this school might not have used it and the next school would use it and when the children move from one school to the other there was no continuity. The parents all pay the same fees so they feel that all parents in the school system should be getting the same thing for their fees. And the principals have to get all the books now through the bookstore and the bookstore only keeps what's adopted in the store and that's all you can have. I'd just as soon not have a [hand]writing book. Always before I've been able to say, "I don't want the writing book," and I didn't get it. Once I have it, I feel obligated to use it because the parents have paid for it. That's the way most of us feel about it.

The principal of the school in which Bonnie, Karen, Andrea, and Charlotte taught communicated this emphasis on uniformity to the teachers by requiring the use of all adopted textbooks, although he unevenly enforced the directive. The cooperating teachers responded to this mandate in various ways. Along with Bonnie's cooperating teacher's reluctant use of handwriting books, Andrea's cooperating teacher eliminated the teaching of original units of study she had created in science and social studies in order to use the texts. However, all cooperating teachers spoke of the value of teacher-developed curriculum, at times taught their own units of study, and usually supported their student teachers' curriculum development work. Even the principal violated his own directive by granting Andrea's request for money to purchase multiple copies of a children's novel and allowing her to deviate from the adopted reading textbooks. He was convinced by her argument that the "better" students were not challenged by the basal readers and the novel would provide this needed challenge. Although there was some leeway for teachers to shape the curriculum to meet the needs and interests of their students, the explicit freedom, expectation, and encouragement to make the curriculum more suitable for a specific group of children did not exist. Unless preservice and experienced teachers provided a convincing argument otherwise or made changes quietly, the principal apparently expected the standard curriculum to be followed. Within this bureaucracy, teaching a caring curriculum was an individual effort.

Two principals also exerted some pressure for teachers to use particular pedagogical styles in their classrooms. One of the men, Linda's principal, evaluated the teachers in his school on the basis of their adherence to his standard of "a really well-managed, quiet, disciplined class." Although neither Linda nor the other teachers in this school discontinued the instructional games and other creative activities which caused more noise when they taught, they did modify their teaching methods when they knew the principal planned to observe. His power to evaluate them made it impossible for the teachers to ignore his pedagogical preferences even if they knew diverse instructional strategies were necessary to make their classrooms more interesting and beneficial for their students. The second principal discouraged the participatory style of teaching that Andrea and her cooperating teacher used by criticizing the arrangement of students' desks in a large square around the perimeter of Andrea's classroom. Because Andrea and her cooperating teacher used large group discussions to foster students' involvement in learning and to affirm the personal knowledge of each child, this physical arrangement of the desks encouraged everyone's participation in these discussions. After observing Andrea's cooperating teacher, the principal asked her if she would consider moving the students' desks into more traditional rows. Although she did not comply with his suggestion, she was disgruntled that he did not understand the value of her classroom arrangement. By discouraging this physical arrangement, the principal also dissuaded the more caring approach to teaching.

Emphasizing Gender Inequality

Other characteristics of bureaucracies which discourage caring include formalized relationships, unequal power, and distance among teachers, students, and administrators (Ferguson 1984; Freedman 1988; Helsel & Krchniak 1972). Ferguson argues that when women as subordinates care for others with less power as well as those with more power, they support existing power arrangements within patriarchy. The caring that these student teachers expressed to their children left the power of their male administrators intact. For the women student teachers in these two schools, the principals reminded them in various ways of their limited power and respect as teachers and as women. Even though these women revealed care for students in multiple ways, they usually were not recipients of caring from their principals. Andrea, Charlotte, Karen, and Bonnie were reminded by the principal of their relatively powerless position in the school during a meeting with him their first week of student teaching. "Don't go trying to change us or telling us what to do. You need to wait until you get into your own classroom where you can make changes. Most of us have been doing this for years and we really don't want to be told what to do" (interview with Andrea). This principal also communicated to the experienced teachers in the school that they did not share the same power he possessed. In addition to the restrictions he imposed on the curriculum and the discouragement he offered to Andrea's cooperating teacher about her participatory teaching style, Andrea observed his "insulting" manner of speaking to teachers during faculty meetings. "He gets up in front and talks to those teachers like he's talking to a class of students. He talks down to them a lot" (interview with Andrea).

The lack of equality between principals, teachers, and student teachers provides an example of the hierarchy within bureaucratic institutions. Because the power accorded people within these hierarchies was divided almost completely along gender lines, the patriarchal nature of schools was evident. When teachers are rewarded in superficial, patronizing ways, principals communicate a lack of respect for teaching and for teachers. Linda's principal's practice of awarding the best bulletin board in the school with a ribbon every month was not considered a serious effort by the teachers to affirm their work (interview with Linda's cooperating teacher). However, the principal viewed teachers as competitors for these limited rewards. "He just thinks that everyone competes for a ribbon. He told me he'd love to give me more than one, but people would get jealous (laughter)" (interview with Linda). When Linda discovered her principal's criteria for hiring teachers included appearance, she was reminded in a very profound way that she was working in a patriarchal institution where women had to please the male administrator in order to get and keep a good teaching position. Because she was interested in finding a teaching position in the local school district, her principal advised her to visit another school in this district and meet the principal.

> When you go there and you observe, afterwards, go to the principal, Mr. _____'s office and let him get a look at you." And I go, "What?" He goes, "Let him get a look at you because he'll hire a pretty teacher over a fat one any day." (Interview with Linda).

Linda was not accorded the same care and respect from her principal as she exhibited toward the children in her classroom. Fortunately, her cooperating teacher supported Linda's efforts to care for her students and together they criticized, ridiculed, and coped with the sexist, degrading treatment from this administrator.

Toward a Feminist Interpretation of An Ethic of Care in Schools

Encouraging the development of an ethic of care in schools is not, by itself, congruous with the goals of feminism. The caring labor that women

189

and others with limited power have given historically has occurred within a patriarchal social-historical context which has not disrupted the various forms of dominance and subordination within patriarchy (Ferguson 1984; Houston 1990). Feminism seeks to restructure personal and public life to protect individual freedoms, to foster gender, racial, and class equality among and within various groups, and to encourage collective action as a way of addressing social problems. A feminist interpretation of caring could lead to interruptions in the ways in which schools support racial, gender, and class dominance.

The caring that the women student teachers in this study communicated to their students were individual acts limited to the privacy of their own classrooms. An ethic of care was not a pervasive aspect of the whole elementary schools in which they taught. Not all members of the school community received as well as gave care. Especially in the case of Linda, Charlotte, and Andrea, their caring labor within their schools was accepted and perhaps appreciated by their cooperating teachers and students, but they were not recipients of care from their principals. Not only did the principals frequently fail to treat the student teachers in caring ways, but they also communicated the bureaucratic constraints which discouraged caring for children. In considering how a feminist interpretation of an ethic of care might become more prevalent in schools, educators could ponder the relationship of justice to caring, the structural changes needed to support caring work and the development of caring communities, and ways an ethic of caring can be infused throughout the curriculum and pedagogy.

Integrating Caring with Justice

An ethic of care cannot simply be infused in schools without considering the equitable distribution of caring labor. When women teachers alone are expected to provide the caring children need and when they fail to receive caring from male administrators and other members of the school community, the division of labor continues to exploit women. Women retain the burden of caring for others while being denied the benefits of receiving care (Houston 1990). If caring always flows from women and people of color to those with more power and status, the more powerful may fail to develop the ability to care for others and may continue to expect caring from subordinate groups (Hoagland 1990). Boys as well as girls, middle-class and upper-class as well as lower-class children, white as well as children of color need to be taught to care for others as part of their socialization process in schools. The withdrawal of caring from those members of the school community who fail to demonstrate caring in their interactions with others is justified when an ethic of care is infused with justice.

Restructuring Schools for Communities of Caring

In striving to build a more democratic, egalitarian school structure in which caring for all people within the school community can thrive, the possibilities for change exist within collective action. Seldom is it possible for an individual to change an organization while simultaneously trying to succeed within the same organization. If an individual strives to infuse justice and caring within a patriarchal, bureaucratic school while being evaluated, rewarded, and/or sanctioned by the administrator of this same school, often the ethical ideal dims, the rewards become scarce, or the sanctions increase. One may protest skillfully within an organization and survive, but one rarely becomes successful (Ferguson 1984). Teachers, parents, community members, teacher educators, and administrators might join together to protect and support one another as they work for transformations. Simultaneously, they would engage in raising the consciousness of each other about ways their behavior support and erode the various forms of inequalities which lead to an absence of caring for some students in schools. Through thinking and living in caring ways, this group can foster genuine social change (Ferguson 1984). Groups can work in these ways:

Accessible Language. We can start with ourselves and our co-workers. We need to develop accessible languages which build on common concerns among teachers, students, parents, community members, teacher educators, and administrators. At times, teachers have used specialized language which separates them from the parents of their students (Noddings 1984). Frequently the language which labels students with certain problems or characteristics tends to objectify them and reduce them to these problems or characteristics. A caring, empathetic, wholistic view of the child becomes lost among the labels. Parents can be understandably alienated by this language. Teacher educators have been known to shroud their descriptions of teaching and schools with a heavy theoretical mist which makes their understandings inaccessible to other members of the school community. Although the unique perspectives of each individual should be preserved, each should also assume responsibility to make their knowledge accessible to other members of the school community.

Cooperative Atmosphere. We need to construct an atmosphere of cooperation, collaboration, equality, and support among all members of the school community. This atmosphere is especially important to children of color and others who have experienced racial, gender, or class discrimination. Such an atmosphere is similar to what Shakeshaft (1987) has described as "the structures of female-defined schools" in which each member of the community is similar to a team member cooperating to achieve group goals. The typical hierarchical ordering of administrators, teacher educators, teachers, parents, community members, and students is transformed into circles and chains of caring (Noddings 1984). In order for this structure to be created, the size of the school must allow for personal, face-to-face interactions. These are the roots of understanding others. However, reducing the size of schools alone is not enough to insure cooperation among teachers, administrators, and students. As Schmuck and Schmuck (1990) discovered in their research in small-town schools, these small schools appeared to be more democratic, but rarely did administrators share influence with teachers, teachers share ideas about instruction with each other, or students have a voice in how schools were run. Perhaps one way to build this cooperative atmosphere is to extend Noddings' (1984) idea of cycles of teaching and administering in order to develop empathy for people in different positions and to experience the challenge of caring for all members of the school community from different perspectives. Just as teachers would have the opportunity to leave teaching for a year and engage in administrative study/work, administrators may choose to return to teaching for a year. Similarly, exchanges can be made between classroom teachers and teacher educators as well as administrators and administrator educators.

Shared Power. Real power must be shared through democratic, participatory leadership. Rather than view power as a finite resource which is to be sought after and held individually, Ferguson (1984, 190) suggests the conception of power as "the ability to empower members to do collectively what they couldn't do alone." Frequently those with the greatest formal power, usually administrators, are the most removed from the students and least likely to know their needs. However, administrators (as well as community members) may be able to procure additional resources more quickly than teachers in response to student needs. Parents and teachers work most intimately with children, are more aware of their needs, and use the resources available to them. By working together through a participatory, democratic governance structure, members of the school community are more able to address students' needs. This governance structure might take the form of a school-site council composed of all vested interests. Decisions made should be real and substantive and could include all important aspects of the school community (Bastian et al. 1985). However, in order for this structure to work effectively, efforts must be made to remain in touch with students' needs and what their experiences of schooling are (Hollins and Spencer 1990). This is especially important for lower-class students and students of color who need more than equal opportunities to include results equal to their white, middle-class classmates (Bastian et al. 1985). Additionally, teachers must have the time and resources during the school day to participate in such a governance structure. To add this responsibility without support to their already heavy teaching loads would lead to the further exploitation of their labor (Zeichner 1991). Finally, this school-site council needs ongoing training programs to enable their work to be successful (Bastian et al. 1985), including training in conflict resolution. This governance structure is a place in which conflicting and diverse perspectives are made public rather than remain suppressed and conflict resolution strategies are used to accommodate, adapt, and reconcile diverse points of view (Ferguson 1984).

Teachers' Increased Authority and Responsibility for Curricular and Pedagogical Decisions. A fourth structural change which can lead to a more caring school community is the elimination of teachers' deskilling (Apple 1986). When teachers have authority *and* responsibility, with input from students, administrators, teacher educators, parents, and other community members, to decide what should be taught to their specific group of students in a particular way, they are able to address together students' needs and to remain intellectually engaged in their teaching. Parents and some community members become significant resources to teachers because of their knowledge of students' lives outside of school. Additionally, a few community members may become paraprofessionals to assist in tangible ways in the development of culturally appropriate curricula and teaching styles (Bastian et al. 1985). Teachers need time as part of their workload to prepare, implement, and evaluate educational plans (Liston and Zeichner 1990), to lead staff development and teacher mentorship programs, and to pursue study, curriculum development, and evaluations and adaptations of school programs to meet students' needs (Bastian et al. 1985).

Curriculum and Pedagogy for Caring. Liston and Zeichner's (1990) recommendations for a teacher education curriculum which supports democratic education have merit for teacher educators concerned about developing teachers prepared to help create caring school communities. They recommend that preservice teachers should focus on an analysis of teaching as work, on conditions which obstruct democratic aims, and on ways teachers develop strategies to deal with these situations. First of all, case studies should be used of teachers who worked to make changes and who recognize the ways schools have harmed children of color. Second, new teachers need to learn about students' cultures and languages in an empathetic way. They need to learn about the kinds of discrimination and repression students of color have experienced, including those in educational institutions. Finally,

Liston and Zeichner recommend the inclusion of the analysis of gender and teaching to question the gendered division of labor in school and the male bias of the curriculum. This analysis could be extended to include the caring division of labor and the possibilities and problems of forming coalitions with other new and experienced teachers to work for changes which would allow caring to flourish within school communities.

Pedagogy can also create caring communities. Just as the size of restructured schools allows for personal, face-to-face interactions among all members of the school community, the size of the classroom must also allow for increased teacher-student interactions. These frequent interactions allow teachers to become exceptionally knowledgeable about each child's background, interests, and needs. This knowledge can be used by the teacher to teach empathetically, by viewing the subject matter as the students do (Noddings 1984) and by building on their background experiences. Pedagogy which responds to students' culture, class, and gender communicates the teacher's care for students and encourages the development of caring among the children.

Conclusion

The development of a feminist ethic of caring in schools enables caring to be given and received by each member of the school community. Such an ethic of caring is rare in schools which more frequently reveal their patriarchal, bureaucratic nature. If the women student teachers had helped to develop a feminist ethic of caring in their schools, they might have been better able to care for their students as well as found the caring they needed to continue and expand their efforts. This ethic of care offers the possibilities for interrupting the oppression some students and their teachers experience.

Bibliography

Apple, M.W. (1986). *Teachers and texts: A political economy of class and gender relations in education.* New York: Routledge.

Bastian, A., Fruchter, N., Gittell, N., Greer, C., and Haskins, K. (1985). *Choosing equality: The case for democratic schooling.* Philadelphia: Temple University.

Bogdan, R.C. and Biklen, S.K. (1982). *Qualitative research for education: An introduction to theory and methods.* Boston: Allyn and Bacon.

Darling-Hammond, L. (1984). *Beyond the commission reports: The coming crisis in teaching* (R-3177-RC). Santa Monica, CA: Rand.

———. (1988). Accountability and teacher professionalism. *American Educator.* 12(4), 8–13, 38–43.

Dobbert, M.L. (1982). *Ethnographic research: Theory and application for modern schools and societies.* New York: Praeger.

Emerson, R.M. (1983). *Contemporary field research: A collection of readings.* Boston: Little, Brown.

Ferguson, K.E. (1984). *The feminist case against bureaucracy.* Philadelphia: Temple University.

Freedman, S. (1988). The doctrine of separate spheres: Its effects on curriculum. *Radical Teacher,* 35, 38–44.

Glaser, B.G. and Strauss, A.L. (1967). *The discovery of grounded theory: Strategies for qualitative research.* Chicago: Aldine.

Gold, R.L. (1969). Roles in sociological field observations. In G.J. McCall and J.L. Simmons (eds.), *Issues in participant observation.* Reading, MA: Addison-Wesley.

Helsel, A.R., and Krchniak, S.P. (1972). Socialization in a heteronomous profession: Public school teaching. *The Journal of Educational Research,* 66(2), 89–93.

Hoagland, S.L. (1990). Some concerns about Nel Noddings' *Caring. Hypatia,* 5(1), 109–14.

Hollins, E.R. and Spencer, K. (1990). Restructuring schools for cultural inclusion: Changing the schooling process for African-American youngsters. *Journal of Education,* 172(2), 89 –100.

Houston, B. (1990). Caring and exploitation. *Hypatia,* 5(1), 115–20.

Lincoln, Y.S., and Guba, E.G. (1985). *Naturalistic inquiry.* Beverly Hills: Sage.

Liston, D.P. and Zeichner, K.M. (1990). Teacher education and the social context of schooling: Issues for curriculum development. *American Educational Research Journal,* 27(4), 610–36.

Noddings, N. (1984). *Caring: A feminine approach to ethics and moral education.* Berkeley: University of California Press.

Patton, M.Q. (1980). *Qualitative evaluation methods.* Beverly Hills: Sage.

Schmuck, P. and Schmuck, R. (1990). Democratic participation in small-town schools. *Educational Researcher,* 19(8), 14 –19.

Schwartz, M.S., and Schwartz, C.G. (1969). Problems in participant observation. In G. J. McCall and J. L. Simmons (eds.), *Issues in participant observation*. Reading, MA: Addison-Wesley.

Shakeshaft, C. (1987). *Women in educational administration*. Newbury Park, CA: Sage.

Spradley, J.P. (1979). *The ethnographic interview*. New York: Holt, Rinehart & Winston.

Zeichner, K.M. (1991). Contradictions and tensions in the professionalization of teaching and the democratization of schools. *Teachers College Record, 92*(3), 363–79.

III

Women Leading: Assimilation,
Acceptance and Resistance

ELEVEN

Advocacy Organizations for Women School Administrators, 1977–1993

Patricia A. Schmuck

"Woman will learn the power of association and she will learn the value of herself" (New York Working Women's Protective Union 1863 quoted in Berg, 1978, p. 143). Those words opened my remarks to the first conference of Oregon Women in Educational Administration in 1977. I had no idea then how prophetic those words would be. That year we were just getting started; advocacy groups had formed in Oregon, Washington, California, Kansas, and Nebraska. The Northeast Coalition of Educational Leaders comprising four states in the East was just getting off the ground, and only a few chapters of the National Council for Administrative Women (formed as early as 1910) still existed. Now, only sixteen years later, advocacy groups for women administrators are in thirty-five states and women's presence in school administration is an accepted fact in most of the United States. Between 1977 and 1993 women in educational administration learned the power of association and learned to value themselves.

What occurred between 1977 and 1993? What happened in the sixteen years between the struggling start of a few women's groups and a full blown national phenomenon? Several events occurred in the 1970s; the spark of the women's movement fired women's consciousness in education; Title IX

199

and equity funding provided support for research and action on women in administration; and finally, women educators informally and formally organized to bring pressure on the educational establishment to hire women in administration. It was a heady time.

A Personal Reflection

My mother, Tekla Halme, asked me as I was growing up, "What will you contribute?" Without a high school education (although she probably completed enough continuing education courses to constitute a masters degree), she who always contributed in some way to her community was named the Volunteer for Michigan in 1985. My mother worked actively in the Red Cross, Girl Scouts, PTA, church, and other local efforts, and then became more radical in her later years when she saw the lack of programs for senior citizens in her own local community of Beaverton, Michigan and set out to organize new programs in the 1970s—from which she now benefits. Her stalwart charity and her undying optimism are my heritage. My contributions have been as an activist for and a researcher on women in school leadership.

In 1958 when I became engaged to Richard Schmuck, I switched my college major to education, following the advice to females of those days that you could always get a job teaching wherever your husband's career might lead. We married in 1959 and I became an elementary teacher in 1960. Dick's career in social psychology took us from Michigan to Pennsylvania, where I taught, and then to Oregon. After having two children in the 1960s I entered the doctoral program at the University of Oregon in Educational Administration in 1973 to become an elementary principal. I had a vague sense my sex would work against me and so I figured I would need to earn "extra" credentials to compete in the marketplace successfully. My intuition about discrimination against women was transformed into a fact of life after I took a course from Henry Wolcott and read his study of *The Man and the Principal's Office* (1975).

As I was searching for a dissertation topic I was inspired by Dick's advice. He was serving then as a member of the Women's Caucus of the American Psychological Association. After returning home from a Women's Caucus meeting in Boston, he suggested, "If you think your sex is against you in obtaining a principalship, why don't you find out why?" So I did. In 1974, I toured Oregon to ask why women were so scarce in educational administration; there were ninety-one women, or about 6 percent, acting as school administrators. I interviewed thirty of them and ten male administrators about why they believed women were so under represented in school administration. My dissertation (Schmuck 1975) received an award from and was published by the National Council of Women in Administration (NCAWE). Little did I know then that between 1973 and 1979 seventy other women across the country would write dissertations on the same topic (see Shakeshaft 1981 and Grady 1990 for citations). The topic of women's place in educational administration was part of a national zeitgeist for research; my dissertation was timely and proved, more over, to be a self-revelation for me. It was through my listening to the experiences of other women that I could see the emerging social patterns of my own life, Through listening to other women's words I found my own voice, and saw my career as an educator in the perspective of gender bias in school administration.

Tips by Paul Goldman, Ann Frentz, and Joanne Kitchell Carlson prompted me to pay my own way to hunt for grant funds in Washington, D.C. in 1974. I didn't know anyone there and had only faint knowledge about the revolutionary legislation, passed in 1972, called Title IX. I visited office after office and talked to person after person learning the machina- tions of Washington, D.C. My timing was fortunate; I discovered the possi- bility of funding from the Women's Educational Equity Act Project and was one of the first grantees when funding became available in 1976.

With those funds Jean Stockard and I co-directed the Sex Equity in Ed- ucational Leadership Project (SEEL) from 1976 to 1979 at the University of Oregon through which we established a state model for achieving sex equity in school administration (see Schmuck 1982; Smith, Kalvelage, and Schmuck 1982; Stockard 1982). With that grant we also helped organize Oregon Women in Educational Administration in 1977, and later wrote successful proposals to start Northwest Women in Educational Administra- tion (including Oregon, Washington, Idaho, Montana, and Alaska) with grants from the Ford Foundation (Project Aware) and the Northwest Area Foundation. From 1980 to 1983, Mary Frances Callan was the NWEA exec- utive director and Elaine Hopson the assistant director. Two books were published on the SEEL project (Stockard et al. 1981; Schmuck et al. 1981); and the project also became a program focus for many doctoral disserta- tions at the University of Oregon (see Kempner 1979; Paddock 1981; Pou- galis 1981; Williams 1980; Edson 1980; Hopson 1985; Matthews 1986; Mattson 1987; Pence 1989). Those years were filled with hope and promise; a hope that we could increase the number of women in educational ad- ministration and the promise that the increased presence of women in school administration would alter the quality of organizational life in schools.

As the Dunlap and Schmuck book came into being, I wondered how we had delivered on that 1977 hope and promise. What happened nationally? Were other groups formed? Where were they? Do they still exist? What is their purpose? Who was involved?

In this chapter I will: (1) describe the methods of the study; (2) present a brief history of advocacy groups for women administrators prior to 1977; (3) document the formation of women's advocacy groups in the United States from 1977 to 1992; (4) suggest new directions for the next decade and finally; and (5) list existing advocacy groups for women administrators with contact names by state.

Method of Study

I distributed a questionnaire in 1991 to all state superintendents, to all members of the Research on Women in Education, a special Interest Group of the American Educational Research Association, to all participants in the Ford Foundation funded Project AWARE, and to all individuals known to me who had done research or written about women in educational administration. I received responses from fifty individuals representing twenty-nine states (often several responses came from members of the same organization), and I made about fifty follow-up phone calls to get more information.

All groups, except the National Council for Administrative Women in Education, were formed after 1970, several did not begin until after 1985. Advocacy groups have varied and changed through time. Some are non-profit corporations with written by-laws; they are affiliated formally with other administrator groups, publish newsletters, employ executive secretaries, have dues-paying members and hold regular meetings and conferences. Others are more informal, have no written by-laws nor constitution, meet regularly or irregularly and have or don't have membership lists. The collective momentum and thrust of the 1970s and 1980s was not new, however, for it was similar to times past when women educators joined together to advocate for women teachers and women administrators.

Before Our Time

Advocating *for* women in education *by* women in education is not new. Efforts to improve women's lot in education first occurred during the women's movement of the early twentieth century when women entered teaching in large numbers. Bystydienski (1987) and Gribskov (1980) explained that teacher organizations, unions in particular, voiced their concerns about women teachers, and women's economic and social advancement. The National Education Association (NEA), has on record as early as 1880 that women were demanding more voice in the decisions of NEA and questioning the norm that supported paying women teachers less than their male counterparts. Bystydienski (1987) argued against the myth that women were passive, inactive union members and showed instead that women teachers in the United States organized on behalf of women and called for radical changes in schooling. And there is evidence that our female forebearers argued against the increasing bureaucratization and hierarchical organization of schools; women often called for more democratic governance, arguing that schools should be governed more by the those who participated in them.

Margaret Haley, first president of the American Federation of Teachers (AFT), in a speech to the NEA in 1904, raised questions about the "professionalism" of teachers. She used the term "factorizing education"—depicting the teacher as an automaton, a mere factory hand—whose duty it was to carry out mechanically and unquestioningly the ideas and orders of those in authority positions (Hoffman 1981, 291). In 1916, Haley organized the union so that rank and file teachers would be elected as delegates and representatives at national conferences; she argued for a more democratic union. Women constituted 60 percent of AFT membership by 1919 and were on the forefront of democratic change in education, as well as the change in status of women's condition in education (Bystydzienski 1987). Mary Parker Follet (1949), an academic in management, long neglected in higher education and only recently rediscovered, argued strongly against the bureaucratic control of officials at the top, and said those who took part in implementing decisions should also be making decisions. Many women then, as today, argued against the principles of scientific management and for more democratic governance and less bureaucratic hierarchy in schools.

At the turn of the century women teachers were not the only educators advocating for changes in the teaching ranks; there were also advocacy groups to support women's entrance and advancement into school administration. In those days women, especially in the west, took an increasing number of executive positions as county superintendents. By 1910, before national suffrage, women's presence was beginning in schools. By that time women could vote in school elections in twenty-four states and they often were elected to county superintendences. In 1922, Edith Lathrop, on the staff of the United States Office of Education, wrote an article urging college-educated women to enter careers in public education because the barriers seemed to be coming down (see Tyack and Hansot 1982, 187). By 1928, according to Gribskov (1980) women constituted nearly two-thirds of county superintendents in the west. Although the accuracy of such demographic data from newspapers may not be totally accurate, Donovan, a journalist, reported in 1910, 53 percent of "supervisory officials" in education were held by women (Donovan 1938). Women elementary principals were so common in the approximately 100,000 school districts in 1926 that the

U. S. Office of Education published an article called, "The Woman Principal: A Fixture in American Schools."

Although women were the majority of teachers and administrators in schools and districts nationwide, they were not among the executives of larger urban school districts. Since women mostly administered rural schools, when Ella Flagg Young became superintendent of Chicago public schools, she was exceptional, as noted in a 1909 editorial which read, "The election of a woman to be the Superintendent of schools in the second largest city in the United States is a violation of precedent. If any man among the candidates had possessed all the qualities recognized in Mrs. Young, her sex might have been against her" (McManis 1916). The concept of the "glass ceiling," although not called that, was proposed as early as 1919 by Louise Connolly in her article called, "Is There Room at the Top for Women Educators?" She wrote, "woman has arrived in numbers only in the lower strata of the upper crust" (see Tyack and Hansot 1982, 840).

The National Council for Administrative Women in Education (NCAWE), is the only women's advocacy group that has survived from the early days. Although NCAWE reports its official startup in 1915 in Oakland, California (see Patterson and Milligan, no date), Gribskov recounts a precursor group formed in 1910 in Seattle (1980). Gribskov, tracing the history of Adelaide Pollack, a principal in Seattle, told this story: "Pollack, then principal of Queen Anne Grammar School in Seattle, invited other Seattle women administrators—elementary principals, vice principals, and the female assistant superintendent—to dinner at her home. The purpose of the meeting was to provide women with the opportunity to discuss educational issues and the special problems faced by women administrators" (Gribskov 1980, 124). Thus, like their modern counterparts, women over eighty years ago gathered in a private dining room for food and discussion about how both to increase their numbers in educational administration and to support each other's efforts to do so.

Between women's entry into teaching and school administration in the early twentieth century and the present time, several important social and cultural events restrained the expansion of women administrators in education:

1. There was a gradual demise over forty years of a strong women's movement in the United States. The 1920 amendment, in which women's suffrage was guaranteed, signaled the end of the first women's movement, while the second did not start until the 1960s.

2. The GI bill, passed after World War II, afforded veterans the opportunity to receive a college education. The mostly male veterans, who otherwise would not have received a college degree, entered the

field of education in droves. Whereas in 1938 men represented 20 percent of teachers, by 1974 they constituted 38 percent of teachers (Neidig 1976). The GI bill resulted not only in more men in education, but it gave rise to a social class distinction between men and women in education. Men more often than women came from lower social classes and rural areas and less often came from professional families and the cities. Public school teaching became a mobility ladder for men; for women it was simply one of just a very few occupations open to them (see Gross and Trask 1976; O'Connor 1970).

3. World War II also ended the prevailing policy nationwide against hiring married women as teachers. As Rosie the Riveter was employed in wartime industry, more and more married women responded to the call of teaching, while many became administrators. As Rosie the Riveter was "pushed" back into the kitchen by the returning soldiers, women administrators too retired and were replaced in the schools by men.

4. Urbanization of the society led to school consolidation; after World War II 100,000 school districts were consolidated to about 16,000 districts. Small schools, often headed by women, were consolidated into larger schools, more often headed by men.

5. The prevailing idea of leadership as "scientific management" and the factory model of schooling separated "management" as a technical scientific field from the craft of teaching.

6. An increased sex stereotyping of "management" as a male domain was legitimized in the growing literature and training programs on administration. "Men manage and women teach" (Tyack and Hansot 1982) became an accepted truism. In fact, studies of education proclaimed it to be a "semi" or "quasi" profession, the criterion being how high the number of women in the field (Etzioni 1969; Lortie 1975). The presence of women, ipso facto, was a criterion to define professionalism, where women dominated there could be no profession.

Those social changes were the factors contributing to the "vanishing woman" in educational administration from 1920–1960. By 1970, women administrators in public schools were on the road to extinction.

In Our Time

By the early 1970s, the second women's movement was in full swing; pressure was on the Congress to deal with sex inequity in public education and Title IX was the outcome (Fishel and Pottker 1977). Along with the legislative support for sex equity in schools, research documented the low status of women in educational administration, financial support for women in administration was provided by federal and private foundation grants, and groups formed all over the country to advocate on behalf of women's entrance and advancement in school administration.

Research in The Academy

Academics began paying attention to the scarcity of women in school administration. Although there were not many published sources about the status of women in educational administration by 1977 (Hare 1966; Fishel and Pottker 1974; Lyon and Saario 1973; Taylor 1973; Schmuck 1975), Shakeshaft found dissertation research to be a highly productive line of inquiry. Of the 114 dissertations written about women in administration between 1973 and 1979, 71 were focused on women in K–12 school administration. According to Shakeshaft, "Dissertation research, by its very nature indicates the trends of a discipline. It reflects the newest directions and current directions of a discipline" (1981, 11). And the published literature on women's status in school administration also started appearing in books, articles and popular magazines.

The first important book publication was Neil Gross and Ann Trask's *The Sex Factor and the Management of Schools* (1976), in which they discussed the behavior of 189 female and male principals of elementary schools and showed that female principals were more involved in instruction and had staffs with higher morale than male principals. Their data about the sex factor remained only a technical report in the Office of Education for over a decade (Gross and Trask 1964); it was published in 1976 as a response to the criticism that, "most studies of organizations have ignored the fact that their members have a gender" (p. 225).

Financial Support

The Women's Educational Equity Act Project of the Office of Education (begun in 1976) and the Ford Foundation Project AWARE (inspired by Terry Saario, housed in the American Association of School Administrators, and led by Effie Jones) between 1979–1985 were the largest sources of support for women in public school administration.

The Women's Educational Equity Act Project (WEEA) provided support for many different kinds of equity projects in schools, among those in school administration were: the SEEL Project (Sex Equity in Educational Leadership) at the University of Oregon (Schmuck 1982); Developing Interpersonal Competencies in Educational Leadership at the University of Cincinnati (Evers 1981); A project of Internships, Certification, Equity-Leadership and Support at the University of Kansas (Adkison 1979); Female

Leaders for Administration and Management in Education in Texas; Women in Leadership Learning in Illinois; and Women in School Administration in Montana (Schmuck 1979).

Project AWARE (Assisting Women in Research and Education) under the Ford Foundation provided support for many state and regional groups including Florida, Arizona, Missouri, New Mexico, Oklahoma, NCEL (Northeast Coalition of Educational Leaders), which included Massachusetts, Connecticut, New Hampshire, Maine, New Jersey and Rhode Island), and the NWEA (Northwest Women in Educational Administration, which included Oregon, Washington, Idaho, Montana, and Alaska).

The financial support by WEEA or Project AWARE provided seed money for many organizations to begin. But many other advocacy organizations were not funded; rather they developed out of the initiative of practitioners and academics who organized on behalf of women administrators.

Defining Obstacles to Women in Administration

By 1977 the obstacles to women's entrance and advancement in educational administration were clear. The obstacles were male administrator attitudes against hiring women as administrators, women's lack of motivation to aspire to school administration, and organizational procedures which perpetuated discrimination in the hiring and advancement of women administrators (see Schmuck 1975; Dias 1975; and an excellent summary in Shakeshaft 1987, chapter 5).

The Old Boy Network

The exclusion of women in state and regional administrator meetings created the first obvious need for change; women were left out. For instance, Kansas Women in Educational Leadership was formed as a dinner club in the early 1970s because the women could not join the men for dinner at the state administrative meetings. In California, women formed a caucus at the state administrator association. In 1975 Barbara Peterson, Jessie Kobayashi, and Doris Prince organized a caucus of the California State Administrators Association. In 1977, the women's caucus of the Oregon Confederation of School Administrators successfully passed a resolution "supporting sex equity in school administration" accompanied by snickers from the predominantly male assembly, and which led to a separate women's organization. Clearly, women felt the male bias of administrator organizations and the prevailing male attitudes against women in educational administration. Judy Adkison noted that administration organizations, primarily male, did not consider gender equity as one of their goals. She said, "Members of administrator organizations do not pay dues in order to add women to the ranks—*and individual members of the organizations may even oppose that objective*" (1979, 48, emphasis mine). That sentiment was echoed in a SEEL project report in 1977.

> "No matter how many publications we put out, or conferences we put on, individuals who believe and act on the premise that a woman could or should not perform administrative jobs will not have their beliefs changed to the contrary. Nationally and in Oregon, it is clear the responsibility of assisting women to find administrative positions is up to us. We hope to do something about it. *We know the formal and informal processes used in administrative recruitment and selection that work to favor men. We need a system that works as well for women.*" (Schmuck 1981).

And that's just what happened—women formed a social system that worked for them.

Women as The Problem

The "underachieving woman" was portrayed in the literature of the 1970s. Charles Schultz, in his inimical fashion of encapsulating a compendium of psychological wisdom and common sense portrayed, in his Peanuts cartoon, the precursor to the underachieving woman. Sally, at the age of five, concludes,

> "I never said I wanted to BE someone.
> All I want to do when I grow up is to be a good wife and mother.
> SO, why should I have to go to kindergarten?"

The popular literature of the time focused on the socialization of females in our society. The argument made was that women didn't want to be administrators because they had not been "socialized" for leadership (see Adkison 1981, for an excellent review). In my own 1975 study, I identified the "Who Me?" woman. The "who-me" woman was one who responded to a request for increased responsibility and leadership (usually from a male boss) with, "Who, ME?"

In 1975, the average woman denigrated her sense of capability, she had not "learned the power of association and the value of herself." Moreover, women teachers were seen as "deficient" in their preparation for leadership and thus advocacy organizations took on the charge to better prepare women to enter and advance in the educational bureaucracy. Conferences, workshops on resume writing, seminars on interview skills, sessions on leadership, and meetings of support groups dominated the calendars and the consciousness of the leaders of women school administrator groups. The call was clear; women needed to be "motivated" to enter administration and they needed to know they would be supported.

Organizational Barriers

Title IX, Title VII, Executive Orders, and other equity legislation provided an important backdrop to the efforts of women advocacy groups to increase the number of women in administration. A few research studies focused specifically on discrimination in hiring women administrators (see Schmuck and Wyant 1981; Timpano 1976; Ortiz 1982).

Affirmative action policies clearly stated procedures for hiring: public notices and screening committees replaced the more informal systems of administrative hiring. The more formal procedures ended the "late night hirings": those where a job announcement was filed at midnight and filled by 2 a.m. Changing the structures which had discriminated against women opened up a pipeline of women who were waiting to be hired. For instance, in 1979, Bertha, a twenty-year veteran teacher who had assumed many teacher leader roles, was called to the superintendent's office. He gave her a brochure about Castle Hot Springs—a special training event for women aspiring to become principals: "Here Bertha, go to this," he said. And she did. And she became a principal, then a superintendent. There were many "Berthas" in the pipeline in 1977 (phone conversation with Dillon 1992).

Both NWEA and NCEL created job banks which matched women candidates with administrative openings. NWEA created the Oregon Network, that sent a list of all women applying for administrative positions to all school districts with openings (Schmuck and Wyant 1981).

The Courts

Although women's advocacy groups *could* have used the law in confronting school districts about discriminatory practices, this was not widely used nor was it generally accepted as a strategy for change. Most women, after all, wanted to enter the system; filing a grievance or a suit against a district where one wanted to be hired was not seen as a wise career move. The common lore was "districts don't hire those who create trouble."

Two exceptions to this common lore stood out in the annals of Oregon. In 1979 in Eugene, Oregon Women in Educational Administration and Lynn George, the only female vice principal in the district, filed a grievance against the Eugene School district for hiring two white male vice principals in high schools. Lynn George's testimony read, "I have been told frequently and earnestly by several building principals that, 'I'd hire a woman if I could find one interested or qualified.' I am reminded of the Seattle School Board memo of 1948 which read, 'Will hire a Negro if a competent Negro can be found.'" The Eugene board did not alter its position, and revealed a "chilly climate" for women in administration in the district while reiterating their affirmative action goals. Now in 1993 in that district, 35 percent of the central administrative staff, including the superintendent, are female, and Lynn who was told she could "kiss her job good-bye," became a respected middle school and high school principal in that district. This is a happy-ending story; the second story does not have such a happy ending.

A woman filed a sex discrimination suit against the Confederation of Oregon School Administrators. She eventually lost the suit, but the filing itself caused divisiveness in Northwest Women in Educational Administration. While she is now an administrator in a large district in Oregon, she left the state for several years following her suit. Although she entered the suit in the interest of *all* women administrators, many women administrators were opposed to such a "radical" action. Women advocacy groups in educational administration have not, by and large, used the courts to fight discrimination and in fact, typically are opposed to such actions.

By the late 1970s several women's advocacy groups emerged across the nation; they formed because they were excluded from the "old boys club," because they had seed money to formally organize, because they were committed to increasing the number of women in administration, because a few courageous souls brought legal action, and because they learned collective action could bring pressure to hire more women administrators.

The Catalysts for Change

The vanishing woman in educational administration took on personal meaning for some women educators. Practitioners, academics, and employees within state departments became the catalysts for change in their state or region. They took individual initiative, funded or not, to breach the tide of vanishing women in educational administration. These are some of their stories.

The California Network of Women Educators

Women seeking administrative positions in public schools found the doors closed against them because of their sex. Doris Prince formed Women Leaders in Education in Santa Clara, California in 1972 and along with Mae McCarthy and Vi Owen convened eighty-two women informally at the San Jose Hyatt House that year to organize women in administration. A few years later, Barbara Peterson started a group in southern California. In 1975 Barbara Peterson and Jessi Kobayashi called the first meeting of the Women's Caucus of the Association of California State Administrators Conference and brought together 120 women administrators. They met because "there should be some way to bring all these California groups together, we could help each other, we could be more powerful together than we were separately" (phone conversation with Peterson and Kobayashi, 1992). Not only did the advocacy groups for women administrators cooperate across the state in forming the California Network of Women in Education (which at one time had about fourteen different regional groups), they were actively engaged with other equity groups and people such as Barbara Landers and Dee Grayson of the Department of Education, and were founding members of the Coalition for Sex Equity in Education.

Career Women in Educational Administration (1975–78)

Doris Timpano organized Career Women in Educational Administration during 1975–78 in Long Island, New York. An informal group was formed and her documentation was one of the first on discriminatory hiring practices in educational administration (Timpano and Knight 1976).

Northeast Coalition of Educational Leaders

Sally Dias, working for the Massachusetts State Department of Education, completed her dissertation about women in educational administration in 1975 at Boston University (Dias 1975). Jackie Clement, then an assistant superintendent in Brookline, and others had published, "No Room at the Top" (Clement 1976). Dias, Clement, Cecilia DiBella, and others called a meeting "because we were startled about the numbers of women in educational administration. We came together on the need for support. We all believed we could be of some assistance" (phone conversation with Dias and Clement, 1992). In 1976 they met at Simmons College and, with the support of Jeanne Speizer and Kathleen Lyman, became members of the Institute for Women in Educational Administration. By-laws were written, funding was received by Project AWARE, and by 1979 NCEL (Northeast Coalition of Educational Leaders) opened its headquarters under the directorship of Lenore Hersey. "The vision for a few had become a reality for many" (Regan 1988). Today NCEL is a volunteer dues-paying organization serving nine states in the northeast.

Castle Hot Springs, Arizona, 1976–1985

Debbie Dillon, self-described as a "radical, naive 26-year-old," was appointed as Sex Equity Coordinator in the Arizona Department of Education by Carolyn Warner, then state superintendent. "No one expected me to do anything. You must remember what Arizona was like in 1976; we hadn't passed the ERA, male administrators attitudes were awful. It was a very conservative place and nothing was happening. I didn't know what to do so I traveled the state to find out *if* anything was happening. Things were happening; there had been a workshop on "Free and Female" at Tucson Valley High School, five women had gone to the 1975 conference that Effie Jones put on for women superintendents, and Myra Dinnerstein at the University of Arizona browbeat me into thinking more creatively. So we put on our first conference at Castle Hot Springs—which was a perfect place for it. Castle Hot Springs is a peaceful oasis, a historical setting of neutrality among the various Indians tribes. At Castle Hot Springs one does not fight. We brought in Jessie Kobayashi, Effie Jones, and Barbara Peterson. In this peaceful oasis we created wonder women" (phone conversation with Dillan, 1992).

Castle Hot Springs was funded by Project AWARE, and reached into Colorado and New Mexico; the program provided an intense three days of interaction, preparation for job interviews, and conversation with administrators. Debbie Dillon left Project AWARE, and at their last Castle Hot Springs conference in 1984, women in Arizona, Colorado, and New Mexico decided to continue as volunteer organizations.

NWEA Training Conference for Women Administrators

The NWEA (Northwest Women in Educational Administration) conference, similar to the program at Castle Hot Springs, invited nominations from superintendents to send promising women administrators to the conference. I addressed the second conference, at Alderbrook Resort in Washington. Then I argued that women had learned the "power of association and the value of herself" and she was replacing the old boy network—one that is informal, unconscious and private—with a new system, one that is formal, conscious and public (Schmuck 1986). John Erickson, then a superintendent of schools in Oregon, the only male to attend the full three days of the women's conference, delivered a speech about the "Politics of School Administration." He betrayed secrets, told stories, and gave advice. He likened administration to playing hardball. He said, "If you can't play hardball, get off the field." Yet I noted the incongruity of his statement: even with equal opportunities for females in athletics, when females play ball, what do they learn to play—*soft*ball.

Women's Advocacy Groups Formed after 1985

By 1985 funding for Project AWARE had ended and WEEA had reduced funding and commitment for equity since the Reagan administration (see Faludi 1991), yet the picture for women in educational administration had changed; the "vanishing" woman administrator was no longer on the road to extinction. The "old boys club" began to incorporate women; in fact, all of the seven advocacy groups constituted after 1985 are formally affiliated with the once male-dominant state administrator organization or their state department of education. Project LEAD (Leadership for Educational Administration Development), funded in 1988, provided some new support for administrator training and several states saw fit to include a focus on women in administration (see U. S. Department of Education 1992). And the NWEA in 1992 forged a new working agreement with the Confederation of Oregon School Administrators. The need for a separatist organization changed since 1977; in 1992 there was a new climate for inclusion.

NWEA/COSA Mentorship Program

In 1987 Boyd Applegarth, then president of the Confederation of Oregon School Administrators, met with me to explore a more harmonious and collaborative relationship between COSA and NWEA. We developed a mentorship program including twenty selected administrative protégés, with a focus on women and minorities, matched with twenty practicing administrators in districts other than their own. The two meet and devise a plan for developing leadership skills. Four annual dinner meetings bring together all protégés with their mentors to share their experience (Pence 1989).

The Future for Women's Advocacy Groups in Educational Administration

"One of the reasons we struggle now is that our original purpose has changed. We have evolved to another stage. We have to change because what we have done is no longer currently compelling or useful," said Barbara Peterson in a phone conversation. I agree. But what is the future? Our heady belief of 1977 was that we could increase the number of women school administrators and change administrator practice.

Has the number of women in administration increased? Yes. The data are clear. The percentage of female principals has risen from 13 percent in 1977 to 34 percent in 1993, most of these are at the elementary school level (Montengro 1993). Deputy and associate superintendents rose from 5 percent in 1977 to 24 percent in 1993, and superintendents from 2 percent in 1981 to 7 percent in 1993. Yet the glass ceiling has not been broken in educational administration, especially in the high school principalship and the superintendency. While equity or parity has not been reached in administration, the trends demonstrate modestly heartening changes.

Has the entry of women in educational administration changed administrative practice? Perhaps. The new call for administrative leadership, which has taken hold concurrently with the push for gender equity, is how women have been stereotyped; it is a call for engagement, participation in decisions,

213

paying attention to the human side of organizations, and raising the place of individual efficacy over organizational efficiency. The restructuring movement calling for the empowerment of teachers, site-based management, and decentralization of authority is in line with the positive stereotypes of female leadership. This leads authors such as Sally Helgeson (1990) to proclaim the *female advantage* in leadership.

Whether gender, as a psychological variable, affects the practice of leadership is still questionable (e.g., that an individual woman administrator will behave differently than an individual man administrator), it seems the theory, practice, and culture of administrative practice is changing as the proportion of women in educational administration increases. Perhaps it is a spurious correlation, yet I am encouraged by the studies in this volume, and my own experience with women administrators who struggle to find their own voice as they bring their female heritage to the bureaucracy of schools, that a more democratic way of administering is emerging, one that views administration in its original meaning, "to minister."

The Future

What of the future? What should be the focus of advocacy groups for women? I have four recommendations:

1. *Women advocacy groups in educational administration should concentrate less on a woman's personal desire for career entry and advancement.* Women's advocacy groups in educational administration have focused almost entirely on the aspirant. To women who would enter educational administration we have given advice, critiqued resumes, and prepared for job interviews. We have done our work well for individual women although more work needs to be done in rural areas and on supporting women for the positions of superintendent and high school principal. A focus on individual women aspirants should be a *part* of an advocacy group's agenda, but not the primary part.

2. *Women advocacy groups in educational administration should focus more on the traditional female stereotyped concerns of child welfare.* Day-care, teenage pregnancy, abused children remain on the periphery of schools, While "the family as first teacher" has successfully operated for many students, more and more students come to school without the academic readiness to perform successfully. Women's groups, in alliance with other organizations, should help refocus the school's concerns to the child's welfare.

3. *Women's advocacy groups in educational administration should better address the problems of practicing women administrators.* Those women already in positions not only grapple with the problems of their job, but often find themselves as a "lone" woman, or in a male dominat-

ed culture that does not value or support their leadership attempts because they are women. Those women need support, yet they eschew another meeting on an already full agenda; they are already over-taxed and over-burdened. Calling a meeting for "support," will not draw practicing women administrators. Many women in administrative positions today have benefited directly or indirectly from the efforts of women's advocacy groups, Although, while they have "drawn water from the well," they sometimes do not know how to "replenish the well" with their already crowded agenda. We must help them find ways to "replenish the well." I have two suggestions:

a) *Make sure that women administrators are included on the program and agenda of conferences in your state.* Women's advocacy groups can assist your state administrators association, school boards association, and teachers groups to assure women's voice is heard. It need not be about a "woman's perspective" but about more general educational matters. Recognition and contact with other administrators can be an important part of women's success.

b) *Establish linkages between women aspirants and women administrators.* The Oregon Mentorship program, in its sixth year, is a easily managed program. It matches twenty protégés with twenty practicing administrators yearly and conducts four dinner meetings yearly to gather and talk (Pence 1989). It has been as important to practicing administrators who have been in the position of teaching about administration, as it has been to the protégés. The program uses the leadership skills of practicing women administrators and allows them to contribute to future administrators; it enables them to replenish the well from which they have drawn.

4. *Women's advocacy groups in educational administration should concentrate, and even celebrate, the values of caring.* They should be in the foreground of calling women and men of all races and ethnic groups into the new forms of leadership, calling for democracy, collaboration and caring (Noddings 1984). The new restructuring movement calls for the administrators to take on the more traditional female stereotype of empowering others, taking a back seat to a wielding authority, and leading through teaching about democratic values, commitment and patience.

Conclusion

Advocacy groups for women administrators should continue to grow and flourish. There is something special and celebratory for same sex members of all races and ethnic groups to come together; perhaps one of the most compelling and powerful experiences that women have in the conferences and workshops for women is the camaraderie, the shared unspoken assumptions, and the revelation of one's experience which is understood. It has been proclaimed as overwhelming, a life experience, something "where my toes met my brain in a new way, I was whole."

I hope women's advocacy groups for women in educational administration will continue to grow and to flourish, but the agenda of 1977 clearly is not the agenda of the future. Even though our past agenda has not been fully realized we have evolved now to a new stage, a stage on which the quality of human existence in schools is the focus. I hope women's advocacy groups in educational administration will continue into the twenty-first century with an even more humanistic agenda than it has today.

Advocacy Groups for Women Administrators in The United States, 1993

AASA Women's Caucus. (American Association of School Administrators), 1975.* Dr. Joan P. Kowal, Superintendent, Volusia County School District, 200 North Clara Ave., P.O. Box 2118, DeLand, Florida 32721-2118. (904) 734-7190.

AASA Women's Advisory Council. (American Association of School Administrators). Eleanor Anderson-Jackson, Assistant to the Superintendent, North Chicago Community School Dist., 2000 Lewis Avenue, North Chicago, IL 60064. (708) 689-6318.

Northeast Coalition of Educational Leaders Inc. Linda Connaly, 83 Boston Post Rd., Sudbury, MA 01776. (508) 443-0064

Northwest Women in Educational Administration. 1977. Christine Tell, Confederation of Oregon School Administrators, 707 13th Street SE, Salem, OR 97301. (503) 581-3141

By State

Alaska. Northwest Women in Educational Administration, 1980. Elaine Hopson, Juneau School District, 10014 Crazy Horse Drive, Juneau, AK 99801. (907) 463-1700.

---

*Indicates year formed when available.

Arizona. 1984. Pat Boykin, Assistant Principal, Alhambra High School, 3839 West Camelback Road, Phoenix, Arizona 85019. (602) 271-2003.

California, San Diego. San Diego Council of Women Administrators (NCAWE), Dr. Michele Marcus, Marston Middle School, Principal, 3799 Clairemont Drive, San Diego, CA 92117. (619) 273-2030.

California, Tustin. Southern Counties Women in Educational Management, Peggy Lynch, Assistant Superintendent, Tustin Unified School District, 300 S. "C" Street, Tustin, CA 96280. (714) 730-7309.

California, Newport Beach. Dr. Barbara Peterson, 232 Hartford Drive, Newport Beach, CA 92660.

California, San Jose. Women Leaders in Education, Santa Clara County, 1972. Kay McDonald, President, 100 Skyport Drive, San Jose, CA 95110-1374. (408) 453-6899.

Connecticut. Northeast Coalition of Educational Leaders. Elizabeth Walters, Windsor HS, 50 Sage Park Rd., Windsor, CT 06095. (203) 688-8334.

Colorado. Jeanette Ray-Goins, Director, Educ. Equity Programs & Services, Colorado Department of Education, 201 E. Colfax Avenue, Room 206, Denver, CO 80203. (303) 866-6680.

Florida. Florida AWARE, 1987. Joyce Skaff, Executive Director, Crown Management Consortium, 1725 SE 1st Avenue, Gainesville, Florida 32601. (904) 336-3640.

Idaho. Northwest Women in Educational Administration in Idaho, 1985. Virginia Foote, McMillan Elementary School, 10901 McMillan Road, Route #4, Boise, ID 83707. (208) 888-6700.

Illinois. Illinois Women Administrators, 1979. Hazel Loucks, Executive Director, Southern Illinois University, Educational Administration, Higher Ed., WHMN Bldg. #0322, Carbondale, IL 62901. (619) 536-4434.

Indiana. Indiana Network of Women Administrators, 1981. Martha McCarthy, Professor, Educational Administration, Indiana University, Bloomington, IN 47405. (812) 855-5362.

Iowa. Iowa Women in Educational Leadership, 1984. Judy Hendershot, The University of Iowa Student Placement Office, Iowa City, IA 52240. (515) 281-5068.

Kansas. Kansas Women in Educational Leadership, 1975. Gail Campbell, Central Elementary School, 1311 Main St., Goodland, KS 67735. (913) 899-6558.

Kentucky. Kentucky Institute for Women in School Administration, 1985. Toni Wilson, Coordinator, Kentucky Institute for Women in School Administration, 1121 Louisville Road, Frankfort, KY 40601. (502) 875-3411.

Maine, Portland. Women in Administration, Maine Leadership Consortium, and NCEL (Northeast Coalition of Educational Leaders), 1989. Betsy McElvein, Chair, Women in Administration, Hall School, 23 Orono Rd., Portland, ME 04102. (207) 874-8206.

Maine, Augusta. Nelson Walls, Director, Maine Leadership Consortium, University of Maine System, 16 Winthrop Street, Augusta, ME 04330. (206) 623-2531.

Massachusetts. NCEL (Northeast Coalition of Educational Leaders), 1975. Carole Thomson, Department of Education, 1385 Hancock St., Quincy, MA 02169. (617) 770-7536.

Maryland. Maryland Network for Women in Educational Administration, 1989. Linda Shevitz, Maryland Department of Education, 200 West Baltimore St., Baltimore, MD 21201. (410) 333-2239.

Michigan. Professional Women's Network. Hattie Brown, Principal, Bennet Elementary, 2111 Mulane, Detroit, MI 48209. (313) 849-3585.

Minnesota. 1991. Jay Norris, Educational Foundation, Bemidji State University, Bemidji, Minnesota 56601. (218) 755-3767.

Missouri, Jefferson City. Network for Women in School Administration, 1987. Judy English, Leadership Academy, Department of Elementary and Secondary Education, Jefferson City, MO 65102. (314) 751-0807.

Missouri, St. Louis. Sharon Shockly Lee, Webster University, 470 E. Lockwood, St. Louis, MO 63119. (314) 968-7070.

Nebraska. Annual Women in Educational Administration Conference. Marilyn Grady, University of Nebraska, 1212 Seaton Hall, Lincoln, Nebraska 68588. (402) 472-3726.

New Hampshire. NCEL (Northeast Coalition of Educational Leaders.) Linda Raines, Asst. Principal, Dover HS, Locust St., Dover, NH 03820. (603) 742-3172.

New Jersey. NCEL (Northeast Coalition of Educational Leaders.) Theodore Martin, One Redford Drive, Clinton, NJ 08809. (908) 735-5045.

New Mexico. New Mexico AWARE, 1981. Sharon Fox, Education Building, 300 Don Gaspar, Santa Fe, New Mexico 87501. (505) 827-6511.

New York, Albany. New York State Association for Women Administrators, 1990. Anne O'Brien Carelli, Executive Director, CASDA-LEAD Center, SUNY-Albany, 135 Western Ave., Husted 211, Albany, NY 12222. (518) 442-3796.

New York, Hempstead. Coalition for the Advancement of Women of Color in Education. Carol Shakeshaft, Professor and Chair, Administration and Policy Studies, Hofstra University, Hempstead, NY 11550. (515) 463-5758.

North Dakota. North Dakota LEAD Center. Rita Kelly, Educational Equity Assistant Director, ND Department of Public Instruction, 600 East Boulevard Ave, 9th floor, Bismarck, ND 58505. (701) 224-2271.

Ohio, Cincinnati. Network for Women in Educational Leadership, 1980. Nancy Evers, Professor, College of Education, University of Cincinnati, ML 0002, Cincinnati, OH 45221. (513) 556-6623.

Ohio, Worthington. Donna Kelley, Evening Street Elementary, 885 Evening Street, Worthington, OH 43085. (614) 431-6520.

Oregon. Northwest Women in Educational Administration in Oregon, 1977. Confederation of Oregon School Administrators, 707 13th Street, S.E., Salem, OR 97301. (503) 581-3141.

Pennsylvania, Pittsburgh. Women's Caucus of Pennsylvania Association of School Administrators, 1985. Maureen McClure, 5 S03 Forbes Quad, Administrative and Policy Studies, College of Education, University of Pittsburgh, Pittsburgh, PA 15260. (412) 648-7114.

Pennsylvania, Philadelphia. Philadelphia Council of Administrative Women in Education (NCAWE), 1970. Marylouise DeNicola, 2340 S. 16th St., Philadelphia, PA 19145.

Rhode Island. NCEL (Northeast Coalition of Educational Leaders,) Josephine Kelleher, Superintendent, Woonsocket, RI, 108 High St., Woonsocket, RI 02895. (401)767-4600.

South Dakota. SD Administrative Women in Education, 1991. Norma Jean Denault, Asst. Superintendent, Rapid City Schools, 300 6th St., Rapid City, SD 57701. (605) 394-5147.

Utah. Utah Women Educational Administrators Association, 1986. Mary Peterson, Utah State Office of Education, 250 East 500 South, Salt Lake City, Utah 84111. (801) 538-7647.

Vermont. Suzanne Ming, RR#2, Box 34A, Lyndonville, VT 05851. (802) 626-3783.

Washington. Northwest Women in Educational Administration in Washington, 1978. Mary Lynne Derrington, Port Angeles Public Schools, Port Angeles, WA 98362. (206) 457-8575.

Wisconsin. 1985. Melissa Keyes, WI Department of Public Instruction, P.O. Box 7851, Madison, WI 53707. (608) 267-9157.

Bibliography

Adkison, J. (1979). Ambiguity, structure and organizational stress in the ICES structure: Linking organizations for educational equity. Project Report: Internships, Certification, Equity—Leadership and Support. The University of Kansas, Lawrence, Kansas.

———. (1981). Women in school administration: A review of the research. *Review of Educational Research*, 51(3), 311–43.

Berg, B. (1978). *The remembered gate: Origins of American feminism*. New York: Oxford University Press.

Biklen, S.K. (1987). Women in American elementary school teaching: A case study. In P.A. Schmuck (ed.), *Women educators: Employees of schools in Western countries*. Albany: SUNY Press.

Bystydzienski, J. (1987). Women's participation in teachers unions in England and the U.S. In P.A. Schmuck (ed.), *Women educators: Employees of schools in Western countries*. Albany: SUNY Press.

Clement, J., DiBella, C., Ekstrom, R., Tobras, S., Bartol, K., and Alban, M. (1977). No room at the top. *American Education.* U.S. Office of Education, 20–26.

Dias, S. (1975). A study of personal, perceptual and motivational factors influential in predicting the aspiration labels of men and women toward the administrative roles in education. Unpublished dissertation, Boston University.

Donovan, F. (1938). *The School Ma'am.* New York: F. Stokes Company.

Edson, S. (1980). Females' aspiration in public school administration: Why do they continue to aspire to the principalship?" Unpublished dissertation, University of Oregon, Eugene.

———. (1987). *Pushing the limits.* Albany: SUNY Press.

Etzioni, A. (1969). *The semi-professions and their organization.* New York: The Free Press.

Evers, N.A., Ross, H.G., Kaminski, N.K., Van Epps, S., Klemt, L.L. (1980). *Developing interpersonal competencies in educational leadership: Instructors' manual for the leadership module.* Cincinnati: University of Cincinnati Press.

Faludi, S. (1991). *Backlash: The undeclared war against women.* New York: Crown Publishers.

Ferguson, K. (1984). *The feminist case against bureaucracy.* Philadelphia: Temple University Press.

Fishel, A. and Pottker, J. (1974). *National politics and sex discrimination in education.* Lexington, MA: Lexington Books.

———. (1977). Women in educational governance: A statistical portrait. *American Educational Research Association Journal,* July-August.

Follettt, M.P. (1949). *Freedom and coordination.* London: Management Publications Trust.

Grady, M. and O'Connell, P.A. (1993). Women in K–12 educational administration: A synthesis of dissertation research. *Journal of School Leadership,* 3(1).

Gribskov, M. (1980). Feminism and the woman school administrator. In S. Biklen and R. Brannigan (eds.), *Women and educational leadership.* Lexington, MA: Lexington Books.

Gross, N. and Herriott, R. (1965). *Staff leadership in public schools: A sociological inquiry.* John Wiley and Sons.

Gross, N. and Trask, A. (1964). *Men and women as elementary school principals.* Final report 2, Cooperative Research Project no. 853, Graduate School of Education, Harvard University, Cambridge, MA.

———. (1976). *The sex factor in the management school.* New York: John Wiley and Sons.

Hare, N. (1966). The vanishing woman principal. *National Elementary Principal,* April, 12–13.

Helgesen, S. (1990). *The female advantage: Women's ways of leading.* New York: Doubleday.

Hopson, E. (1985). Evaluation of Northwest women in educational administration. Unpublished dissertation, University of Oregon, Eugene.

Hoffman, N. (1981). *Woman's "true" profession.* Old Westbury: Feminist Press.

Kempner, K.M. (1979). A conceptual framework for the evaluation of planned change. Unpublished dissertation, University of Oregon, Eugene.

Lortie, D. (1975). *School Teacher.* Chicago: University of Chicago Press.

Lyon, C. and Sarrio, T. (1973). Women in public education: Sexual discrimination in promotions. *The Kappan,* 2(55), 120 –24.

Matthews, E. (1986). Women in school administration: Support systems, career patterns and job competencies. Unpublished dissertation, University of Oregon, Eugene.

Mattson, S. (1990). Oregon women elementary principals: Their attitudes about leadership goals, mission, and sex equity. Unpublished dissertation. University of Oregon, Eugene.

McManis, J. (1916). *Ella Flagg Young.* Chicago: A.C. McClurg.

Montenegro, X. (1993) Women and Racial Minority Representation in School Administration. Arlington, VA: American Association of School Administrators.

Neidig, M. (1976). The rise and decline of women administrators. *American School Board Journal,* June.

Noddings, N. (1984). *Caring.* Berkeley: University of California Press.

O'Connor, J.F. (1970). Changes in the sex composition of high status female occupations: An analysis of teaching. Unpublished dissertation, University of Illinois.

Ortiz, F. (1982). *Career patterns in education: Women, men, and minorities in public school administration.* New York: Praeger.

Paddock, S. (1981). Male and female career paths in school administration. In P. Schmuck, W. Charters, and R. Carlson (eds.), *Educational policy and management: Sex differentials.* New York: Academic Press.

Patterson, C. and Milligan, V., (no date). The history of NCAWE (National Council of Administrative Women in Education). Unpublished paper from Barbara Stockton, Washington, D.C.

Pearson, C., Shavlick, D., Touchton, J. (1989). *Educating the majority: Women challenge tradition in higher education.* New York: Collier Macmillan.

Pence, J. (1989). Formal and informal mentorship for aspiring and practicing administrators. Unpublished dissertation, University of Oregon, Eugene.

Pougiales, R. (1981). A case study of a social change project. Unpublished dissertation, University of Oregon, Eugene.

Prentice, T. and Alison, M. (eds.) (1991). *Women who taught: Perspectives on the history of women and teachers.* Buffalo: University of Toronto Press.

Regan, H. (1988). *Northeast Coalition of Educational Leaders, Inc. Annual Report,* Sudbury, MA.

Sadker, M., Sadker, D., Klein, S. (1991). The issue of gender in elementary and secondary education. *Review of Research in Education.* Washington, DC: American Educational Research Association.

Schmuck, P. (1975). *Sex differentials in public school administration.* Arlington, VA: National Council of Women in Educational Administration.

———. (1979). *A state of the art conference: Women in educational leadership.* Unpublished conference papers, Asilomar Conference, CA.

———. (1982). *Sex equity in educational leadership: The Oregon story.* Newton, MA: Education Development Corporation.

———. (1986). Networking: An old name, a new game. *Educational Leadership,* February, 60–61.

Schmuck, P. and Spencer, W. (1981). Clues to sex bias in the selection of school administrators: A report from the Oregon network. In P. Schmuck, W. Charters, and R. Carlson (eds.), *Educational policy and management: Sex differentials.* New York: Academic Press.

Shakeshaft, C. (1981). Women in educational administration: A descriptive analysis of dissertation research and paradigm for future research. In *Educational policy and management: Sex differentials,* P. Schmuck, W. Charters, and R. Carlson (eds.). New York: Academic Press.

————. (1987). *Women in school administration*. Los Angeles: Sage.

Smith, M.A., Kalvelage, J., and Schmuck, P. (1982). *Sex equity in educational leadership: Women getting together and getting ahead*. Newton, MA: Educational Development Corporation.

Stockard, J., Schmuck, P., Kempner, K., Williams, P., Edson, S., and Smith, M. (1980). *Sex equity in education*. New York: Academic Press.

Stockard, J. (1982). *Sex equity in educational leadership: An analysis of a planned social change project*. Newton, MA: Educational Development Corporation.

Taylor, S. (1973). Educational leadership: A male domain. *Phi Delta Kappa*, 2(55), 124–28.

Timpano, D. (1976). Sex discrimination in the selection of school district administrators: What can be done? Washington DC: National Institute of Education.

Tyack, D. and Hansot, E. (1982). *Managers of virtue*. New York: Basic Books.

U.S. Department of Education. (1992). *Strengthening support and recruitment of women and minorities to positions in education administration*. Washington, DC: Superintendent of Documents.

Williams, P. (1980). The impact of anti-sex discrimination laws on the employment of Oregon school principals. Unpublished dissertation, University of Oregon, Eugene.

Wolcott, H. (1975). *The man in the principal's office*. New York: Holt, Rinehart and Winston.

TWELVE

The Trouble with Change: A Conversation between Colleagues

Willi Coleman and Patricia Harris

The larger issues that face women in education—and women in society as a whole—are often reduced in reality to a personal, daily struggle. What follows is the story of two women (one white and one black) who were friends and colleagues, and who had their relationship shaken by events that veered beyond their control.

The voices we use are our own. We are not speaking "for" other women of our race or class. Rather, we are exploring our own intertwined history in order to enhance our future.

Much has been written recently on the need for feminist research to include issues of importance to women of color. The phrase "women and minorities" has become an integral part of present day political rhetoric.[1] It is used with regularity in discussing the elimination of oppression throughout society. In most instances there is little question as to how—or if—women and minorities fit together historically, politically, or programmatically. When discussed at all, the question is most often couched in the language of "How do we add women of color" to our program? The broader and more critical issue is to revise our visions of "women's issues" and "racial issues" so that in both instances race and gender are given equal consideration. This is the story of one campus where women's and racial issues left the realm of theory and became an agonizing reality.

San Luis Obispo, California, is a city of 42,000 people. It is situated directly between Los Angeles and San Francisco on the central coast of California. Nestled in a lovely valley between the Coast range and the Pacific Ocean, it has for the last fifteen years been steadily attracting refugees from the smog of southern California and from the crowds in northern and central California. There is virtually no heavy industry in the area: the biggest employers are the State of California and the County of San Luis Obispo; and its population is overwhelmingly white upper-middle class.

Just north of the center of town sits California Polytechnic State University. Established in 1901 as a vocational high school, Cal Poly admitted women as part of the first class, but then excluded them for many subsequent years. For a long time, female students were concentrated in the areas of home economics and physical education, but they now make up 42 percent of the student population, and are well represented in every major. Cal Poly is known at the "lily" of the Cal State system. In a state where minorities make up 43 percent of the population, Cal Poly has retained an ethnic imbalance overwhelmingly in favor of whites. Add to that, a faculty composed for the most part of white males; and you have a campus that goes beyond feeling "chilly" for females and ethnic minorities. The climate is described by many as hostile and threatening to both groups.

Until 1989–90, Cal Poly was the only California State University with neither a Women's Studies nor an Ethnic Studies program. While there were campus-based informal advocacy groups for each program, their members continually felt a sense of invisibility and powerlessness. Although never in overt opposition to one another, the advocacy groups seemed to run on parallel tracks with very little crossover and no integration from one group to another.

One of the few visible events for women on campus was an International Women's Day celebration, which was first observed in the early 1970s under the aegis of the then Dean of Women. She nurtured that special day and other women's programs until 1981, when Willi Coleman, newly arrived on campus, began to take over some of that dean's duties. Under Coleman's direction, Women's Day became Women's Week and it became more firmly entrenched as an annual event of interest.

By 1984–85, Women's Week had become an event that was important to many people on campus. Faculty members welcomed the opportunity to present papers in their own community, staff members had a chance to be relieved of their duties and listen to a speaker or two, and students were able to learn outside of the classroom in a campuswide conversation.

Patricia Harris (PH): I happened upon Women's Week within a few months of beginning a new job at Cal Poly. I went to hear a speaker on African-American women. The speaker was so eloquent and inspiring, I was (much to my chagrin) moved to tears during her presentation. That speaker was Willi Coleman. I was inspired and emotionally touched by her. It had been almost five years since I had been involved in women's issues. I had been concentrating on sheer survival, raising two daughters as a single mother. Now I wanted to be back in the company of women, working for common goals. The next time I saw an announcement for a Women's Week planning meeting, I was there.

Many of the women who would eventually identify themselves as the "core group" for women's issues on campus started to work on the planning of Women's Week in 1985. Women struggled with pride to work together with minimum concern about status. Coleman, as leader, had the final say in case of deadlock, and she presented the agenda for each meeting, keeping the group on task as necessary; but otherwise there was very little formal group structure. The "core group" was one of the rare social settings on campus where there was no status differentiation between faculty and staff. Tasks were assigned to whomever volunteered for them. For staff women especially, the group's dynamics were liberating. Women's Week was an event to break out of job descriptions and try new things. New strengths and talents emerged for all participants. In a happy coincidence, at this same time, State lottery money became available to the University for special projects that would not otherwise be funded. Women's Week was one of those special projects, and in the next few years, continued its steady growth, supported by the funds of California gamblers.

PH: I started out in the group rather quietly, new to the campus and somewhat awed by the women with Ph.D.s. I soon realized that within this group, while visionary ideas were welcomed, it was up to each woman to carry her ideas to fruition. We used to joke that if you suggested it, you were put in charge of it. Since I was employed at the time as a clerical assistant, performing tasks that were rarely challenging, Women's Week meetings became the focus point of my work week. I discovered competencies and abilities I had never been aware of. One of the first projects I undertook was to bring a black women's repertory group from San Jose to perform Ntozake Shange's "for colored girls who have considered suicide when the rainbow is enuf." I did everything, from negotiating their contract to having the tickets printed, including hosting a cast party after the performance. The only disappointment was that Willi didn't come to the party.

Over the next five years, Women's Week grew from a day of modest events to a week-long extravaganza, attracting thousands of participants from the campus and community. Community planners began to coordinate their events with Women's Week, so events spilled over from the campus into the town. Responding positively to Coleman's prodding, women of color were invited to become members of the group, and programs were organized with a thematic focus suggesting acceptance of differences among women.

Working together on the planning committee created strong bonds among the women involved. In addition to weekly meetings, the women shared much of the rest of their lives. By 1988, the group expanded to create a Woman's Coalition, drew in other women who were not engaged in Women's Week per se, and produced a quarterly publication, featuring writing and art of men and women at the university. The Women's Coalition had a year-long spurt of vibrant activity, but in 1989, with its members suffering from the burn-out that seems to be endemic to women's groups, it faded away. Among the casualties was Coleman, who had organized the group and served as its leader for many years. While feeling many of the same "burn-out" symptoms expressed by other group members, she had an additional concern.

> Willi Coleman (WC): For almost nine years I had been the only woman of color to regularly participate in the planning group. While others had occasionally attended, the only way I could ensure having another women of color present was to pay someone as a student assistant. This quasi-solution lasted for a year, but when it became clear that the group was ready to continue the situation without making any fundamental changes I realized that it was going to have to be I who made the change. What followed was a complete and thorough break between the group and myself. While relations remained cordial, there was very little comprehension of my insistence that the group would continue to be monoracial unless attempts were made to more seriously incorporate the concerns of women of color. The usual pattern of focusing on inclusive language and of attempting to bring specific "big name" women of color as speakers had not effectively opened the group to women of color.

At this point three staff women volunteered to assume responsibility for co-ordinating the upcoming Women's Week, and the program was assured of existing for at least one more year. At the end of their 1990 tenure, the tired triad vowed never to volunteer for that responsibility again. They felt the need for someone to be in charge, and wanted to have women's issues validated by the creation of a women's center, with a full-time director to run it, and Women's Week.

> PH: I fully expected to have a chance at the position of director. I had been involved in Women's Week for several years, and during the last year had been one of the three coordinators. I even helped write the job description for the

position we requested. While Willi would have been a logical choice, considering her qualifications and experience, I somehow assumed that she would not be interested. In our infrequent conversations during the past year, Willi had seemed quite interested in teaching full-time, and had not expressed much concern with what was going on with Women's Week. I never really questioned her as to why she was no longer interested; and instead threw myself into the campaign to create a woman's center. These were heady times for us, many of whom had come of political age during the 60s. This was throwback to that time—we were ready to take over the Administration Building if we had to.

Quickly gathering support, a kind of grass roots drive for a women's center began. Petitions were circulated, community support was enlisted, and resolutions were presented in the academic Senate. The effort was empowering to the women who were part of it. They were finally going to get a place of their own. It was out of their feelings of empowerment that the seeds of an upheaval that would ultimately split the campus were sown.

The women who were the driving force in the campaign for a women's center were predominantly majority culture women. The place that they envisioned was one where they would feel comfortable. When they noticed that women of color were not significantly engaged, they expressed a certain kind of peevishness: "once again, *we* have to do all the work, and *they* will reap the benefits." They never questioned their implicit belief that what benefited them would benefit all women.

> WC: The group was unaware of or chose to ignore the work of women and men of color who had waged a continuous and often public battle to make ethnic diversity a part of university life. Focusing on the impact which an "essentially all-white university" was having on both white and nonwhite students; men and women of color, joined by a few white males, were increasingly involved in documenting and calling attention to the escalating racism on campus. The group's activities ranged from meeting with administrators, to a letter-writing campaign, and agitating for a formal Ethnic Studies program. Concurrently, students via ethnic clubs and organizations regularly programmed events and speakers that focused on issues ignored by the rest of the campus. I concentrated my energies on working with the Committee on Ethnic Diversity in order to make gender a central issue within the proposed Ethnic Studies program.

Even those majority culture women who were familiar with the Ethnic Studies campaign failed to see a connection between the two groups. They also failed to see the fiscal storm clouds gathered on California's horizon. By the middle of the 1989–90 academic year several issues converged. There was, first, the threat and then the reality of California's budgetary deficit. Faced with the loss of a hundred million dollars in funding, California State University trustees prorated the deficit throughout the twenty-campus system.

The impact at Cal Poly included a 10 percent increase in student fees, shorter library hours, and elimination of some programs and "streamlining" of others. In accordance with regulations, lists of impending layoffs were drawn up and expected raises were delayed.[2]

Second, Women's Week needed a home and the demands for a women's center and an ethnic studies center continued to escalate. Women's Week was particularly vulnerable. Heavily staffed by volunteers, funded with "soft" money, with no official home in a particular department or division, but with a high demand for campus wide services, it presented a serious liability for any administrator who might willingly agree to assume responsibility for it.

At this point, the vice president for student affairs (an African-American woman) agree to house the women's center in Student Affairs, if the monoracial nature of the center was addressed. The Center for Women and Ethnic Issues was born. However, what could have been a solution also became a battleground. With tenure of less than three years on campus, the vice president had clearly established a new direction for student affairs. She had sent out an unmistakable message, reemphasizing the division's commitment to welcoming, serving, and working with diverse ethnic groups. She also created opportunities to discuss and respond to the 1990 census report describing California as an increasingly multiracial, multicultural society. Communication of her fundamental commitment to a multicultural university, however, was not clear to the women who had been agitating for a women's center. Their understanding was simply that they were finally getting a place of their own, even though they would have to share it.

At that point, the situation got ugly. Unconscious racism and the arrogance of white privilege reared its ugly head. Not being privy to any of the internal machinations that led to the creation of a Center on Women and Ethnic Issues, the white women who were presented with it as a fait accompli interpreted the administration's decision according to their own worldviews.

PH: We felt cheated and manipulated. We were sure that we had amply demonstrated the need for a women's center and we fully expected the administration to pay attention to our demands. Now we were getting a center, but it wasn't what we wanted. There was talk of a conspiracy—after all, Willi Coleman, who was appointed to direct the new center, was the vice president's friend. Willi had withdrawn from the Women's Week last year, without even telling anyone why. There was a recurring image of young men hanging out in what should have been a women's center—an image with racist overtones. It was sometimes articulated, but didn't even need to be, that these would be young, black men—probably with huge radios playing rap music. There was a feeling that in combining women's issues and ethnic issues, the administration had thrown a bone to the two stray dogs of the campus in order that they might tear each other apart over it. What went unrecognized in general was that there might be concomitance in women's and ethnic issues. The feeling on the majority women's part was that we had always tried to include women of color in our events' planning. We had tried to do the right thing—now why were we being punished? That feeling disclosed the unconscious racism that existed. Why was having to join forces with people of color—men and women—felt to be a punishment? Perhaps it wouldn't have felt that way if we had been allowed the luxury of choosing such an alliance. Perhaps having no choice in the matter is what made it such a bitter pill to swallow. But, perhaps if we had a choice, the alliance may never have been forged.

WC: It was clear to me that the primary issue was to get women's programming institutionalized. Time was of the essence since the budget and state regulations regarding expenditures were in flux. With long-term state employees being laid off, the campus could not create a new position—director of the center. However, administrators—as always—had the power to move employees within their own divisions. The vice president, exercising the same power and authority as white males in her position, offered the job to the most qualified person in student affairs. Not only was it personally insulting but also, I thought, astoundingly politically naive, for people whom I considered friends to choose to ignore both my academic qualifications and my time in the trenches. I had a Ph.D. with research focus in multicultural women's history, plus seventeen years of involvement with women's issues in colleges and universities, including the creation and administration of a women's center at Yuba College, Marysville, California. Additionally, I was already a part of the division of student affairs, which made it administratively more feasible to appoint me director of the new center.

In protesting the combination of women's and ethnic issues, the women's advocacy group now began to mirror traditional university hierarchical behaviors. Staff women who had assumed primary responsibility for women's programming previously found themselves increasingly shut off from influence as faculty women began more and more to assume the mantle of leadership. Also, direction began to come more from women who had very little previous involvement. While the open and informal nature of the group's structure had had a positive effect in the past, now established norms of consensus and support began to break down.

PH: Looking back, it's strange to see how easily we accepted this mode. We staff women looked to faculty women to call meetings with the administration, and we felt powerless to do so. We trusted the faculty women to speak for us, and it wasn't until I was invited to one of these meetings that I began to feel uncomfortable with the situation. It was a lunch-hour meeting, and the vice president for academic affairs made it clear that he would rather be somewhere else, and that this was really something we could have cleared up among ourselves. To my

231

surprise, I agreed with him. At this point I was ready to concede that we had not gotten what we wanted, and get to work with what we had. I could identify with the pain that some of the women still felt at having come this far only to see the door slammed in their faces; but for me, the pain was beginning to recede and I wanted to get on with it. Willi was not present at these meetings.

Each woman engaged in the strife resolved the conflicts in her own way. Some withdrew from the group entirely, a painful loss for them and the others. Many moved their attention to the arena of Women's Studies—feeling that if the center was not going to be a "women's place," they would create an alternative place of their own. The problem with that tactic was that women's studies at Cal Poly was an "orphan" field, housed in Liberal Arts, but with no funding, no release time for coordinators, and minimal institutional support. Some women stayed with the core group that evolved around the new center and served on its advisory board. They tried to redefine oppression in terms not only of gender, but also of race and class. Each of these individual choices was made in a highly emotional, economically strapped, and politically charged situation.

WC: At about this time I had moved to what was a new, but increasingly clear position for me. I was unwilling to invest much more of my time in the education of majority culture women. To me the work at hand was to continue the momentum which had clearly surfaced around the new center. The center was now a reality and my feeling was that we could choose to work together or allow our disagreements to continue to destroy any possibility of alliance. Recognizing Pat's struggle to understand the dynamics of the whole gender and race issue, and in honor of the friendship we had shared, I was willing to make one last tangible effort to bridge the gap. I gave her a reading list.

PH: I reconnected with Willi, and tried to repair the fabric of our friendship, which had been stretched but not completely torn. We met and had innumerable phone conversations that summer. Willi was so angry that she scared me, in part because I carried such guilt that I felt I deserved to be the object of her wrath; but in time I began to understand more and more why she was angry. At one point she suggested that I lead a group in studying African-American feminist writings. I felt in no way qualified to do so, but armed with the reading list Willi provided, I ordered enough books to keep me occupied all summer. I immersed myself in the writings of bell hooks, Johnetta Cole, and Paula Giddings, but it was a mimeographed copy of Peggy McIntosh's "White Privilege: Unpacking the Invisible Knapsack;" that really served as the one clarifying piece that brought everything else into focus. It was the lens under which I examined my emotions and reactions of the past year, and which I used as a guideline in dealing with issues that continued to erupt.

Meanwhile, the Center for Women and Ethnic Issues thrived. Attracted by the center, and unfettered by a knowledge of its troubled history on campus, students came with fresh ideas and an untrammeled, naive enthusiasm. By the end of its first year, responding to the students, the neophyte center had become home to many projects and groups. Without being conscious of it, the students were following the most effective path toward forging true coalitions across class, race, and gender boundaries: they were working together on projects that had captured their individual interests. The reproductive choice group, for instance, is the most diverse. Its membership encompasses men and women in all shades between black and white. Another group has formed a film production company, and is seeking grant money to create videos on rape, child abuse, and sexual harassment. A black sorority gravitated toward the center, bringing its own agenda and incorporating its ideas into the ongoing events and groups. There has been no question of how to "fit in" issues that that are important to women of color, because these young women have taken matters into their own hands. If it is important to them, it is by virtue of their enthusiasm important to everyone at the center.

All of this movement has been informally-initiated and self-propelled. The women faculty and staff who were seasoned in the struggle to create the center now accept that they alone will not have the final say in what the center is about and have made their individual choices in response to that political reality. Those who are still engaged are now "shifting gears" to participate with students in shaping the future direction of the center. Work goes on: redefining women's issues so that race and class—as well as gender—are central to the programs that we create and support.

> PH: I still feel saddened at times, when I look around at a meeting and realize how few of my old friends are present. Some of them are actively involved in women's studies now, some are busy with individual projects of their own. I try not to wax nostalgic, however, and instead concentrate on the new talent that has emerged and new friendships that are evolving. I am pleased with what the center has become. It is a center for women, but it excludes no one. It is a center for ethnic issues, but it is comfortable for people of all colors. It is not a retreat from the world, but rather a center of activity and a broader base for political action.

> WC: For me, the continuing evolvement of the center is a microcosm of what must occur within the women's movement as a whole. People who are part of the center are already accepting of the concept of equal commitment to the issues of gender and race. I feel released from the obligation of having to educate majority culture women about my personal and historical reality and instead can concentrate on the future—which belongs to all of us.

233

The center is still too new to serve as prototype for other institutions, but there are some specific lessons we've learned that may apply to others. First, learning to live with ambiguity is a milestone on the way to maturity, especially through the uncharted paths of feminism and ethnicity. Second, sharing control, as we did, may be the only way to keep a vision alive. Finally, a crucial element of leadership is the ability to listen, guide, and follow.
For the two of us, our evolving working relationship and friendship has transformed our own lives, and has certainly changed the way we envision the future of the Center for Women and Ethnic Issues. It remains to be seen whether or not "our center" will transform the institution.

Notes

1. Norma Riccuci, *Women, minorities and unions in the public sector* (New York: Greenwood Press, 1990); Alison M. Konrad, and Jeffrey Pfeffer, "Understanding the hiring of women and minorities in educational institutions," *Sociology of Education*, 64(3), 141; "Promotion and tenure of women and minorities on medical school faculties," *Annals of Internal Medicine*, 114 (1).

2. *CSU Stateline*, California State University, September 1990 and October/November 1991; *Mustang Daily* (Cal Poly), 4 April 1991; *Cal Poly Report*, 31 October 1991; *The CSU Academic Senator*, 8 November 1991.

THIRTEEN

Administrative Women and Their Writing: Reproduction and Resistance in Bureaucracies

Joanne E. Cooper

> Power is the ability to take one's place in whatever discourse is essential to action and the right to have one's own part matter.
>
> —Carolyn Heilbrun, *Writing a Woman's Life*

This study provides a special opportunity to witness how women in administration think privately about their professional work. The research addresses the question, "What are administrative women's reflections on bureaucratic pressures?" Through an analysis of the activity and meaning of journal writing to ten senior-level women administrators, ways in which their personal discourse both reproduces and resists bureaucratic pressures are revealed. Reading the journals of these administrative women allows us to look at how they think about inclusion and resistance to bureaucratic life. Their writings, which reveal efforts to empower themselves and to effect organizational change, may prove instructive to women in educational administration.

Effects of Bureaucratic Life

Ferguson's definitive critique, *The Feminist Case against Bureaucracy* (1984), describes the pressures faced by women working within complex or-

235

JOANNE E. COOPER

ganizations. A discussion of Ferguson's points about the multiple dilemmas women confront in organizations provides a context for the examples of journal writing in these ten women administrators I studied. According to Ferguson, in addition to the everyday problems of managers (e.g., budgetary problems, questions of curriculum, personnel problems, etc.), women in educational organizations face particular dilemmas related to gender expectations and role relationships. Educational bureaucracies, such as schools and colleges, have been conceived and constructed by men and have historically been dominated by men, especially at the upper levels of administration. Women enter such organizations as "the other." Women in administration thus face pressures due to their gender, their position as token women in a predominantly male world, due to their tenuous status as organizational members, and due to their role as managers in the top levels of organizations.

First, women face pressures to conform to male bureaucratic structures and norms, to speak and behave in the rational, linear modes that constitute the way of life in bureaucracies. As administrators, women are identifiably different. They clearly do not "fit in" because they are not male. Ferguson (1984, 107–8) described the pressures faced by tokens, those who are visibly "different from the main stream in sex, race, age, language or some other salient trait":

> The token is highly visible and thus stands out, getting attention from superiors, subordinates, and peers that both creates performance pressures and also exaggerates the contrast between the token and the ordinary personnel.

Thus, both the pressure and the social distance from colleagues isolate women.

Rosabeth Moss Kanter's classic work (1977) on women as tokens who represent all women, reports that those in the token positions face a number of dilemmas and contradictions. Tokens are the quintessential "individuals" in their organizations because they stand apart from the mass of their peers. Yet they lose their individuality and sense of self because they are pressured into taking stereotyped roles and into playing the part of the token. Kanter found that self-repression and refraining from personal expressiveness are part of the culture in any large organization, but that those are especially true for people taking on a token role.

Minnich (1984, 184) clearly defined the dilemma of prefixed or token persons, such as women vice-presidents or women principals: "To want and need the approval—and the jobs—offered by the very world that sees us as 'women in general' first and individuals as a very poor second . . . that accepts us only as long as we are willing to be exceptions or to assimilate, is twisty, painful, and familiar to us all." As marginal persons who are defined by their marginality first and their individuality only as a very poor second, women in educational administration need a place for self-definition, a place to define themselves as individuals rather than as exceptions.

Self-definition for administrative women then entails not only who they are, but who they are against the backdrop of the bureaucratic worlds in which they live. They struggle to live in male-dominated worlds that often do not accept them and yet tempt them with the promise of inclusion. For women, organizational inclusion is often won at the cost of trivializing themselves from their female peers. The dilemmas faced by women in authority also include decisions about how to try to change their bureaucratic worlds while trying to secure a place in them (Jacobson 1985).

Second, as organizational members, women face pressures to conform, to follow and enforce rules, to adhere to and reproduce or support bureaucratic procedures. Bureaucracies impinge on both men and women in a variety of ways. Ferguson (1984, 8) claimed that "the institutions of mass society converge on the individual in ways that induce conformity," thus erasing individual identity and replacing it with normalized behavior in the form of rules to "make" organizational members "behave" (Arendt 1958, 40).

Beyond pressures for conformity and isolation, women face further layers of pressure within bureaucratic structures. A second layer arises as individuals move up the organizational structure. Ferguson (1984, pp. 105–6) states that the higher one moves in the organization, the more important impression management skills become. . . . At the top levels officials require more demonstrations of loyalty to the organization and to each other in order to compensate for the relative absence of formal rules. Thus, women, like all administrators, are expected to show more loyalty and commitment to the organization as they move into positions of higher and higher authority. They also are more easily swept into the chaos of complex organizational life (Peters 1987), an experience which can be both disorienting and exhausting.

Methodology

Sampling

This study examined "native" journal-keepers, those who had kept a journal for a year or more and who held senior-level positions within their organizations. It was qualitative in nature in that the data appeared in sentences and paragraphs rather than numbers. This study was part of a larger study of reflective practices in administrative women (Dunlap 1989).

Sampling in this study followed two of the three procedures suggested by Burgess (1984). In part, the sampling was one of judgment and opportunity and in part, it used a snowball technique. The members of the Northwest Women in Educational Administration and the members of a women's leadership seminar held on a university campus were asked to nominate peers from various organizations that they believed were effective managers or administrators. The criteria of selection required that each subject be nominated by two peers and hold a senior-level position within their organization; in other words, they had to supervise at least two levels of administrators below them. Nominees were then asked if they kept a journal or a diary. Ten women journal-keepers were interested in participating in this study. Of the ten, six were educational administrators, such as a director of continuing education, a director of graduate studies, and an elementary school principal. Of the remaining administrators, two were in the field of business, a corporate vice-president and a CPA, and two were hospital administrators, a director of nursing, and a director of community relations. Their years of experience ranged from three to twenty-seven.

Procedures

Each participant was given an initial information sheet to provide background, after which I conducted on-site observations and in-depth interviews. Participants were interviewed two or three times in a setting of their choosing. The interviews were semistructured; a series of questions and accompanying probes were covered, but not in any particular order. Topics were explored as they emerged in the interview and included questions about how and why each participant kept a journal, when and where they wrote, what they used their journals for and in what ways it had been most useful to them. They were asked what they thought keeping a journal had taught them, how it had affected their life both personally and professionally, if there were things they did not write in the journal, if they ever went back and reread what they had written, if they shared it with others, and so on. The interviews ranged from one to three hours in length and took place in private homes, in offices at work, in school buildings at the end of the day, in restaurants, and in cars. These people were all extremely busy and were interviewed wherever and whenever possible. Participants were asked to contribute any diary excerpts they felt comfortable reporting. In some cases, excerpts were read aloud. In some cases excerpts were photocopied. In one case, an entire diary was donated to the study.

All interviews were recorded and transcribed. Confidentiality was insured through the use of code names and numbers. The analysis followed Miles and Huberman's (1984) general qualitative procedure of data reduction, data display, and conclusion drawing/verification. In part, participants were asked to assist in the reduction of data by generating metaphors for themselves as journal-keepers or the journal-keeping process. Guided by Glaser and Strauss's (1967) model of the discovery of grounded theory, the concepts generated here are derived through a comparative analysis. Conceptual categories were derived from the data and the evidence from which the category emerged was used to illustrate the concept.

Results

Although there are many reasons for keeping a diary or journal (Cooper 1987) and many ways in which journals are used (Cooper and Dunlap 1991), this study focused on the effects of life in bureaucracies and responses to bureaucratic pressures which can both be found in the personal writings of these administrative women. The women in this study all live and work in bureaucracies. The activity of writing is an attempt to make meaning of both their public and private lives and to help them form cohesive identities as members of these bureaucratic organizations. The bureaucratic pressures outlined in Ferguson's work (1984), to conform, to demonstrate loyalty, to fit in and to reproduce bureaucratic rules and functions are evident in these women's writings. Two major results of these pressures, stress and isolation, are clearly illustrated. In addition, evidence of these diarists' efforts both to reproduce and resist bureaucratic functions can be seen.

Stress and Isolation

The pressures these women face can be dissected into categories, those faced by all members of bureaucracies, those faced by administrative members, and those faced by women as token organizational members. Yet in reality, these pressures have a cumulative effect on women in administration. These multiple stressors are experienced simultaneously. Administrative women often do not have or take the time to sort out the cause of the pressure they face. They are too busy trying to cope, as seen in the following journal entry:

> Talking to myself, here's a great line: "Don't lose it at this time, lady." You appreciate little words of wisdom captured painfully on the page. So . . . where am I? Fried from the surging and suffering whiplash from the sudden stops.

This woman does not stop to define where the pressure is coming from. She merely offers words of support and advice and goes on to name her response to the stress she is feeling.

In addition to stress, isolation is a by-product of the bureaucratic and administrative lives these women lead. Ferguson (1984) has clearly outlined the ways in which bureaucracies break down social networks, replacing them with rigid role definitions, thus isolating organizational members. Bureaucracies continually pursue stability through the mechanism of control. Bureaucratic functioning is predicated on the need to eliminate uncertainty through rational management. In the process, bureaucracies isolate members through role definitions that do not acknowledge members as whole or individual persons. This system of roles isolates human beings by cutting them off from both others and themselves (Ferguson 1984).

Kanter's work (1977) described the isolation tokens experience in the workplace. Administrative work, which can be "lonely at the top" adds a third layer, leaving no doubt that one of the greatest pressures administrative women face is that of isolation. Colleen Bell (this volume) reports on the great lengths women in the superintendency will go to in seeking some solace against the isolation they feel. The following journal excerpt reflects that isolation and illustrates how journals function as support:

> It's just one of those little blobs that I just wrote really quickly . . . and it ends with a statement about where am I going to find help at two-thirty in the morning . . . and there wasn't anybody I was going to call at two-thirty to say . . . I'm not doing very well here."

The journal seems to function as a support mechanism here, a place to turn at hours when no one is around. In addition, private writing helps diarists to keep in touch with themselves, with what they are feeling and thinking. Their writing then becomes a compensation for the ways in which prescribed role behavior isolates organizational members from themselves, as well as others. Although journal writing may provide women solace and help them regain a sense of who they truly are, the very activity of private writing might tend to isolate them all the more. Kanter (1977) asserted that female administrators suffer from their aloneness, while the dynamics of male interaction around them may create a pressure for them to seek advantage by disassociating themselves from female peers and hence to remain alone. She further asserted that even the best coping strategies under these circumstances may have some internal repercussions, ranging from inhibition of self-expression to feelings of inadequacy and, perhaps, even self-hatred.

Reproduction and Resistance

In writing about their public and private lives, and in examining their personal identity and social interactions, The women in this study offer a nonbureaucratic vision of collective life to heal the breach between public and private life and to replace bureaucratic forms with a different vision of organization. Their writing may thus be seen as a form of resistance. Yet these women are after all administrators; they hold some power to control and regulate the lives of others. As administrators they experience enormous pressure to conform to the established procedures that keep the the institution running effectively. In a sense, they are practicing bureaucrats at the same time that their writing and thoughts resist some bureaucratic procedures.

Using Bureaucratic Norms Evidence of the effort to both conform to bureaucratic norms and to control them can be found in the journals of these administrive women. One response to the chaos of administration is to increase control of the self. Self-control is a typical bureaucratic response and so it is not surprising to find it employed by women who have been successful in those bureaucracies. The following excerpt describes a director of education's efforts to provide the self with rules or guidelines:

> I can remember writing things down, particularly in the first few years I was in administration, of things I wanted to remember about how to interact, what were some kinds of rules. I wanted to remind myself of situations I didn't want to get in again . . . some things about reacting, not responding immediately to something you're not completely sure about . . . and giving myself enough time to really think about something before I made a decision. I wrote those down, and I wrote them down directly after experiences I had that were not particularly successful.

Controlling the self through one's own rules and goals is one way to deal with the bureaucratic rules and goals women face. This woman's efforts to set down written rules for herself is one way of understanding bureaucratic demands and of "fitting in" or succeeding by adhering to those demands.

Yet more is going on here than just setting goals and making rules. In the next passage, a corporate vice-president reflects on who she is and who she wants to be in the workplace. Her efforts to define herself and her own goals are a form of resistance. She states:

> This is the kind of thing I do at work a lot, frankly. I sit down and say, wait a minute, you know, I'm getting swept away by a lot of stuff going on here, let me remember what's important to me. . . . Recently, when I'm feeling like I don't know what's going on, I want to set some rules for myself because that's the way I'm going to be able to sort my way through it. . . . I have a sheet of goals in my desk. I write this down and have it right in the center drawer of my desk. I pull it out and I read it and go, "OK, I got what I'm doing." And a lot of it is, have a positive attitude, you know, basics, nothing real esoteric here, but just the way I want to live my life, who I want to be. And you can lose that pretty easy under the pressure of things pulling you different ways. . . . So it's an anchor.

Given the enormous pressure to adhere to impersonal, male-defined, bureaucratic demands, the writing of these women reflects both conformity and resistance. Their written rules and goals help them both to conform to the norms of bureaucratic life and to resist the pressure of outside forces.

Honoring Rational and Subjective Epistemologies A second form of reproduction and resistance to bureaucratic life can be found in these women's epistemological choices, choices about whether to honor subjective feelings more or rational thought. The writing of these women can make them more conscious of their feelings and put rational thought in perspective. When they reflect on who they are in the workplace, an examination of their own identity can provide them with choices, thus helping them to reflect on resistance. One woman wrote:

> I had a thought at the symphony tonight. Feel I am more and more able to select the right reaction for a situation, tune it to the appropriate mental, emotional, social part of my brain and being, so that I'm using logic and reason when it's called for, using common sense, emotions, spirit, when they're called for.

Here we see her choices at work, choices about whether to use her rational side or her affective side to respond to a particular problem or situation. The use of logic and reason follows bureaucratic functioning, while emotional or spiritual responses do not. Simply providing herself with choices is a form of resistance to an organization which demands automatic disinterested rational responses.

A second example of epistemological pressure is reflected in the following passage describing the demands for rational, administrative thinking, the requirement that administrative women think in rational modes, in the bureaucratic manner of their male counterparts. In coming to grips with these epistemological demands one woman wrote,

> I trusted a feeling of calm that embraced me as I thought about my school administration test. After all, it was just explaining my own work, but unrelatedly or abstractly so, (and that) left me writeless. But I must say I struggled for some logical piece of information and tracked it back to the cortex of my mind. Maybe I'll get them counted correct. . . . I'm feeling compelled to say goodnight Pat, sleep tight, and don't worry . . . the bedbugs . . . won't bite.

In this passage we witness the bureaucratic pressures for rational thought processes which can, in effect, silence women in the workplace. Max Weber, famous for his theories on the nature of bureaucracy, argued that the quest for rationality was itself a mode of domination (Morgan 1986). This woman's journal functions as a place for her to reflect on the domination of rationality and provides personal support for her affective struggles.

Adhering to Personal Value Systems The pressure to perform placed on all administrators as they move up the organizational hierarchy tends to push them toward rushed and automatic responses. One woman, a director of continuing education, said when she was offered the job she has now, her boss was fired and she was asked to replace him: "I was told on a Friday, and . . . the dean said, 'Well I'm telling you Friday so you'll have the weekend to think it over.' And I said, 'I don't need to think it over. I'll take the job.'" She was asked to replace her boss, continue to do her job (no one replaced her), develop new programs, and continue to bring in the same amount of income per year that the unit always had. She stated:

> But I don't regret it because, you know why I did this? I did not do it for money or prestige. I did it to see how my character is developing because it would force me to be visible, and to develop qualities I needed and not to hide from the bad ones I had. It would either make or break me.

This woman has been very successful by organizational standards. She has managed to meet the budgetary goals of the organization with half the staff. She has survived by keeping her eye on who she wants to be, not the goals she "should" meet. She is conscious of the pressures her job places on her and resists those pressures by adhering to her own code of behavior.

> Along with the . . . common ordinary code of behavior for being a professional, I have my own personal one and it's real important to me and it's very much a caring kind of a mode. I wouldn't say that there's an absence of evil, but let me give you an example. We have a board in the office . . . where we keep enrollment figures . . . and a lot of how I'm judged is by (the) income (from enrollment). I've had three male bosses since I've been there. Every one of them would hover over the mail every day, see what the enrollment was, watch it go up on the board, and either pat themselves on the back and say, "I'm OK because my enrollment figures are good," or "Oh god, I must not be OK." And I just shake my head. I look at those things and I think, "Isn't that great that that course is going to go," or "I don't have to cancel this one." . . . I've been so into the process that I wasn't even aware 'til three months ago that we were going to make this income figure. It wasn't that I didn't care, I did, but I knew I was doing the best I could and there was . . . nothing else that I could do.

This woman adheres to and reproduces bureaucratic procedures in doing the best she could do to meet the organization's goals. Yet she simultaneously resists bureaucratic pressures by defining her own personal code of behavior, one she interestingly alludes to as "an absence of evil."

Conclusion

In response to bureaucratic pressures, women in administration have learned to reflect on their organizational lives in order to survive and advance in the hierarchy. They carry their female views with them into the male bureaucratic realm and must consciously put some of them aside to "succeed" in this world on its own terms. Yet the women in this study continue to resist some of the organization's most central tenets, by carrying out a private discourse with themselves through their journals and by resisting the depersonalized relations bureaucracies encourage. Even as they resist, however, these women actively recreate and passively fall victim to male dominance. As Ferguson claimed (1984, 24), "It does us no service to ignore or downplay either of these sides, nor to overlook or simplify the complex dialectic by which they are intertwined." Instead of overlooking or simplifying administrative women's response to bureaucracy, this study subjects their personal writing to the scrutiny of the public eye in an effort to unveil the "complex dialectic" at work in everyday lives.

Ten women's journals reveal ways in which they simultaneously conform to and resist bureaucratic procedures. Scrutiny of their journals allows us to see how they traverse the territory between inclusion and resistance to life in bureaucracies. Their writings allow us to understand the dilemmas women face in the struggle between assimilation and exclusion, and provide us with the experiential data needed to begin to transform bureaucratic workplaces. The journals reveal the day-to-day issues, obstacles, ambitions, problems, and solutions that women in managerial positions face. Reading them moves us from the theoretical to the practical, from potential power to possible action.

Through their efforts to define personal value systems in their writing, these journal-keeping administrators have learned to use narrative power to produce "texts which . . . teach us what it means to be knowing creatures, what it means to know ourselves as selves. They teach us about the relationships between cognition and emotion, between reason and passion, between the mind and the body, between epistemology and politics" (Pagano 1990, 12).

Administrative women, with their lists, goals, and journals, are claiming their place in the discourse of their professions, moving from reflection to action, and making a difference in their organizational workplaces. Through their resistance to bureaucratic pressure, with deliberate efforts they are transforming the small spaces they occupy. Granted they are part of the bureaucracies that stifle human growth and potential. Granted they use the rational, linear goal-setting procedures so prevalent in the institutions they inhabit. Yet they are, as Heilbrun stated (1988, 18), taking their place "in whatever discourse is essential to action." By moving from discourse to action, and claiming their right to have their own part matter, these women can function as influential agents of change.

Bibliography

Arendt, H. (1958). *The human condition.* Chicago: University of Chicago Press.

Bell, C. (1995). 'If I weren't involved in schools, I might be a radical': An analysis of women superintendents' gender consciousness. In D. Dunlap and P. Schmuck (eds.) *Women leading in education.* Albany: SUNY Press.

Burgess, R. G. (1984). *In the field: An introduction to field research.* London: George Allen & Unwin.

Cooper, J. E. (1987). Shaping meaning: Women's journals, diaries and letters, the old and the new. *Women's Studies International Forum,* 10(1), 95–99.

Cooper, J. and Dunlap, D. (1991). Journal keeping for administrators, *The Review of Higher Education,* 15(1), 65–82.

Dunlap, D. M. (1989). Differences between men and women administrators in four settings. Paper presented at the annual meetings of the American Educational Research Association, San Francisco, March.

Ferguson, K. (1984). *The feminist case against bureaucracy.* Philadelphia: Temple University Press.

Glaser, B., and Strauss, A. (1967). *The discovery of grounded theory: Strategies for qualitative research.* New York: De Gruyter.

Jacobson, A. (1985). *Women in charge: Dilemmas of women in authority.* New York: Van Nostrand Reinhold Co.

Heilbrun, C. (1988). *Writing a woman's life.* New York: W. W. Norton.

Kanter, R. M. (1977). *Men and women of the corporation.* New York: Basic Books.

Miles, M. B. and Huberman, M. A. (1984). *Qualitative data analysis.* Beverly Hills, CA: Sage.

Minnich, E. (1984). Hannah Arendt: Thinking as we are. In C. Ascher, L. DeSalvo, and S. Ruddick (eds.), *Between women*. Boston: Beacon Press.

Morgan, G. (1986). *Images of organization*. Beverly Hills, CA: Sage.

Pagano, J. (1990). *Exiles and communities: Teaching in the patriarchal wilderness*. Albany: SUNY Press.

Peters, T. (1987). *Thriving on chaos*. New York: Harper & Row.

FOURTEEN

Women in Educational Administration: Views of Equity

Evelyn Nelson Matthews

What do women administrators think about women administrators? Is there one unified voice, or are there differences in how women are viewed? Do their career paths influence their views of themselves and their views of other women in administration?

To answer these questions, I conducted twenty-nine in-depth interviews with women superintendents, assistant superintendents, high school principals, and assistant principals in Oregon public schools. I asked questions about careers, issues confronted by women administrators, sex-role stereotyping, sex discrimination, and perceived problems of isolation. Women expressed their opinions regarding many of these issues—anti-sex-discrimination laws and separate professional organizations for women. From these interviews, four distinct points of view emerged: activists, advocates, isolates, and individualists.

Women categorized as "activists" cared passionately about issues of gender equity and actively supported efforts to correct the imbalance of women in educational administration. "Advocates" supported women, joined advocacy organizations, and expressed the view that women bring unique strengths to school administration. "Isolates" detached themselves from issues related to equity; most didn't believe that sex discrimination really existed, and, in most cases, never gave this issue much thought or even saw it as a problem. Lastly, "individualists" believed the individual, male or female, took precedence over the group. They did not promote women nor did they believe in any kind of countermeasures to correct the sexual imbalance in school leadership. In reality, these four categories are not discrete—they may be regarded as on a continuum that represents the points of view of individual women. Furthermore, this continuum represents points of awareness whereby each women's experiences, including her administrative career path, has created the lenses through which she views issues of sex equity in administration.

I examined how the women in this study viewed the following issues: (*a*) women in administration, (*b*) men in administration, (*c*) their own careers, (*d*) support for other women, (*e*) their experiences of sex discrimination, (*f*) their opinions about remedies to overcome discrimination such as the courts and legislation, and (*g*) their opinions regarding advocacy organizations designed to support women in educational administration. A matrix showing the interaction of points of view and issues of sex equity in administration is displayed in the appendix. Categorization by Women Administrators' Points of View Regarding Issues Related to Sex Equity in Educational Administration.

An interesting pattern began to emerge as I examined the data related to perspectives of sex equity issues and to sources of support women received as they entered and advanced in administration. Each woman discussed sources of support as coming (*a*) from people in the district in which she was teaching—her principal or some other significant person in the district; (*b*) from people or organizations outside her district, such as friends or organizations outside the district; or (*c*) from her own personal initiative—women who persevered in spite of obstacles and lack of support from district sources.

Moreover, the source of support was closely tied to career patterns. A woman who acquired her first administrative position in the district in which she last taught had a one-district career pattern and support came most often from district sources. A woman who moved to a different district to obtain her first administrative position had a two-district career pattern and received support from outside sources or from her own initiative. Table 1 shows that women who have one-district career patterns overwhelmingly receive district support: 86.6 percent of those entering administration and 73.3 percent of those advancing in administration. On the other hand, women with two-district career patterns enter or advance in administration through their own initiative or outside sources: 57.1 percent enter administration through their own initiative. And as the following analysis will show, these women did, indeed, speak in different voices.

Different Voices: An Analysis of Points of View

Activists

Women in the activist category—which includes women from all four positions: superintendent, assistant superintendent, principal, assistant principal—demonstrate an active involvement in issues related to sex equity, from the local school level to the national level. They are concerned about national issues such as current threats to affirmative action guidelines and Supreme Court rulings that limit sex and racial gains. They speak of their struggles to overcome sex-role stereotypes and sex discrimination. They are knowledgeable about sex-equity laws and use them to their advantage and to the advantage of others. Their lives have been touched in a manner that propelled them to become active participants.

Nearly all of the women in this category (83 percent) entered administration by their own initiative; all have two-district career patterns. Some activists struggled and persevered a long time before getting their first administrative position. Clearly, they entered administration because they had a mission—they cared deeply about a particular cause or issue and that motivated them to continue to pursue administration.

One activist said of her entry into administration,

> I thought, "There's absolutely no college teaching for me. I want to be a school administrator. This is exactly what I want to do." I think that one of the reasons I got hooked on administration was because it dawned on me that school administration was where you could begin to make some things happen.

After persevering for many years to enter administration, another described her mission:

> I had some very definite ideas on opportunity for people and on avenues that could be opened up for people through education. I think the education system not only discriminates against women, but it discriminates against minorities to a major degree and, even though we have seen progress there, that's still a problem. I think I'm able to influence policy and behavior of teachers to a tremendous degree and I think behavior eventually changes attitude. But even if behavior doesn't change attitudes, if I am able to change behavior to allow young people more opportunities, that is very satisfying. . . . To me, it has been very rewarding to be able to influence the philosophy of the schools and the behavior of teachers.

Activists are older than women in the other categories—an average of six to ten years; 50 percent are married. Furthermore, most activists had experienced a change in consciousness similar to what many women went

TABLE 14.1
Sources of Support for Women in Educational Administration by Type of Career Pattern

	Women in Category		Sources of Support							
			Entering Administration						Advancing in Administration					
			District		Own Initiative		Outside		District		Own Initiative		Outside	
Career Pattern	n	%	n	%	n	%	n	%	n	%	n	%	n	%
One-District Career Pattern	15	51.7	13	86.6	2	13.4	0	0.0	11	73.3	2	13.3	2	13.3
Two-District Career Pattern	14	48.3	3	21.4	8	57.1	3	21.4	5	35.7	3	21.4	6	42.9
All Women in Study Total	29	100.0	16	55.2	10	34.5	3	10.3	16	55.2	5	17.2	8	27.6
Mean Percentage														

TABLE 14.2

Characteristics of Women Administrators, Career Patterns, and Sources of Support by Points of View Regarding Sex Equity in Administration

| | Women in Category | | Age | | | Percentage Career Pattern | | Sources of Support | | | | | |
| | | | | | | | | Percentage Entering Administration | | | Percentage Advancing in Administration | | |
Category	n	%	Mean	Range	% Married	One-District	Two-District	District	Own Initiative	Outside	District	Own Initiative	Outside
Activists	6	20.7	50.2	45–53	50.0	0.0	100.0	0.0	83.0	17.0	33.0	33.0	33.0
Advocates	11	43.0	43.0	35–54	63.0	55.0	45.0	64.0	18.0	18.0	55.0	18.0	27.0
Isolates	5	17.2	44.0	32–47	100.0	80.0	20.0	60.0	40.0	0.0	80.0	20.0	0.0
Individualists	7	24.1	40.8	27–45	86.0	71.0	29.0	86.0	14.0	0.0	71.0	0.0	29.0

through during the women's movement and consciousness raising groups of the 1960s and 1970s. In describing her transformation, one assistant principal said:

> I know the event, actually. I had again left a position to go with my husband to a new job. We sat down on the couch and were talking about, "Could I go back to school? Maybe get my degree?" And he agreed to let me return to college as long as I was able to maintain the house and keep the children and do all those other things—as long as it didn't interfere. My reaction? I was absolutely thrilled that this person gave permission. I started back to school and there was talk in the universities, and I read articles and books; and suddenly, I guess it was gradual, but it seemed like practically overnight, it just dawned on me that I had submerged myself, my identity, into everything else. I absolutely didn't know who I was.

Forming new groups and identifying with other women is essential in the transition to a new consciousness and women in this category valued their female relationships. One woman said, "I think the fact that NWEA (Northwest Women in Educational Administration) was there gave me a lot of permission."

Huws (1982) and others (Berger and Luckmann 1967; Rowland 1984) stress the importance of making connections with other women who may be going through similar changes. Huws argues:

> The group plays an enormously important role in affirming this change in personal identity and social reality. The group's language . . . is the principal means by which this affirmation is achieved (Berger and Luckmann 1967). In order for the initial conversion to become a permanent change, continued involvement with the group which shares the same identity and worldview is essential. This is true whether the larger society is actively hostile and oppressive or merely unsupportive of the new identity. Feminists know how important, indeed essential, group support is. (pp. 408–9)

One woman who had moved to a smaller district missed the support she had received from female colleagues in her larger district where there were more women in leadership roles: "Because of the size of the district, this has been very . . . almost uncomfortable for me, because of my lack of support groups or my female colleagues."

Reflecting on her struggle to become a high school principal, another said:

> I began to be more influenced by the women's movement. And there is no question but that the people who were radicals paved the way for those of us who came later. There is absolutely no question that nothing would have happened if people sat back and denied. So I owe a great deal to the people who were re-

ally abrasive, unpleasant, ugly. It allows those of us who wanted to be a little more approachable and less assertive and less abrasive to do that. So I have no illusions and I think it's too bad that people don't recognize that there have been a lot of people who basically sacrificed their careers and made it easy for us.

Women in this category have taken an important step—to become conscious of what they know and to take responsibility for their own experience. If women undertake this task, schools will benefit because women bring dimensions of experience "which are not taught as knowledge in our schools" (Child 1981, 125). Many authors have elaborated upon the characteristics assigned by sex in our culture (Bernard 1988; de Beauvoir 1949/1952; Goh 1991; Grambs 1976; Hatcher 1991; Oakley 1981; Stockard et al. 1980).

Child (1981) describes this phenomenon and how it is translated in schools this way:

> In our culture, we tend to dichotomize our experience between dimensions designated objective/subjective, thinking/feeling, rational/intuitive, abstract/contextual, active/passive, etc. We tend to think about these polarities in either/or terms rather than both being necessary parts of the whole. Further, we tend to value one over the other creating an imbalance with powerful consequences for our understanding of the creative imagination, morality, and consciousness itself. Feminine experience is usually equated with the devalued polarity (subjective, feeling, intuitive, contextual, passive, etc.) at all levels from symbolic representation to everyday interactions. . . . Feminine dimensions of experience are exactly those which are not taught as knowledge in our schools. Curriculum tends to focus on the value of rational thinking, scientific facts and information, logical structures and objectivity. Questions of the nature of intuition, the creative imagination, subjectivity, and emotional orientations are usually not explicitly included. (pp. 122, 125)

The task of examining knowledge and taking responsibility for their experiences is difficult, particularly for women in male-dominated professions. As Bernard (1979) claims, "Women have been taught to see the world—even their own experiences—through male eyes" (p. 270). But activists have struggled and persevered to overcome obstacles in achieving leadership roles in schools. At some point in their careers they developed a "change in consciousness . . . a transition in how one understands the world and one's place in it" (Huws 1982, 408). The activists' taken-for-granted views of the world had been disrupted—perhaps, for some, it was within their personal lives, or, for others, within the course of pursuing careers in administration. These women turned to their own initiatives for support, and, somewhere along the way, they became very involved in the cause for equity in administration.

Advocates

A theme that permeates the career experiences of women in the advocate category is support—support for other women and support from other women. There are pronounced differences in the degree to which women in the various categories support each other, but the advocates consistently exhibit support, regardless of the issue being analyzed. Advocates not only support other women in administration, they express a concern about the inequities in school administration and a desire to remedy it. One women mentioned both the superintendent and board members as being crucial to the advancement of women in administration. In addition, advocates strongly support an advocacy organization for women. A principal emphasized:

> I think just the moral support and the networking is important . . . initially I thought that [the advocacy organization] should be a short-term kind of thing until we get the thing remedied. But the statistics don't show that we're getting it remedied. I mean the balance and the numbers.

They believe that women bring particular strengths to administration and they attribute these strengths to women's socialization in this culture. One woman said:

> I think there are some important traits that I think it is easier for women to develop in our culture than it is for men, and one of them is a sensitivity to where other people are. It helps enormously with your communication and with knowing when to make a particular decision and knowing when to ask questions of people that you are working with. Like just picking up on cues. Now I don't think that it is a woman's natural trait. I think that our society makes it very easy for women to become strong in that area and less easy for men to develop those kind of strengths. And they are very useful.

Another woman was aware of many of the same strengths and she, too, attributed them to socialization:

> We have a tremendous instinctual ability to read behavior and some men have it, too. But I think that as I just circle the halls in the morning, I can tell which teachers are really feeling bad, which ones need support, where the kids are. You can almost feel the tension if it's there. And you can also feel the excitement or the happiness or the relaxation. But we're more attuned to that because, I think, of the way we're brought up.

Many other women in this category mentioned these same characteristics: "Willing to negotiate." "A lot of patience." Regarding men, one woman said:

I don't think patience is a virtue of very many men. They haven't had to be patient. And they haven't had to learn to build their schedules around crying babies and wet diapers and their meals, and so forth. And I think it builds in a capacity to be a patient and tolerant person and not have to have everything right now.

Still another administrator emphasized women's background:

I think women are probably culturally trained to have some real strengths in administration and that is empathy. I don't sense that among some of my male colleagues. Just human-relation skills. And I feel there are so few women in administration—there's so much talent out there that's never been tapped. They are in the background and have those skills. They are already skilled, but they are like gifted underachievers.

Many of these same themes run through Gilligan's (1982) analysis of female moral development. Women in the advocate category exhibit many of the same characteristics that Gilligan defines: "Sensitivity to the needs of others and the assumption of responsibility for taking care lead women to attend to voices other than their own and to include in their judgment other points of view" (p. 16). And she observes, "The reluctance to judge may itself be indicative of the care and concern for others that infuse the psychology of women's development and are responsible for what is generally seen as problematic in its nature" (1982, 17). She describes how women see relationships as webs or networks rather than as hierarchies. Eventually, Gilligan develops a path of moral development for women which reaches a level of interdependence and truth (1982, 106–27).

The path that Gilligan describes is evident in the description of strengths and characteristics which women bring into administration. Related to that observation, many of the women in this category feel that schools would be better if there were a balance of men and women in administrative positions. These women reach out to others, whether in support of women coming up or to their immediate colleagues, be they men or women. Many do not describe a transformation of reality such as some women in the activist category, nor do they seem to see the world through males eyes, as Bernard (1979) describes. Their connections with both men and women seem natural and comfortable to them. This was illustrated by two women who described their connection to NWEA. One woman explained it this way:

I tried to recruit women here in the district and had a hard time. A lot of the women did not, and I can name at least ten of them, did not want anything to do with it. And I don't know why. They were afraid, I think, of being tagged with a women's group, being somehow criticized by men, which is silly, but that's what they thought and they just weren't amenable to joining a women's group.

Another women acknowledged that she had some fears of entering into a male-dominated field:

It was scary. This district has quite a number of women administrators, but they do not—or many of them do not—make contact with the other women administrators in the state or the women's administrative organization and I did not understand why they were unwilling to do that. And it's fear—I think a lot of it has been fear on their part—that if they rock the boat, then their position might be in jeopardy. But I think that more and more of us are beginning to realize that, yes, it is scary, but we do have each other and there are also some other folks out there who are willing to help us.

Thus advocates, who enter administration in about equal percentages from one-district and two-district career patterns and who receive support from all three sources (district, outside, and their own initiative) when entering into and advancing in administration, value relationships with both men and women. They advocate for women; they want to bring equity into school administration. On the other hand, women in this category have not experienced the barriers that were faced by their colleagues in the activist category. They have not entered into administration in the same ways, nor have they had the same experiences as women in the other two categories. Hence, their points of view are different, reflecting their experiences in educational administration and shaping their views of sex-equity issues.

Isolates

Women in the isolate category, all of whom are married, are detached from issues of equity in administration. They have a certain naiveté about the problems of sex discrimination in educational administration and the measures that have been taken to increase the numbers of women in leadership positions. Upon entering into administration, 60% of these women had district support and 40% pursued administration under their own initiative. As they advanced in administration, 80% received district support—the highest percentage for any of the four categories of women. Their comments regarding entry into administration reveal this entry pattern. One woman, recruited into this position by her male supervisor, stated it this way: "If, even six months before I became a principal, they had said I was going to be one, I would have laughed them out of the place."

The issue that particularly distinguishes isolates from the women in the other categories is their responses to instances of discrimination. Some acknowledge that it could exist for others, but deny any instances of discrimination in their own careers and, in fact, are not aware of discrimination in their whole area. For example, 1 woman insisted, "I don't think we've experienced it in this community or this area." Another woman maintained:

> I have never found a man in this state not to be supportive. Even men who were not supportive of women in an administrative position, sometimes give the best input as to why because when they talk to you they are frank and they usually have a very good reason why they don't think that a woman should be in that position, which is very helpful [so you can] work to make sure you don't do that particular type of thing. I have never run into a man who had a bias that was frivolous.

In response to a question about discrimination and its effect on her career one principal said:

> I haven't felt that; in fact, I've felt the opposite. I have been to meetings where I'm the only woman with a slew of men and I get this royal treatment of door openings and "May I serve you?" and so forth. I have never felt they didn't value my opinion; in fact, again, the opposite. As a woman, I was often asked, "Well, how do you feel about this?" and getting a point of view.

Another woman echoed her sentiments:

> I have never felt that I have ever been discriminated against, in fact, I felt the opposite in that I have been pushed more than I have been denied because every job or opportunity I've been asked to apply, or asked to interview, or people have told me to get in there and do it, rather than me knocking on the door. People come to me to say, "We need you," "We want you," "Come in and be our counselor," or "Come and apply for this job."

In her district, which has a low percentage of women administrators, this woman acknowledged that:

> Logically there should be more women and there must be women out there that have the qualifications that could do it, but I don't know what you do about it and I don't know what I would tell someone. I've never come in contact, or had anyone say to me, "I applied for this job and this job and this job, and I'm not getting it and I think it's because I'm a woman." And, I don't know.

One of these women answered in a manner that indicated she was treated as a token—as a symbol rather than as an individual member of the group (Kanter 1977, 208). Kanter describes skewed groups as "those in which there is a larger preponderance of one type over another, up to a ratio of perhaps 85:15" (p. 208). And indeed, women in the isolate group have an average of only 15% women administrators in their districts, whereas the percentage of women administrators in the other groups is higher: activists have an average of 26.2% women administrators in their districts; and 19.5% for both advocates and individualists. Thus isolates can be viewed as a skewed group with the likelihood that those in the minority have the potential to be treated as tokens. Kanter contends that in skewed groups those in the minority "can appropriately be called 'tokens'; for . . . they are often treated as representatives of their category, as symbols rather than individuals" (p. 208).

Tokens are treated in a variety of ways be the majority members of a group. They are highly visible, thus making their performance more public than that of the "dominants" (Kanter 1977, 212–14). Kanter found her tokens to have developed a "public persona that hid inner feelings . . . and [they] were forced into the position of keeping secrets and carefully contriving a public performance. They could not afford to stumble" (p. 214). This was verified by one administrator in the isolate group who revealed, "There are times I wonder why I'm doing this to myself. I know I will not be able to let my guard down. And I think that probably none of us should."

Tokens are often treated as category members. As Kanter explains, "Those women who were few in number among male peers and often had 'only woman' status became tokens: symbols of how-women-can-do, stand-ins for all women" (p. 207). Kanter adds: "Women were treated as symbols or representatives . . . regardless of their expertise or interest, they would be asked to provide the meeting with 'the women's point of view'" (p. 215). Some women in Kanter's study "seized this chance to be a symbol as an opportunity to be included in particular gatherings or task forces" (p. 215). "Furthermore, those women who sought publicity and were getting it in part for their rarity developed a stake in not sharing the spotlight. They enjoyed their only-woman status" (p. 220). Some of these women then kept other women out of the organization by "excessive criticism of possible new-hires or by subtly undercutting a possible woman peer" (p. 220). This resulted in the organization keeping its skewed status.

Furthermore, if women in situations such as those described by Kanter do not have a vocabulary and a theory to explain their situation, they lose much of their decision-making power about their own actions. Mueller (1973) discusses the importance of language, communication, and knowledge of a system if a person is not to be manipulated by those in authority; whereas a person with "linguistic and cognitive abilities . . . can consciously choose to support or oppose the political system and articulate interests other than those which are predefined" (p. 85).

This situation describes the women in the isolate category. They did not speak of keeping women out nor did they speak of recruiting women into the administrative ranks. They did not visualize themselves as advice-givers or as role models to other women. As one woman said, "I've never seen myself as an advice-giver; I could share my experiences—I just never know if my personal experiences are applicable or are that much of a guide." Asked about being a role model for others, another woman replied, "I don't have that feeling at all."

Detachment from issues of sex equity are apparent in statements which isolate these women from their peers:

> I'm not a real strong women's-lib person. I guess I feel like if you've got the credential and you've got the experience and can project that you can get a job. And if you're not confident, then you shouldn't get it.

Another woman said:

> I am not one to really push the women's thing and I guess it's because I have always felt I could do whatever I wanted, it didn't make any difference, and I just assumed that everyone else could, too. I just haven't had the time and the energy to fight for the other women or for their opportunities either.

Clearly, women in the isolates category were treated as tokens—as symbols for all women. Likewise, their responses often mirror those of the women in Kanter's study, taking pride in their status of being the "only women" and having opportunities to give "the woman's point of view" on various issues. To be a woman in a skewed group situation does indeed require a knowledge of theory and a vocabulary if one is to have an awareness of the situation and a choice about one's actions.

Individualists

Women in the individualist category are more concerned with the attributes of individuals, be they men or women, than with the cause of sex equity in administration. Many women in this category were recruited into administration by male administrators within their districts. One woman said of her entry into administration in which her male superiors had persuaded her to take on quasi-leadership roles and then appointed her to a temporary position of principal before it became permanent:

> I have a lot of good feelings about the way I came into where I am. It makes me feel good in many ways that someone else kept saying, "You have the capabilities, you have the features that we want, you have the things that we need."

And another woman recalled her entry into administration:

> Funny thing, after I was into my master's program for a year, the second year it became the "in" thing for women to get into administration. All of a sudden,

boom, there were all these women. And I know the guys used to protect me and said, "You were here first! They're just jumping onto the bandwagon." There were so many of them that just didn't belong. They haven't got the patience for it; they haven't got the personality; they haven't got the guts. Some of the gals were in there just because they were women.

In contrast to her own attributes:

I am kind of a unique woman in that I have never let the "different sex" stop me. I have always teased: I could out-drink, out-smoke, and out-swear any of the guys I needed or had to. And I find it a compliment that they consider me one of the guys—I am one of the guys.

Most woman in this category had serious concerns about separate advocacy organizations for women. Some of their statements follow:

It's difficult for me since I didn't experience some of the frustrations that some of the women are experiencing. It is real hard for me to put myself in their place. So I don't see a separate organization having much influence. I know there are some men who have more influence when positions open up.

Another concedes:

I really have a hard time identifying with people who feel they need that kind of support. And I don't think they're going to be happy. I think you have to really learn how to work with all kinds of people, be it men or women. And you sort of have to play the rules of the group that's there and if you go in and try to change those rules you're going to feel resistance. And I think the approach that you need to have in working with men, you learn how to play the same way. And I guess that's my feeling and I have never joined the women's group because I really don't agree with them.

And this women is quite blunt:

I don't want to increase women in educational administration. I am not necessarily a supporter of picking out women to get them to get involved simply because they are women. I guess I have trouble with the idea of promoting women because they are women or promoting blacks because they are black or promoting whatever. I would feel very, very bad if I thought that I was principal of this school because I was a woman.

A theme running through many of these comments is a fear of alienating men; in reality, they have alienated themselves from women. These women have received district support as their major source of support and they seem to view women coming into administration as a threat, particularly women who won't play the rules the way those in the majority have written them. Bernard (1979) argues that some women have learned to see the world through men's eyes—"the male prism" (p. 270). Speaking of female scholarship, which is applicable to women in educational leadership, she notes:

> The history of female scholarship and research is, in fact, one in which women have been taught to see the world—even their own experience—through male eyes. Many of them have been so well taught that they have been alienated from other women. (p. 270)

What is the price of being co-opted by men? D. E. Smith (1975) argues:

> We have difficulty in asserting authority for ourselves. We have difficulty in grasping authority for women's voices and for what women have to say. We are thus deprived of the essential basis for developing among ourselves the discourse out of which symbolic structures, concepts, images, and knowledges might develop which would be adequate to our experience and to deviating forms of organization and action relevant to our situation and interests. In participating in the world of ideas as object rather than as subject we have come to take for granted that our thinking is to be authorized by an external source of authority. (p. 365)

And that external source of authority for some women is the male voice. Clearly, a dilemma exists for these women in administration. As they enter arenas dominated by men, they adapt and they adopt the male behavior, values, and concerns (Carlson and Schmuck 1981). Others try to live in both worlds—trying to integrate their world of work with their private world, each with its own set of disparate values. As Grambs (1976) points out, not only does the woman selected become indistinguishable from her male sponsor, she "also may show a willingness to take on the role of permanent protege" (p. 299). Moreover, women who have been socialized into administration by men, who have been appointed to positions, who have not "experienced the frustrations that some of the women are experiencing," deny the validity of these experiences for other women. One woman said:

> I really have a hard time identifying with people who have felt that they had to fight to be heard or fight to get along, because I haven't had to do that. I really think that we, as women, when we keep reminding that women need to be treated differently, that we always are planting a vision that we are different. It really has bothered me when I have gone to meetings and heard people say, "You should get a woman in that job." I never want a job because I'm a woman.

I think we scare off the men sometimes when we try to force and push women to be there. And I have found with the men that I've worked with, that you just go in and you're there and never constantly reminding them them you're a woman, and pretty soon it's just natural that you're there. Sure, you have on a skirt and they have on pants, and they may like their jock stories, but you can enter into those if you want to.

Individualists seem to be at a point of awareness whereby they devalue their own experiences and their own identities in favor of the "more powerful" majority. In speaking about women who "choose to enter the male world," Huws (1982) observes:

In these male dominated milieus, they quickly become aware of the extent to which feminine knowledge, values, concerns, modes of thinking and ways of behaving are either ignored, patronized or scorned. Moreover, they may find that being a woman automatically makes them second-class citizens in their field of work. Not surprisingly, many women in this situation go through a period of alienation from other women during which they seek to identify totally with male behavior, values and concerns. Others find, however, that they are alienated not just from other women, but from their own selves as well. This occurs in spite of the fact that they may savour immensely the rights and responsibilities which are theirs in the public arena. (p. 406)

Women at this point have adopted a judgmental attitude toward other women in administration—particularly toward those women who are advocating for other women. The very thing that these women are striving to achieve—"working and making the right impression and not being any different than anybody else"—points to the very thing that is lost: their unique experiences as women, and the values and beliefs that accompany that experience. In their efforts not to be different, they have, instead, defined their reality through the male prism—discounted their own experiences in favor of the male majority.

Summary and Conclusion

In summary, women who are activists strongly support the cause of equity in administration. They are active on committees, locally and nationally; they are aware of national issues—legislation, court cases, affirmative action suits. Many developed their activist's perspective by overcoming obstacles and confronting discrimination in their pursuit of administrative careers. All had two-district career patterns; most entered into administration through their own personal initiative. No one was persuading them to take administrative positions as was the experience of women in some of the other categories.

Advocates are supportive of other women and clearly believe women bring unique strengths to the schools in which they administer. They have both one-district and two-district career patterns and receive support mainly from district sources. These administrators seek to build networks and liaisons with their colleagues.

Isolates enjoy their status of being one of the few women in administrative positions in their districts—they stood out and they liked it. Their opinions, as women, were sought out and this gave them special attention. None of them perceived that they had experienced discrimination in their careers and, furthermore, they were not aware of discrimination in their area or in the state. The overall percentage of women administrators in their districts is low—only 15 percent, putting them in the status of tokens. These women truly seemed isolated from issues surrounding gender equity in administration and from the theory and language to give them explanatory power.

Individualists, on the other hand, strive to model themselves after their male colleagues who, in most cases, recruited them into administration. They work hard not to offend male administrators and want to be indistinguishable from their male colleagues. They resent women who advocate for gender equity in administration and are very opposed to separate advocacy organizations for women. These women had made it into administration with district support—86.0 percent, by far the highest percentage of all the four categories. They want to fit in with the majority and take pride in the fact that they were recruited into administrative positions by their male superiors.

Women do speak in different voices. And this study suggests that patterns of careers and sources of support may be two important reasons why women express differing points of view regarding issues related to sex equity in educational administration. Indeed, "the essential dialectic of society . . . can be summed up in the proposition that society exists only as individuals are conscious of it" (Berger and Luckmann 1967, 78).

Despite the focus on women in school administration during the last two decades, the percentages of women in positions such as superintendencies and high school principalships remain very low. (Harvey 1986, 511). Women continue to face discrimination in their efforts to achieve higher level administrative positions (Cann and Siegfried 1990; Goh 1991; Murgai 1991). Bernard (1988) urges educators to address these more subtle forms of discrimination, the "inferiority curriculum," that keep women from achieving their potential and defining their own reality. Now is the time for women and educators to emphasize programs that celebrate and enhance the natural skills and abilities that women bring to leadership positions (Helgesen 1990; Skakeshaft 1986). Schools throughout the nation are striving to find structures and leadership models that will serve students of the twenty-first century. Women have much to contribute to that effort and must be included at all levels of administration and decision-making.

Bibliography

Berger, P. L., and Luckmann, T. (1967). *The social construction of reality: A treatise in the sociology of knowledge.* Garden City, NY: Anchor Books.

Bernard, J. (1979). Afterword. In J. A. Sherman and E. T. Beck (eds.), *Essays in the sociology of knowledge.* Madison: University of Wisconsin Press.

Bernard, J. (1988). The inferiority curriculum. *Psychology of Women Quarterly,* 12, 261–68.

Cann, A. and Siegfried, W. D. (1990). Gender stereotypes and dimensions of effective leader behavior. *Sex Roles,* 23, 413–19.

Carlson, R. O., and Schmuck, P. A. (1981). The sex dimension of careers in educational management: Overview and synthesis. In P. A. Schmuck, W. W. Charters, Jr., and R. O. Carlson (eds.), *Educational policy and management.* New York: Academic Press.

Gilligan, C. (1982). *In a different voice.* Cambridge, MA: Harvard University Press.

Goh, S. C. (1991). Sex differences in perceptions of interpersonal work style, career emphasis, supervisory mentoring behavior, and job satisfaction. *Sex Roles,* 24, 701–10.

Grambs, J. D. (1976). Women and administration: Confrontation or accommodation? *Theory into Practice,* 15, 293–300.

Harvey, G. (1986). Finding reality among the myths: Why what you thought about sex equity in education isn't so. *Phi Delta Kappan,* 67, 509–12.

Hatcher, M. A. (1991). The corporate woman of the 1990s: Maverick or innovator? *Psychology of Women Quarterly,* 15, 251–59.

Helgesen, S. (1990). *The female advantage: Women's ways of leadership.* New York: Doubleday.

Huws, G. M. (1982). The conscientization of women: A rite of self-initiation with the flavour of a religious conversion process. *Women's Studies International Forum,* 5, 401–10.

Kanter, R. M. (1977). *Men and women of the corporation.* New York: Basic Books.

Matthews, E. N. (1986). Women in educational administration: Support systems, career patterns, and job competencies. *Dissertation Abstracts International,* 47, 1138A. (University Microfilms No. 8613362).

Mueller, C. (1973). *The politics of communication.* London: Oxford University Press.

Murgai, S. R. (1991). Attitudes toward women as managers in library and information science. *Sex Roles,* 24, 681–99.

Oakley, A. (1981). Interviewing women: A contradiction in terms. In H. Roberts (ed.), *Doing feminist research.* London: Routledge & Kegan Paul.

Rowland, R. (ed). (1984). *Women who do and women who don't join the women's movement.* London: Routledge & Kegan Paul.

Shakeshaft, C. (1986). A gender at risk. *Phi Delta Kappan,* 67, 499–503.

Smith, D. E. (1975). An analysis of ideological structures and how women are excluded: Considerations for academic women. *Canadian Review of Sociology and Anthropology,* 12, 353–69.

Stockard, J., Schmuck, P. A., Kempner, K., Williams, P., Edson, S. K., and Smith, M. A. (1980). *Sex equity in education.* New York: Academic Press.

Appendix: Categorization by Women Administrators' Point of View Regarding Issues Related to Sex Equity in Educational Administration

I. Women in Educational Administration

Activists

> Believe women are capable administrators and will continue to be; are proud of women coming in; appreciate the "radicals" who paved the way for those who came later; urge women to help each other but also to look at the power structure; believe it is important for women to go after principalships; connect with women administrators in their districts.

Advocates

> Feel deep responsibility for those coming up; want to see women coming up because women approach things completely differently; want more women in educational administration; identify with other women; have strong support feelings for and actively support other women administrators; believe women are strong administrators.

Isolates

> Do not have a commitment to other women's careers (e.g., "I could do whatever and assumed everyone else could too"); did not want to be seen as advocates for women; believe women can get jobs on their own; have no time or need to develop in depth relationships with other women in administration (e.g., "So this isn't a time, I don't think, at least from any experience, where you are going to be able to develop a lot of in-depth relationships with females").

Individualists

> Have a hard time identifying with other women who have "had to fight to be heard or fight to get along" (e.g., "It's real hard for me to put myself in their place"); judgmental towards women aspirants (e.g., "Some of the gals were in their just because they were women" and "they have to have a certain personality structure"); accept double-standard that women have to be better than men, "but frankly, that doesn't bother me. For one thing, the job gets done better and that's nice."

II. Men in Educational Administration

Activists

See themselves as alternate to the norm of men as administrators (e.g., "I think opportunities are going to be much more open to us [women] as we present ourselves as an alternative"); see numbers of women and men in administration as important (e.g., "I had a real obligation to look for a superintendency"); see distinctions in the way colleagues are groomed for administrative positions compared to women; are not afraid to speak out for sex-equality issues (e.g., "And I do speak out and tell people that I represent superintendents; sometimes my views may be somewhat different from the mainstream, but I am here and we are a force to be reckoned with"); speak positively about professional relationships with male colleagues; expect to be treated like professionals; see themselves as more competent than many of the men in administration (e.g., "I knew I could do so damn much better than they. I mean, to watch the incompetence for the number of years that I did and simply the fact that the person was male gave him the opportunity to go into administration").

Advocates

Use various strategies to work cooperatively with men (e.g., "I think that I have always had a real support from the men that I've worked for, but I seek that out and establish it partially myself" and "I move carefully and am trying to develop a trust relationship with him, and yet I can do my own thinking and acting, too, without that being a challenge to him"); are not as comfortable being around men when they are the only woman (e.g., "I would go to the meetings and there would be all men, they would tell men jokes and men-type things . . . sort of as though I weren't there. I feel very good, very relaxed about it now that there are two of us . . . we just refuse to be ignored" and "It's been really helpful to have at least one other woman . . . to confide in even if we don't always have the same concerns").

Isolates

Make no distinctions between men and women in administration; defer to men in positions of leadership (e.g., "even men who you knew were not supportive of women in administrative positions sometimes give the best input as to why"); see men only as supportive (e.g., "I have not felt anything but support and sometimes that's why I have trouble identifying [with women] when I'm hearing about nonsupport").

Individualists

See themselves as "one of the guys"; see people as people and do not make distinctions between men and women (e.g., "My identification is

267

more with accepting people as people rather than having anything to do with job, position, or numbers of people"); are proud that men in administration saw their strengths and encouraged them to pursue administration; are concerned about alienating men (e.g., "I think that we have alienated some of the men just by kind of drawing away [and forming separate organizations]"); want to work within the existing structure (e.g., "I think the approach that you need to have in working with men, you learn how to play that same way").

III. Themselves in Relation to Career in Administration
Activists

See themselves as essential in promoting women in administration (e.g., "Women who are in the field and touching base, if not daily, all the time with all these actors" and "I know that as a result of my being in the hiring position at one point in time . . . our district had as many women administrators as any district in the state"); are aware of being role models to other women and to the girls in their schools; have worked hard to dispel the image that "women don't work well together or support each other"; see themselves as feminists and actively supporting causes for sex equity in education; acknowledge that they have to be persevering, to "make your own luck"; see themselves as being perceived differently from men in the role (e.g., "The teachers here were a little suspicious and I knew I was different from what administrative experiences they had").

Advocates

Discuss women who have been role models to them and see themselves as role models for women coming up; are interested in theory and research about women in male-dominated roles (e.g., "I had all sorts of support books that deal with all kinds of experiences. . . . I read Kanter's book. . . . I read a lot of things that supported what I thought should be done or identified some of the problems I felt"); are aware to the affirmative action policies and their effects on their careers (e.g., "And I know the make-up of this district well enough to know that they are in a great need of women administrators—particularly at the secondary level—so if I indicate to them that 'Hey, I'm ready to make a move' then I'm sure that will happen"); express the feeling of being judged differently, of being scrutinized more carefully (e.g., "There was that sense of questioning" and "There was a lot of curiosity about what it was going to be like and the coaches were very nervous").

Isolates

Are not comfortable in the position of advice giver or role model for other women (e.g., "I've never seen myself as an advice giver"); have limited experiences with sex equality issues (e.g., "My perceptions are very limited, but I do not find the women who are really qualified and the type of women who can achieve in administration are in it").

Individualists

See themselves as successful administrators who made it through their natural leadership qualities (e.g, "I think if you are a strong leader they don't really care [if you are a woman] as long as you take the bull by the horns and go for it"); consider themselves unique (e.g, "I am kind of a unique woman in the sense that I have never let the different sex stop me").

IV. Giving and Seeking Support

Activists

Develop formal and informal support networks with women administrators (e.g., "We got together regularly and that's not just officially. We'd call each other up and get together and have a glass of wine once in a while"); notice whether or not women in the district are supportive of each other; go to women outside of the district for support; support males and females, but go to special efforts to seek out and support women coming up; maintain support networks by telephone when they move on to different and sometimes more isolated districts; seek ways to support women who are interested in administration; scrutinize the qualitifications for job openings to assure that women can qualify (e.g., "look for the minimum qualifications and disregard some of those stereotypical qualifications that really aren't necessary to the job"); have a commitment to women (e.g., "I feel a real dedication to other women—to try to give them a leg up. . . . I have tried to let women know when I felt there was a job opening that was appropriate for them. I have encouraged them to take the plunge"); believe it is very important for women in administration to support each other.

Advocates

Feel a sense of responsibilty and pride for women coming up; join advocacy organizations for women in administration (e.g., "I probably call a lot more individuals who are in the women's organizations now that I've gotten to know them"); call on other women for support; support women by requesting women administrative interns to be placed in the building (e.g., "I actively call on other women"); support women by speaking to women's groups when given the opportunity; help other women with interviewing techniques; want to see women join professional organizations and become involved in leadership roles; want to support women in order to see more women in administration (e.g., "especially in the high school principalships—we need more"); frequently mention the support they have received from other women.

Isolates

Promote women and men with no special emphasis given to promoting women (e.g., "There are several men and the same number of women and there was nothing intentional about it" and "I don't know if they need any more encouragement than qualified men who are reluctant to get their feet wet"); do not consider going to women, just because they are women, for support; do not consciously develop relationships with women; most day to day support comes from men.

Individualists

Support others with no distinction between men and women (e.g., "I am not necessarily a supporter of picking women out to get them to get involved simply because they are women"); have not given much thought to supporting women (e.g., "I just really haven't given that much thought, to be really honest. I guess I keep my eyes open to any promising person to go into administration, male or female"); are reluctant to give support to any but the best women (e.g., "And they really have to have a certain personality structure to be an administrator. I don't think you can just train for it").

V. Experiences of Sex Discrimination

Activists

Acknowledge discrimination exists at many levels and deal with it (e.g., "I told them I had no intentions of standing still for that. And, as far as I could see, they could either make it right by me or expect that I probably would not be back" and "It's covert"); believe that sex discrimination has affected their careers (e.g., "The sense of discrimination would come in the kinds of questions . . . absurd questions, just absurd. I have experienced a lot of this"); are cognizant of the present political scene, nationally and locally, that makes this issue even more relevant (e.g., "And then, with the new Supreme Court ruling on basic nonsupport for affirmative action"); recognize subtle discrimination.

Advocates

Discuss instances of discrimination in their careers, from pay inequities to stereotyping (e.g., "I think that I lost the discipline vice principalship because they feel a man needs to do that"); are aware of discriminatory questions in interviews; discuss the public's perception of differences in ability to do the job; acknowledge that some staff members have difficulty working with a woman administrator—"a woman boss"; maintain their integrity in working with issues of sex discrimination; grow in their knowledge of discrimination and try to be aware of it when it is happening (e.g., "It meant that I was going to stand up for something that I felt was right").

Isolates

Report that they have not been discriminated against (e.g., "I don't think that we've experienced it in this community or this area" and "I have never found a man in this state not to be supportive"); do not believe that their sex makes a difference (e.g., "I haven't felt it [being a woman] to be a detriment"); attribute low numbers of women in educational administration to other causes (e.g., "We are very low on females in administration so it might be interpreted as being discriminatory; on the other hand, this district hires a lot from within and I don't think we have too many females with credentials").

Individualists

Describe differing degrees of discrimination in their own careers, from "Oh, yes, of course" to "No, I really haven't"; speak of discrimination happening in other districts, not in their own (e.g., "I felt some frustration as I watched some appointment, not in this district, but around some other districts, where I saw some men appointed and I had some feelings of, 'Gee, you're not even getting an opportunity to apply'"); do not identify with discrimination experienced by others (e.g., "I really haven't [felt any discrimination] and that's where I guess I have a hard time identifying because I'm sure there are some—and I don't know how to identify them"); minimize instances of discrimination in their careers (e.g., "I think it was really unique . . . really minuscule").

VI. Strategies and Remedies to Overcome Discrimination

Activists

Consider the impact beyond themselves (e.g., "The law will begin to prevent some of the injustices of the past" and "It needs to have impact for other people"); appreciate the people who have paved the way for them (e.g., "There are a few brave souls who have dared to sue at, I think, extremely great personal expense—and I'm not talking about money"); Don't have any "pat" answers, but believe it must be a personal decision to sue; balance the costs and the benefits of considering a lawsuit (e.g., "Sometimes you can undo with too much of a fuss what you have worked so hard to do"); respect individual decisions regarding lawsuits (e.g., "I guess that it has to be a personal decision"); believe strongly that women must help those coming up (e.g., "We're going to have to work from within to make sure that we're helping the women one-on-one and making the opportunities available").

Advocates

Believe that "grass-roots" efforts are most effective (e.g., "It has to be the women who take the initiative"); urge women to build support networks and encourage each other and help develop skills; enjoy coming up with strategies to combat sex discrimination; urge women to continue being involved even when they are busy administrators themselves (e.g., "It is important to continue to be involved"); believe that school districts should have specific programs to promote women; need to pursue instances of discrimination through appropriate channels, then take legal action if necessary; take sex-equity laws seriously and do not believe they should be overlooked (e.g., "I don't think you should sit still and let irresponsible things happen. . . . I wouldn't duck").

Isolates

Are uncomfortable with lawsuits as a remedy to sex discrimination (e.g., "I think women have to be real careful about lawsuits . . . they do more damage than they do good"); do not believe women should use their sex as a reason (e.g., "I don't think it is right to use being a female . . . there must be another reason and, see, that could be totally unfair"); accept judgements of other (e.g., "I would just accept that someone made that decision and in their judgment I wasn't the best qualified"); believe that women are too quick to "jump on the bandwagon of discrimination"; do not want to set themselves apart from men by using the law or other remedies.

Individualists

Would go through district channels and then pursue a lawsuit if they were discriminated against; believe that too many women use being a woman as an excuse; would have to give very serious consideration before pursuing a lawsuit because "I may be damaging some relations"; believe that they would have to be personally mistreated before pursuing a lawsuit (e.g., "I probably wouldn't fight it. If I were mistreated, I would stand up for myself"); put themselves above remedies (e.g., "Even if they told me 'It's because you are a women and we wanted a man,' that's probably where it would end with me because 'If you don't want me, I don't want you'").

VII. Advocacy Organizations, such as NWEA
Activists

Support organizations that advocate for women, formal or informal; see the broad implications of why women form such organizations (e.g., "The real impact of groups like that has been to create awareness of women as a force in the country"); recognize the opportunity for women to get together and come up with strategies and remedies to the problem of underrepresentation of women in leadership roles.

Advocates

Believe that advocacy organizations examine issues and problems not addressed by other professional organizations; are not worried about alienating men by belonging to such organizations (e.g., "I get questions, 'Well, what is the purpose anyway?' and, then I explain it as professionally as I can"); believe the organization should exist until the numbers of men and women in administrative positions evens out; see the organization as helpful in getting administrative positions; see opportunities for leadership in the organization; support an organization that provides networking and support to women who work in isolated districts; see the organization as highly supportive, both personally and professionally.

Isolates

Do not see a need for an organization that singles out women (e.g., "And in my head I can't figure out really why that is necessary"); have higher priorities than belonging to such a group; do not have the ties or the energy to become involved in issues addressed by advocacy groups.

Individualists

Do not believe in having two separate professional organizations (e.g., "I have not been supportive of a separate organization. I really feel that we need to save up in the organizations that we've got"); are concerned that the organization alienates men in administration; do not have time to go to meetings; believe that women should do things as their own merits, not having "an organization like that promoting me" and "If you start giving special treatment, you don't have to work for where you are."

FIFTEEN

Women Principals' Views on Sex Equity: Exploring Issues of Integration and Information

Patricia A. Schmuck and Jane Schubert

During the past two decades there has been a modest increase of women school principals and assistant principals. In 1974 women were 15% of principals and assistant principals, their representation grew to 17% in 1980, to 21% in 1985, and to 27% in 1990 (see Jones and Montenegro 1991).

Women who became principals in the last two decades were beneficiaries of the national attention directed at women's absence in educational governance. Women were encouraged to seek administrative positions by passage of Title IX, by federal directives for affirmative action, by initiatives such as Project AWARE, (sponsored by the Ford Foundation and under the auspices of the American Association of School Administrators), by research and action projects supported by the Women's Educational Equity Act Project, by technical assistance supplied by the Sex Desegregation Centers, and by the resources and services of regional advocacy groups such as the Northwest Women in Educational Administration and the Northeast Coalition of Education Leaders. In addition, an explosion of knowledge in the 1970s and 1980s about women's lives and experiences established a supportive cultural context for women to seek positions in formerly male-dominated roles (Schmuck 1975; 1981; Gross and Trask 1976; Pottker and Fishel 1977;

Biklen and Brannigan 1980; Havens 1980; Spender and Sarah 1980; Adkison 1981; Ortiz 1982; Shakeshaft 1987).

At this time attention was also directed to the experience of students in school. Title IX was introduced in 1972 that disallowed discrimination on account of sex in any school receiving federal funds. In the 1970s and 1980s there were scholarly books as well as articles in the more popular educational press showing how schools maximize sex differences in teacher behaviors, outcomes and opportunities for students (Frazier and Sadker 1973; Fischel and Pottker 1977; Guttentag and Bray 1976; Stockard et al. 1980; Sadker and Sadker 1985; Fenema and Ayer 1984; Klein 1985).

Many women became principals when national sentiment and mandates actively supported and encouraged equal employment and equal educational opportunities, yet we know little about how these women view their responsibility to provide equity in schools. For example, will female administrators give attention to equity policies and practices in public schools? Will women administrators be sensitive to gender and race discrimination and bias? Will they advocate for equity in their schools and districts?

Adkison studied state and district school officers charged with implementing equity mandates; she found women and minorities were stronger advocates for equity as compared to white men who administered the compliance of regulations. She argued individuals who have personal experience with institutional discrimination will be more sensitive to bias, and be stronger advocates for change (1982). Adkison's work suggested that women, who had to face overt and subtle discrimination in their career paths to the principalship, would, from their own experience, become equity advocates and that the placement of women in school governance might better shape local policy and practice toward greater sex equity for employees and for students. With this premise in mind, we began an exploratory study of the attitudes of women principals toward sex equity.

Method of Study

To explore women principal's views on equity we interviewed nineteen women principals in Oregon, California, and Arizona using the critical incident technique (Flanagan 1954; Fivars 1980). The critical incident technique consists of procedures for obtaining behavioral descriptions.

The key features of the critical incident technique are that:

- Interview questions are open-ended, so respondents do not choose from a predetermined set of answers.
- Responses focus on actual events; descriptions of events must be explicit about what an individual actually did.

- Responses include statements of outcomes so the consequences of an event are known.
- Descriptions of events must contain contextual information so a reader will understand what happened without being present.

Each principal was asked to describe at least one event in each of the following areas: (1) to identify an important overall school policy or practice for which the principal was responsible; (2) to identify a specific policy or practice about sex or race equity for students for which the principal was responsible, (3) to describe their own career path, especially about their experience with race or sex discrimination in their pursuit of the principalship, and (4) about their perceptions as to whether being female made a difference in how they performed their job as a principal.

We conducted telephone and personal interviews for about one hour with nineteen women principals. Since this was an exploratory study we chose to talk to women principals we knew, fifteen of whom had participated in at least one conference on women in administration. Our sample, shown in Table 1, represents a mix of employment history, age, level of school, and ethnicity.

The results are organized by each of four themes: (1) educational concerns, (2) equity concerns, (3) perceptions of discrimination and, (4) perceptions of being a woman administrator.

Concerns of Women Principals

When queried on the first question, "Describe an important school policy or practice for which you are responsible," *none* of the principals

TABLE 15.1

Profile of Interviewees

School Level	N	Years as a Principal 0–5	6–10	11–15
Elementary	11	7	4	
Middle	3	2		1
High	5	1	2	2
				Total = 19

30–35	36–40	Age 41–45	45+
3	4	7	5
			Total = 19

Black	Asian	Ethnicity Hispanic	White
4	1	1	13
			Total = 19

raised a policy or practice that directly focused on equity concerns. Examples were varied and centered on general improvement in instruction or creating better working conditions for staff. For example, responses included creating more uniform discipline policies for students, changing a tracked homogeneous system of ability grouping of students toward greater heterogeneity, increasing teacher sensitivity of students perceived at risk of failing, increasing parental involvement with special needs students, and to increase staff participation in school wide decisions. These are laudable goals, and consistent with the findings asserting that women principals, as compared to men principals, tend to be more concerned with instructional leadership and that they foster greater faculty participation in running the school (Gross and Trask 1976; Charters and Jovick 1981; Shakeshaft 1987).

Equity Concerns of Women Principals

Responses to the second question, "Please describe a school policy or practice which addresses sex or race equity concerns for which you are responsible," yielded twenty eight different examples. We categorized the twenty-eight examples into four levels (see Schmuck et al. 1985 for a more complete description of the categorical levels).

Level 0 means no example was given.

Level 1 indicates a single classroom event has taken place, usually an "awareness" happening, such as displaying posters on equity laws or about sex-stereotyping in toys or games, asking "role models" to speak in class, or encouraging a girl or minority student to be a school leader. These we interpreted as modest, passive gestures toward providing equity.

Level 2 suggests a more serious effort at addressing equity concerns at the school level but one which falls short of incorporating a general equity policy into the educational system. Examples include a staff development program on an equity topic, a career awareness day, observing Black History Month or Women's History Week. These events usually engage a group of students or educators for a short time.

Level 3 indicates that equity enters the educational enterprise as a normal way of doing business. Such practices include; selection committees using nonsexist and nonracist criteria for selecting class resources, establishing recruitment policies for classes where some groups of students are under-represented, or eliminating sexist and racist disciplinary practices. At level 3 equity concerns become part of school practice and policies; there is an expressed concern for recognizing race and sex as critical criteria for determining fairness in school life.

TABLE 15.2
Distribution of Equity Level Response

		Number of persons at each response level	Number of equity examples given
Level 0	No examples given	5	—
Level 1	A single classroom event	8	17
Level 2	A single schoolwide event	2	4
Level 3	Ongoing schoolwide events	4	7
		Total: 19 persons	Total: 28 examples

Table 2 shows the distribution of equity concerns at their *highest* level of response expressed by the nineteen interviewees. That is, individuals citing level 3 examples may have given level 1 or level 2 responses also. There were five individuals who gave no response, eight gave only level 1 responses, two gave at least one example of a level 2 response and four gave at least one example of a level 3 response. There were twenty-eight examples given.

There is a mixture of responses on the continuum. At Level 0, five principals gave no response. "I haven't thought about that" or "We don't discriminate in this school" were common responses.

At Level 1 eight principals gave seventeen different examples. "Being a women, I am a role model for female students" was mentioned five times. Other examples were single events such as displaying posters for Women's History Week, or inviting a woman or minority to speak to a class. In most cases individual teachers had taken on a specific activity for their students, but there was no organized or school sponsored event for which principals had taken on a leadership role nor made this a schoolwide concern.

At level 2, two principals reported schoolwide events such as celebrating Martin Luther King Jr. Day, an inservice teachers on sex equity, or observations of Women's History Month.

At level 3, four principals reported continuing and concerted schoolwide efforts to address student inequities. Two of the principals were African-Americans and they served predominantly African-American students. Two principals were white and focused on sex inequity. Examples included school assemblies on race or sex with follow-up activities in the classroom, efforts to decrease tracking for poor and minority children, and text book adoption committees which reviewed texts for sex or race stereotypes. These activities were on-going and part of the day-to-day practices of the school.

In our assessment, only four out of nineteen principals (all at the elementary level), directly addressed sex or race inequity. While we prodded for more specific examples that have been reported in the literature about sex and race bias such as, "Do you look at student outcome data, especially in math and science, with regard to sex or race bias in achievement?," or "Have you looked at your discipline records to see if there are differences by race or sex in student infractions," or "Do you see any peer pressure on the basis of sex or race," no principal had investigated any of these areas nor indicated a plan to do so.

Perceptions of Career Discrimination

We asked, "Please tell us about your experiences in gaining the principalship," and then probed further, "Did you experience any discrimination as a female seeking the principalship?"

The majority of our interviewees, especially those who attained their positions within the last five years, reported experiencing *no* sex discrimination in their careers. They cited support and encouragement from their peers and superiors. Yet many of these same women reported differential treatment because of their sex. One said, "There is a parent club run by two men; they tried to railroad me out of the parent club." A black female reported, "The community did not want to accept me. It was a blue-collar working-class community. That was hard." Another black woman said, "No, I've not experienced discrimination. I've been in the right place at the right time. The civil rights movement and the feminist movement all occurred in my life. I haven't suffered discrimination professionally. Of course, sometimes people have been less than accepting of me." These women principals reported differential treatment on the basis of sex but did not label this behavior as "discrimination."

Only two women gave examples of sex discrimination. They cited instances of unfair competition, lack of access to information or being mistreated by the system. These two women, who had become secondary principals before 1980, reported active discrimination opposing their efforts to obtain a principalship. Although these two women reported discrimination on the basis of sex, both ranked low on the equity continuum; one gave no evidence of promoting equity in her school and the other gave a level 1 response.

Although different treatment was noted, it was not called "discrimination" by most interviewees. Even those few women reporting instances of discrimination did not translate their personal experiences into an educational agenda to prevent such experiences for their students or teachers.

Perceptions of Being A Woman Principal

In response to question 4, "Does it make a difference that are a woman in the principalship," *all* respondents answered "Yes." All the principals said they faced unique issues because they were women. While most claimed they had not experienced discrimination, they understood they were unique as women and as principals. One high school principal was often asked by her staff how she managed her traditional role as a wife and mother and her nontraditional role as a high school principal, "Who cooks your family's dinner when you are here so late?" Another woman reported that profanity was always followed by an apology at administrative meetings. Another reported a parent delegation visited the superintendent because they believed she could not be "tough enough."

We pushed further. We asked the question, "Do you consider yourself a feminist?" *All* women interviewed rejected the label "feminist." One experienced high school principal who reported facing sex discrimination in her long career in one metropolitan school district said it was "sad" that women couldn't help each other but that it would be "political suicide" for her to belong to a women's group. She went on, "No, I don't consider myself to be a feminist; I'm reasonable and logical." She also went on to say, "But I must be careful with my male colleagues. Perhaps I am a feminist because I am often at odds with my colleagues because I am woman."

Another woman, a first-year principal, belonged to a formal women's administrative organization and an informal support group of women administrators in her district, also responded, "No," she did not consider herself a feminist. She reported, "I've always hated the cattiness of women, some of my best friends are men." She stated most of her support came in the district from other women principals yet in her school her support came from the few men on the staff; she deplored the women teachers who are "housewives who just want to get out of the house. They are not professionals, they have no career aspirations." Yet she concluded the interview speaking at length about the strain of simultaneously balancing the demands of school and family life. Apparently she realized no dissonance between her struggle as a professional educator and a wife and mother and the experiences of women teachers in her building.

What did we learn from talking to this small sample of women principals? We find several uneasy contradictions in their reports. While *all* the women principals acknowledged their femaleness made a difference in their role as principal, seventeen denied any discrimination in seeking their positions. Yet even those who denied experiencing any sex discrimination reported, "people have been less than accepting of me as a woman." While five principals acknowledged their special role as model for other female students and staff, they also reported "bending over backwards to not give preferential treatment on the basis of sex." While all the principals proudly gave examples of being instructional leaders and paying attention to the needs of students, only four principals had taken active leadership to address race or sex inequities in their school. Why? How do we resolve these apparent contradictions? What sense can we make of their reports? What did we learn from this small sample of women to explain their general lack of attention to gender differentials in school practice?

In the following section we offer two explanatory themes. First, women principals want to become integrated into the prevailing administrative culture; they want to deny their unique status as minorities, and their identity as women in a predominately male administrative culture. Second, women principals, like men principals, are uninformed about how school policy and practice intentionally or unintentionally serve to perpetuate sex inequity.

Integrating into The Dominant Culture

Our interviewees revealed struggles over their personal and professional identity as women and as administrators. They must continually encounter the traditional stereotypes of being women from their staff, their colleagues, the community, and their superiors. They must even encounter researchers, such as us, who ask them pointed questions about their role as women administrators which they would rather ignore. Many women reported positive instances of "not being treated like a woman, but just another administrator." Several said, "I just want to be one of the guys." Their hope was to be judged by their competence, and not by their sex.

Understandably these women want to forget about their unique role as women and as administrators, it plagues them in unsettling ways from many fronts. Women principals are constantly reminded they are not part of the mainstream. Yet they want to be part of the mainstream of administration in their districts, they want to be integrated into the culture of their administrative peers.

The rise to school administration entails subtle socialization into the new role. New principals, male and female, voice the difficulties in the transition from the role of teacher to the role of administrators (Duke et al. 1984; Hart 1995). Loneliness and the changed nature of their interactions with former teacher colleagues often surprise those becoming administrators (see Louis 1980). New principals, who have interacted with teachers as peers, are suddenly thrust into new role relationships which can be uncomfortable and confusing. Women administrators face the inevitable problems inherent in any role change. In addition, they face the unique problem of moving from a teaching culture which is predominantly female, especially in the elementary school, to an administrative culture which is predominantly male.

The predominantly male administrative culture and the predominantly female teaching culture differ considerably; they differ on educational concerns, perceptions of power and influence, the people with whom one interacts and the type of work to be done. Women administrators must learn the ropes of their new administrative culture; in addition, they must leave the predominantly female culture of teaching. Women administrators often must choose between their same-sex culture of teachers and the other-sex culture of administrators. One principal reported that the women teachers in her building, "think I should better understand their problems because I am a woman." She went on to say how she "bends over backwards" not to give preferential treatment to women teachers. "I want to be an effective administrator, not an effective woman," she reported.

Women administrators also must decide whether to affiliate or not with women's groups. While some see it as "political suicide," others take a more sanguine view. One first-year principal was part of an informal women's group in a district where the number of women elementary principals had risen appreciably. She reported the importance of "this group, they supported me, they give me the inside scoop, they advise me." "But," she cautioned, "we, as women, don't want to splinter off, we need to work with men, too." Politically, and personally, women administrators are torn between being segregated into a culture of women and being integrated into a culture of men.

In an article called "The Denial of Personal Discrimination," Faye Crosby reported that working women acknowledged that sex plays a discriminatory role in the working lives of women in general. Yet they deny any disadvantage to themselves individually, and do not perceive themselves to be "victims" of sex discrimination. She notes: "It is as if women were completing a syllogism. The major premise states: 'Women are discriminated against.' The minor premise states: 'I am a woman.' But instead of the expected conclusion, 'therefore I am discriminated against,' women seem to say, 'Phew, that was a close call.' Such reasoning smacks of denial" (1984, 372).

In our study all women reported their femaleness made a difference in their jobs, yet only two principals noted behaviors which they labeled "discriminatory," although several women reported examples of differential treatment such as, "they have been less than accepting of me because I am a woman." How can we make sense out of the fact that they received differential treatment, yet deny the fact of personal discrimination?

Crosby, focusing on the social psychological argument of Allport's (1954) theories on prejudice, argues that minority members try to accommodate to the opinions of the majority group and internalize the dominant group's negative perception of themselves. Such people have been referred to as "Uncle Toms," or "Tio Tacos." What is the label we can give to women principals, who must constantly face their femaleness, yet who want to be integrated into the dominant administrative culture? Betty Crockers? Women must resolve the fact that they are "women" and they are "administrators." Thus, these women see themselves as "exceptions," they argue, I am not like other women, I am not a victim of sex discrimination, and my femaleness will not affect the work I do. As they disassociate themselves from their own female identity, they do not take up the cause of working toward sex or race equity in their schools. As one woman principal said, "I would be rendered ineffective among my peers if I took up every gender issue." Thus, she took up no gender issues.

Information about Equity and Feminism

All of our interviewees rejected the label of "feminist." Furthermore, these women, even those who see themselves as promoting women in administration, hold relatively negative and traditional stereotypes about women generally. They posit an explanation of "individual deficiency" (e.g., women teachers have no career ambition, they just want to get out of the house), but do not see the structural or cultural factors which perpetuate gender segregation in educational institutions. While they recognize the unique problems facing them as women administrators, they take a personalized and even idiosyncratic view of themselves as "exceptional." Women principals, even those who have attended workshops on women administrators, have little information from feminist literature or the literature on factors which perpetuate gender segregation in educational institutions. Gender issues are not included in their pre-service programs, in-service training, or professional associations.

Pre-Service Programs in Higher Education

Pre-service programs for teachers and administrators seldom incorporate theories about how schools perpetuate gender and race inequality in the society. Howe (1979) showed that women's studies courses are increasing and focus on women's experience in the culture, yet such courses are seldom available in schools of education (see McCormick 1995).

All states require the administrative certificate; there are nearly 300 educational administration programs (Murphy and Hallinger 1987). The dominant philosophy in training school administrators is the objective, value-free social science inquiry into organizational settings. The social science theory movement is chided by those who claim departments of educational administration fail to discuss relevant social issues and pay no attention to issues of sex, race or social class (see Yeaky, Johnson, and Adkison 1986). Departments of educational administration provide the first level of professional socialization for administration, and equity concerns are excluded. Not only does the curriculum represent a male bias, women, now a majority in many certification and doctoral programs, continue to face unique difficulties in their student roles. Webb (1986) reported the efforts of four departments of educational administration which addressed the psychological and structural factors which discriminate against their women students. It should be noted that these four schools—University of Oregon, Rutgers, University of Arizona, and University of Georgia—were all chosen as exemplary models of departments attempting to provide equal educational opportunity for their female students yet each report points out how their women students are disadvantaged. Male or female administrators' have little or no preparation for developing an equity agenda in their roles as school leaders. Given this context, we can better understand why women administrators do not address equity in their schools; they had no opportunity to do so in their preparatory programs. We might better ask, how is it that any administrator develops an equal educational agenda in his or her school?

Professional Associations

Professional associations take responsibility for the continued professional development of administrators. Issues of equal educational opportunity and employment vie with other important school issues such as finance, excellence, reductions in force, declining test scores, capital improvements, educational reform, and demographic changes. Whereas equity concerns were on the agenda of professional associations when the federal mandates emphasized compliance with Title IX, now it appears that the appetite for equality has abated at the federal level and professional associations have put equity on the back burner.

Many women administrators, however, have some exposure to equity concerns. Fifteen of our interviewees had attended equity conferences, workshops, or meetings about women in administration. What do prospective women administrators learn at such meetings? They learn how to write resumes, how to deal with sexist questions in job interviews, how to cope with sexist attitudes on the job and how to successfully cope with being a "lone" woman in an administrative meeting.

Such compensatory programs for women aspiring to leadership have been successful in assisting women to enter administration, but these individualistic approaches have not assisted women administrators to build an equity agenda for schools nor to change existing bias in school practice. Advocacy organizations for women administrators are too narrow in their advocacy. They advocate individual self-interest in career mobility, but do not promote a sense of responsibility for providing equality for students and other employees. They encourage individual women to advance in their careers, but do not teach women administrators to encourage other females to seek similar positions. They provide support for individual women, but do not imbue a sense that support received should be support returned.

Our sample of women administrators lacked the information to be sensitive to inequity in school organizations. They lacked the skill to intervene and alleviate inequitable practices. Indeed, when we described an equity agenda with some of our interviewees many were surprised, "I had not thought of that," was a common response. Women educators, like men educators, have not "thought about" how schools subtly or blatantly perpetuate inequality.

Conclusion

While there are more women administrators today than twenty years ago, our exploratory study indicates that changing the gender representation of principals will not, alone, change equity practices in school. Of the nineteen principals interviewed, only four elementary principals revealed an active agenda for equality; two were African-American principals concerned about racial equality, two were white principals concerned about sex equity. Women principals appear to adopt the prevailing norms of the administrative culture which ignores issues of equity. Although women principals face unique problems of identity and integration, they do not translate their personal experiences into professional actions to assure greater equality for students or employers. They take a personalized view of their experience; they see their experiences as individual, even idiosyncratic, and fail to comprehend the more fundamental concept of how gender serves as a segregating factor in the culture of educational institutions. Although we applaud continuing efforts to reach gender equity in administration and believe women have successfully demonstrated their administrative competence, we cannot presume because a woman is in charge, challenges to inequity will be made. We must continue to educate female and male educators about inequality through the universities and professional associations. Women's professional associations, especially, have taken too narrow a view; they should provide a more comprehensive and critical view of how our schools perpetuate inequality.

Bibliography

Adkison, J. (1981). Women in school administration: A review of the research. *Review of Educational Research*, 51(8), 811–48.

————. (1982). Advocates and administrators: Perspectives on the title co-ordinator's role. Paper presented at the annual meetings of the American Educational Research Association, New York.

Allport, G. (1954). *The nature of prejudice*. Reading, MA: Addison-Wesley.

Biklen, S. and Brannigan, M. (1980). *Women and educational leadership*. Lexington, MA: Lexington Books.

Charters, W. W., Jr. and Jovick, T. (1981). The gender of principals and principal-teacher relations in elementary school. In P. Schmuck, W. Charters, and R. Carlson (eds.). *Educational Policy and Management*. New York: Academic Press.

Crosby, F. (1984). The denial of personal discrimination. *American Behavioral Scientist*, 27, (3), 371–86.

Duke, D., Isaacson, N., Sayor, R, and Schmuck, P. (1984). Transition to the principalship. Paper presented at the annual meetings of the American Educational Research Association.

Fenema, E., and Ayer, M. J., (eds.) (1984). *Women and education*. Berkeley: McCutchan.

Fishel, A. and Pottker, J. (1974). *National politics and sex discrimination in education*. Lexington, MA: Lexington Books.

————. (eds.). (1977). *Sex bias in schools*. New Jersey: Fairleigh Dickinson University Press.

Fivars, G. (1980). *The critical incident technique*. Palo Alto: American Institutes of Research.

Frazier, N., and Sadker, M. (eds.). (1973). *Sexism in school and society*. New York: Harper & Row.

Gross, N. and Trask, A. (1976). *The sex factor in the management of schools*. New York: John Wiley and Sons.

Guttentag, M. and Bray, H. (1976). *Undoing sex stereotypes: Research and resources for educators*. New York: McGraw-Hill.

Hart, A. W. (1995). Women ascending to leadership. In D. M. Dunlap and P. A. Schmuck (eds.), *Women leading in education*. Albany: SUNY Press.

Havens, E. (1980). Women in educational administration: The principalship. Unpublished paper. Washington DC: National Institute of Education.

Howe, F. (1979). The first decade of women's studies. *Harvard Educational Review*, 49, 413–21.

Jones, E. and Montenegro, X. (1991). *Women and minorities in school administration.* Arlington, VA: American Association of School Administrators.

Klein, S. (1985). *Handbook of sex equity in schooling.* Baltimore: Johns Hopkins University Press.

Louis, M. R. (1980). Surprise and sense making: Newcomers experience in entering unfamiliar organizational settings. *Administrative Science Quarterly, 25,* 226–51.

McCormick, T. (1993). Teacher education programs. Unpublished paper.

Murphy, J. and Hallinger, P. (1987). *Approaches to administrator training.* Albany: SUNY Press.

Ortiz, F. (1982). *Career patterns in education: Women, men and minorities in public school administration.* New York: Praeger.

Sadker, D. and Sadker M. (1985). The treatment of sex equity in teacher education. In S. Klein (ed.), *Handbook for achieving sex equity through education.* Baltimore: Johns Hopkins University Press.

Schmuck, P. (1975). *Sex differentiation in public school administration.* Arlington, VA: National Council of Women in Educational Administration.

Schmuck. P., Adkison, J., Peterson, B., Bailey, S., Glick, G., Klein, S., McDonald, S., Schubert, J., and Tarason, S. (1985). Administrative strategies for institutionalizing sex equity in education and the role of government. In S. Klein (ed.), *Achieving sex equity through education.* Baltimore: Johns Hopkins University Press.

Shakeshaft, C. (1987). *Women in educational administration.* Beverly Hills: Sage.

Spender, D. and E. Sarah (eds). (1980). *Learning to lose: Sexism in education.* London: The Women's Press.

Stockard, J. (1980). *Sex equity in educational leadership. An analysis of a planned social change project.* Newton, MA: Educational Development Corporation.

Webb, D. (1986). Disequity in programs of educational administration. Paper presented at the annual meetings of the American Educational Research Association, Washington, DC.

Yeaky, C. C., Johnson, G. S., and Adkison, J. (1986). In pursuit of equity: A review of research on minorities and women in educational administration. *Educational Administration Quarterly, 22*(3), 110–49.

SIXTEEN

"If I Weren't Involved with Schools, I Might Be Radical": Gender Consciousness in Context*

Colleen S. Bell

Scholars and students of social interaction often assume that marginalized people will hold enlightened perspectives and offer special insight into the unequal social arrangements we all inhabit. Ferguson (1984) summarizes these assumptions:

> Those who are marginal in the dominant society, who experience life in more than one "world," have access to more than one point of view. Thus those who stand on the fringes of established roles can offer insights less available to individuals more thoroughly and consistently integrated into the established categories. (p. 178)

Similar expectations of those "on the fringes" are evident when we examine this phenomenon in the field of education. In some cases, expectations go beyond marginal persons offering insights to include motivation to

*Research for this paper was supported in part by the AAUW Education Foundation, the US Department of Education's Office of Educational Research & Improvement, the University of Tulsa, and Hamline University. I would like to thank Susan Chase, Michelle Collay, and Ann Weaver Hart for comments on earlier drafts of this paper.

act exceptionally. For example, Adkison (1982; 1983), in reporting a study of Title IX coordinators, argued that persons who have experienced institutional discrimination will recognize bias more readily than others and will be more active in fighting it. It is important to note the connection between the experience and awareness of discrimination on the one hand, and pro-equity activism on the other.

Similarly, Schmuck and Schubert (1995) initially expected that women in principalships would be equity advocates because they had experienced discrimination and had gathered information on equity through workshops. The questions Schmuck and Schubert posed at the beginning of their inquiry into the sex equity attitudes of nineteen women principals capture their expectations:

> Will [an] increase of women as administrators improve the infusion of equity policies and practices in our public schools? Will women administrators be sensitive to discrimination and biases in school curricula? Will equity issues be part of the agenda of women administrators? (1995, 280)

Schmuck and Schubert were "disappointed, frustrated, alarmed, and angered" (1988, 11) by the results of interviews with these principals. A majority of the participants—in the same conversation—denied experiencing sex discrimination *and* reported being treated differently than men. Some of them actively supported women's causes and at the same time distanced themselves from the label "feminist" or disparaged other women educators. And overall, Schmuck and Schubert found among this group "little attitudinal support or action to foster equity practices in schools" (1995, 290).

How should we interpret the gender consciousness of women who make—as Schmuck and Schubert found these principals did—seemingly contradictory claims about their experience and commitments? How ought we interpret the disconnection of action from consciousness and experience when this occurs?

One way of exploring this question is to continue studies of the kind Adkison and Schmuck and Schubert have done, examining closely the perspectives of women whose lives hold clues to enlarged understanding. Women in school administration are both members of a majority (women in education) and members of "the few" (women leaders in schools); their positions as female leaders put them on the fringes of groups of teachers and of administrators. Administrative women's experiences encompass both authority and influence as leaders, and isolation and exclusion as women in a male-dominated occupation. How do they interpret and manage these tensions? What forms of reconciliation between their opposing statuses are reflected in their perspectives?

One purpose of this paper is to explore the notion of gender consciousness as it surfaces in interviews with women who lead K–12 school districts.[1] I analyze two individual superintendents' thought and action and the institutional context in which they are intertwined. A second purpose is to evaluate the usefulness of several strategies for understanding and interpreting gender consciousness.

Developing An Understanding of Women's Gender Consciousness

Hochschild's (1974) "Making It: Marginality and Obstacles to Minority Consciousness" provides a useful beginning for developing an understanding of how marginality shapes consciousness and action. As she reviews twelve autobiographical accounts of successful professional women—many of whom have entered male dominated occupations—Hochschild focuses on "why the very women who are most likely personally . . . to suffer prejudice and discrimination, often resist thinking of women as a minority group" (1974, 194). Hochschild observes that although there is substantial evidence of discrimination against women in the professions, "few women in the society at large have minority consciousness" (p. 194). She notes that, like many other women, the twelve professionals whose stories she reviews express an ambivalence toward discrimination. Although they offer specific examples of discriminatory experience, they often summarily deny having suffered discrimination. This stirs Hochschild's interest in the dynamics of "not what makes a woman successful, but rather, how being successful makes her feel less like other women" (p. 194).

Hochschild's explanation is essentially that a woman faces various obstacles in her life on the fringes of male-dominated professions as she attempts to unite two roles that have been defined as contradictory, that of woman and that of professional. These obstacles include "de-feminization" (in which her identity as a woman is questioned and her ties with other women are cut through "compliments" such as "She's a fine analyst. She thinks like a man.") and "de-professionalization" (in which her ties with male colleagues are cut and her professional identity is undermined by claims such as "She slept her way to the top").

Like men, women in the professions must prove themselves to employers. However, unlike men, women must prove themselves to be different from a negative stereotype of others like them (i.e., women in general). This often pressures women into doing their own "de-feminization" by encouraging them to differentiate themselves from other women. In the context of

290

such pressures to disaffiliate from other women, it is not surprising to find women in the professions refusing to identify with feminism and the women's movement as Schmuck and Schubert's principals did. Hochschild summarizes a perspective that might be adopted by the woman who wishes to be integrated into a male dominated profession:

> Her sex is already a point of latent tension and to "come out" as a feminist, even a sweet and reasonable one, only feeds into the existing fear that one is, in the minds of others already "bunched up under the heading 'women'." (1974, 198)

Hochschild's contribution to the question of women's gender consciousness is the idea that ambivalence about the women's movement is one consequence of ideological and structural barriers to the development of a minority consciousness that could emerge from identification with other women.

A second resource in understanding the gender consciousness of women in male-dominated occupations is a 1985 paper by Gerson and Peiss in which they observe that many writers on gender consciousness assume gender consciousness is an either-or phenomenon; that is, either one has it or one doesn't. This formulation, the authors point out, ignores "the possible varieties of feminist and female consciousness" and they propose that "viewing forms of gender consciousness along a continuum produces a more useful conception of consciousness [than the either-or conception]" (1985, 324).

Gerson and Peiss identify three types of consciousness, arrayed on a continuum: gender awareness, female/male consciousness, and feminist/antifeminist consciousness. Gender awareness is the least critical of these three perspectives and, as the authors put it, "means that people may associate or correlate certain phenomena with one gender group or another, but there is no evaluation of the ultimate significance or meaning of these attributions" (1985, 324–25). The second type of consciousness Gerson and Peiss identify, female (or male) consciousness, goes beyond trait attributions characteristic of gender awareness to acknowledge that reciprocal rights accompany gender-based obligations in this gender arrangement. Feminist (or antifeminist) consciousness, the third type Gerson and Peiss identify, "involves a highly articulated challenge to or defense of the system of gender relations in the form of ideology, as well as a shared group identity, and a growing politicization resulting in a social movement" (1985, 326).

Gerson and Peiss further advise thinking of consciousness as a phenomenon that can shift as people interact; that is, consciousness is not a steady state. This notion connects closely with Ferguson's writing on the development of women's consciousness. "Consciousness," says Ferguson, "is not an object, but a process, an ongoing interaction with others" (1984, 178). Ferguson reminds us that an individual has potential to rethink experience and undergo change as a result of her relationships with others, that an individual "both creates herself and is created through these connections" (p. 178). In this sense, any attempt to understand gender consciousness that disregards change over time will produce short-lived understanding.

Given its dynamic nature, scholars must explore women's gender consciousness by examining the conditions and contexts that shape its development and expression. Two theorists—Ferguson (1984) and Westkott (1979)—have articulated this point most clearly. Ferguson asserts:

> Instead of judging the content of consciousness, feminist discourse looks to judge its *context,* distinguishing between situations that are relatively autonomous and those that are relatively manipulative. Consciousness as a temporal process is judged by its authenticity, its integrity: is it developed in a context of freedom and community, where connections with others are rooted in equality, not domination; or is it shaped by institutional links with others that express and enforce the values/interests/knowledge of the powerful? (1984, 178–79)

The issue of whether women's gender consciousness is shaped by conditions of autonomy or manipulation is critical in understanding the content of consciousness. For women who work in school administration, relations of dominance characterize their situations much more thoroughly than do conditions of autonomy, simply because of sex-segregated sex-stratified social arrangements in public education (Bell and Chase, 1993). Expressions of gender consciousness, therefore, will reflect these conditions. In studying women's expressions of gender consciousness in male-dominated environments we must consider how such expressions reflect contextual forces.

Ferguson's emphasis on the importance of context echoes Westkott's (1979) earlier critique of conventional social science's misinformed assumptions about women. Westkott noted that social scientists assume a fit between consciousness and action. Arguing that women's experiences are full of tensions and contradictions that emerge from problematic social arrangements, Westkott went on to say that it is not surprising—given women's simultaneous belonging and alienation—to find women opposing the very conditions to which they conform. In other words, while women participate in an organization they may simultaneously resist or become critical of its practices. Westkott continued: "Such a dissociation between conforming behavior and consciousness emphasizes the crucial importance of women's consciousness in patriarchal society" (1979, 429). Westkott drew attention to the possibility that if consciousness is split off from activity, it may become a sphere of freedom for women. While women often need to demonstrate visible conformity in their actions, consciousness is private and not subject to others' scrutiny in the same way as action.

Taken together, the approaches of Hochschild, Ferguson, Westkott, and Gerson and Peiss suggest several strategies for understanding the gender consciousness of women in positions such as the superintendency:

1. Focus on barriers to group identity ("minority consciousness") and affiliation among women.
2. Recognize consciousness is dynamic and attend to the context in which consciousness develops and is expressed.
3. Concentrate on apparent contradictions or tensions between consciousness and action.

In order to ascertain what these interpretive strategies might add to our perspective on the gender consciousness of women in school administration, I examine the thoughts and experience of two superintendents as described in interviews. I chose these two women's interviews because they are at odds with each other in some important ways; their differences pose a challenge to interpretive strategies drawn from the literature. To what extent can these strategies shed light on women's gender consciousness in various forms? To what degree can these strategies enlighten us about the role of marginality in producing consciousness and action that challenge structures of inequality in educational organizations?

The Focal Interviews

Pauline and Cynthia are two white superintendents whose interview transcripts I examine in what follows. Their interviews were conducted in 1987 during the earliest phase of a four-year co-investigation[2] of women's experience in the superintendency. Both were the first women to occupy the superintendency in the districts where they worked; both headed districts that enrolled a significant majority of white students.

Pauline headed a small-town district in the Midwest. She was beginning the second year of her second superintendency when we interviewed her. Her first superintendency was in a prestigious suburb of a Midwestern city. Pauline had had more than five years' experience as a superintendent and four years' experience in another major administrative role at the time of our interview. She had earned a Ph.D. and was in her mid-fifties. Our interview with Pauline took place in her office and lasted about two hours.

Cynthia spoke as superintendent of a small-town district in the Southwest. When we interviewed her, she had been heading this district for over a year and had previously led an urban district in the Southwest for four years. Cynthia had extensive experience in school administration, having served as department chair, assistant principal, principal, curriculum director, and assistant superintendent prior to the superintendency. Cynthia held a doctorate and was in her mid-forties. Her interview extended over six hours in two sessions, about a month apart.

Pauline

In talking with us about her career, Pauline emphasized the role of two male mentors who pushed her into applying for superintendencies. One of these men was a university professor and the other was the superintendent of an urban district in which Pauline was an administrator in the mid-1970s. As one of the first women in the state to break into the superintendency in that decade, Pauline had been quite visible.

Affiliation and Gender Consciousness[3]

There are two primary instances of disaffiliation evident in Pauline's interview. The first—in Pauline's response to a question about whether her gender had been an issue in her hiring as superintendent—shows signs of the pressure Hochschild described as de-feminization. Pauline told us: "I've never thought of myself as a woman. I've always thought of myself as being an educator." While our question asked about being a woman in a male-dominated occupation, her response denied the relevance of sex and focused on the profession.

Another instance in which Pauline asserted disaffiliation occurred when we asked, "Is there a statewide organization for women in educational administration?" She had a lot to say about this:

> Yes, but I object to it. There are two or three women [who] . . . have tried to start a separate organization. . . . They meet, you know, in little restaurants in little groups and I don't have any time for that at all. . . . I have absolutely no time for women's groups. Now I will and always have given a lot of time to developing mentoring relationships and I've had a lot of intern women administrators. And I see that as a much higher priority than [to] go and have cookies and cake and dinner with a, bunch of women. . . . I will not belong to a separate women's organization . . . because the real power is in the [state organization of superintendents].

She continued talking about an organization for women that some administrators in the state had organized:

> [It's] very bitchy oriented. Very bitchy, you know. The women who belong to it call and say, you know, "They invited us to their, their meeting and then they had a golf tournament and you couldn't play golf" or you know, "Women couldn't go into the bar" or you know, "They treated me like this." I said, "So? Didn't you know the rules before you went there?" I don't have any time for them. You may or may not agree with me, but I don't have any time for them. . . . This little [local] group is just, you know, it's their rationale to complain. To be organized so they can complain as a group, you know, kind of thing.

Susan, my collaborator—to clarify Pauline's point about this group—paraphrased: "So it's not the fact of women getting together that you object to, but what they do when they get together." Pauline expanded on that:

> Yeah, what their goals are. Yeah, if . . . you're going to be . . . a superintendent, belong to the superintendents' group and work on those agendas that are important to the superintendents. Those issues that are strictly women's issues—like you know, getting a job—not much is going to happen through the superintendents' group. You're going to have to, you know, help each other through the networking process, I think.

This statement raises two questions. First, it is not clear how getting a job is an issue "strictly" for women. Pauline may have meant that women ought not expect that their getting jobs will be an issue of central concern to a group of superintendents such as the state district administrators' organization (in which 3 percent of members are women), although that organization treats job placement as one of its tasks. It is also not clear whose network Pauline was referring to when she said, "You're going to have to . . . help each other."

Susan followed with a clarifying question about networks. The next interchange in the interview shows the intensity of Pauline's disaffiliation with women and her identification with men in school administration.

> *Susan:* Is there a women's network? You've talked about mentoring and supporting.
>
> *Pauline:* Yeah, I think the women's network, my network is more male oriented . . . simply because my contacts are nationwide from the experiences I've had . . . I know a lot more male superintendents.

Susan's question about networks followed Pauline's mention of the group of women in her region, but Pauline's response focused on established networks of men in the field. Pauline's disaffiliation was so strong that although she began to respond in terms of "the women's network," she almost immediately reinterpreted the question in terms of her own network which "is more male oriented." The fact that Pauline's network was composed primarily of men is not unusual in a field where 96 percent of a woman's colleagues are male. However the disjuncture in this exchange occurred because our question was based on experience with other women in the superintendency who *did* talk about networks of women and Pauline's experience did not include such networks.

As the first woman to hold a K–12 superintendency in the state and as a result of her efforts to break into the state organization for superintendents, Pauline was a highly visible person. When we interviewed her female peers in the region, some of them noted Pauline's years of experience and connections in the superintendency. One of these colleagues commented on her "style" as well: "If there's a woman in our ranks today who reminds me of the old-style male superintendent, it's Pauline." This observation captured Pauline's explicit disaffiliation with women and her identification with male colleagues.

Context of Pauline's Consciousness and Action

Male-dominance in social arrangements in schools limits the relative autonomy of women superintendents in their work situations. A good example is the following incident Pauline told us about when we asked whether she had ever experienced sex discrimination.

> When I was a curriculum coordinator, the male coordinators . . . [were] paid more than the female. [Another woman in administration] wanted to challenge it and I would not support her in challenging. . . . I could see what was happening to her. She never got into the inner circle.

We asked Pauline to explain why she had declined to support the complaint and she went on:

> Politically it just wouldn't have worked. It would have, you know, hurt all of us at that time. I knew the superintendent. He wasn't interested in being hassled . . . if you wanted to get ahead, you didn't do those things.

This work situation could surely be described as constraining. Pauline understood the superintendent's preference for not being "hassled" and acted on that basis. Power relations were at work in ensuring that those "outsiders within" (Hill Collins 1990) would not question the rules; it was quite clear to Pauline what actions and attitudes the reward structure would promote and what would be punished. She was also clear that her decision not to support her female colleague was shaped by that reward system.

Tension between Action and Consciousness

In this section I examine two instances of tension between Pauline's consciousness and experience on the one hand, and her action (defined to include explicit reasoning rather than overt action in one case) on the other.

The first example arose when Susan asked Pauline to summarize how women should think about getting into the superintendency. Pauline's advice was:

> You've got to be comfortable with yourself. You've got to be able to do the job and then, you know, want to do it to the best of your ability and use all your resources.

Pauline went on to say that some women fail because "they don't use resources" or they "aren't sure enough when they go into the job" or "their goals haven't been clear enough." In these comments Pauline seemed to be assigning responsibility for failure to individual women themselves. Then Pauline commented on how difficult it would be to be "stuck out in the middle of nowhere." She felt "privileged" to have been placed in a large urban area with plenty of resources. In these follow-up remarks Pauline acknowledged the importance of organizational support structures and social arrangements. The tension here is between her reasoning about other women—about whether individual women or their situations (or some interaction of these) are responsible for women's failure—and her experience of having access to urban networks and resources. Pauline points to women's own motivations and capacities as sources of their individual failures even while she acknowledges her own advantage and access to social and organizational supports that make her success possible.

In the second instance, although Pauline asserted that she had more important things to do than spending time with "a bunch of women," she said she has spent time mentoring individual women aspiring to administration, such as a high school teacher who interned with her the previous summer. Mentoring individual aspirants while refusing to participate with groups of women in administration seems contradictory. The contradiction may arise from the male-dominated occupational context, however. Kanter (1977) has convincingly documented how women's minority status creates visibility in a male-dominated field, as well as pressure to conform and blend in with the majority. Other informants in this study have told us that when women superintendents get together at state administrators' meetings they are often teased by male peers about engaging in subversive activity. For these structural reasons, Pauline may find it less problematic to support women individually than in "a bunch."

Cynthia

As she reviewed her career history, Cynthia identified the first time she understood that being a woman would make some kind of difference in her career; she was a first-year teacher at the time. More than two decades later, she has been the first woman to serve in almost every role she has occupied since she left the classroom.

Affiliation and Gender Consciousness

In discussing the dynamics of women's organizations—particularly those which she has helped to create—Cynthia offered the following analysis of what women do when they get together, specifically "telling war stories" (stories about discrimination):

> I'm so bored with war stories but I, now I find myself telling some occasionally when I go with the women superintendents because we really don't have anybody else who's been through some of this stuff. . . . I don't like it but I find us doing it. . . . And when I go to these conferences [for women administrators] . . . it just wears me out to hear about it continually.

As Cynthia went on, we heard an understanding of women's agenda that differed markedly from the one Pauline articulated. In fact, it sounded almost as if Cynthia was responding to Pauline's assertion that women administrators who get together are "bitchy" or complaining:

> Some women quit going to conferences [like that of our statewide organization for women administrators] . . . because they will say "Well, all they do is sit and bitch about what happens to them." Well, they're asking for help when they do that. They're not . . . playing "Can-you-top-this-one?" What they're saying is, "How do I handle this?"

As we continued discussing sources of professional support, Cynthia talked about her reasons for wanting to meet with other women who are superintendents. While it is important for all women to gather together so that aspiring and entry-level women have some support, Cynthia observed, women's needs vary across stages of professional development. She did not think that superintendents learn much from statewide meetings for women in administration, so the women superintendents in that organization needed another place "to share and to learn." Essentially they created their own place by meeting informally. Although Cynthia acknowledged learning some things from joint meetings with her male colleagues in the superintendency, she believes she has learned more from the women who are superintendents than from the men who are superintendents.

When we laid out an understanding of what Cynthia meant—"so what they deal with is different because they're men, not women, and maybe some of the things that they do are different because they face a different set of perceptions from other people"—Cynthia responded, "That's right, exactly. Exactly." In this affirmation she seemed to be agreeing that there is something women bring to their informal advising sessions with each other, some shared understandings that reside in the gendered experience[4] of women in the superintendency.

As one of the co-founders of a statewide organization for women in school administration, Cynthia has been forced to acknowledge the range of others' attitudes toward it. The strength of her own commitment to women's organizations has led her to argue with women who feel the pressure to disassociate themselves from the organization. She recounted:

> I've been told by some of the women superintendents as recently as last week that it [the statewide organization for women administrators] became very strident and a couple of them had real trouble associating with it, so they got my twenty-minute lecture on "I don't care what you think, you owe it to those women to be a role model."

Cynthia was also instrumental in organizing a national organization for women in school administration and described herself as one who had "a real bias about the fact that once we've made it to the superintendency we must keep . . . talking to the other women. . . . It's an obligation I want to fulfill." Cynthia's work to organize women's groups and her sense of duty are evidence of strong affiliation with women in school administration. After examining the context of her work, I introduce an instance of Cynthia's disaffiliation and then look at contradictions between Cynthia's consciousness and action.

Context of Cynthia's Action and Consciousness

One clue to the context that shapes Cynthia's work and consciousness was found in her response to our question about informal meetings the women superintendents in her region held. When Susan asked, "Do the men superintendents know you're doing this?," Cynthia's response was:

I doubt it. I don't tell them, you know, it just doesn't come up. And I present it—when I'm going to be gone for that afternoon—that I've gone to a superintendent's meeting. And I ask my secretary not to write "women superintendents" on my calendar. Isn't that a shame? But I mean, I do, because I don't want that to become the issue, because the professional associations are helpful. . . . I doubt if the men know we're doing it. I think it means too much to each of us to make a big deal about it.

The group was important to Cynthia and potentially threatening to male colleagues; therefore it had to be kept quiet to remain out of jeopardy. Two acknowledgments are embedded here: first, that if the men superintendents in the state knew the women were getting together they wouldn't like it, and second, that if the men found out, the women's meetings would have to end. Cynthia points out that gender rather than "professional associations" would then become focal. Once again, because women are a numerical minority they are both isolated and highly visible. For these women superintendents, separate meetings provide a supportive professional setting that their work situations do not; at the same time, their meetings are threatening to men because they are separate from the male majority. Interestingly, it was here that Cynthia and her peers created something akin to the "conditions of autonomy" that Ferguson identifies, however temporary those conditions are. The fact that the women gathered outside of their work situations to provide support and a hospitable environment for one another is a likely reason the meetings would have posed a threat to male counterparts.

We asked Cynthia about whether she had experienced outright sexual discrimination and her first response pointed to one of the most common constraints women working in male-dominated fields identify: being excluded from traditionally all-male organizations. She said:

You try joining the Rotary in [Small City, USA]. . . . Even if I could, what would I lose by doing something like that? . . . I think there'd be people who'd be against me because they'd see me as a radical female trying to get into Rotary or Kiwanis or Lions . . .

But she went on to identify a strategy she had employed in her previous position as a "way around some of that discrimination." As superintendent, she had paid the civic club membership for one of her principals and went as his guest to every meeting in order to meet face-to-face and shake hands with the community power-brokers. At the point in the interview where Cynthia offered this story, Susan asked, "Was that a way of making it appear that you weren't a radical woman trying to get in?" Cynthia affirmed that interpretation: "Um-hm, um-hm. You see, if I weren't involved in the business I'm in, I might be radical."[5] She continued:

Because I'm tired of it, and uh, there's real discrimination when somebody dis-
agrees with the decision a female has made because it's always, "Who does *that*
woman think she is?" *That* woman. Now a male superintendent makes the same
decision. It's not "Who does that man think he is?" It's maybe, "Who does he
think he is?" or "Why did he do that?" But with a woman it's always, "Who does
that woman think she is?" or "What does *that* woman think she's doing?" It's so
that the woman becomes the problem instead of the issue.

In her emphasis on *that* woman, Cynthia points to the woman's being one
of a few and to the emphasis making visible her isolation, uniqueness, and
problematic presence. The verbal strategy Cynthia has identified reinforces
men's dominance in positions of power in a way similar to that of "gatekeepers' talk" (Chase and Bell 1990). Specifically, in analyzing the individual woman's actions without acknowledging the context within which she
acts—pointing to "*that* woman"—a speaker is "blind to the processes that
recreate men's dominance of positions of power" (Chase and Bell 1990,
174). An utterance as simple as "*that* woman" can highlight individual actions and obscure systematic obstacles to fair participation.

Tension between Action and Consciousness

Two complexities arose in our interview with Cynthia that demonstrate tension between consciousness and action. The first of these was evident in Cynthia's language and had to do with whether women are seen as active agents
or victims of the system. After repeated references to ways in which the system is structured unequally for women and men, Cynthia argued that
women ought to think in terms of "choices" they make. She told us, "I never
use the phrase 'Pay the price' and I try to work on women not to do that.
You just make your choices." The distinction in this language—"choosing"
versus "paying the price"—could be interpreted as a psychological survival
strategy for women whose gender (something they cannot choose) subjects
them to inequitable treatment in the sex-segregated, sex-stratified field of
school administration. Cynthia's distinction was designed to emphasize
women as actors rather than as acted upon; the tension lies between her emphasis on taking action and her experience of being acted upon and discriminated against, as recounted in our interview.

A second example in which ways of thinking and doing pulled against
each other for Cynthia arose toward the end of our discussion of sex discrimination. The following example comes from that discussion. It centers
on the importance of gender in shaping interaction and interpreting experience, and relates closely to the tension between being an active subject and
being "subject to."[6]

Cynthia had been describing how interactions and experience are different for women and men superintendents because of others' expecta-

tions, essentially acknowledging that a superintendent's gender makes a difference. In the course of follow-up inquiries we asked Cynthia if she felt she—as a woman—has had to "prove herself" to the school board. Her immediate response was:

> No. I have had to prove myself as a professional educator. I've been fortunate in the boards that I've worked for, I've not sensed a negative attitude about women, but then I think that I wouldn't be working for them if that negative attitude were there.

De-feminization—apparent in this response where Cynthia asserted her identity as a "professional educator"—stands in sharp contrast to the affiliation with women Cynthia expressed throughout the interviews. Immediately following this interchange, intending to discover whether she had perceived the presence of women on her school board as a form of support, we asked Cynthia how she felt about the fact that there were women on her board. Three of her seven board members were women. "Does it matter to you that there are women on this board?" Susan asked. From her reaction—"No, I love it"—it was apparent that Cynthia heard our inquiry as a negative one, as an inquiry about women board members' negative attitudes toward women superintendents. Cynthia immediately told a story about a female board member she had once worked with who "would rather see me dead . . . than alive." Our miscommunication in this exchange reveals both Cynthia's assumption about having women on the board (it could be negative for a female superintendent) and ours (that having women on the board would be positive for a woman in the superintendency).

Susan followed with the question we had intended to raise, "What about the other side, do you ever feel it as a positive thing? An advantage that there are women on the board?" Cynthia's thoughts on the issue revealed the difficulty of taking gender into account without stereotyping:

> *Cynthia:* Yeah, but when I try to isolate a specific, I don't know. I think the positives are that sometimes the women understand better what I am trying to do in curriculum. Ah, women tend—I'm generalizing and I hate it when I do that— but I think the women tend to be more demanding on details and that's good.
>
> *Susan:* Um-hm.
>
> *Cynthia:* But no, I guess I really view all of them as board members and try to relate to them as individuals.
>
> *Susan:* Um-hm

Cynthia: Yeah, you know I think that's a terrible question for you to ask me because I think that's saying it's okay for me to treat women board members differently from how I treat men and you see I treat them as individual board members. I told you, you know, there are some I knew I had to call weekly, some I needed to call every other day, and some, you know, "call me when you need me" kind of thing.

Susan: Um-hm.

Cynthia: And I can't put those as male or female characteristics.

Susan: Um-hm.

Cynthia: I didn't mean to attack, but you know—

Susan: Right.

Cynthia: I think we, we perpetuate some of the biases ourselves by asking "Is it different because—" Or I know one time I was interviewing . . . and I talked to the consultant and he said, "Well, we specifically asked the board did they care if the candidates, if there were women in the candidate field." And I said, "How dare you? You made it an issue by asking. Wouldn't you just put the best professional educators . . . in the pool?" And he didn't agree with me but I think sometimes it's, we say it's okay for it to be an issue by even asking.

While Cynthia demonstrated sensitivity to gender earlier in the interview (e.g., noting the value of women superintendents' meetings together), in the interchange above she felt compelled to adopt a gender-neutral stance by emphasizing her competence and "professional" status.[7] It seemed that our direct question about potential advantages of having women on the board pushed her into this position by focusing on her gender rather than her profession, a move that emphasized her uniqueness and isolation in the same way that the speaker who refers to "*that* woman" does.

Our question also raised the possibility of gender bias in favor of women. Cynthia had repeatedly made a point that the context of leadership differs for women and men in the superintendency—an argument for gender sensitivity—but here resisted what she felt was our attempt to generalize about gender as a force structuring interactions with women and men on her board. In opposition to our query about gendered interactions which she seemed to perceive as biased and bound by gender, Cynthia insisted that she "relate[d] to them as individuals," an approach which claims to be gender-neutral. This shift in Cynthia's argument is similar to what we have identified elsewhere: some school board members' strategy of removing gender from discussions—claiming gender neutrality—as a defense against the charge of gender bias (Chase and Bell 1990). Cynthia's emphasis on proving herself as a "professional educator" brought competence and merit to the fore and asserted the irrelevance of gender.[8]

Thematic Summary and Discussion

I set out to examine how marginality shapes expressions of gender consciousness among women in the male-dominated public school superintendency. I have a fundamental interest in how women experience maledominated leadership positions, and in marginality because it is thought to produce insight. I have asked whether marginality does produce insight, and if it does, whether this insight can be acted upon. Following Hochschild I listened for affiliation and disaffiliation among women; following Ferguson, I focused on context and not just judgments about the content of consciousness. From Westkott I took a cue to attend to tension between action and consciousness. Taken together, these ways of looking at gender consciousness and its expression help us understand how a context of maledominance in organizations shapes women's experience.

Affiliation as An Expression of Gender Consciousness

Affiliation is an expression of social identity. One's affiliations may communicate solidarity and loyalty, or desire for social mobility. Affiliation is shaped in part by power relations in social environments. In this sense, affiliation is political and may reflect power structures in organizational contexts.

In the case of women in the superintendency, professional relationships with powerful people can facilitate career mobility and activate resources required to accomplish tasks. Because of women's underrepresentation in the superintendency, women are generally not among the power-brokers. Consequently, affiliating with women is sometimes viewed as a waste of time or even as an act of self-destruction (Bell 1990). Hochschild (1974) has labeled disaffiliation or deliberate distancing from women "de-feminization," whether women distance themselves from women or others do it for them.

Each interview examined in this chapter showed examples of defeminization. Pauline and Cynthia both resisted our questions about whether the fact of being a woman had influenced others' assessments of their work as superintendent. Each emphasized her professional performance as relevant to such an assessment and her gender as irrelevant. In assuming that gender interacts with professional status and asking how this works, our questions created tensions by linking two identities—woman and administrator—that have been defined as contradictory. It seemed that Pauline and Cynthia were protesting our focus on their gender because they wanted it to be irrelevant in evaluations of them as professionals.

Alongside this common experience of de-feminization, there are striking differences between Pauline and Cynthia when we explore issues of affiliation as an expression of gender consciousness. While Pauline asserted, "I don't have any time for women's groups," Cynthia was committed to arguing with female colleagues who wanted to dissociate from other women in school administration. Cynthia asserted an obligation on the part of experienced female administrators to provide for others what they had already achieved by urging, "You owe it to those women."

One way of understanding this contrast may be to go back to Pauline's and Cynthia's early career histories. Cynthia, having taught in a male-dominated field (math), had forged strong linkages with other women, worked to protect those associations, and felt she had much to learn from her female colleagues. Pauline's experience in a traditionally female field (home economics) may have convinced her that it is "men's work" that is valued in education and the world, and thus encouraged her to distance herself from women and "women's work."

Contexts in Which Consciousness Develops and Is Expressed

School administration has been associated with stereotypically masculine characteristics (Adkison 1981) and men have dominated school aministration—particularly the secondary principalship and the superintendency—since those positions were created (Hansot and Tyack 1981). In 1991–92, 5.6 percent of the nation's K–12 superintendencies were held by women (Bell and Chase 1993). In an environment as male-dominated as the superintendency, being a woman is inescapably "an issue" because women are visible, isolated, and a numerical minority.

Pauline and Cynthia share a great deal in terms of the context of male dominance in which they work. As women in the superintendency, both have experienced the scarcity of women in the occupation and their own visibility and isolation. They have witnessed the same patterns of sex segregation and stratification. Neither one talks of the field as a site wide open to unfettered achievement. Cynthia cast the field as conservative, comparing it with the corporate world which she believes offers women greater opportunity. Pauline acknowledged that certain behaviors are rewarded and others punished and acted on the principle that careers are made by skirting rather than actively combatting systemic problems of inequality.

Focusing on the *context* in which consciousness develops highlights how male-dominance shapes women's experience. Women in the superintendency operate under conditions of reduced autonomy in spite of their positions of power; that is, they do not define the conditions under which their work will be evaluated by others, by the powerful. As women their actions are visible; they are pressured to conform closely to organizational norms or risk being suspect as professionals. There are few other women with whom they can affiliate, and if they do, this may be seen as subversive. In a system where men and the masculine are standard and valued, it is better for one's career to de-feminize—as Pauline did—than to risk de-professionalization.

Even if one overcomes obstacles to the development of gender consciousness and affiliates with other women—as Cynthia did—there are times when, in a male-dominated context, the need to assert one's identity as a professional will override one's identity as a woman. In male-dominated occupations, the identities of "professional" and "woman" are defined as contradictory; women are required to choose between them. In Cynthia's case, when her gender excluded her from a gathering place for community power-brokers, she attended as the guest of one of her administrative staff members. To openly challenge exclusive membership might have led to de-professionalization, that is, being seen "as a radical female trying to get in." Being "a radical female" suggests disorderly conduct such as breaking rules rather than following them, and seeking admission through pressure or force rather than competence and merit.

When Cynthia said, "You see, if I weren't involved in the business I'm in, I might be radical," she alluded at once to her notions about changing the membership rules and to the conservative occupational context of which those rules are a part. Being a professional in her occupational context seems to involve not openly challenging the rules. Clearly, Pauline would not be mistaken for radical, and Cynthia was acting strategically in order to keep from being so identified.

Tension between Consciousness and Action

In the introduction to this paper, I suggested that we try to understand why women like Schmuck and Schubert's (1995) principals would describe discriminatory experience and at the same time, deny that sexism affects them. One of the possible explanations that has emerged in the process of discussing Pauline's and Cynthia's interviews is that contexts within which women work—in this case, male-dominated contexts—create contradictory expectations, environments, and messages. Male-dominated contexts are not hospitable to women in the ways that they may be to men.

Pauline vehemently opposed an organization for women in school administration and chose to participate instead in the "superintendents' group" (the state-level organization for school district administrators). At the same time, Pauline said that she devoted time to sponsoring internships for individual women. Why is it acceptable to mentor individual women but not be active in women's organizations? My interpretation of these apparently contradictory assertions—that women's groups are undesirable but supporting individual female aspirants is worthwhile—points to the male-dominated context of school administration. Pauline's ambivalence toward advocacy for women, I argue, is a result of her simultaneous belonging and not belonging. Although she has experienced prejudice and discrimination (e.g., lower pay than men for equivalent work), she resists thinking of women as an excluded group and she refuses to engage in collective activity to challenge discrimination. Pauline's choices suggest that her values and behavior approximate the dominant group's, and that she understands what is required to join the "inner circle." Her choices are interpretable in the context of her contradictory statuses as outsider and insider.

In talking with Cynthia we noted her resistance to our suggestion that as a woman, she might have been required to prove herself to the school board. Cynthia's response was to deny the relevance of gender and to underscore her affiliation with "professional educator[s]." In the context of Cynthia's critical perspective on sexism in educational administration and her efforts to organize women for collective action in the profession, this instance of disaffiliation was startling and seemed contradictory. However, women in male-dominated occupations are often called upon to distinguish themselves from a negative stereotype of women; to emphasize her competence as a superintendent was a way for Cynthia to do this.

As the interview went on we noticed a related tension in Cynthia's talk about her work. In contrast with her consistent sensitivity to the significance of gender in school administration throughout our conversations, in one interchange Cynthia adopted a gender-neutral position, insisting that she treated male and female board members "as individuals." This occurred when we asked whether it mattered that there were women on her board. Both her first response ("No. I love it.") and her second response (roughly, that women understand curriculum issues and are more detail-conscious than men) acknowledged that gender matters and tapped into stereotypes about women. Cynthia then explicitly resisted her own generalizations about women and chastised us for suggesting that "it's okay . . . to treat women board members differently from . . . men." It seems contradictory to say that gender matters and simultaneously assert gender neutrality.

Cynthia's gender consciousness—built on experiences of discrimination and an awareness of herself as a member of a socially stigmatized group—did not immunize her against others' charges of gender bias. Her sensitivity to gender pervaded our conversations and Cynthia was obviously very much alert to the influences of gender in her world. But in the face of a question about possible advantages of having women on her board, Cynthia's response was to remove gender from the discussion. Its removal does contradict her more pervasive commitment to gender sensitivity but is explicable if we understand the conditions under which she was speaking. Importantly, those conditions included the presence of two female researchers who were studying the effects of gender bias in the superintendency, specifically in board–superintendent relations. Cynthia perceived our interest in the dynamics of gender bias as potentially perpetuating gender bias. By asking about it we were somehow reinforcing it. In fact, Cynthia had spent a good deal of her energy fighting implicit and covert sexism. To be faced with an explicit, overt acknowledgment of its workings and to respond to an invitation to explore ways gender might work in women's favor in a male-dominated context may have seemed too much like disloyalty, defection, or an act of treason against other women in the superintendency.

Concluding Observations

What do these analyses imply for practitioners and scholars interpreting experience and understanding action?

First, marginality can result in pro-equity action if marginalized people develop a sense of identity among themselves ("minority consciousness") and are able to collaborate politically to reform an organization. A major obstacle to the development of a feminist (or other "minority") consciousness is disaffiliation. Particularly in male-dominated professions such as the superintendency, pressure to disaffiliate from other women arises from women's need to prove themselves different from a negative stereotype of others like them.

For women who are practitioners in male-dominated fields, this implies that reluctance toward networks of women and ambivalence about women's rights and feminism are barriers that must be overcome if one is to have female colleagues and collaborate to change the profession. Pressure to disaffiliate from other women comes from sexism in an occupation's traditions. Yielding to this pressure will result in women's isolation and inability to build solidarity with other women in the occupation, and will ultimately inhibit collective political action for social change.

For scholars these notions about consciousness and marginality are particularly important as they relate to the social context. Feminist theorists have identified the advantages of women's outsider status (summarized in Harding 1991) in knowing and analyzing the social order. Questions surrounding the connection between insight and action are a next step; fewer feminist theorists have dealt effectively with the relationship of consciousness to action.[9] Notions about marginality and minority consciousness explored in these interviews may be useful in developing theories of women's action in male-dominated contexts. An example of how this might work is offered in Schmuck and Schubert's study on the nineteen principals' gender equity commitments. According to the authors, principals "personalized" sex discrimination rather than seeing it systemically (1995). Schmuck and Schubert also observed that the women wanted to be "integrated" into rather than "segregated" from their male colleagues. These preferences and the absence of pro-equity action are predictable when one takes the context into account.

Secondly, when a woman's action contradicts her experience or an expression of her consciousness, look to the context in which she is acting for clues to understanding the contradiction. Tensions or contradictions often arise from the organizational environment; in Westkott's (1979) words, women sometimes oppose the very conditions to which they conform. Consistency or "fit" between women's consciousness and action should not be assumed.

For practitioners and scholars this observation implies the importance of acknowledging contradictory perspectives in women administrators' work lives, perhaps even seeking them out. While it is definitely the case that women in school administration have "insider" status (vis-à-vis school practice and policy), they also have "outsider" status (vis-à-vis school leadership and policymaking in general). The value in being on both sides of the boundary lies in "the possibility of seeing the relation between dominant activities and beliefs and those that arise on the 'outside'" (Harding 1991, 131–32). Both practitioners and scholars can benefit from noticing this dual status. We must also attend to the question of whether, and under what conditions, those learnings will be transformed into action.

For scholars the observations about minority consciousness also imply some questions about racial and ethnic consciousness and their relation to gender consciousness. Hochschild's barriers to minority consciousness are not limited to women's experience. There are other social identities—such as race and ethnicity—that act in a way parallel to gender. How is gender consciousness shaped by and interactive with ethnicity, race, social class, and other aspects of identity? Are there ways in which one's ethnic and class consciousness facilitate or impede the development of gender consciousness?

Finally, taking to heart Ferguson's charge to evaluate the context in which women's gender consciousness develops, we might seek contexts for study in which women's consciousness develops amidst "connections with others [that] are rooted in equality, not domination" (1984, 179). What would we learn about gender consciousness by observing "context(s) of freedom and community" and talking with women whose awarenesses are shaped by them?

Notes

1. These in-depth interviews are part of a larger study of women superintendents and gatekeepers to that occupation in the United States. The twenty-seven participating superintendents come from diverse racial and ethnic backgrounds (white, black, Hispanic, Asian-American, and American Indian), geographic regions, (South, West, Midwest, and Central), and district sizes (200 to over 50,000 enrollment). Each superintendent spent from two to twelve hours with two co-investigators, discussing her district, her career, her perceptions of the profession, and her perspective on gender issues. Nine husbands of superintendents, forty-four local school board members, and eight state level observers also participated in interviews. All interviews were taped in their entirety, transcribed, and the transcripts checked for accuracy. Superintendent transcripts range from 40 to 130 single-spaced typescript pages, totaling nearly 3,000 pages of text. Other transcripts range from 20 to 50 pages, yielding an additional 2,000 pages. Field notes and transcribed debriefings generated by the co-investigators are a third source of data upon which the study draws.

2. This co-investigation was conducted with Susan E. Chase, a sociologist with whom I worked for four years at the University of Tulsa. We co-conceived the project, conducted all interviews jointly, and have co-authored a number of papers based on this study. For these reasons, her contributions in the interviews are an explicit part of the paper. The analyses laid out in this paper, however, are my own responsibility.

3. I use the term "gender consciousness" to refer to what Hochschild called "minority consciousness." Hochschild's use of the term "minority consciousness" in the 1970s was meant to draw attention to numerical imbalances and the resulting structural pressures against affiliation. The term "minority" has come to imply something different in the 1990s.

4. For development of the idea of a gendered structure in public schools, see Chase and Bell (1990) and Martin (1991).

5. The original quote was as it is here in the text; I have modified it for the title of the paper.

6. For a more thorough discussion of the distinction between being a subject and being subject to, see our chapter in Rogers and McMahan's forthcoming *Oral History Interviewing*.

7. The way I make sense of this draws substantially on Jane Roland Martin's (1985) tripartite distinction among orientations to gender as social force. Martin identifies three positions: a gender-bound position (in which gender is the only difference between persons that matters), a gender-blind or gender-neutral position (from which it is argued that gender makes no difference at all), and gender-sensitivity (a position that asserts the importance of being aware of the workings of gender).

8. See S. Chase's (1988) chapter in A. Todd and S. Fisher for a more elaborate discussion of this dynamic.

9. Patricia Hill Collins (1990) is one who has. In *Black Feminist Thought* she discusses the insider-outsider stance as essential to black women's activism.

Bibliography

Adkison, J. A. (1981). Women in school administration: A review of the research. *American Educational Research Journal,* 51(3), 311–43.

Adkison, J. A. (1982). *Advocates and administrators: Perspectives on the Title IX coordinator's role.* Paper presented at the annual meetings of the American Educational Research Association, New York.

Adkison, J. A. (1983). Administrators and advocates: Perspectives on the Title IX coordinator's role. *Journal of Educational Equity and Leadership,* 3(2), 149–64.

Bell, C. S. (1990). Gender and the meaning of professional relationships for women in the superintendency. Paper presented at the annual meetings of the AERA SIG Research on Women in Education, Milwaukee.

Bell, C. S. and Chase, S. E. (1993). The underrepresentation of women in school leadership. In C. Marshall (ed.), *The new politics of race and gender,* 1992 Politics of Education Association yearbook. London: Falmer.

Chase, S. E. (1988). Making sense of "The woman who becomes a man." In A. Todd and S. Fisher (eds.), *Gender and discourse: The power of talk.* Norwood, NJ: Ablex.

Chase, S. E. and Bell, C. S. (1990). Ideology, discourse, and gender: How gatekeepers talk about women school superintendents. *Social Problems,* 37(2), 163–77.

———. Interpreting the complexity of women's subjectivity. In K. L. Rogers and E. McMahan (eds.), *Oral history interviewing: Essays on interactional processes.* New York: Lawrence Erlbaum.

Ferguson, K. E. (1984). *The feminist case against bureaucracy.* Philadelphia: Temple University Press.

Gerson, J. M. and Peiss, K. (1985). Boundaries, negotiation, consciousness: Reconceptualizing gender relations. *Social Problems,* 32, 317–31.

Hansot, E. and Tyack, D. (1981). *The dream deferred: A golden age for women school administrators.* Policy paper no. 81-C2. Stanford: Center for Educational Research at Stanford.

Harding, S. (1991). *Whose science? Whose knowledge? Thinking from women's lives.* Ithaca, NY: Cornell University Press.

Hill Collins, P. (1990). *Black feminist thought: Knowledge, consciousness, and the politics of empowerment.* Boston: Unwin Hyman.

Hochschild, A. (1974). Making it: Marginality and obstacles to minority consciousness. In R. B. Kundsin (ed.), *Women and success: The anatomy of achievement.* New York: William Morrow and Co.

Kanter, R. M. (1977). *Men and women of the corporation.* New York: Basic Books.

Martin, J. R. (1985). *Reclaiming a conversation: The ideal of the educated woman.* New Haven: Yale University Press.

Martin, P. Y. (1991). Gender, interaction, and inequality in organizations. In C. Ridgeway (ed.), *Gender, interaction, and inequality.* New York: Springer-Verlag.

Schmuck, P. A. and Schubert, J. G. (1995). Women administrators' views on sex equity: Exploring issues of integration and information. In Dunlap, D. and P. Schmuck (eds.), *Women leading in education.* Albany: SUNY Press.

Westkott, M. (1979). Feminist criticism of the social sciences. *Harvard Educational Review,* 49(4), 422–30.

SEVENTEEN

The Glass Ceiling Reconsidered: Views from Below

Mary Woods Scherr

The glass ceiling is an image representing obstacles that prevent women from advancing to the top of their careers. Although women have a full view of the top of the organization, they bump against an invisible shield of resistance and can rise no further. In educational administration the top of the organizational ladder is the superintendency.

Researchers have predicted that as more women occupy line positions in school districts (such as assistant superintendents or directors), we would see more women join the ranks of the superintendency (Schmuck 1982). This has not been the case, however. Only about 4 percent of district superintendents today are women, even though more than 20 percent of line district office positions are filled by women (Schuster and Foote 1990). Have these women risen to a glass ceiling? Can they rise with a view to the top and proceed no further? Or, are there other explanations for the small percentage of women holding superintendencies?

Method of Study

To answer these questions, I interviewed thirteen women who belong to the potential pool for future superintendents. I wanted to learn about

313

their aspirations and hear their views of the superintendency. The subjects for this study were thirteen women who are assistant superintendents or directors in one southern California county, representing union and unified school districts and ranging from student enrollment of less than 2,000 to over 30,000. The length of time they had held a district office position varied from six months to nine years. Eleven of the women worked for a male superintendent and had never worked for a female superintendent. Two women, who worked for the same female superintendent, had been in their positions for only six months at the time of the interviews.

The interviews, which varied in length from fifty minutes to two hours, included questions about each woman's career background, her views of the superintendency, her perceptions of the daily life of a superintendent and whether or not she aspired to the superintendency. To learn about individual perceptions, I asked open-ended questions and invited additional comments. Each woman received a transcript of the interview and a request to modify the transcript to assure that her perceptions were recorded as accurately as possible (Blackmore 1989). Data analysis was guided by Glaser and Strauss's (1967) method for grounded theory in which themes and dimensions are derived from the data by comparative analysis.

Four of the thirteen women aspired to become a superintendent, another was unsure but thought she might "down the line," one was retiring, and the remaining seven assistant superintendents or directors did not intend to become superintendents. While these women had a view to the top, they chose not to pursue the superintendency. The way they saw the role enacted may not have been congruent with their views of themselves nor their preferred ways of working since they saw the role as one which is primarily traditional, controlling, hierarchical, political, and public. Both the aspirants and nonaspirants gave substantially similar views of the superintendent's role. This chapter first focuses on their views of the superintendency and second discusses alternative ways of looking at the position that more women may find appealing.

Views from Below: Images of The Superintendency

Interviews with district women administrators included several questions designed to learn how they perceived the role of superintendent. Analysis of the interview data revealed three dominant themes: The power inherent in the role, the political nature of the superintendency, and the public nature of the role.

The Power Inherent in The Role

The superintendency was seen as a powerful role, one that was responsible for most of the change and action within a district. One woman said:

> The power of the position [enables the superintendent] to make lots of changes. . . . If you can get the OK from people, you can go, you can move, you can allocate resources.

Another woman stated:

> I find it to be a very powerful position . . . direct influence on the instruction . . . direct relationship with the community and a direct relationship on the morale of the employees of the district.

She concluded by repeating slowly, "A very powerful position."

Most of the interviewees saw the superintendent as a person of strength, who used the formal authority of the position as an opportunity for direct action:

> No other position gives an individual the opportunity to create and dream what needs to be done and to meet the needs of children in the district. . . . You have the power and influence to see that the dream comes through.

One woman described the superintendency as the "ultimate power position":

> If the superintendent has a very strong vision he/she is in the ultimate power position to work with the board, the community and the staff to lead the group. As an assistant [superintendent] you are always still an assistant, you aren't ultimately in the driver's seat.

Another administrator expressed a similar view: "If your goal is to impact education, then the chance of achieving that goal is greater than in any other position."

Other women emphasized the superintendent "is in the top position," "is the one who can drive the direction of the district," "can establish the vision," and "can make lots of changes."

In addition, these women described superintendents as "the chief administrator," "the CEO for the district," the one in the "top paid position," and the "corporate manager of a major business or industry." The tone of their voices as well as their words often indicated their perception of the superintendency as a position of high status, authority, and control.

The women who plan to become superintendents apparently assumed that since schools are complex, bureaucratic, and hierarchical organizations, superintendents need to wield power in the ways they described: directing, driving, and establishing power. The women who do not plan to become superintendents may not see themselves wielding power in these ways and therefore, did not aspire to a role they did not "match."

The Political Nature of The Superintendency

The political nature of the superintendency, which included working with elected members of the school board, was frequently mentioned as a negative aspect of the position. In response to a request to describe the superintendent's role, one woman replied: "The position is exceptionally challenging and difficult because of the politics and visibility." Another woman said:

> The first word that comes to mind is politician . . . they have a tremendous responsibility for networking in the community with businesses, certainly with board members who are elected officials—which is a whole different ballgame.

One administrator, who did not wish to become a superintendent, offered this specific reason: "I see it [the superintendency] as a much more heavily political role than I would like to play in education."

Nearly all of the thirteen women mentioned work with board members as a major part of a superintendent's political work. One woman stated: "He's the principal decision-maker, even though the board is the nominal decision-maker. He guides them, informs them, molds them. He's the politician."

Several comments focused on the skills required in working with board members: "You have to develop a lot of patience [with board members] and wait to bring people along." A few gave bitter descriptions of board members. For example, "They have no idea about a school district and they have their own agendas."

Furthermore, the board contributed to job insecurity; the "politics of the job" made the superintendent vulnerable to the actions of the board. One woman explained:

> The average length of the superintendency is rather short. . . . I think you are taking a risk when you step out there, you are the one who is ultimately responsible for everything, if there are any problems, if there is any turmoil in the district, it is probable the superintendent is going to go.

Another woman offered a more graphic description of the dilemma faced by a superintendent:

> Your security and your career is predicated on five elected board officials . . .
> you must be in harmony with three of them at any one time otherwise you're
> out on the street.

Board members were seen as those who had their own agendas, often
represented special interest groups, sometimes had little knowledge about
the school district, and were often responsible for the short tenure of superintendents. Those who expressed a long term commitment to their career did not want a temporary role; those who wanted to focus on education
rather than "politics" wanted to stay in an education role. Again, perception
of a role that could not be changed appeared to influence these women's
choices more than a perceived glass ceiling.

The Public Nature of The Superintendent's Role

The women administrators described superintendents as necessarily
highly visible in public meetings, at civic functions, and in community organizations. They felt that being "so much in the public eye" and fulfilling
"expectations of a very active role in the community" accounted for much
of the job's stress. One woman explained:

> There is a personal liability you pay in your free time, social time, and personal
> time—whatever that may be. Unless you choose not to participate in any social
> service or community organizations. . . . I think a superintendent has to do
> that . . . what you are saying is that my time is your time, community, and I will
> give my all for it.

Others spoke of the stress which comes from "working with diverse
groups, demanding groups." For example: "Sometimes you are out there
with your neck on the line and lots of people are ready, willing and able to
be there and take shots at what you are trying to accomplish."

The press was also blamed as a cause of job-related stress: "Some superintendents are subjected to public hangings with some editors if they take
stands on issues which may not be popular."

The long hours required to do the job was also related to the public nature of the position. The following phrases were typical: "All consuming,"
"tremendous demands on time," "your life isn't your own," and "eighteen-
hour days." Yet, when probing further, I frequently found that the woman I
was interviewing worked nearly as many hours as the superintendent she was
describing. In a few cases, her hours were longer "because I can't delegate
as much as he does."

Another participant described the superintendent as needing "to be
aware of everything that is happening in the district," which she felt was "ex-
traordinarily stressful." One woman said:

I suspect that you never have it all out of your mind. There would never be a time to be completely free of the worry of the scandal of something happening because the security system down there or the fields here or a teacher may be in serious difficulty. . . . Every decision you make has the possibility for disaster. Anything can blow up at any time.

The political and public aspects of the superintendency were closely intertwined. Working with a lay, elected board required major amounts of time and a "lot of patience to bring people along." And taking an active role in the community in addition to the responsibility for the entire district could result in an "all consuming" job with "eighteen-hour" days. The amount of time required, job insecurity, pressure from special interest groups and from the press created stress that some women considered "too big a price to pay." Two women felt that the public and political commitments would crowd out what they liked best. As one woman explained: "I have always liked the curriculum development and instruction . . . if I could keep my hands in curriculum . . . with a superintendent's role I don't know how that would be possible."

Discussion of Alternative Views of The Superintendency

The women administrators in this study saw the superintendent's role as powerful, political, and public. Although several women described their superintendent as a "team builder," or as one who practiced "shared decision-making," the predominant words and phrases these women used to describe the superintendent's role are those associated with formal power in bureaucratic, complex organizations: "Establish the vision;" "move, allocate, and make changes;" "drive the direction of the district." This language suggests decisiveness, action, goal orientation, and a high degree of autonomy, authority, and power for the superintendent.

Similar language was found in the interviews with 144 Oregon school administrators, reported by Kempner (1989). Administrators admired superintendents who could "make things happen" and possessed a "can do" attitude. Kempner submits that the culture of education is:

> Based upon conceptions of control and authority drawn from the metaphors of business, the military, and athletics. Those individuals who do not possess these characteristics, notably women and minorities, face extraordinary difficulties in entering and surviving in educational administration. (p. 119)

The women interviewed for this study had entered and survived in school administration and had been promoted to central office positions, in several cases the next highest position to the superintendent. It is, there-fore, not surprising that many of them have adopted the dominant language and metaphors of the profession, which are associated with bureaucracies.

Several recent studies have reported alternative ways of looking at the superintendent's role within a bureaucratic organization. A new way of look-ing at power, proposed by Dunlap and Goldman (1991), considers profes-sional power as "facilitative"—a type of power that differs from traditional, authoritative power typical of large, bureaucratic organizations. Facilitative power "is exercised and actualized through others on the basis of trust and reciprocity" and involves "a relationship between professionals who behave as peers rather than as superiors or subordinates" (p. 22).

In a study of women superintendents, Bell and Chase (1989) found that women superintendents talked about "trusting and investing in their staff members," frequently used teaching metaphors, and integrated "a focus on followers with a focus on achieving tasks" (p. 10). They recognized that "an organization *is* its people." When they felt it necessary, they conformed to "bureaucratic norms, procedures, and language" but they also resisted "the dehumanizing aspects of bureaucracy" (p. 11). They employed strategies that "de-emphasize hierarchy, that facilitate the participation and growth of staff, and that emphasize the value of staff contributions and abilities" (p. 14), they also candidly admitted that shared decision making reduced the demands on their time.

"What goes on in the classrooms and relationships with teachers and other staff" were strong commitments, which Bell and Chase interpreted as "examples of women's 'submerged voice' and as a 'voice of resistance' in the face of bureaucracy's dehumanizing aspects" (p. 17).

In a study of administrative women, Cooper (1994) also reported that the women both reproduced and resisted bureaucracies. Drawing on the work of Ferguson (1984), she discussed the "multiple dilemmas" that women face in working within educational bureaucratic organizations as a context for her analysis of their journal writings. She identified three cate-gories of bureaucratic pressures: those faced by all members within the or-ganization, those faced by administrators, and those faced by women as token members. Women administrators who are tokens face unusually strong expectations "to conform to male bureaucratic structures and stan-dards, to speak and behave in the rational, linear modes that constitute the norm for life in bureaucracies" (p. 3). In her analysis of their journal writ-ing she discovered that administrative women attempt "to empower them-selves and to effect change within their organizations" (p. 2).

The political aspect of the superintendency that was discussed in the greatest detail by the women administrators was the difficulty of working with a lay school board. The "politics of the job" resulted in job insecurity, they reported. This is a standard topic in administration textbooks. For example, Konnert and Augenstein (1990) warn: "Successful superintendents must never forget that they are employees of the board of education" (p. 113). The women district administrators were fully aware that a superintendent "works for a lay board" and that the average tenure of urban school superintendents has dropped to two and one half years (Urban Superintendents 1992).

Bell and Chase found that "negotiating authority with one's school board continues to be one of the most problematic issues for district leaders. The women district administrators cited in this study also strongly felt that this was indeed a problematic area. They spoke of the need for a superintendent to spend a major amount of time with board members "influencing" and "guiding" but the context indicated that concern for the superintendent's authority as the chief officer of the district was a continuing issue. If "an organization *is* its people," the school board members need to be included as part of the organization and "trusting and investing" in staff members can be extended to board members. Teaching metaphors are also appropriate in describing a superintendent's role with the board and community. Shakeshaft (1986) reported that "women . . . are likely to view the job of principal or superintendent as that of a master teacher or educational leader while men view it from a managerial, industrial perspective" (p. 118). The women interviewees, however, had had minimal or no experience with women superintendents.

The political and public nature of the role significantly contributes to the power of the superintendency. Public schools are governed by elected public officials who conduct their business in public meetings. Because the superintendent is "in the top position," he/she becomes the spokesperson for the district and the district's representative at public functions. It is precisely because the superintendent is "so much in the public eye" the he/she has tremendous power to influence, to promote coalitions, and to encourage collaboration.

A collaborative process that involves members of the staff, the school board, and the community is vital for the development of a district vision that receives commitment and engenders community pride. The superintendent's political and public roles can provide the link between school and community for the necessary coalition building.

The women administrators in this study did not describe the development of a vision as a comprehensive, collaborative process involving members of the staff and the community. Three women referred to a district committee that included one or two community representatives, but most spoke of the superintendent as the one who had "an opportunity to bring people toward his or her vision," as the one with the ability "to establish the vision," or "to drive the direction of the district." Fullan (1992) has pointed out that administrators can be blinded by their own vision and "feel they must manipulate the teachers and school culture to conform to it" (p. 19).

According to Pitner (1981), women superintendents spent "more time with community members who were not parents" than did male superintendents (p. 289). The women also taught administration classes as adjunct professors, sponsored women teachers "for leadership positions within and outside of the school district . . . [and] spent their unscheduled time handling curriculum and instructional matters" (p. 289). Pitner's study, therefore, indicated that women superintendents continued a teaching role, fostered relationships by sponsoring women teachers, and stayed committed to curriculum and instructional matters—a commitment several women administrators in this study feared would not be possible for a superintendent.

Conclusion

Seven of the thirteen women district administrators in this study did not aspire to become superintendents. The glass-ceiling phenomenon may be a partial explanation for the low percentage of women in the superintendency, but does not appear to be an adequate one. This is not to say that barriers and biases against women no longer exist. The interview data, however, suggest that the perception of the role may also explain why some women don't want to be superintendents. The women in this study saw the superintendency as powerful, political, and public. They saw the power derived from the formal authority of the top position in the district. They did not view power in alternative ways nor express an understanding of power as interwoven with the political and public aspects in essential, powerful ways that enable a public school superintendent to change schools for the benefit of students and society. On the contrary, even the women who currently aspire to the superintendency tended to view the political and public aspects as a disadvantage to being a superintendent.

These views of the superintendency, which reflected a traditional, control and direct approach, were based primarily on their experiences of working with male superintendents. Although we do not know nearly enough about women superintendents, research on women's psychological development (Gilligan 1982; Miller 1987); on women's ways of knowing (Belenky, Clinchy, Goldberger, and Tarule 1986); and on women's ways of leading (Astin 1991; Helgesen 1990; Rosener 1990) suggests there may be gender-related differences in how the role of the superintendency is fulfilled. That research has emphasized the tendency for women to value relationships and collaboration. Others (Sergiovanni 1992; Fullan 1992; Shakeshaft 1986; and

Foster 1989) are challenging the traditional organizational theory of schools that is dominated by concepts of hierarchy, power, and authority and endorse the concepts of collaboration, community, and relationships.

More women might find the superintendency appealing if they had different conceptions of the role and different models suggesting the collaborative nature of the position. Women who plan to become superintendents may also benefit from alternative views of the position. If district administrators perceived a superintendent's primary role as one of commitment to relationships, with all members of the staff, with board members, and with community members; if they realized teaching and community metaphors were as important in administration as in the classroom; if they knew some superintendents continued to be involved with curriculum and instruction; and if they saw the political, public nature of the position as an opportunity for coalition building more women might aspire to the superintendency and become mentors and role models. Women below the glass ceiling might then see more superintendents who resist the pressures "to conform to male bureaucratic structures and standards" (Cooper 1994), who seek to empower themselves and who use facilitative power to transform schools into humane learning communities for students, teachers, and administrators.

Bibliography

Astin, H. and Leland, C. (1991). *Women of influence, women of vision.* San Francisco: Jossey-Bass.

Belenky, M. F., Clinchy, B. M., Goldberger, N. R., and Tarule, J. M. (1986). *Women's ways of knowing: The development of self, voice and mind.* New York: Basic Books.

Bell, C. S. and Chase, S. E. (1989). Women as educational leaders: Resistance and conformity. Presented at the annual meetings of the American Educational Research Association, San Francisco.

Blackmore, J. (1989). Changing from within: Feminist educators and administrative leadership. *Peabody Journal of Education,* 66(3), 19–40.

Cooper, J. (1995). Administrative women and their writing: Reproduction and resistance in bureaucracies. In D. M. Dunlap and P. A. Schmuck (eds.), *Women leading in education.* New York: SUNY Press.

Dunlap, D. M. and Goldman, P. (1991). Rethinking power in schools. *Educational Administration Quarterly,* 27(1), 5–29.

Foster, W. (1989). The administrator as a transformative intellectual. *Peabody Journal of Education,* 66(3), 5–18.

Fullan, M. (1992). Visions that blind. *Educational Leadership,* 19(5) 19–20.

Gilligan, C. (1982). *In a different voice.* Cambridge, MA: Harvard University Press.

Glaser, B. G. and Strauss, A. L. (1967) *The discovery of grounded theory.* New York: Aldine.

Helegesen, S. (1990). *The female advantage.* New York: Doubleday Dell.

Kempner, K. (1989). Getting into the castle of educational administration. *Peabody Journal of Education, 66*(3), 104–23.

Konnert, M. W. and Augenstein, J. J. (1990). *The superintendency in the nineties.* Lancaster, PA: Technomic.

Miller, J. B. (1986). *Toward a theory of women's development.* Boston: Beacon.

Pitner, N. J. (1981). Hormones and harems: Are the activities of superintending different for a woman? In P. A. Schmuck, W. W. Charters Jr., and R. O. Carlson, (eds.), *Educational policy and management: Sex differentials.* New York: Academic Press.

Rosener, J. B. (1990). Ways women lead. *Harvard Business Review, 68*(6), 119–25.

Schmuck, P. (1982). *The Oregon Story.* Wellesley, MA: Education Development Corporation.

Schuster, D. J. and Foote, T. H. (1990). Differences abound between male and female superintendents. *The School Administrator, 47*(2), 14–19.

Sergiovanni, T. J. (1992). Why we should seek substitutes for leadership. *Educational Leadership, 49*(5), 41–45.

Shakeshaft, C. (1986). Female organizational culture. *Educational Horizons, 64*(3), 117–22.

The Urban Superintendents. (1992). *The Urban Superintendents' Sounding Board, 1*(1), 1–3.

IV

Shaping Alternative Visions of Leadership: An Agenda for A New Century

EIGHTEEN

To Walk the Red Road as School Leaders

P. J. Ford Slack and Patricia Cornelius

> Walking the Red Road . . . is a way of love
> and respect for nature and a belief in the
> simple truths of family, caring, humor,
> and sharing.
>
> —A Red Lake Ojibwe elder, 1989

Introduction

This chapter attempts to capture, through story and discussion, how people in one primary culture can contribute to understanding others. The story is about an Anglo woman and an Ojibwe woman working as principal and superintendent in a Native American school. Here, story is both research methodology and an honoring of the Ojibwe belief in story as truth.

The discussion that follows the story is our constructed meaning of this story in terms of the considerably more linear, masculinist traditions of Western educational "science." While we constructed this discussion with many friends and colleagues from several cultures, it is ultimately our voices that attempt to find a sung harmony among the different voices and cultures.

The Setting

The Bug-O-Nay-Ge-Shig School is located on one of the six reservations of the Chippewa tribes in northern Minnesota. Known as the "Bug School," it sits in a beautiful eighty-acre site of cedar and white birch forests, lakes, and eagle-breeding areas. It was established in 1976 as a Bureau of Indian Affairs (BIA) magnet school in response to parental and teacher protest over the perceived poor treatment of native American children in the local public schools (Chase 1991). By 1984, the school had expanded to include kindergarten through twelfth grade. Today it serves over 600 students from ten public school districts. Buses travel more than 3600 miles each day to transport children from homes which are located on reservation and non-reservation land across northern Minnesota.

This is an unusual school. It embraces an open-enrollment policy with a mandate to serve any and all Indian children. "Children," in this context, were described to me by one member of the school staff as including all Indian students from any tribe. "Family" was used in a much broader sense than that typically implied by the Euro-American traditional model of family as a singular descendent tree with two parents and children and other, directly blood-related relatives. In the Ojibwe sense, family includes not only parents, children, aunts, uncles, grandparents, and so on, but also neighbors, friends, co-workers, and others who touch on the lived lives of the school. Aides, bus drivers, teachers, janitors, kitchen staff, parents, and so forth, are expected to function as the school family that comes together in happiness or crisis. Since every child is seen as a son or daughter, the question that is asked in a time of crisis is not, "Why doesn't the family do something?" but, "What do we need to do as family to protect, support or help this child?" This concept of family is woven into the school through open classrooms, the teen wellness clinic, the nursery, small class sizes, flexible school hours, and the availability of all staff at all hours to the children.

This broad concept of family can also be seen in the absence of some traditional features of a public school. There is no traditional school board and there is no teachers' contract or union. The Parent Advisory Council represents the major villages and towns of the student population. While the goal is to have an all-tribal school staff, many of the certified teachers and staff are not tribally affiliated because of insufficient numbers of certified tribal people. Regardless of tribal or nontribal status, current staff are expected to act as part of the family. What that means is not clearly spelled out for a white person, like myself, coming in to the school, nor, I discovered, is it always clear to those who have lived their lives as members of the tribal family. It is something learned and lived over time.

The Situation

I first met Patty Cornelius when she was a student in my educational administration class at nearby Bemidji State University. As a new resident of the state, I knew little about the schools of my students. I soon discovered that most of my students had gone to school with Ojibwe students, and often had them in their own schools. But like me, they knew little about the Ojibwe school, avoided talking about the reservations, and generally talked about Ojibwe people as being "outside" of the education community. As a member of the class and a member of the Ojibwe people, Patty began to wash away our ignorance. She was an open, honest spokesperson for her people and her school. She soon brought all of us to a deeper, personal understanding of the biases perpetuated in educational staff evaluation systems that I had been trying to discuss in the class. I think that we all learned more about the issues that arise when one culture is dominated or suppressed or not understood by the predominant culture. Patty subsequently received many invitations from other class members to speak about her experiences and her school at the public schools in the area.

When Patty came to my class, she was the elementary principal of the Bug School. Within the year, she had been asked to be the superintendent of the school, and she had asked me to serve as the new elementary principal in her place. Our roles changed dramatically. The story that follows is about our first year together as principal and superintendent. It is about community and about being "insider" and "outsider," in the language of Hubbard and Randall's thoughtful 1988 book on that subject. It is about hierarchy and role, and it is about "top-downness" and "bottom-upness." It is also about constructing personal and shared meaning out of complex events in complex lives. After we tell our story, I will come back to discuss community, hierarchy and roles, and constructed meaning in terms of what this might mean for a better understanding of women leading in education.

Patty and PJ's Story

Patty: I remember the first class with PJ. She had asked us to do a project on supervision or professional development related to our school. I knew that most of the people in the class would not know much about BIA (Bureau of Indian Affairs) schools or Ojibwe life. So, I was different because of the school and because of my tribe. I was also different because I was a woman and relatively younger than my classmates. The other members of the class were white men who were administrators in public schools and who were older than me.

When I presented my project, I remember that the room got very quiet. I was afraid that I wasn't doing the right thing, that I was an outsider again, and that I had messed up. But PJ didn't seem upset so I continued and later, PJ and my classmates told me how much they had learned and many of the other administrators asked me to come to their schools and talk about the Bug School and tribal life.

PJ: Patty's presentation in class was amazing. In an hour she had helped these veteran practitioners more than all of my articles and books and dramatic teacher pacings. She also turned to me after her presentation and said, "PJ, the theories are interesting but do not help me address the problems and challenges of my school and my students." She was also very kind not to point out that this blindness to tribal reality and needs had gone on for close to five hundred years. I understood that while my university status and my Ph.D. gave me an insider edge on the one hand, Patty was the insider when viewing practices from her culture.

Later we talked about what had happened in class and began to use the "insider-outsider" images to help us understand the problems presented to each of us in our professional worlds. Patty certainly knew her world better than I could, yet was quick to point out some of the stresses presented to her as a woman trying to lead in a role traditionally filled by white males, even in the Ojibwe culture. I tried to describe my world of academic rituals and practices, where I had insider status but often felt like an outsider because of my beliefs, my background (not administration, but special education and science), my gender—even my hair (bright red, naturally curly, long, and uncontained).

We came to respect each other as friends and colleagues. I was still shocked when she asked me to join the Bug School family as principal. Nevertheless, I was quick to accept her offer. I was not happy in my new faculty position, and I could not resist the chance to experience another culture from "inside." Besides, I was honored to be asked and I knew that I could depend on Patty to help me in my new role.

Patty: When I was asked to be superintendent, there had never been an Ojibwe woman in that role. The superintendency had been the domain of men and I was taking over the role from an ex-Marine whose administrative style seemed straight out of the Desert Storm ethos that permeated the country that year. While I was an insider to the school, I was certainly different in terms of having attended universities and being in leadership roles. And I was much younger than previous leaders, too. Age is a significant factor in the Ojibwe community where wisdom is associated with revered elder status. People saw me as capable of leadership, but I didn't fit the model of revered elder-as-leader in my own community.

PJ pointed something else out to me. In one of our conversations, she said, "You are very attractive, too, and—you know how pretty women in powerful positions get treated—as if they are dumb or worse." She asked if that was the same for the Ojibwe, and I had to admit that it was something that was so pervasive that I mostly hated even thinking about it.

I knew there were lots of issues for both of us, but I was sure glad that PJ would be there working with me while we tried to face or go around the issues when they arose. There was so much work that needed to be done; I just hoped that we would have a chance to do it together, learning as we went along, and finding ways of leadership that would work for everyone.

PJ: It was amazing watching Patty in her first days of the superintendency. She had been an open, caring principal who walked around the halls and classrooms of the school and who knew every teacher, staff person and child by name and family. She took this same honest style to her new role. She seldom seemed to give direct commands. Instead, she listened to the stories of the people of her school, and she told her stories in turn. Somehow, a decision would emerge. I couldn't always tell exactly what had happened.

On the other hand, some of the things she did looked like every school I had been in, and the way I felt as "her" principal felt like other schools, too. The first days were confusing and hectic. There were confusing bus routes that got kids in at different times. There was no privacy; I was in a room with four other people and most of the school supplies. All my "principal" things were on a rolling typewriter table that doubled as a desk. I remember standing next to the teachers' mailboxes on the first day, listening to them gruble. Patty hadn't shown up to introduce me, and I could hear a superintendent-like male voice bellowing nonsense from the PA. I remember thinking that couldn't be Patty. Where was the welcome, the rolls, the warmth?

Later, Patty helped me laugh at this. I accused her of being like the trickster in switching persona on me; I came expecting my friend Patty and instead I got some disembodied male superintendent who was "getting even" for all the theory and nonsense of educational administration by thrusting me into a place where nothing I knew made sense. People poured in the front door, all three phone lines were ringing, there was country Western music playing, and some male superintendent was on the intercom. Somebody yelled, "Who is the principal, anyway, and what about this no smoking policy?" Before I could answer, that person left. No one paid attention to the woman pressed up against the receptionist desk, waiting for someone to show her her new supply room office. I felt tricked, and powerless. Patty interrupted my tirade, laughing, and said,

> Well, isn't that a Western interpretation—it isn't me that's the trickster—it's you—you tricked yourself. That is always what Coyote does. I'm not sure I ever saw you as someone who had fallen victim to their own knowledge but this is a funny story you are telling, isn't it?

Of course, she was right. Later in the year, when I felt like I could find my way around a little more, I could talk to her about the first days. Eventually, I could laugh about it. I found out later that she arrived late because she was busy at home helping bus drivers over the CB base stationed in her kitchen. That reality had never occurred to me. It was my Western self that expected her thirty minutes early, coffee cup ready, with open arms to welcome me.

When she did arrive, it was like entering Oz. The same teachers who not ten minutes earlier were sour and complaining were now smiling at Patty, shouting greetings, giving her hugs.

Our days were like marathons. Each of us was constantly available to students, teachers, staff and community. I believe that a principal is not an office, but should be public, a person, *there*. Of course, saying this in class, writing articles, and giving papers is one thing; *doing* it is another.

Patty: I was really impressed with how "public" PJ could be—most Anglo's could not tolerate the lack of privacy and the noisy interruptions that made up a day at our school. Later, when we talked, I was often surprised by her reactions and impressed with her ability to weave language all around her experiences. Once, she was yelling about what people expected of us, and she said Anglo teachers had old visions of leadership,

> where they expect us to be captain of the team, general of the troops, messiah of the lost spirits, rock star to idolize, guru to meditate with, the Lee Iaccoca of education, the "can-do" leader of Desert Storm, the robo principal of scientific technology, the Christopher Columbus exploring education, and don't get a run in your nylons, or cry . . .

I told her I was glad she didn't teach me all of this before I accepted the superintendency, but I was also amazed at her ability to put words to our experienced leadership lives. We both tried to be open and human and ourselves. We tried to be a healthy part of the family and model in our actions what we thought was caring behavior in a family. We tried to get those old man models out of our heads, and tried to help others do the same. We had a vision of compassion that was more process, I guess. Leadership meant striving to be open, humorous and compassionate. The learning came through the joy of the journey together instead of reaching a particular destination.

PJ: Humor was very important through that difficult year. Many times at the end of the day we would sit in Patty's office telling stories of our day. We would often find ourselves telling stories to make us laugh. Secretaries in the office would shout Ojibwe one-liners to us that usually stopped us in our linear planning tracks. Once we were planning a big elementary awards assembly and Patty decided to make a leadership statement by riding into the assembly on the biggest, fanciest bike, given for three years of perfect attendance. I told her to make sure there was air in the tires, and someone shouted about the amount of air all of us women generated. Someone else yelled that we need even more because the newspaper was coming to cover the event, and we were all laughing uncontrollably.

Looking back, I see the importance of our daily humor and daily stories in easing the pain of the day. The humor also helped us construct a broader meaning to events that surely looked smaller and meaner without the context of humor and time. For example, Patty once began to muse about what the location of the school meant to her:

> Did I tell you, PJ, that my sisters and I used to pick berries back here? Here where the school is—maybe even under my office. This area, where the school is now, used to be an eagle breeding station. That is why there are so many eagles here in the spring. I don't think as a young girl I ever imagined that there would be a school here . . . here in all of this beauty . . . a place for laughter and growing . . . or that I would be the superintendent, riding a bicycle into the gym, and you laughing.

She taught me that the Ojibwe concept of leadership was one of storyteller, humorist, teacher—one who must first give away all possessions in order to demonstrate trust in the people. The women, at that time, selected, taught, guided, and eventually chose the male leader.

Through her stories, I came to understand how her people had chosen her to be a new leader in a new time. As a child, she had attended public schools where she had been called dirty and stupid by the teachers and where her major learning came from other students and not from the teachers who mostly ignored the Indian children. She was a good student, in spite of the treatment. She said she did all the things that were expected of an Indian woman after graduation from high school: marriage, a job as a secretary, two children, a move back to the reservation. But then she entered a paralegal program at a local community college and met a counselor who thought she could be an excellent teacher. She said,

> Heck, all I wanted to do was finish this darn paralegal course. I was tired between working a job, taking care of the babies, and going to school. But, he started to coax me into thinking about teaching as a profession and I started taking education courses at the state college.

333

She soon found out she was a good teacher and she soon found her teaching home in the new Ojibwe school where the Indian children were not outsiders but were at the heart of the school. She became a master teacher and then began to help with administrative duties.

After she became superintendent, I saw Patty use her experience, humility, and storytelling talents to make murky areas clear to parents and to defuse tense situations. One evening early in our year together, there was a tense Parent Advisory Council meeting where many of the parents thought that the school was in serious trouble and it was the superintendent's fault. They were angry and vocal. Many demands had been made for changes.

Patty started the meeting with a story about a female student with family problems who made a rash decision to take a car and was ultimately arrested but then returned to the school for help. She talked about the three different social service agencies she had to call to get help. She talked about the different teachers and social workers and counselors who helped. The story ended. Not a sound came from one member of the council. Patty smiled, looked at each member, and asked for help. One by one, the council members asked a question, or offered a solution. Other stories emerged to assist with the problem-solving around the school's needs. It was not as direct as most public school meetings I had attended, but the problems got solved and everyone left satisfied with the evening's deliberations.

Patty: I guess that the role of principal, superintendent, or other leader in our culture is that of storyteller, teacher, maker of meaning, family member—mother, auntie, uncle, grandparent, father—or trickster—the principal as human in helping to build community. Most of what I had learned in the university about being a principal had hidden relational roles and focused on control roles that just didn't make much sense to me in my world. Leadership values espoused by the Ojibwe are community and family focused. They are integrated in the leader role as an important link between the current education changes being proposed and in how an individual walks in community. I don't think that the woman issue has to get in the way, any more than the age issue, or the color issue, or anything else other than the focus on lovingly applied skills toward the good health of the family.

I see the Bug School as not like most other schools in many ways, yet in many ways like all schools. School is about family and caring and being here, taking responsibility for the students no matter who you are, what your position, what your skin color. The way we do this is by telling our stories, and by listening to each other with respect and caring. This can't be dictated by a theory or by a person, and it never sounds the same in a retelling. And that is how our lives are constructed—out of the relationship, the family, the story.

Discussion

Having told this story, we want to discuss community, hierarchy and roles, and my constructed meanings of those concepts within the Ojibwe culture.

Community

The story that we have told is about the first year together as a white woman principal and an Annishinabe woman superintendent in a Minnesota school. I learned from this Ojibwe school that "school" is about community and family. It is also about being "insider" and "outsider," often at the same time. Over the past ten years, the educational literature has revealed the tension between a desire to be individuals, while searching for elusive community. Bellah and co-workers (1985) discussed the predominantly white middle-class search for community in a dispersed society that puts independent individuality as the highest goal for each person. In fact, our search for lost community has often carried us into conflict with the very people who could teach us about the community they live every day.

In an attempt to widen our horizons about educational practice, Shulman (1987) and Schon (1987) have written extensively on the subject of reflection, reflective practice, and reflection in action. Dunlap and Cooper (1989) took concepts from Schon (1987) and Belenky and co-workers (1986) and explored how leaders solve problems by using various forms of journal writing. Their findings reveal creative and innovative strategies for solving problems in a leadership role. However, their study also illuminated the isolation in the daily routine of these leaders, managers, and principals. While these individuals may be called upon to create community in their workplace, it is the continued isolation of the individual which may be problematic in our search for creation of communities within schools.

The principalship framed as a "humane" role places the focus not on the individual, the technologist, the manager, the charismatic, or the competitor, but on the leader as one of the educational community's storytellers. The leader becomes a collaborator in the making of meaning.

Hierarchy and Roles

School leadership is also about hierarchy and roles. No matter how personal our interactions with each other and the larger school community, we were still defined by the roles we played and the hierarchy of the roles within the school. However, we had more opportunity than either of us had understood at the beginning of the year to mold and change how we viewed the roles and how others saw the roles and us filling the roles. There was still "top-downness" and "bottom-upness" to some of the events of our daily lives but, more significantly, the focus was on the child at the heart of the family/community/school, instead of roles and job descriptions. A student's problem was our problem; there was little time spent on assigning blame according to role or job type.

Perhaps the most striking insight for me from this year was the persistence of old metaphors of leadership, even in a different cultural setting and even with the active and conscious work of two leaders committed to identifying and using new metaphors. I had written about the persistence of old metaphors of leadership (Ford Slack 1992) and I guess that I thought that identifying the problem was almost the same thing as solving it.

The old metaphors of leader as male, as hero, as controller, are alive in our mind's eye today. We try a new way, and just when we least want the old images to emerge, there they are messing up our new process. I remember at one point asking my teachers to make a decision. I was told, "You're the principal; you decide." You can guess that a lot of stories had to be told before we were able to sweep aside old ideas of role and hierarchy and move beyond them to a mutually conceived solution.

It is possible to mediate confusion and conceptual anxiety with love and humor, but now I think that pain is the inevitable companion of finding new and better ways to lead in schools. But we have choices about how much pain, and whether to suffer alone or together. I am convinced that we have much to learn about how to help ourselves and others emerge on the brighter side of hard transitions with a minimum amount of pain and a maximum amount of support, laughter and companionship (see Rosaldo 1989, Takaki 1993, Turner 1986 for thoughtful ideas about change and transition in community).

Constructing Meanings

School leadership is also about constructing personal and shared meaning out of complex events in complex lives. For example, reservations hold many images for Native Americans and non–Native Americans. A reservation is a place both real and surreal. It is, in one view, a division of land and people created by treaties, federal law, belief in manifest destiny, and broken promises (Pevar 1992; Weatherford 1991). In another way, it represents both separation and betrayal between colonized Americans and Native Americans, at the same time it represents home and an honoring of ancestors and self. The meanings are constructed.

Conclusions

What does this mean for a better understanding of women leading in education? Besides giving us a broader understanding of community, insiderness and outsiderness, hierarchy and roles, school leadership, and constructed meanings, it also focuses our attention on the role of stories and storytelling/storylistening in good administration.

Patty, like every good storyteller, is also first and foremost a good listener. She listened to problems, family adventures, imaginary quests, dark journeys, and warrior-like tales of escape and triumph. She responded to students, teacher, and parents through an assortment of stories, fables and narratives that fit each situation. In other words, she communicated her leadership *in community*. Gardner (1989) and others have documented that stories can "open our minds" in an organizational setting as well as in our private moments, and that storytelling is an imminently acceptable form of constructing meaning for humans in many settings. In fact, Boje (1991) and others argue that storytelling is the preferred sense-making currency of human relationships among internal and external stakeholders in organizations.

The shared story of Patty and PJ is also an example of an ethno-graphic case study using biographic/autobiographic storytelling as the research method (Witherell and Noddings 1991; Rosaldo 1989). It is a method that yields unique meanings. I systematically gathered and recorded our stories. When I drafted this chapter, it was discussed, interpreted, laughed about, and revisited by many people on Leech Lake Reservation over many months. The tapes and journals and chapter drafts formed a basis for long conversations and more storytelling that finally led to this version for this book. Meanings are here, constructed in a way still unusual in Western science.

And, perhaps most significantly, the story of two leaders at one school helps us see how very important the real voice of each person is in each setting. Acting as a leader through our own voice, life, and experience is the beginning of leadership (Takaki 1993). Listening to other's stories and telling our own is not excessive personalization but is, instead, a hope for transformation of our schools.

Note

A special thanks and blessings to the women of Leech Lake and White Earth Reservation who spent many hours telling stories and checking drafts of this chapter. Nadine Chase, Shirley Fisher, Carol Jenkins and Carrie Ortiz of Leech Lake Reservation, our teachers and friends, your voices are now in the conversation.

Bibliography

Aiken, L. (1991). Tribal law and federal government. Unpublished excerpts from lectures. University of Minnesota, Duluth.

Belenky, M., Clinchy, B., Goldberger, N., and Tarule, J. (1986). *Women's ways of knowing: The development of self, voice, and mind.* New York: Basic Books.

Bellah, R. et al. (1985). *Habits of the heart.* Berkeley: University of California Press.

Boje, D. (1991). The storytelling organization: A study of story performance in an office-supply firm. *Administrative Science Quarterly,* 36, 106–26.

Chase, N. (1991). Conversations and stories with tribal elder and board member on the founding of the Chief Bug-O-Nay-Ge-Shig School. Cass Lake, MN. Transcripts taped by authors.

Christiansen, R. (1991). Five cultural competencies for teacher of Ojibwe children. Curriculum guidelines presentation, Minnesota Indian Education Conference, Rochester, MN.

Dunlap, D. M. and Cooper, J. (1989). Journal keeping as an example of successful reflective practice among administrators in government, business and education. Paper presented at the annual meetings of the American Educational Research Association, San Francisco.

Ford Slack, P. J. (1992). Whose democracy? Paper presented at the annual meetings of the University Council for Education Administration, Minneapolis.

Gardner, H. (1989). *To open minds: Chinese clues to the dilemma of contemporary education.* New York: Basic Books.

Hubbard, R. and Randall, M. (1988). *The shape of red.* San Francisco: Cleis Press.

Kristeva, J. (1977). *About chinese women.* New York: Urizen Books.

Pevar, S. (1992). *The rights of Indians and tribes,* ed. N. Dorsen, ACLU. New York: Bantam.

Rosaldo, R. (1989). *Culture and truth: The remaking of social analysis.* New York: Beacon Press.

Red Lake High School Students. (1989). *To walk the red road: Memories of the Red Lake Ojibwe people.* Red Lake, MN. Project Reserve, The Red Lake Tribal Offices.

Schon, D. (1987). *Educating the reflective practitioner.* San Francisco: Jossey-Bass.

Shulman, L. (1987). Knowledge and teaching. *Harvard Educational Review,* 56, 1–22.

Senese, G. (1991). *Self-determination and the social education of Native Americans.* New York: Praeger.

Sergiovanni, T. (1987). *The principalship: A reflective practice perspective.* Boston: Allyn and Bacon.

Takaki, R. (1993). *A different mirror: A history of multicultural America.* Boston: Little, Brown and Co.

Turner, F. (1986). *Beyond geography: The Western spirit against the wilderness.* New Brunswick: Rutgers University Press.

Weatherford, J. (1991). *Native roots: How the Indians enriched America.* New York: Crown Publishers.

Witherell, C. and Noddings, N. (eds.). (1991). *Stories lives tell: Narrative and dialogue in education.* New York: Teachers College Press.

Zinn, H. (1980). *A people's history of America.* New York: HarperCollins.

NINETEEN

Women's Working Worlds: A Case Study of A Female Organization

Patricia Valentine

A feeling of high energy and dynamism, mixed with some nervous tension was apparent when I first entered the school of nursing. In the halls, the strong impact of female gender became readily apparent as I watched the predominantly female students milling about, chatting with one other while moving through the corridors to the classrooms. A poster hanging in a faculty member's office reinforced the perception of femaleness: "When God created men, *She* was only kidding." Outside the main office, individual pictures of mostly female students, faculty and staff further cemented the feeling of a female domain. Upon entering the faculty lounge, a major area for faculty interaction, I was greeted by a group of slim, well-dressed, youthful-looking women. The lounge was a small cosy room with couches arranged into three conversation areas. Another area included a counter and a sink with a rack holding a variety of coffee mugs that hinted at the heterogeneity of the faculty. The coffee maker was close by. Upon opening the refrigerator door, I was faced with shelves overflowing with brown-bag lunches and a home-baked cake. Scattered around the lounge were several female-oriented magazines such as *Homemakers, Chate-*

laine, The Magic of Scarf Fashion, Working Women, Wedding Bells, and a *Tupper-ware catalogue.*

In the lounge, pregnancy and child care were frequent topics of conversation because three faculty/staff members were pregnant. One pregnant women mentioned that she did not have an adequate coat to cover her expanding abdomen, two others were looking forward to upcoming maternity leaves but pondering whether they would return to work. One of them was trying to predict the sex of her baby by the amount of movement in the uterus.

It was not unusual for children to be in the lounge. One day when I walked into the lounge, one of the part-time faculty members had a child in tow. I had seen this child previously when the mother had an appointment with the director. Another day, I observed an eleven-month-old baby on the couch with his obviously pregnant mother bending over him, waiting for his father to collect him. When children were in the lounge, all attention was focused on them.

The above scenario depicts social aspects of a female organization. What does research on a women-dominated organization teach us about the form of leadership that evolves and how women function in such an organization? Since I have spent most of my life working with women, this type of situation, along with the incorporation of a feminist perspective, stimulated this area of research. The purpose of the following chapter is to describe aspects of the work culture in a Canadian hospital school of nursing. This description will delineate the distinctive views that the female nurse educators brought to the workplace that produced a different organization from the male-dominated organizations usually described in the organizational and the administrative literature.

Until very recently, most of the organizational and the administrative literature, including the literature on educational organizations, has emanated from studies of men in organizations, using a male perspective, males as investigators, and generalizing the findings to both women and men. If women were studied, it was usually because they were considered deviant; they did not fit the male model (Stanley 1984, 194). More recently the literature has included studies on women in organizations, but few have been case studies on women in female-dominated organizations. Nursing is a profession that provides fertile ground for investigating the perspective women bring to the workplace because it is about 96 percent female and is one of the oldest and largest professions dominated by women.

Bernard (1981), a prolific writer over the past four decades on women, work and family maintains that "[t]he female world is worthy of study in and of itself, quite apart from its impact on the male world" (p. 1). This statement served as a guide for this research.

The Female World

Bernard (1981) developed the conceptualization of "two worlds" one of males and one of females. Her writings, which have focused on the "female world," defined it as "a system of beings with some common characteristic that is considered a unity" (Bernard 1981, 23). In another article, Valentine and McIntosh (1990) compared the development of the female world with the development of the world of nursing showing that they evolved in concert with one another. Studies of women in other female-dominated organizations such as elementary school teachers and social workers revealed a similar conclusion (Biklen 1987; Freedman, Jackson and Boles, 1983).

The conceptualization of the female world includes female culture, a term that according to Bernard (1981), defies definitional consensus. One cultural conception focuses on sex roles (Lee and Gropper 1974). In this approach, female culture is viewed as a product of the female role just as the male culture is a product of the male role. These cultures contain elements such as "rituals, roles, dress customs, gestures, communication patterns, reference groups . . . [and] visible properties and practices of sex role as it is reflected in everyday life" (Lee and Gropper 1974, 371). Other aspects of female culture are different from male culture (Bernard 1981; Jacobson 1982). For example, there is occupational segregation by gender (Blaxall and Reagan 1976) in nursing and elementary school education; marriage is experienced differently by both genders (Bernard 1972); rules or norms developed by women are different from those developed by men whether legislated or crescive in nature (Bernard 1981). However, until recently, culture-specific data on women has largely disappeared from the record because such information was considered of little interest (Jacobson 1982). Bernard (1981) believes that recognition of the female culture as part of the female world, independent from the male culture and world, will have considerable benefits for female understanding. Therefore, this study emphasized the female world instead of using the male world as the norm against which to judge or to contrast the female world.

Description of Study and Setting

The research was carried out in a Canadian hospital school of nursing that consisted of 220 students, a director, assistant director and 40 nurse educators, all of whom had a minimum of baccalaureate education with three faculty members with master's degrees. All participants were female. The instructors' ages ranged from thirty to fifty years with twenty-one married, three divorced, twelve single, and one whose arrangement was described as "cohabiting."

The data were collected by attending teaching-team meetings, full faculty meetings, and selected committee meetings over a twelve-month period as well as by talking with faculty during lunch and coffee breaks in the faculty lounge where most faculty congregated. Six faculty members served as key participants for the research although the study included all faculty members. There were three types of data: copious documents circulated to the faculty, transcribed audio tapes of two sets of interviews with the six key participants and abundant field notes. I carried out two interviews of 60 to 90 minutes with each key participant: one during the first six months and the second during the final month of study. The key participants either confirmed, disconfirmed or noted exceptions to the constructs that were generated from the study. The grounded theory method was used as the guiding research approach in this case study (Glaser and Strauss 1967; Glaser 1978; Strauss and Corbin 1990).

When the study commenced, the administrative structure consisted of the director, the assistant director/coordinator, two coordinators and two faculty members with other administrative duties. A management team composed of the director, the assistant director/coordinator and two other coordinators was responsible for the administration of the school. This structure changed during the period the investigator was studying the organization. When the assistant director resigned, the structure was flattened by assigning curriculum duties to one team coordinator. Along with three teaching teams, there were eight committees that reported to full faculty meetings which were held on a monthly basis.

Most of the activity in the school revolved around the three teams that were responsible for teaching the curriculum. One teaching team taught the first year, another the second year, and a third team taught the last four months of the program which was referred to as the third year. Team meetings were held twice a month and lasted from 90 to 120 minutes. All instructors attended these meetings.

Link between Home and Work

A more detailed description of the school's female culture will sensitize the reader to the themes of home and work that permeated this environment. There was a strong interaction between work and home. The impact on the work lives of the nurse educators of child care and household management is described along with the dilemmas these activities created in their pursuance of further education.

Marriage, Childbearing, Childrearing and Work

The fecund environment became increasingly apparent as I spent time in the school: childbearing and childrearing were main topics of conversation. For example, in introducing herself during an orientation session, one administrator spontaneously mentioned the ages of her children and told an anecdote about them. The new staff members followed her lead and mentioned their family or lack thereof. One instructor added that their dog was "their child." The youngest instructor in the group declared she was not married and had no plans to marry in the immediate future.

At the same orientation session, a staff member who was obviously pregnant announced when her maternity leave would start. Concurrently, the names of the other faculty members and staff who were currently on maternity leave or who would be going on maternity leave that term were announced. When faculty members gave birth, it was treated with special attention. The births were announced immediately with details on the length and the type of labor and delivery and the upcoming date of the baby shower.

Along with the concerns of expectant faculty members, came the concerns of those instructors who had children such as: the costs of child care, the problems of having a precocious 3½ year-old daughter who terrorized the 18-year old babysitter, the difficulties of managing two sets of twins, the concern about whether an eleven-month-old baby was sick or merely teething, and one instructor's son's "disastrous" first day at school. At the end of the first term, two faculty members resigned due to the pressures associated with trying to work and to care for several young children at home.

Ill children were taken seriously. Faculty members often shuffled timetables to accommodate instructors who had sick children at home. For example, one day the timetable was rearranged so an instructor with a sick child could teach at the beginning of the day and then go home. Another day, a faculty member arrived late for a meeting because her child became sick overnight, and she had to make other arrangements for him in the morning. This was accepted without question. When she arrived, the coordinator's first question was about her child's health.

Along with children, household management was central to the nurse educators' lives. The instructors' remarks made it clear that they were largely responsible for both the care of their children and the management of their households. As one key participant indicated:

> [they] all take the majority of the responsibilities for their children, they may go to day care or a babysitter, you talk to most of them and they're the ones that make the arrangements; they are the ones that drive the kids and pick them up, arrange all the extra activities for their kids.

This statement was supported when team members tried to arrange to meet after work for a drink and all the problems of having major responsibilities for meal preparation and child care surfaced. One Monday morning when one instructor commented on how tired her colleague looked, the colleague replied that she had spent all weekend on household chores instead of taking time off for rest and relaxation.

The multiple expectations of these women were affirmed by one key participant when she talked about the expectation of bringing home-made food in for work-related events: "Women [feel] compelled to be successful in so many areas: they have to be successful in their job, they have to be wonderful mothers, wonderful homemakers, wonderful wives and [home baking shows] what a wonderful homemaker you are." Another key participant concurred pointing out:

> Yeah, it's amazing some of these women have two and three children at home, and they are working full time and yet able to contribute to committees as well, not just the fact that they have home responsibilities, but they have an outside life . . . as well as their work life.

As indicated above, although these women were professionals who worked outside the home, the traditional concerns of wives and/or mothers spilled over into the workplace. My field notes included the observation that these women appeared to weigh their careers equally with their family and outside life. However, one key participant, pointed out that family and/or friends were given first priority by most faculty members.

Marriage, Childbearing, Childrearing, and Graduate Education

Pursuit of graduate education was another expectation for the nurse educators. During an orientation session, a new instructor prefaced her remarks by declaring that she was obviously the oldest person in the group and then mentioned she had two sons, adding that she could not pursue any further education until they were older. Another instructor disclosed that she had obtained her baccalaureate degree with reluctance, and her husband would need to be convinced before she could pursue advanced studies. During one interview, one key participant who was single talked about the employment expectation of obtaining a master's degree:

> If I find it tiring even thinking about it, when you think of marriage, small kids and the income that's needed and . . . on top of that the expectation, that they start working on [a master's degree], that is going to take a lot of time, energy [and] money.

345

Two of the key participants in the study had children. When discussing career plans, one key participant, a single parent, indicated that she would work for two or three years, perhaps taking courses toward her master's degree. When her child was older, she would attend university full time. She finished by saying "once he is in school, I think things will be better." The other participant who had two children was taking a university course towards her master's degree. Both women preferred not to stay at home full time. Although they felt guilty at times, they came to realize that their children had not suffered appreciably from their working outside the home. However, both acknowledged that they would not be able to work in many other nursing jobs and raise their children at the same time. They admitted that flexible hours and being able to work at home when they did not have commitments in the school were "perks" that helped to assuage the guilt. One key participant added that although "flex time" sometimes permitted her to go on a field trip with her child or to a Christmas concert, she often worked at home in the evening and had to say to her kids: "Look, I'm really sorry about this week, Mommy is really busy."

Relationships in the Workplace

For the nurse educators, relationships were a crucial part of the workplace. Relationships provided the context for most work activities. The following section will describe how relationships had an impact on the way the work was carried out in the school. The description will include: the importance of camaraderie, the necessity of a supportive environment, the interpersonal function of food and social events, the cohesion building aspects of meetings, the cohesive element of the arrangement of tables during meetings. The manner in which decisions were made, questions were formulated, and curriculum was developed also included an interpersonal element.

Camaraderie

For the nurse educators, camaraderie was a strongly held value. Although there were cliques and some tension areas in this faculty group, there was also strong evidence of camaraderie. For example, one colleague brought another colleague a corsage as a token of friendship. After entertaining at home, instructors often shared the remaining food with their colleagues. One instructor offered to loan a roomy coat to a staff person when she became too pregnant for her own coat.

According to one key participant, the promotion of fellowship was the objective of "Up Group," a committee that had as its "mandate to act as a positive influence on students and faculty and to plan activities for facilitating this." She emphasized that the focus was first on students, then faculty. "Warm Fuzzy Week," planned by this committee and celebrated in mid-December, was an attempt to promote comradeship among the nurse educators. Each instructor was assigned an anonymous partner to whom she was to give a small, inexpensive present each day for a week. At the end of the week, the gift-givers were identified. The previous year, one instructor's small gifts culminated in a live rabbit. When the investigator asked one key participant why Warm Fuzzy Week was adopted, she responded: "To facilitate warmer relations between management and staff." Another way of promoting harmonious working relationships in one teaching team was through the exchange of small gifts at Christmas.

Support

Support mechanisms as essential was one construct arising from the study. Support was a term that constantly came up in daily conversations and at meetings; the existence of one supportive colleague in the school was tantamount to a satisfactory work life. The relationships instructors tried to foster were "more than just working relationships; they strove to be friends" (Valentine and McIntosh 1990, 366). Acting in a supportive manner was also an important aspect of the team coordinators' roles. Coordinators took this responsibility seriously and often helped new instructors carry out their teaching responsibilities.

Food and Social Events

Relationships underpinned two other constructs generated from this study: food as a facilitator of, and social events as integrators of, relationships. Food and social events, "which blended together and complemented each other" (Valentine and McIntosh 1990, 357), were used to facilitate interaction among the nurse educators and "'to bring faculty closer together' to foster common action" (Valentine and McIntosh 1990, 365). Food was viewed as the panacea for many situations and was a strong ingredient of a variety of celebrations such as births, birthdays, marriages, end-of-term parties, and various graduation events. Food and social events were also used to try to ameliorate conflict and to try to get the work done more collaboratively. During the twelve-month period, there were at least fifty-five different social events.

Meetings

Meetings as cohesion builders was a fourth construct emanating from the study. The considerable number of meetings held in the school were used to get the work done. However, they also served as mechanisms for trying to integrate the nursing faculty into a "smoothly functioning unit"

(Valentine and McIntosh 1990, 367). When the investigator suggested that meetings along with food and social events were used as integrating mechanisms, three participants agreed, one commenting that: "In many cases, that is part of the purpose of those types of activities."

Seating Arrangements

All team and full faculty meetings were held in one particular room. The importance of the facilitation of communication among instructors was demonstrated by the arrangement of tables. The tables were arranged in a circle, in an oval or a large square or diamond depending on the number of participants. When the tables were unsuitably arranged, faculty members rearranged them prior to the commencement of meetings. When I asked the key participants to comment on the arrangement of tables, their responses suggested this arrangement allowed for equity of space, eye contact, and cohesiveness among the nurse educators: "I think it's so everyone is in an equal position to speak; so everyone has a view of the other . . . face-to-face; to promote eye contact among group members; again I think it has to do with cohesiveness and probably—when I speak with people I like to see who I am speaking to—to try to have everyone included."

Decision-Making

The investigator's field notes indicated that decisions were made at the faculty committee meetings, the full faculty meetings, and the teaching team meetings. Although few decisions were made at full faculty meetings, most decisions were reached by consensus. Only five motions were voted on over a twelve-month period. Three motions concerned the disbursement of money for professional purposes, another to determine the restaurant for the end-of-term luncheon, and the fifth to ascertain which instructor would give the convocation speech. Formal motions were rarely initiated at the team level. For example, in the third-year team, there were only three motions voted on over the four months they worked together. Over a four-month period, the first-year team voted on seven motions while nine motions were voted on in the second-year team over a twelve-month period.

The six key participants were asked the question: How were decisions made in the school? Their responses and the field notes revealed that the majority of decisions were made by group consensus by the teaching teams; a small number of decisions were voted upon: "Generally issues were brought forward and discussed thoroughly by a high proportion of faculty [team] members and usually resolved on the basis of this discussion." For example, to ensure consensus at third-year meetings, the coordinator usually asked instructors to comment if they failed to remark on issues. Since student representatives had recently started attending second-year team meetings, it was suggested that they attend the curriculum revision meetings for the next year. When the coordinator asked: "Is the *feeling* of the group that we want to invite students? Do we want to vote? The answer to the second question was 'no.'" Thus, the decision in favor of the student representatives was made by consensus. At one first-year team meeting, the coordinator asked team members: "Would everybody be happy with . . . ?" when referring to three particular suggestions. Participation in decision-making at the team level was high; often questions posed by team coordinators were to determine if there was mutual agreement on issues while student responses were always given serious consideration.

Questions

The types of questions raised in the three teams had strong similarities; they were mainly used to determine if there was consensus, to get further information, or for clarification on issues. Emotional words that showed a concern for interpersonal relations were frequently used in posing questions. The questions often included reference to *feelings* or to *meeting the teams' needs*.

Examples of questions posed by the coordinators in the three teaching teams were: "Would everyone by *happy* with . . . ; I am wondering how you would *feel* being at the front of the class for introductions?; I don't know how the group *feels* about it?; Do you *feel* comfortable with the level at which we are doing this?; Would that *meet the needs* and expectations of everyone?; Would you *feel* more comfortable if the words were in . . . ?; Are we all clear on the process?; What's the *feeling* of the group?; Give me ideas on how we want to handle this in our [team] and *meet our [team's] needs?;* Well, what do you want to do?; How are things coming?; Is timetabling going the way you want it?; Are you *feeling* any better now?; Does that *meet our [team's] needs?"* This approach was used for all team meetings during the period the investigator was observing them.

Curriculum Development

The approach to curriculum development was similar for all teams. The first part of each team meeting consisted of "feedback" where instructors received feedback on content that had been presented during the previous two weeks and the second part was "correlation" where instructors who would be teaching the content or were responsible for arranging for guest lecturers, overviewed content that was to be presented during the ensuing two weeks of classes. All meetings consisted of previewing or reviewing content areas, asking faculty members for their comments and concerns, and giving serious consideration to students' comments and concerns. Suggestions were often made for improving the curriculum content, especially for the following year.

Almost every page of the summary of my field notes contained feedback from faculty members on various aspects of the teaching process. For example, in the third-year team, there were ten entries on the preceptorship experience for students while in the second-year team there were twenty comments from faculty regarding a particular quiz. During a ten-minute discussion about the level of one examination question, all but three second-year faculty members commented for a total of thirty-five comments. In the first-year team, there were twelve comments on one lecture.

Discussion

The description of the school's culture does not sound like the usual depiction of work culture in the research literature. The school had norms, rituals, gestures and communication patterns that are unique to female culture (Bernard 1981). The school's culture revealed a bridging of the private world of the home and the public sphere of the workplace. The home-like milieu of the lounge included women's magazines, "woman talk" and homemade "goodies." Childbearing, childrearing and household management played major roles in these women's lives and posed dilemmas in trying to fulfill career goals and to maintain family harmony. Another reason for the strong focus on childbearing and on childrearing stemmed from the fact that the nurse educators assumed major responsibility for their children and for their households. Therefore, blending home with work was part of their reality. It was difficult, if not impossible, for the instructors to compartmentalize their lives. Instead, family life was integrated into the workplace. Helgesen's (1990) study of four American women executives revealed that they were unable to separate their private life from their work life but "saw their own identities as complex and multifaceted" (p. 26). Their homemaking experiences provided them with a wide array of skills that had major relevance for work outside the home. Having to maneuver effectively on a daily basis in both the public and the private spheres contributed to better psychological integration or a state of personal wholeness, a factor that Helgesen's (1990) women managers attributed to their incredible energy. Lamphere's (1985) study of American women who worked in blue-collar industries, and "[brought] the family to work" (p. 520) by staging various life cycle celebrations such as birthdays and baby showers, found these rituals facilitated the creation and the maintenance of "worker solidarity." Acker's (1992) study of British elementary school teachers indicated "a strong sense of community sustained by rituals" (p. 18) similar to the ones found in the nursing school where the many celebratory occasions helped to humanize the workplace by establishing bonds of friendship and bridging age divisions (Lamphere 1985).

The interaction among the nurse educators revealed a work environment that was strongly focused on faculty-to-faculty, faculty-to-staff, and faculty-to-student relationships. For example, the various gestures of friendship and the objectives of the Up Group were evidence of the attempts to foster warm relations among faculty, students, and staff. The four constructs emanating from the study of the school indicated this striving for connection whether through the use of food, social events, meetings, or supportive gestures. As Gilligan (1982) and many other researchers (Belenky, Clinchy, Goldberger, and Tarule 1986; Berzoff 1989a, 1989b; Chodorow 1978; Helgesen 1990; Loden 1985; Lyons 1983; Miller 1986, 1984) have found, women tend to see the world through relationships, "a world that coheres through human connection rather than through systems of rules" (Gilligan 1982, 29). More recently "feminist theories have come to extol women's empathic atunement and connection to others as valuable dimensions of their adult development" (Berzoff 1989a, 97). Loden's (1985) study of 200 women and 50 men in a wide variety of organizations and entrepreneurial businesses in the United States suggested that women leaders believe that "positive satisfying relationships" (p. 118) lead to productive individuals. Some administrators/managers contend that the ability to focus on relationships facilitates getting the tasks done (Statham 1987).

In the school, the organizational structure consisted of minimal hierarchy and during the study the organizational structure was flattened. Gilligan's (1982) research suggested that women prefer a nonhierarchical approach to relationships. Neuse's (1978) research indicated that in order to encourage others to participate, women willingly ignore formal hierarchy and minimize their personal power. Naisbitt and Aburdene's (1986) book *Reinventing the Corporation* concluded that hierarchical organizational arrangements are fast becoming obsolete in todays corporations and are yielding to "an environment for nurturing personal growth" (p. 72) with a "networking style" (p. 72) of management that includes all players as resources. They proposed the lattice or grid as the structural model for the new corporate economy. This model is similar in many respects to the web described in Helgesen (1990) and Loden's (1985) female models of management. The school had a web-life structure that encouraged full participation by faculty members.

Intimacy in the workplace, a value that is usually not talked about by women leaders, but is practiced by many of them under the guise of other labels, is a factor that Loden (1985) contends is necessary for contemporary

351

organizations but is still unacceptable to most business leaders. However, it has been a part of Japanese management for some time (Ouchi 1981). The striving for camaraderie through the Up Group and through Warm Fuzzy Week, the facilitating of communication through the arrangement of tables during meetings, the requiring of a supportive work setting that included striving to become friends with work colleagues are indicative of the value placed on intimacy in the school. In a study of British elementary school teachers, Acker (1992) found that these teachers showed a similar "concern and compassion" (p. 13) for one another.

As indicated previously, few decisions were voted on in the school. Most decisions were made by consensus by the teaching teams after considerable discussion and input from instructors and students. The team leaders saw "themselves primarily as empowerers, the individuals responsible for encouraging greater autonomy among group members" (Loden 1985, 118). Muller and Cocotas's (1988) study of sixteen American women health-care executives, described their management style as "consensus building [and] working as a team" (p. 74). According to Loden (1985), having input into decision-making tends to create a feeling of ownership in the final decisions, even if the original ideas are not accepted. This cooperative climate for discussion also minimizes the "win-lose element of voting" and directs the energy of the group towards "reaching decisions that every member can accept" (Loden 1985, 125). Research by a firm that has developed decision-making exercises on wilderness survival for management development programs found that out of forty-eight teams studied, the all-female managerial groups that used consensus as the decision making method reached the best technical decisions (Lafferty and Pond 1974).

The questions posed at the school's team meetings were used to produce consensus, to solicit information, to derive clarification on issues, and often included reference to *feelings* or *meeting the team's needs*. These questions were usually phrased to encourage "community building" (Bernard 1981; Shakeshaft 1987, 181), often referred to meeting the affiliative needs of the instructors (Kahn 1984) and showed "courtesy, gratitude, respect and appreciation" (Shakeshaft 1987, 181). As Shakeshaft (1987) stated, "women show respect for their audience through listening, echoing, summarizing, polite speech and nonantagonistic responses" (p. 181). The questions asked by the nurse educators usually expressed feelings that are typical of interaction among women, according to Helgesen (1990). The four women managers in her study were "keen observers of both the content of interactions and the process or method used to communicate" (p. 142).

Tannen (1990), a linguist, who studied videotapes of children and adults talking to same-sex best friends found that "at every age, the girls and women sit closer together and look at each other directly . . . and anchor their gaze on each other's faces" (p. 246) just as the nurse educators found it essential during meetings to have the seating arrangements maximize eye contact.

The approach to curriculum development where the nursing instructors commented on the lectures given the previous two weeks followed by an overview of the content to be taught in the next two weeks was an example of what Loden referred to as "employee participation." This occurs when women "[put] cooperation ahead of competition and [seek] input and support from all members of the group" (p. 126). The majority of the women leaders in the health care industry studied by Muller and Cocotas (1988) "described their management style as participative and person oriented" (p. 74). Just as the school's structure included a variety of mechanisms for optimizing information dispersal (team meetings, full faculty meetings), Helgesen's (1990) study of four women executives, revealed that they structured their days to include time for sharing as much information as possible; "it was a deliberate process, a major goal of every day" (p. 27).

The women in Loden's (1985) study contended that organizational effectiveness was facilitated by the two-way communication that resulted from holding regular staff meetings; the frequent meetings held in the school served the same purpose. According to Helgesen (1990), this propensity to sharing is derived from women's orientation to relationships which locates them in the midst of the activity rather than at the top; for women, "it's more natural to reach *out* than to reach *down*" (p. 27). This weblike structure "facilitates direct communication, free-flowing and loosely structured, by providing points of contact and direct tangents along which to connect" (Helgesen 1990, 50). The web puts one at the core, a critical element of feminine leadership (Helgesen 1990; Loden 1985).

Loden (1985) concluded that a female leadership model exists. Her female leadership model includes an operating style that is cooperative, an organizational structure that is based on a team approach with the basic objective being quality output, a problem-solving style that is intuitive/rational, and several key characteristics such as "lower control, empathic, [and] collaborative with high performance standards" (Loden 1985, 63). Although Loden's research dealt with profit-motivated organizations, several of the characteristics were present in the nursing school, a human service organization. As has been described previously, the school's main thrust was toward collaboration or cooperation, with "teamwork" being the major way the work was carried out. A constant striving for quality teaching was apparent in the mechanisms used to monitor the curriculum, that is, the bimonthly review-preview process that utilized the feedback of students and instructors as the basis for continually revising the curriculum. During team meetings, empathy was exhibited through the tolerance for, and encouragement of, the expression of feelings in the phrasing of questions at team meetings. According to Loden's (1985) women executives, "productive human interaction involves the exchange and expression of both thoughts and feelings" (p. 142).

Conclusions and Implications

One major conclusion of this study is that the school had a distinctive culture that is usually not portrayed in the traditional organizational and administrative literature. The manner in which women approach work and management should be studied for its contribution to work organizations rather than being treated as deviant. Before making comparisons with organizations that use a male perspective, organizations that are staffed largely by women should initially be studied to determine the contribution such analysis could make to the organizational and the administrative literature. Another conclusion is that a feminist perspective was crucial for initially sensitizing me to the concept of a female world. This perspective also provided the impetus, the knowledge base, and the confidence necessary to legitimize research on an area that has often been invisible, devalued, or trivialized.

What implications does this research have for future organizations? Since this study and others suggest that women view work outside the home as only one part of themselves, this factor needs to be considered in the structuring of organizations. Having to manage both daily work outside the home and work generated from inside the household is usually not given much credence in organizations where there is a mixture of women and men, ones in which there is a preponderance of men, or ones where women predominate. Instead, women's issues are usually ignored. This needs to be rectified by accommodations such as flex time and special arrangements when children are sick. More workplaces need to have child-care facilities on the premises, a policy that has been recommended many times.

Recognizing that supportive relationships are important to women workers suggests that organizations need to build in this kind of structure. For example, women should not be in isolated jobs where they have no network of female colleagues. This has major implications for the token woman in organizations.

Finally, the integration into the organizational and the administrative literature of the literature on women's experiences will help to change organizations so that they better meet the needs of women. Some of the research, to date, suggests that female leadership models such as those that utilize weblike structures, if allowed to grow and flourish, have the potential for making positive contributions to administrative practice as well as to the organizational and the administrative literature. These types of structures would help women begin to realize that the mode of operating in organizations that feels comfortable to them is different from the traditional male mode. This insight will enable them to ignore the courses and manuals on management that stress how to act like men. Instead, women will be free to develop leadership styles that have the potential for humanizing the workplace and for improving the health of organizations.

Bibliography

Acker, S. (1992). *Gender, collegiality, and teachers' workplace culture in Britain: In search of the women's culture.* Paper presented at the annual meetings of the American Educational Research Association, San Francisco, California.

Belenky, M., Clinchy, B., Goldberger, N., and Tarule, J. (1986). *Women's ways of knowing: The development of self, voice and mind.* New York: Basic Books.

Bernard, B. J. (1972). *The future of marriage.* New York: Basic Books.

———. (1981). *The female world.* New York: The Free Press.

Berzoff, J. (1989a). From separation to connection: Shifts in understanding women's development. *Affilia: Journal of Women and Social Work,* 4(1), 45–58.

———. (1989b). Fusion and heterosexual women's friendships: Implications for expanding our adult developmental theories. *Women and Therapy,* 8(4), 93–107.

Biklen, S.K. (1987). Women in elementary school teaching: A case study. In P. Schmuck (ed.), *Women educators: Employees of schools in the Western world.* Albany: SUNY Press.

Blaxall, M., and Reagan, B. (1976). *Women and the workplace: The implications of occupational segregation.* Chicago: University of Chicago Press.

Chodorow, N. (1978). *The reproduction of mothering.* Berkeley, CA: University of California Press.

Freedman, S., Jackson, J., and Boles, K. (1983). Teaching: An Imperiled Profession. In L. Shulman and G. Sykes (eds.), *Handbook of Teaching and Policy,* New York: Longman.

Gilligan, C. (1982). *In a different voice: Psychological theory and women's development.* Cambridge, MA: Harvard University Press.

Glaser, B. and Strauss, A. (1967). *The discovery of grounded theory: Strategies for qualitative research.* Chicago: Aldine Publishing Co.

Glaser, B. (1978). *Advances in the methodology of grounded theory: Theoretical sensitivity.* Mill Valley, CA: Sociology Press.

Helgesen, S. (1990). *The female influence.* Toronto: Doubleday.

Jacobsen, H. (1982). Women's work and women's culture: Some further considerations. In C. Gallant and J. Gow (eds.), *Women's culture: Selected papers from the Halifax Conference.* Ottawa: Canadian Institute for the Advancement of Women.

Kahn, L. (1984). Group process and sex differences. *Psychology of Women Quarterly,* 8(3), 261–81.

Lafferty, C. and Pond, A. (1974). *The desert survival station.* Plymouth, MI: Human Synergistics.

Lamphere, L. (1985). Bringing the family to work: Women's culture on the shop floor. *Feminist Studies,* 11(3), 519–40.

Lee, P. and Gropper, N. (1974). Sex-role culture and educational practice, *Harvard Educational Review,* 44(3), 369–410.

Loden, M. (1985). *Feminine leadership or how to succeed in business without being one of the boys.* Toronto: Random House.

Lyons, N. (1983). Two perspectives on self, relationships and morality. *Harvard Educational Review,* 53(2), 125–45.

Miller, J. (1984). The development of women's sense of self. *Work in Progress* no. 12. Wellesley: Stone Center Working Papers Series.

Miller, J. (1986). *Towards a new psychology of women* (2nd ed.). Boston: Beacon Press.

Muller, H. and Cocotas, C. (1988) Women in power: New leadership in the health industry. *Health Care for Women International,* 9(2), 63–82.

Naisbitt, H. and Aburdene, P. (1986). *Reinventing the corporation.* New York: Warner Books.

Neuse, S. (1978). Professionalism and authority: Women in public service. *Public Administration Review,* 38(9/10), 436–41.

Ouchi, W. (1981). *Theory Z: How American business can meet the Japanese challenge.* Reading: Addison-Wesley.

Shakeshaft, C. (1987). *Women in educational administration*. Beverly Hills: Sage Publications.

Stanley, L. (1984). How the social science research process discriminates against women. In S. Acker and D. Piper (eds.), *Is higher education fair to women?* Guildford, Surrey: SRHE & NFER-NELSON.

Statham, A. (1987). The gender model revisited: Differences in the management styles of men and women. *Sex Roles,* 16(7/8), 409–29.

Strauss, A. and Corbin, J. (1990). *Basics of qualitative research: Grounded theory procedures and techniques*. Newbury Park: Sage.

Tannen, D. (1990). *You just don't understand: Women and men in conversation*. New York: Ballantine Books.

Valentine, P. and McIntosh, G. (1990). Food for thought: Realities of a women-dominated organization. *The Alberta Journal of Educational Research*, 36(4), 353–69.

Valentine, P. (1992). Nurse educators and decision making: A female perspective. *Canadian Journal of Nursing Administration*, 5(3), 10–13.

TWENTY

Leadership from The Classroom: Women Teachers as A Key to School Reform

Vivian Troen and Katherine C. Boles

W̲e write this chapter to bring the accumulated wisdom of six women teacher leaders to others interested in the issue of teacher leadership. We appreciate our interviewees' willingness to expose themselves to our scrutiny in order to help others who are embarking on teacher leadership in school reform. We begin the chapter with descriptions of the projects we studied in order to set the stage for the subsequent analysis of teacher leadership. The next section of the chapter provides a theoretical framework for our study and identifies themes common to all the projects. We then examine the effect of leadership efforts on the individual teachers initiating the projects and on the school as a whole, and we conclude with the implications of our findings and some suggestions for further research.

The Teacher Leadership Projects

The projects these teacher leaders initiated were restructuring efforts and altered the school environment in some way. Historically, such teacher initiatives have been rare, and given the subordinate roles played by teachers in schools, this phenomenon should come as no surprise.

We have organized the projects into two categories: school/college collaboratives and curriculum reform efforts. The names of the projects and the teacher leaders have been changed to protect their anonymity.

School-College Collaboratives

The Highland College Experiment. Pauline Curran is an elementary school teacher in a small town. Reflecting on her years of classroom experience gave her insights into the need for improving the training of student teachers while simultaneously giving veteran teachers strategies for working with preservice teachers. She believed a collaborative approach to preservice undergraduate education could provide some solutions to these problems, and as a result, she attempted to initiate a dialogue with the student teacher supervisor at nearby Highland College. To her surprise, she was immediately rebuffed.

"I was pretty naive at the time," she says, "I thought they would welcome the opportunity to collaborate with classroom teachers in building a stronger program. I was wrong. For years and years, universities have run pre-service training, and the message I was getting was that they were not about to share their authority and control."

She tried different levels of the college hierarchy, but received no attention until, on her own initiative, she sought and obtained a small grant. At that point a college faculty member became "mildly interested" and agreed to a formal meeting to discuss Pauline's ideas.

After pulling together a coalition of college supervisors, classroom teachers, and student teachers, Pauline published a handbook for cooperating teachers to use during the student teaching practicum. This handbook is now in use in many parts of her state and serves as a model for cooperation among the various constituencies of preservice training.

The success of the handbook helped other teachers in her building realize that the role of cooperating teacher needed additional clarification, and the project expanded to include more teachers in the school.

At the heart of the program is the teacher leader/on-site coordinator (initially Pauline Curran) who facilitates meetings for cooperating teachers to develop strategies to enhance the student teaching experience. A second component designed by Pauline is a seminar series for student teachers taught by classroom teachers. Seminar topics include mainstreaming of special education students, whole language strategies, and behavior management. Classroom teachers also serve as guest lecturers at college practicum courses.

Pauline went on to design the third program component, a Cooperating Teacher Study Group. The group meets during the school day while student teachers are teaching. Facilitated by a college supervisor, group discussions center around current literature concerning classroom practice and educational theory. According to Pauline, the study group has inspired teachers to use new strategies in their classrooms.

The program is now in its third year.

The O'Neill School/Sprague College Partnership. This middle school/graduate teacher education project was initiated by Maureen Agostino, a math teacher in a large urban school.

"It occurred to me that there were three components of the profession that needed attention," reports Maureen. "First, student teachers in my school were set up for failure because of the lack of understanding and communication between college instructors and classroom teachers. In addition, new teachers were giving up and leaving after only one or two years on the job. And isolation and stagnation seemed to be the inevitable lot of those teachers who stayed in the profession. I thought all three of those areas could be attacked with a coordinated effort between the school and the college."

Maureen approached Sprague College with the idea of forming a collaboration with a twofold purpose: to bridge the gap between theory and practice for preservice teachers, and to create professional development opportunities for experienced faculty.

Like Pauline, Maureen was stunned by the college's lack of interest. "They don't take you seriously if you're a classroom teacher," she says. "After all, you don't have your doctorate and teach in college, so how could you have any worthwhile ideas about educational reform?" But Maureen wasn't finished. "I went home and screamed at the walls," says Maureen, "but they hadn't seen the last of me. I was not about to give up."

Maureen wrote grant applications, consulted with others who were involved in school/college partnerships, kept visiting the college and pushing the faculty, and finally arranged a serious meeting with college faculty that resulted in a school/college partnership. Obtaining grant money, as in Pauline's case, seemed to be the turning point. "When you show up with money in your hand, they begin to pay attention," she relates.

Now in its second year, the O'Neill School/Sprague College Partnership consists of a cluster of teachers and student interns who are at the school site for a year-long practicum. Collaborative teaching has lowered the student-teacher ration; teachers report they feel more accountable to one another for the quality of their lessons; and children benefit from more thoughtful lesson planning.

Teachers in the collaboration serve as adjunct college faculty members, presenting at college courses, and participating in a study group on classroom-based research, taught by a college faculty member.

As part of her ongoing battle, Maureen is fighting to have teachers paid for their extra work.

The Consortium for Improved Teaching and Learning. Disquieted by the isolating nature of classroom teaching, two elementary school teachers in a suburb close to a major city began regularly to reflect on their practice. Their initial discussions centered around team teaching as a strategy to reduce classroom isolation.

Two years of planning by Tamar Vine and Bella Katz included article writing and lecturing to try out their ideas, lobbying with their principal and school system superintendent, numerous trips to call on the state commissioner of education in order to obtain funding, agitating with local colleges and universities to try and drum up interest in their plan for a school/college collaboration.

Their plan consisted of forming teaching teams with several objectives: increase the clinical aspect of preservice teacher education, provide special needs children with all remedial services within the regular classroom, offer experienced teachers an expanded role in the training of novice teachers, and provide teachers with opportunities for alternative professional options in research, curriculum development, and pre-service teacher education *during the school day.*

A spate of grant proposals and fund-raising initiatives resulted in several state grants, a donation from a private foundation, and some funds moved from elsewhere in the school budget.

The current, much-expanded collaborative project is now in its fifth year, and consists of two colleges and teaching teams in three urban and four suburban schools. It is accomplishing what its teacher leaders set out to do: form collegial teams, mainstream bilingual and special needs students, bring full-time graduate interns into the classroom, and provide new professional roles for full-time teachers.

"We were lucky to have the initial support of a sympathetic principal and one college faculty member who understood what we were trying to do—and gave us encouragement," recalls Tamar. "In other areas and at other levels, we kept hitting walls of resistance. We just learned how to go through them or work around them."

Curriculum Reform Efforts

The Writing Project. Veronica Miller is a second-grade teacher in an urban school. Doing research on the writing of children in her classroom, she discovered that writing could lead children into developing positive strategies of problem solving.

"It suddenly came to me that there was an opportunity to encourage children to reach higher levels of thinking than they had been capable of in the past," Veronica recalls, "and that led me to form a plan for writing a specialized curriculum for whole language teaching for kindergarten through third grade."

She had given herself a difficult assignment. First, she had to confront and overcome opposition from the school principal, who was not pleased that she had spent long hours working on her own time to develop a better curriculum. He would have preferred her to concentrate on delivering the citywide curriculum. She implemented her new curriculum in her own classroom but she was never allowed to work with other teachers in her own school. She, therefore, went (practically undercover) to work with teachers in other buildings in her system.

Even more upsetting was the negative reaction she received from parents who said she was a "bad teacher" because their children weren't getting lots of worksheets and instead she was teaching them in "not a regular way."

"That really hurt," says Veronica. "I shed a lot of tears over that experience, but I was convinced that raising the aspirations of my students by empowering them to gain new insights into their own creative process was something I had to do."

She disregarded the system's mandated curriculum. She wrote numbers of grants. She designed and held workshops. And she finally overcame both resistance and hostility to provide teachers (not in her own building, unfortunately) with a new curriculum that today, two years later, is also encouraging them to use classroom-based research to improve practice.

"Teachers can be encouraged to look beyond the immediacy of the moment—to reflect on their teaching and on the children in their classes," says Veronica. "It just takes a lot more effort than you think it should."

The Mount Whitmore Project. Desperate for space in her overcrowded rural K–8 school, Theresa Fournier began looking at the accommodations in a local arts center. The building was up for sale, and Theresa devised a feasible plan to obtain the space for the school's seventh and eighth grades. Convincing the school board and the theater's board of directors was not as easy as devising the plan, and another difficult step in the process was forming a collaboration with the art teacher and the other seventh and eighth grade teachers.

With assurances that the arts facility would be obtained by the school, the newly formed group designed a curriculum that effectively integrated the arts and computer technology into the seventh and eighth grade academic curriculum.

After a full year of exceptionally hard work, the team is still optimistic that the plan can be put into effect. However, the building has not yet been acquired and the project is in danger of collapsing because of recent political maneuverings regarding the use of the building.

The Community Outreach Project. Teacher leader Olivia Cameron developed a program that increased parent participation in the school, brought arts and foreign language into classrooms, and increased children's experiences with "Real Work"—working in the community using community resources as a primary learning source. Recognizing that other schools in her rural school district could benefit from the work she had done in her own school, Olivia organized a group of teachers from her school district and wrote and obtained a large state grant to expand her ideas to the three other schools in town. Olivia's goals were twofold: to broaden the scope of community participation in the schools by creating programs and curricula that necessitated the positive involvement of the community, and to give children a sense of purpose and meaning in their learning in order to improve academic performance.

Five mini-schools were created from the earlier, more traditional three-school configuration. Children now remain in their mini-school for three or four years. "Real Work" projects are being instituted in the various schools, and increased communication between the schools and the community has been facilitated by frequent meetings organized to more actively involve parents and other community members in the life of the school.

Background of Teacher Leadership

The school reform reports of the late 1980s make strong and compelling recommendations for teachers to provide leadership in restructuring the nation's schools (Carnegie 1986; Holmes 1986). The reports emphasize the importance of creating new roles for teachers that both recognize the centrality of classroom teaching and extend teachers' decision-making power into schoolwide leadership activities.

Teacher leadership initiatives, though, run contrary to the norms of school teaching in the United States. Since the mid-nineteenth century, teaching has been accepted as woman's work, or, as Catherine Beecher called it, "woman's true profession." Woman's role was to follow, not to lead. David Tyack referred to the newly feminized schools of the nineteenth century as "pedagogical harem(s)" where many women taught and a few men directed. As Strober and Tyack (1980) report:

From the beginning, sex segregation was part of the design of the urban graded school. . . . By structuring jobs to take advantage of sex-role stereotypes about women's responsiveness to rules and male authority, and men's presumed ability to manage women, urban school boards were able to . . . control the curriculum, students and personnel. . . . Given this purpose of tight control, women were ideal employees. With few alternative occupations and accustomed to patriarchal authority, they mostly did what their male superiors ordered. Differences of gender provided an important form of social control. (p. 500)

Teachers work in isolation, segregated from one another in "egg-crate" classrooms (Lortie 1975). Indeed, they function much like nineteenth-century factory workers who would have deemed it inappropriate or useless to tell the bosses how to restructure the assembly line. There has been an expectation of top-down mandates with little input from practitioners. This should come as no surprise, since teaching has traditionally been a low-status job for women in the United States.

The teacher leadership literature of the 1980s and 1990s ignored the critical role that gender had played in the history of the American schoolteacher, but did challenge the top-down nature of schools.

The first phase of this literature focused on what *should* happen vis-à-vis teacher leadership. *A Nation Prepared: Teachers for the 21st Century* (Carnegie 1986) emphasized the importance of providing leadership roles for teachers, thus restructuring the role of the teacher in the organization. *Who Will Teach Our Children?* (1985), the report of the California Commission on the Teaching Profession, and Devaney's "The Lead Teacher: Ways to Begin" (1987), a paper prepared for the Task Force on Teaching as a Profession for the Carnegie Forum on Education and the Economy, projected the role these newly empowered teachers would play in America's schools. Hypothetical sketches portrayed restructured schools and classrooms where a reorganized school day and a multilevel career path for classroom teachers offered new stimulation and avenues for teachers' professional growth. The reports envisioned less rigidly structured organizations where teachers' roles are flexible and extend beyond the boundaries of the classroom.

The second phase of the leadership reform literature made the difficult leap from report to reality by documenting what *is* happening in teacher leadership—cataloguing the experiences of teachers in newly created teacher leader roles. Ann Lieberman, in her study of seventeen teacher leaders (1988), views teacher leadership as a means of "fashioning new ways of working with the school community." However, her study indicates that even when school districts identify teacher leaders and give them leadership positions in schools, the work of teacher leadership is not easy. Lieberman describes the number of organizational and administrative skills these teacher leaders had to learn, and she states that they learned "without exception . . . about the school culture as if it were a new experience for them" (p. 150). They discovered how hard it was to develop trust among teachers and "they were confronted with the egalitarian ethic held by most teachers—the belief that teachers are all alike" (p. 151). Patricia Wasley's (1990) study of three teacher leaders supports Lieberman's findings and provides a more in-depth understanding of the dilemmas and demands confronting teacher leaders.

Though the teachers Wasley studies continue to teach at the same time as they provide leadership in their schools, a large number of teacher leaders have left classroom teaching to assume their leadership positions. Those who have continued teaching often assume positions such as mentor or peer coach, roles that support collegiality and collaboration, but do not provide "direction or determination" (Cooper 1988, 51). In addition, most of the teacher leadership positions have been determined not by teachers, but by "higher-ups" in the school organization.

Little attention has been paid in the reform literature, however, to teachers who have *created* their own leadership roles and have exerted that leadership *without* leaving classroom teaching. Maintaining their roles as classroom teachers, while assuming leadership roles beyond their traditional position in the school hierarchy, these teachers have facilitated change in their schools. Ignoring this critical group of teachers interested in leadership for school reform limits the definition of teacher leader and overlooks a possible means to professionalize the role of teacher.

The purpose of teacher leadership is to alter the hierarchical nature of schools, allowing practicing teachers to reform their own work and the work of other teachers.

The goal of this chapter is to force the discussion of teacher leadership to address how teachers can be leaders and continue to be classroom teachers. It also adds the dimension of gender.

Methodology

For the purpose of this research, and because we are looking for new models of teacher leadership, each of the teacher leaders we chose to study:

1. Teaches children during at least part of the school day.
2. Exerts influence beyond her isolated classroom, playing an important role in the larger arena of school and school district.

3. Has initiated a project to improve the school as well as to "redesign [her] work and augment [her] formal authority" (Johnson 1990, 348).

Such a sample acknowledges the centrality of care-giving and nurturing to the definition of teacher, while broadening the definition of teacher leader to include curriculum development, research, and policymaking beyond the classroom's four walls.

An outstanding teacher, admired by parents and colleagues alike, did not match our definition of a teacher leader unless her influence extended beyond her own classroom. Teacher leaders could not be "former teachers," such as those described in Lieberman's study. Thus, a full-time staff developer, though valued by colleagues, did not qualify for our study.

Nor were we looking for examples of the "empowered teacher" (the teacher who has been appointed to an existing or newly-created leadership position). Myrna Cooper, in her article "Whose Culture Is It, Anyway?" defines empowerment as "derived power . . . the licensing by others . . . to act somewhat free of direction in specified areas of performance. Empowerment is less than power. To be a colleague, a helper, a 'developer' does not a leader mean" (p. 50).

In our sample, authority was not *given* to the teachers and none of the teachers had the advantage of positional power and established leadership roles. They had exerted their leadership in entrepreneurial ways beyond defined boundaries. and their projects involved school restructuring, college collaborations, parent/community outreach, and curriculum reform/research.

We restricted our sample to *women* teacher leaders. The vast majority of schoolteachers are women, and it would be naive not to acknowledge the importance of gender in any study of teacher leadership. We chose to interview elementary teachers only, due to the preponderance of women at that level, and because our own long experience as teachers in elementary schools made us more cognizant of the issues confronting elementary teachers. We selected six women teacher leaders from urban, suburban and rural settings ranging in age from their late thirties to early sixties, with between fifteen and twenty-five years of teaching experience; five are white, one is African-American; five are married, one is single.

These teacher leaders were recommended to us by other teachers, school administrators, central office administrators, or college faculty members. Each was recognized by all four of the above constituencies as a teacher leader who had influenced other teachers. The teachers were interviewed at length in a semistructured interview, using the attached interview guide. Subsequent personal conversations with the subjects and their colleagues rounded out our data.

Overview of The Findings

This section examines the characteristics of teacher leaders, describes how these teachers define teacher leadership, and highlights teachers' motivations for asserting leadership, the collaborations that sustained these teachers and the barriers that confronted them. Teacher leadership as a vehicle for professional development, the importance of collaboration in women's leadership efforts, and the concept of power in teacher leadership round out the study. All this is set in a feminist context and highlights the potential of teacher leadership as a source of school reform.

Common Characteristics of Teacher Leaders

Each teacher leader was passionate about the project she had initiated and confident of its importance to children and teachers. She had a clear vision for school reform, and, above all, each of these teacher leaders was persevering, willing to promote her vision until it became a reality. Each was undaunted by bureaucratic constraints, unafraid to tackle the system that didn't meet the needs of the children she taught. As one teacher commented, "Being willing to take a dive, I think, is what's different about me."

The teachers were all in mid-career with over fifteen years classroom teaching experience. This phenomenon is consistent with Erikson's theory regarding adult development—that is, during middle adulthood, achievement and recognition become central developmental objectives. From Erikson's point of view, it would not be an accident that self-initiated teacher leaders tended to be between 40 and 60 years of age (Erikson 1950). The teachers in our study had been teaching and nurturing children for many years; now they wanted to "'jump outside' the frames and systems authorities provide and create their own frame" (Belenky et al. 1986). The experience of these women is consistent with a higher level "way of knowing" described by Belenky and co-workers in *Women's Ways of Knowing;* these teachers succeeded in effectively *integrating* knowledge that they felt intuitively was personally important with knowledge they had learned from others" (p. 134).

Our sample of teacher leaders, deeply committed to classroom teaching, were regarded as excellent teachers by colleagues, administrators and parents. One had been named statewide "Teacher of the Year." Another had, over the course of her career, been awarded both state and national fellowships. All demonstrated their enthusiasm for learning by attending numerous professional conferences, regularly taking and teaching workshops and college courses, and pursuing advanced degrees.

Teacher Leadership Defined

As teachers defined teacher leadership a common theme emerged: the importance of currently practicing teachers acting as catalysts for other teachers' learning. The interviewees expressed this notion in a number of ways.

> Teacher leadership is classroom teachers motivating other teachers to create a new attitude in a school, an attitude that respects teacher learning. I like to think my role as teacher leader is to encourage teachers to pursue professional development.

> Teacher leadership is a group of classroom teachers banding together to provide a quality education for kids. It's thinking with others who work directly with kids about issues that concern these kids.

These quotes highlight the importance of relationships to these teacher leaders. This should come as no surprise, given the findings of Jean Baker Miller, Carol Gilligan and others. Gilligan (1982) suggests that women's sense of self and of morality revolves around issues of responsibility for, care of, and inclusion of other people. It was clear that these teachers felt the same.

One teacher leader we interviewed synthesized what was implicit in the other quotes, when she observed, "I believe teacher leadership is all about conversations and relationships. I like to think of myself as a facilitator for teachers to follow their own interests and desires."

The definition—being a catalyst for teacher learning—was broadened by some teachers to include taking responsibility for restructuring efforts. One project leader contended, "The only way schools will improve is through *inside-out* change. Practicing teachers must change the structure of schools, whether it's the ill-designed 40-minute period or the competitive isolation inherent in most schools."

Motivation

Dissatisfaction with the status quo was the primary motivator of the project leaders. The problems addressed by the teachers can be divided into two categories: those dealing with child-related issues and those affecting the adults who work in schools.

Issues of curriculum were a top priority for these classroom practitioners. Much like the teachers in McLaughlin's study (1988), the teachers were more interested in teaching and life in the classroom than they were "in moving vertically into quasi-administrative or expanded teaching functions or horizontally into administrative or central-office resource positions" (p. 24). As one teacher in our sample stated, "I was looking for a new way to be involved with education without leaving the classroom. It's a way to be a boss, and still be a teacher—still be with kids."

The teacher leader whose vision had propelled her to become a teacher researcher and initiate a literacy program for young children in an inner-city school stated, "I knew that what I wanted to do had to be connected to the classroom. I had no desire to be a principal because I want to always have a strong connection to kids."

The teacher involved in integrating the sciences, arts and humanities into one interdisciplinary curriculum for seventh and eighth graders, remarked, "I'm really interested in questions of curriculum. I'm not at all interested in questions of leadership or questions of administration. I've never thought about it."

Teachers whose projects were solely focused on adults were influenced by the desire to eliminate teacher isolation and improve preservice education. As one teacher said, "the deteriorating quality of student teachers was a major impetus for my wanting to revamp traditional student teaching." Another teacher stated, "I was a cooperating teacher and I had a student teacher I didn't know what to do with, and I knew there were many other teachers in my building just like me."

The motivation to professionalize teaching was addressed by three of the teacher leaders. One of them said: "Whenever I talk about this project at a conference or a workshop, I always say that you must provide meaningful professional development for teachers. That's the only way we'll get teachers to think about improving the way they teach the kids."

Collaboration

The importance of collaboration was highlighted by each of the participants in our study. "I built my project through collaborations and alliances," was the way one teacher phrased it.

Jean Baker Miller, in *Toward a New Psychology of Women*, explains this aspect of women's behavior. She writes: "One central feature (of women's development) is that women stay with, build on, and develop in a context of connections with others. Indeed women's sense of self becomes very much organized around being able to make and then maintain affiliations and relationships" (p. 83).

As a first step in their leadership efforts, teachers sought sympathetic colleagues in their buildings. One suburban teacher described a colleague in her school as an important element in her success: "I never could have done this without my 'partner in crime,' my teaching partner. When I was ready to throw in the towel, she had the energy to keep going, to consistently be a source of strength and inspiration."

From their first connections, the leaders "spread the word," convincing other teachers that it was in their own self-interest to be concerned with the broader goal of school reform. Because the leadership of the teachers in our study was not positional, they *had* to attract others to their ideas (i.e., create their own following), using interpersonal skills, hard work, and personal contacts.

This is not dissimilar from the experience of women leaders in business. Rather than "the traditional command and control style" identified with male hierarchical leadership, Judith Rosener, in a study on the ways women lead, states that businesswomen engage in "interactive leadership" that encourages participation and facilitates inclusion (Rosener 1990, 120).

The teachers leaders we studied looked to parents and community members as natural allies. When asked to define her greatest source of support, one teacher responded quickly: "My greatest support comes from the community and from the parents. In the things that have mattered a lot to me, I can rally the community behind me. I've had to do that a few times."

In another project, parents supported the teacher's initiative by contacting foundations to fund the project because they felt their children had been so well served by the project's restructuring efforts.

Noting that her work with the local arts center had been initiated by a conversation with the center's director, another teacher stated, "I went to breakfast with the director and I asked if she thought it was possible for us to move into the now vacant space in her building. I didn't go through anybody. . . . Because she was a friend, I wanted, from one friend to another, to know whether or not it would be a good idea."

Teachers approached colleges with their ideas. In each of the three college collaborations, teachers initiated their partnerships to redesign the clinical aspect of pre-service education by increasing the role of the classroom teacher. Such collaboration also enabled teachers to pursue teacher research, curriculum development, and to participate in study groups during the school day rather than the more traditional staff development that occurs after the school day.

One of the project leaders involved in a school/college collaborative remarked: "I used to think that teachers had all the expertise necessary to educate pre-service teachers. But then I realized the importance of a strong symbiotic relationship between higher ed and the school. The practical was not enough. Theory was essential. And theory and practice could be a powerful combination."

In one case the school principal was an ally to the teacher's reform efforts, in another the former principal served as a mentor offering advice and encouragement, but mention of the principal is notably absent from descriptions of allies and supporters, and in two cases the principal was a decidedly negative force against teacher leadership. In any discussion about principals, it is important to note the lack of an existing paradigm for the role of the principal in teacher leadership.

Power

The school reform movement is replete with buzzwords such as "shared decision-making," "school-based management," and "the professionalization of teaching." Inherent in these concepts, but often overlooked in discussions of their implementation, is the issue of power. Power is a limited commodity in schools, and the established hierarchy places teachers in a low-power position, making it difficult for teacher leaders to be acknowledged as credible forces of change.

Rosabeth Moss Kanter, in *Men and Women of the Corporation* (1977) defines power as "the ability to get things done, to mobilize resources, or to get and use whatever it is that a person needs for the goal he or she is attempting to meet."

Teachers wield power in only one domain—that of the classroom. Our survey confirms Susan Moore Johnson's analysis of the domains of decision-making in schools, in which she reports that though decisions about "classroom policy—what to teach, how to use time, and how to assess progress" (Johnson 1989b) are made by teachers, other important decisions that affect teachers' work, such as scheduling, class placement, assignment of specialists and the allocation of supplies are made by those at higher levels of the school's bureaucracy. Teachers are generally powerless to affect school-wide policy, and this very fact makes it difficult for leadership to emerge from among the ranks of teachers.

And, when teacher leaders do emerge and begin to affect policy and the larger domains of the school, another phenomenon occurs. The teacher must confront not only the principal, but also the ambivalence and often the resistance of teacher colleagues to the leadership of another teacher. Kanter accounts for this phenomenon by stating that when individuals experience "low opportunity," it "leads to 'passive resistance' or foot-dragging from the sidelines; a feeling of powerlessness leads to inappropriately tight control and turf-mindedness" (1983, 406) Thus, in order to take a leadership role in the school the teacher leader must wrestle both with those above her and those equal to her in the school hierarchy.

When we asked our teacher respondents to define power, they often sidestepped the question, and remarked that the word power conjured up negative visions of authoritarian bosses. Our respondents were not alone in that perception. Dunlap and Goldman note that "Power is fundamentally domination; it carries connotations of manipulation and prohibition at best and oppression and negativity at worst" (p. 9).

When pressed, however, the teachers consistently stated that power meant the freedom to control the work they did. One teacher echoed the sentiments of many when she defined power as "decision-making, the freedom to create—and playing hardball." Another teacher defined power as having control over her future. There was an equating of power with control—control over change, curriculum, budget, professional development, pre-service training.

The "zero-sum" view of school leadership implies that there is only a limited amount of power in the school. If principals fear they will be relegated to becoming operational managers as a result of teachers taking on new leadership roles, then teacher leadership will not succeed. If teachers question the leadership of other teachers and wonder, "Who does she think she is?" then teacher leadership will remain a rare occurrence. But if those in schools begin to believe that power is not a "zero-sum," that power can be shared, and that by sharing power with others the quantity of power for each participant increases, our study demonstrates that teacher leadership could actually be a powerful catalyst for the professionalization of teaching.

The issue of power has only begun to be analyzed, and more discussion of this topic is clearly necessary. Though the word is seldom articulated by teachers, the issue of power merits a long, hard look in any discussion of teacher leadership and school reform.

Issues and Barriers Confronting Teacher Leaders

The road to teacher leadership is strewn with obstacles and roadblocks. An obstacle frequently specified by the respondents is the lack of support from other teachers for their leadership efforts. This difficulty is directly related to *the egalitarian nature of teaching.*

Historically, teaching has been an "unstaged career" (Lortie 1975, 83) where all teachers are equal, and where the responsibilities of the first day on the job are the same as on the day of retirement. Teachers do not take on increased responsibilities consonant with their increasing skill. Therefore, teachers find it difficult to accept one of their own as a leadership figure. As one teacher leader stated, "When you work in a school and you decide on taking leadership, the reaction is, 'Who does she think she is?'"

These teachers' accounts confirmed Edson's (1987) and O'Connor and Boles' (1992) findings that women leaders frequently encounter jealousy, competition, and lack of support from other women educators. One teacher leader in our study attributed her greatest source of stress to "other teachers' reluctance to change—teachers, love 'em, hate 'em. They complain and let you do all the work!"

Two other teachers had similar comments:

Other teachers stress me out. They're aware of their inadequacies but don't care. Teachers are so resistant to change! I think it's despicable that teachers refuse to use new curriculum even when it would be better for kids.

When I got all these grants and I was Teacher of the Year for the state, it was hard, because the people right around you don't want to recognize your expertise. . . . It's much easier to go somewhere else, and tell somebody else. They think you're wonderful—but not on your home turf.

It is ironic to note that though teacher leaders found their first allies in one or two sympathetic colleagues in their schools, once the teacher leaders began to extend their purview to larger numbers of teachers, other teaching colleagues became a source of considerable resistance.

The teacher leaders discovered the difference between *collegial and congenial relationships among teachers.* Many schools offer friendly, congenial work environments; but few offer a professional, collegial work environment that makes the school "as educative for teachers as for students" (Shulman 1983). The teacher leaders in our sample focused on establishing collegial relationships—relationships where mutual growth and learning are explicit goals. Despite having increased the number of their own and their peers' collegial associations, they lamented losing some of the congenial relationships they had enjoyed prior to their leadership initiatives.

As one teacher stated:

Being a teacher leader—it costs you! You can never be totally in with the other teachers. What it costs is, I can't be in the teachers' room. I don't belong in the same way. You give up your friends, but I say it's for a higher purpose. I see things differently. The payoff—teachers can talk about teaching and controversial issues like tracking in a safe environment that I've created—That's a biggy!!

Carol Gilligan uses the metaphor of a web to describe how women often feel when they differentiate themselves from other women, that is, assume leadership in an egalitarian work setting. She describes this phenomenon as, "[women's] wish to be at the center of connection and the consequent fear of being too far out on the edge" (p. 62).

Another teacher reiterated the effect of this loss of connection. "I feel more isolated from the rest of the school. As more energy goes into the project, less energy goes to the rest of the school. I feel less in touch."

These words also echo Philip Jackson's in his article, "Lonely at the Top: Observations on the Genesis of Administrative Isolation." Jackson contends, "the person in charge of an organization . . . is somewhat more vulnerable to feelings of being alone." Though these teacher leaders are not "in charge of an organization," nor do they aspire to be principals, they, too, are confronted by "the forces that threaten to encapsulate . . . administrators, surrounding (them) with a shell that separates (them) from others in the organization that (they) serve" (Jackson, 1976, 14) and are isolated from their colleagues.

Each of the teacher leaders we interviewed worked in a school with a male principal, and a number of the teachers blamed *administration* for the difficulties they encountered as teacher leaders. As one subject stated:

> Support isn't there from administration. They don't recognize the importance of making teaching the best it can be. There are objective standards that aren't adhered to. My principal called my efforts "cute." Cute doesn't describe serious-minded people.

Another echoed these sentiments when she described her efforts to implement substantive school change.

> It's about decision-making. Playing hardball. Letting people know you're serious. My principal said to me, "Why don't you tend to your knitting?" and "Don't you ever stay home with your kids?" I took it as a way to push me back, a way to keep me in my place. The hierarchy is male in education.

Only in one instance were parents considered an obstacle to the teacher leader's reform efforts. This teacher remarked that *parents* in her inner-city school were not supportive of the changes she had brought to reading and writing. As she reported: "I work with the urban poor. Within that framework parents don't see that change is inevitable. They hold on to what they think is good education—even if it's not good for their child in this time."

Another set of obstacles related to *time* and institutional *structure.* The difficulty of juggling leadership and classroom responsibilities was sometimes overwhelming.

One teacher remarked:

> I think the biggest obstacle is the time factor—that if you're really seriously doing your job, it's very time consuming. It's hard to take a lot of time out to talk with other people and be out of your classroom . . . keep growing and working . . . out giving workshops and that kind of thing. I think that time is really the hardest factor, at least initially.

Calling "time" the biggest source of stress, another teacher remarked:

> It's time—keeping on top of my classroom and doing the other work of seeing that things get done. Another source of stress has been that I've had to learn to slow myself down in order to get other people on board.

Teacher Leadership as A Vehicle for Professional Growth

Though professional growth was not the primary goal of any of the projects we studied, sophisticated professional development was accomplished by all the teacher leaders in their projects. Professional development for these teacher leaders, and the many teachers whose work they affected, no longer occurred at afternoon workshops mandated by central office and tolerated by teachers. It was an outgrowth of the work that teachers did together. These collaborative ventures reflect current feminist theory that the most substantive growth occurs in conjunction with others to whom we feel connected and for whom we care.

Teachers felt their projects had stimulated and deepened their conversations about teaching; improved classroom teaching was the result.

> This project has made me more aware of my teaching. I want to be the best I can be. It makes me want to try new things, and find out if I can do them. I'm not boring. I've added a new dimension to my teaching.

> Teachers who research the classroom can learn to teach better. Looking beyond the immediacy of the moment and reflecting back enables me to be a more effective teacher.

In addition, these teachers acquired skills not generally thought of as essential to successful teaching. They learned to communicate more effectively with other adults, to build coalitions, listen to peers, work behind the scenes to achieve their goals, develop strategies for innovation and change. They spoke passionately and in detail about having become more politically savvy.

> I know how to present now (at college classes and conferences), to speak to different audiences. People appreciate my knowledge and my honesty. I talk about the real issues in education.

Another teacher noted, "Working with student teachers has made me more cognizant about what and how I teach. I really think about integrating theory and practice."

Teachers were more self-confident, both professionally and personally, as a result of the new roles they had created for themselves.

> I feel better about myself. I can now say with conviction to other people that I'm doing something that's educationally and pedagogically sound. It's not just a frill. I feel much more professional.

Clearly, our interviews with teacher leaders confirm Roland Barth's comment in *Run School Run.* "Staff development . . . is most fruitful when it is an incidental outcome of other school functions thoughtfully undertaken" (1980, 147).

Conclusion

The Carnegie Report states that "the key" to the successful reform of schools "lies in creating a profession . . . of well-educated teachers prepared to assume new powers and responsibilities to redesign schools for the future" (p. 2). Our study demonstrates that such teachers already exist, and it is likely that their ranks could be increased if the structure and the culture of the school allowed teacher leadership to flourish.

The teachers we studied succeeded *despite* the structure of the schools in which they worked. Despite administrators who cautioned them or thought they were "cute," despite other teachers who questioned their right to take authority, and despite the bureaucratic structure which placed them in a low-power position, these teachers prevailed.

Teacher leaders are primarily interested in the improvement of teaching and curriculum for children. Their leadership interests come second. Each had a vision of how she thought her school should change. That vision was meant to directly meet her needs, the needs of the children she taught, and then to affect other teachers and children.

Relationships and feelings of connectedness, so important among women, changed when these women took leadership. Though many of their colleagues saw them as important figures in the school, others viewed these teachers as threats. Why does connectedness change when female teachers take leadership? Can female teachers maintain relationships with other women when they are in a power position? How can we redefine power and leadership in feminist terms? This is indeed fertile ground for further investigation.

Most studies of teacher leadership have focused on teachers' leadership role in mentoring and peer coaching—more common examples of the way women lead. Women's propensity to devote themselves to the care and empowerment of others has been amply documented by Miller, Gilligan, and others.

Our study demonstrates that teacher leaders can assume leadership in a larger arena—the arena of school reform—and it also indicates the difficulties and obstacles that teachers can expect to encounter when they choose to undertake such leadership activities. This study encourages us to expand our vision of what teacher leadership could include. The teacher leaders we interviewed struggled, and to a large extent succeeded, in claiming new territories of teacher leadership in school reform.

Education cannot afford to ignore the talents of teachers with vision and leadership potential, who are ready, willing and able to assume leadership roles. Policymakers, boards of education, administrators, and unions should aggressively seek out teachers with expert leadership qualities so that schools can more effectively educate our children, the key to America's future.

Bibliography

Barth, R. S. (1980). *Run school run.* Cambridge, MA: Harvard University Press.

Belenkey, M. F., Clinchy, B. M., Goldberger, N. R., Tarule, J. M. (1986). *Women's ways of knowing: The development of self, voice, and mind.* New York: Basic Books.

Boles, K. C. (1991). *School restructuring by teachers: A study of the teaching project at the Edward Devotion School.* Unpublished doctoral dissertation, Harvard University.

California Commission on the Teaching Profession. (1985). *Who will teach our children?* Sacramento, California: California Commission on the Teaching Profession.

Carnegie Forum on Education and the Economy. (1986). *A nation prepared: Teachers for the twenty-first century.* New York: Carnegie Forum on Education and the Economy.

Devaney, K. (1987). The lead teacher: Ways to begin. Paper prepared for the Task Force on Teaching as a Profession. New York: Carnegie Forum on Education and the Economy.

Edson, S. K. (1987). Voices from the present: Tracking the female administrative aspirant. *Journal of Educational Equity and Leadership,* 7 (Winter 1987).

Erikson, E. (1950). *Childhood and society.* New York: W. W. Norton.

Gilligan, C. (1982). *In a different voice.* Cambridge, MA: Harvard University Press.

The Holmes Group. (1986). *Tomorrow's teachers.* East Lansing, MI: The Holmes Group, Inc.

Jackson, P. (1976). Lonely at the top: Observations on the genesis of administrative isolation. Paper presented at the annual meetings of the American Educational Research Association, San Francisco.

Johnson, S. M. (1989). Schoolwork and its reform. In J. Hannaway and R. Crowson (eds.), *The politics of reforming school administration*. New York: The Falmer Press.

———. (1990a). *Teachers at work*. New York: Basic Books.

———. (1990b). Teachers, power and school change. In William H. Clune and John F. Witte (eds.), *Choice and control in American education. Volume 2: The practice of choice, decentralization and school restructuring*. New York: The Falmer Press.

Kanter, R. M. (1977). *Men and women of the corporation*. New York: Basic Books.

———. (1983). *The change masters*. New York: Simon & Schuster.

Lieberman, A., Saxl, E. R., and Miles, M. B. (1988). Teacher leadership: Ideology and practice. In A. Lieberman (ed.), *Building a professional culture in schools*. New York: Teachers College Press.

Little, J. W. (1987). Teachers as colleagues. In V. Richardson-Koehler (ed.), *Educators' handbook: A research perspective*. New York: Longman.

———. (1988). Assessing the prospects for teacher leadership. In A. Lieberman (ed.), *Building a professional culture in schools*. New York: Teachers College Press.

———. (1990). The persistence of privacy: Autonomy and initiative in teachers' professional relations. *Teachers College Record*, 91(4).

Lortie, D. (1975). *Schoolteacher*. Chicago: University of Chicago Press.

McLaughlin, M. W. and Yee, S. M. (1988). School as a place to have a career. In A. Lieberman (ed.), *Building a professional culture in schools*. New York: Teachers College Press.

McLaughlin, M. W. and Marsh, D. D. (1990). Staff development and school change. In A. Lieberman (ed.), *Schools as collaborative cultures: Creating the future now*. Bristol, PA: The Falmer Press.

Maeroff, G. (1988). *Teacher empowerment*. New York: Teachers College Press.

Miller, J. B. (1986). *Toward a new psychology of women*. Boston: Beacon Press.

———. (1991). Women and power. In J. Jordan, A. Kaplan, J. B. Miller, I. Stiver, and J. Surrey, *Women's growth in connection: Writings from the Stone Center*. New York: The Guilford Press.

National Commission on Excellence in Education. (1984). *Meeting the challenge of a nation at risk.* Cambridge, MA: USA Research.

Powell, A. G., Farrar, E., and Cohen, D. K. (1985). *The shopping mall high school.* Boston: Houghton Mifflin.

Rosener, J. B. (1990). Ways women lead. *Harvard Business Review,* 68(4) Nov.–Dec.

Sarason, S. B. (1971). *The culture of the school and the problem of change.* Boston: Allyn and Bacon.

Shulman, L. S. (1983). Autonomy and obligation: The remote control of teaching. In L. Shulman and G. Sykes (eds.), *Handbook of teaching and policy.* New York: Longman.

Sizer, T. R. (1984). *Horace's compromise: The dilemma of the American high school.* Boston: Houghton Mifflin.

Sklar, K. K. (1976). *Catharine Beecher: A study in American domesticity.* New York: W. W. Norton.

Strober, M. and Tyack, D. (1980). Why do women teach and men manage? A report on research on schools. *Signs: The Journal of Women in Culture and Society,* 5(3).

Tyack, D. B. (1974). *The one best system: A history of American urban education.* Cambridge, MA: Harvard University Press.

Wasley, P. A. (1991). *Teachers who lead: The rhetoric of reform and the realities of practice.* New York: Teachers College Press.

TWENTY-ONE

Women Principals—Leading with Power

Kathleen S. Hurty

> Women's entry into the public sphere can
> be seen not merely as the result of con-
> temporary economic pressures, the high
> rate of divorce, or the success of the femi-
> nist movement, but rather as a profound
> evolutionary response to a pervasive cul-
> tural crisis. Feminine principles are enter-
> ing the public realm because we can no
> longer afford to restrict them to the pri-
> vate domestic sphere, nor allow a public
> culture obsessed with Warrior values to
> control human destiny if we are to survive.
>
> —Sally Helgesen

The reconceptualization of power is a lively current topic. In both academic and popular texts there are increasing challenges to traditional
theories of power. Women are leading the debate.

Rosabeth Moss Kanter's work on power, powerlessness, and empowerment in organizations was pace-setting in its focus on power as capacity and
efficacy rather than domination and control (1977, 1979, 1989). Carol Gilligan (1982) contrasts hierarchy and webs as ways of thinking about structured relationships of power and proposes that as we reinterpret women's
experience in terms of their own imagery we can move from inequality to
interconnection. This, she argues, contributes to the understanding of human development and provides a basis for generating new theories beneficial to both women and men. Kathy Ferguson (1984) argues that both our
speech and our institutions will be transformed by looking at the submerged

380

and devalued experience of women, and by bringing the language of power to light in order to alter that power. In Ferguson's view, feminist discourse embraces the values of care, connection and commitment to participatory democracy—a model not universally applicable to all women nor exclusive of all men. Sharon Welch (1990) believes there are alternative systems of thought and action already existing in our world and finds described in the literature of African-American women an attempt to exercise and create a different sort of power. Drawing on these resources, Welch proposes a feminist ethic of risk. Diane Dunlap and Paul Goldman (1991) propose that facilitative, interactive power is more useful in school reform than top-down vertical systems of authority. Judy Rosener (1990) challenges the "command and control" leadership style frequently associated with men and suggests that women tend to use "interactive" leadership which encourages participation, shares power and information, enhances self-worth, and gets others excited about their work.

In the popular vein, Dorothy Cantor and Toni Bernay (1992) analyze stories from the new cadre of women in political leadership and argue for WomanPower, which, among other aspects, sees strength rather than weakness in tenderness and caring. Journalists Sally Helgesen (1991) and Sherry Suib Cohen (1989) are among those who have explored women's stories and experiences to help shape a new power agenda in the corporate world and in the public debate.

Women do have power as school leaders but have seldom articulated the dimensions of that power. With but a few exceptions the educational research community has not focused its attention on women in the principal's office, in order to understand the concepts of leadership and power.[1] Listening to the stories and examining the work ways of women in school principalship in order to understand the concept of power from their perspective as school leaders is therefore an essential task.[2] Such work offers new insights for the transformation of schools and other institutions and points us toward new ways of understanding and using power in the twenty-first century. In fact, schools would be well-served in seeking women as administrators. Consider this recent finding by Schmuck and Schmuck (1990) in their study of small-town schools. Male administrators, coming frequently from the coaching field, tended to see communication and teamwork as "unidirectional and hierarchical, as a kind of military teaming." In contrast:

> with only one exception, every female administrator we interviewed and observed was more aware of and skillful in the give and take of interpersonal communication. Most instances of collaboration, involvement, and shared influence took place in the school that had female principals. In those places, we saw teamwork, excitement, and enthusiasm.

The reconceptualization of power proposed in this chapter is based on my study of a selected population of women leaders: seventeen elementary school principals in a large urban school system.[3] This study was a vehicle for exploring the possibility that women leaders espouse and practice a different theory of power than is typically assumed or thought to be prevalent in male-dominated organizational settings. The power themes that emerged do indeed point toward new theoretical perspectives on power and have the potential of broadening our understanding of educational leadership. Enlarging the definition of power to include these women-identified elements of power provides creative resources to shape and transform the schools and organizations of the future. While rooted in the experiences of women in the principalship, these power and leadership resources are not limited by gender, nor applicable solely to educational settings.

Exploring Power Theory: A Personal Story

My early years as an elementary teacher were marked by little attention to the concept of power. I made the assumption, as did many of my colleagues, that I had little power and that there were "ways around the system" to get creative things done, when necessary. Not satisfactory, but livable. Then, as I became involved with other teachers, parents, and school arts administrators in the creation of an arts magnet school within the district, new notions of participatory decision-making strongly appealed to my sense of hope for the transformation of schooling. I decided to pursue graduate studies in order to learn more about the possibilities of school–community collaboration and I enrolled in graduate school with ideals in my pocket. By this time I was principal of an elementary school. It was not long before issues of power came to the fore.

As I tried to refine my administrative skills with a focus on the facilitation of children's learning by enabling teachers and parents to work with administrators in the development of creative school settings for active learning I became increasingly frustrated. The more I read in the required texts the more I perceived a disjunction between theories of administration and the practice of "principaling" from an enabling perspective. My frustration was symbolized by what seemed an incredible mismatch: the definitions of power in textbooks with what was required to facilitate good education born out in my experiences as teacher and principal.

The textbooks seemed to suggest that to wield power as an administrator I had to be more controlling, less trustful, more tempered toward domination and subordination, less open in communication, less tolerant of uncertainty, more coercive, less collaborative. That did not match at all what I had found to be effective either in the classroom or in the principal's office. What I came to call the "power over" model proposed in those traditional tests didn't match with what I now know as the "power with" model evident in effective schools.[4] The power possibilities I longed to know more about didn't have a name then, but I began to look into women's ways of using and talking about power to search for some concrete clues.

It was a participatory quest. The design of the research was a grounded theoretical field study in a large West Coast school district. I observed and interviewed seventeen female elementary school principals who were ethnically diverse and differed in age and years of experience, but who were identified by the district as effective principals. I listened to these women talk, I shadowed several of them during their work day, I participated in their school site activities, I talked with staff members and parents and students. I came to appreciate the courage of these women school leaders despite the difficulties of administering a school in a troubled district and in a time of complexity. I began to understand that while they were unique individuals with differing stories, their ways of describing their world of work and their approaches to it contained remarkable similarities.

The questions and ideas continued to develop as I watched and listened and as I searched the transcribed data for segments of articulated experience that fit into an integrated meaningful whole. I began to see a match between these shared experiences as mothers/teachers/principals and the administrative gifts of women *leading with power*.

I knew that I had often felt powerless both as a teacher and as a principal to do all that I knew was right for kids, and at first I took some small comfort in noting I was not alone. Feelings of powerlessness are common to women in school leadership. In lunchroom conversations we commonly talked about "those at the top" who made our lives miserable by their rigid hierarchical ways of thinking. We fell readily into the trap of thinking we had no power because power, in this unchallenged view, meant control over people, money and resources. In the interviews, when the principals were told that the "next set of questions will deal with power," they frequently responded, "this won't take long because I don't have any!" These women saw themselves as having little "power over" in the traditional bureaucratic organizational structure of the school district.

Yet, when these women, effective principals in a large school district, were asked for their own definition of power, an equally common theme emerged. After pondering the question they consistently said "for me, power is the ability to get the job done." When asked how they got the job done, their responses provided a clear way of defining power through women's experiences in school leadership. If indeed power is the ability to get the job done, then *how* they went about getting the work done is what gives meaning to an authentic definition of power, identified through and validated by their experience. The picture that emerged was a vision of "power with," power redefined out of their daily struggles to get the job done, the job of educating children in a challenging urban multicultural school district.

Because of the reigning ideology of power, these women had not thought of what they were doing in power terms. But when they began to name the strategies and resources they used for doing their work effectively, thus naming their own power tools, a whole new view of power came to the fore. It was an "aha" experience for them as they sought to name the power they possessed. They began to analyze and critique this broadened definition of power derived from their own experience, and critiqued as well the traditional definitions of power that had not accounted for these women-identified ways of working powerfully. These women really knew that they could bring their personal and political resources to bear in this complex school district and in this community. Their stories and their strengths were "narratives of perseverance and survival" in an often inhospitable environment. Jean Bethke Elshstain's (1990) perspectives in her helpful discussion of feminism as civic discourse suggests that "women, from a double vision that straddles power and powerlessness," may hold the key to the development of new forms of power.

The authenticity and integrity of female experiences, often hidden or missing from the public historical record created in the main by men, can be appreciated as contributions to more fully accountable stories of human development. If this happens a more human and more humane world is likely to ensue. These elements of a new power theory may fall strangely on "administrative ears." They may be dismissed as too soft, too emotional, too non-decisive, too risky. On the other hand, schools are being administered effectively according to those responsible for evaluating effectiveness. This way works! It remains to be seen how both men and women in the principalship will learn from these perspectives on leadership and power.

Learning from Contemporary Women Principals

In the talk and actions of these seventeen women principals, whose stories and ways of working form the case study data, I observed creative empowerment strategies at work that gave a distinctive picture of effective leadership. These women were emotionally committed to the education of the children in their care, competent in curriculum and instruction, energetic in engaging teachers and parents in decision-making, and creative in their abilities to work with people toward needed change. They agonized over the lack of resources, the apathy, the bureaucratic hindrances to action, the lack of caring, the impersonalisation of the larger system, the breaking down of evaluation into "scientific tidbits" for isolated analysis. They pondered how to help children learn and grow toward maturity, and how to solve problems of school management. They had dreams of what could be, while working with what is. They got tired, angry, frustrated, and shared those feelings honestly. Yet they also enjoyed their work, and found a sense of fulfillment in doing it well and being at the center of the creative transformation of their schools. They made the choice to "work around" bureaucracy, to act collaboratively with others, to "turn things around" despite the constraints. They had little hope that change would come rapidly. But they envisioned a future beyond bureaucracy, and worked toward that possibility.

Here were women leading in the "power with" mode, utilizing the resources of their own experiences as women. Five distinctive elements of this kind of power came to light: (1) *emotional energy*, a willingness to use, honestly and openly, a full range of emotions in their work with teachers, students and the community; (2) *nurtured growth*, the ability to nurture even small evidences of learning and development; (3) *reciprocal talk*, talking *with* rather than *at* others by listening to and learning from other points of view; (4) *pondered mutuality*, keeping others in mind in the reflective rumination used in making decisions; and (5) *collaborative change*, working with and involving others in the transformation of schooling. These are available attributes which bring new, qualitatively distinctive dimensions to the concept of power. Borrowing from Helen Regan (1995) I would suggest that these are among the elements of power, defined by those below the fault line in the pyramid model, which are critical to the reconstruction of schooling in the "double helix mode." Regan uses this metaphor as a way of talking about school leadership (teaching and administering) as intertwined, connected and interactive. Let's look at these elements in detail.

Emotional Energy

How often the accusation has been leveled in institutional settings that "she wouldn't make a good leader because she is too emotional!" The presupposition is that in rational bureaucracies emotions are to be left at the door. Women (or men) who show too much emotion are not thought to possess the controlling kind of power needed by suitable leaders. Yet, emotional energy invested in school leadership and decision-making has proven effective for the women in this study.

Consider this illustrative issue. The learning process is frequently interrupted for some children. Their lives become a series of uncertainties and adjustments to strangeness. It takes time for teachers to build a learning framework for the child who is beset by this constant trampling on fragile growth. It takes time for the child to readjust, to feel strong and certain again, able to cope with the lively life of yet another burgeoning elementary classroom, to find a comfortable space for learning. It takes time for the principal to know the children and their families who stream through the schools in these times of social restlessness.

One principal's story speaks to this all-too-common dilemma. Informed that a student's mother was taking her daughter out of school, the principal spoke with concern and frustration: "I'm so sorry. There must have been a rift. Latricia was doing so well here. She needed some order in her life and her grandparents were giving her that. It so hard on this little one to be moved around so much when she is just beginning to make good progress and feel comfortable with herself." Principals have to deal with such educational ambiguities all of the time. Is it child abuse to pull a child in and out of schools and fracture their just-budding confidence and achievement in learning, or are children tough and flexible and able to adjust rapidly to new situations? Is this a family tug-of-war or a problem on its way to a solution?

This principal did not hide her emotions as Latricia came to say good-bye. She put her arms around the listless little girl, gave her a hug, and suggested she say hello to the principal at the new school who was a friend of hers. She made an attempt to foster some human connection by promising to tell the other principal that Latricia was coming. The principal empathized with Latricia's sadness and fear, although she could not stop the parent from taking the child from the grandparents' home; nor prevent the pattern from continuing. She had followed Latricia's progress while at the school and worked with the grandparents to help build up her confidence, caring deeply about what happened to this pillar-to-post child. She could have chosen a bureaucratic response by directing the secretary to fill out the necessary transfer papers and instruct the parent what to do, impersonally sending this child and her mother on their way—another case of transiency, another "L" for "left" in the attendance register. In bureaucratic school systems it is easy to assume that the principals' function is to dispatch things, such as books, materials, students, teachers, to their appropriate slots, like widgets in an efficient "objective" assembly line. But this principal was far from impersonal in her ways of dealing, not only with Latricia, but with a schoolful of children.

The human exchanges I observed as these women principals went about their work, rather than being casual and routinized, gave evidence of emotional energy at work: tending to feelings of children, teachers, parents; expressing anguish over behavior that affected others; generating enthusiasm, showing compassion, and sharing anger and joy. Such awareness of feelings produced some word or gesture of caring: a nod of acknowledgment, an accepting tone of voice, humor to ease tension, a hug, a smile of welcome, tears, enthusiasm and excitement or anger in language, eyebrows knit in concern. These acts communicate a range of feelings. They are the behaviors of "acting with" another person in a way that acknowledges the personhood of the other, and shows sensitivity to the others feelings.

Emotional energy provides the power dynamic for "feeling with" another. It is doing the emotion work required in interpersonal relationships and engaging others in productive emotional labor. As energy it is a dynamic power source that can be employed both personally and interpersonally. Emotional energy may be explicit, that is, observable when displayed or shared; it may also be implicit, hidden within actions or language, invisible and unmeasurable. Leaders who use resources of emotional energy to empower rather than exploit others provide an example of human connectedness and community. As Arlie Hochschild (1983) suggests, emotion "functions as a messenger from the self, an agent that gives us an instant report on the connection between what we are seeing and what we had expected to see, and tells us what we feel ready to do about it."

Nurtured Growth

These women principals believe strongly that the primary emphasis in their work is the nurturance of children's growth. When one principal was asked about her philosophy of education she responded without hesitation, "the focus, of course, is on children!" The responsibility to manage an organizational structure or administer a program or resolve labor-management disputes, is, quintessentially, in the service of nurturing children's learning. Such an emphasis requires the commitment to recognize children's right to learn and to help children develop their abilities fully. As one principal emphasized: "education exists for boys and girls . . . every child has the right to an education as far as his/her capabilities and potential will allow." The conviction was clearly stated that "all children can learn . . . you fit the curriculum to the child—you don't fit the child to the curriculum—you plan the curriculum around the child's needs." While this principal articulated interest in efficiency and orderliness, she did not lose sight of the human growth-nurturing character of schooling. Growth is nurtured, said another principal, when you

> treat kids with dignity and respect. . . . You need to observe them enough to be sensitive to what they need. And you need to trust them, ask them about things, not give them too much that they don't ask for, and be there for them, ready and available without hovering. . . . There is a close kinship between what I want for my own kids and for kids in general.

While guarding against the stifling characteristics of hovering over-much, these principals seemed to articulate the positive interactional qualities of needing to be, at times, a mother hen: "I like working with the children—that is the first thing—and I like working with the parents and I like helping the teachers problem solve. . . . What they really needed was a kind of *mother hen* to listen to their problems and their concerns and to brainstorm with them." And nurturance is important for teachers as well as for children:

> I have the strong conviction that good teachers not be neglected, that good teachers must be nurtured. On the other hand you have to work with your teachers who are not making it. I try to do that in a positive and constructive way. . . . I make it clear what I am looking for and how we can turn it around, yet I let them know I want to be supportive and demonstrate my supportiveness in specific ways. I work closely with the instructional support team, so it is a team effort. We collaborate. I have the benefit of their thinking.

Central to these principals' professed belief was the focus on nurturing children's growth and the expressed conviction that schooling is for the purpose of fostering this growth and development for each child, requiring collaboration between teachers, parents, principal, and students. Such a view corroborates McCormick's (1995) learner-centered strategies of feminist pedagogy. An emphasis on the whole child and his/her needs rather than on a program, or the maintenance of an organization, or the furtherance of careers may seem a self evident requirement for school leaders, not a matter of choice. However, actions sometimes belie words, and while most principals would acknowledge, if pressed, that schools are for nurturing children's growth, what often happens is that bureaucratic rule-making, legislative policy, collective bargaining issues, or personal ambition draw adults away from that primary emphasis.

The grammar of nurtured growth, then, is the grammar of "with-ness." The frequent use of the preposition "with" suggests there is an interactive quality to nurturance: feeling with, working with, deciding with, being with. Such an emphasis moves away from the negatively stereotyped concept of "mother hen" within a patriarchal culture of language to a more positive and dynamic concept of mothering and nurturing in the sense of an interactive stimulation toward growth, a process of turning things around, a keen sense of how to observe signs of growth.

Growth happens over time and is marked by plateaus and valleys. A nurturer recognizes even minute evidences of growth and gives support and encouragement. There is a dynamic interactive quality about nurturance, for to be effective it can neither commandeer change nor be oblivious to it. Nurturance requires trust, reciprocal obligation, and the willingness to let go. Nurturance need not be arranged hierarchically, for peers can nurture growth through avenues of mutual stimulation. While bureaucracies foster impersonal relationships, nurturance of growth is a power principle of interpersonal organizational structure.

Reciprocal Talk

Another theme from my observations of women principals is that of reciprocal talk. Many principals have to face the dilemma of overcrowding. A new sixth-grader had just enrolled in one school I visited and the principal considered this a big problem because each of the three teachers in the sixth grade had thirty-three students in his/her class, a size considered much too large already. Public schools do not have the choice of turning children down; they have to find an appropriate placement. Quickly the principal went over to the cluster office to see the teachers before class started. She laid out the facts: "We have to take the child for at least twenty days while I see what alternative arrangements I can make. How shall we solve the problem?" The teachers questioned her about the district policy on teacher overload and she explained the next steps she would take for a more permanent solution. Thought was given to drawing straws. I don't know anything about the child," the principal commented as the others paused. "Well, I'll take him," volunteered one of the teachers, followed by obvious sighs of relief. The principal was appreciative, but continued painfully, "I'm really sorry. I had promised I'd do everything to keep class size down. I asked you to trust me, and now we have to take another child. When our classes jumped up so high I called all the other schools, but 6th grades are full all over. I'll try to find another way."

In examining this exchange we see illustrated the pattern of "reciprocal talk" that seemed to be typical of this principal's style of leadership. Communication that involves both listening and speaking is typical. Reciprocal talk implies turn-taking, both answering and asking questions, listening and responding to what is said. Reciprocal talk is a form of decision-making that the principal used informally throughout the day. Reciprocal talk is also a power strategy useful in building trust both at the school site and in relationships with "downtown." One principal described the need to keep confidentialities and to be trusted as one who keeps them. Establishing that trust involves talking with people in informal ways, being available to people, being willing to talk things over, advise if requested, and honor confidentiality.

"Taking a look at the absurdities" of a bureaucratic system is essential if one desires to engage in reciprocal talk, for the pyramidal arrangement of bureaucratic systems mitigates against reciprocity. Dale Spender (1980) uses the terms "dominant" and "muted" to describe the worlds of public discourse which men and women inhabit within patriarchal organizations. The dominant speak, far more frequently than they listen. Monologuing, rather than dialoguing, is the preferred strategy of those who see power as control over conversations, meetings, and board deliberations. Women have a long tradition of what Spender calls "cooperative talk"—developed in part through consciousness-raising groups and other formal and informal exchanges. Reciprocal talk is both listening and speaking. Women are often presumed to be good listeners, but now it is time to connect the broader notion of reciprocal talk with the power dynamics of organizational leadership.

To hear and speak to what others say about issues under consideration is to "play fair" by reciprocal talk. It seems rather straightforward; nonetheless it is not always practiced in hierarchically arranged organizations. Reciprocal talk implies listening to get a "feel for" the perspective of the other and to verify understanding. It is a checking out of ideas or plans with those who are likely to be affected. Reciprocal talk also implies sharing one's own perspective in ways that respect the integrity of the other. In the use of reciprocal talk the principals showed that their own talk was shaped by, or sensitive to, the dynamics of the conversation itself.

Sensitive turn-taking in talking and listening is not usually perceived as a power strategy. Yet these women insist such a strategy is essential to "getting the job done." Since they define power as the "ability to get the job done" and since they model "talking with" others in accomplishing the goals of the school, in decision-making and in problem-solving, it becomes clear that reciprocal talk is a resource of power.

Pondered Mutuality

A fourth theme generated by these women's articulated experience is that of pondered mutuality. The principals I interviewed gave indication of ruminating toward decisions. To ruminate is to meditate, muse, or ponder— to chew again or over and over. It is turning things around in one's mind, in order to turn things around in school. Rumination is a form of reflection. One principal describes her internal resources: "I do a lot of meditating. Not the formal kind, but I find that quiet times on my own help me turn inward and work things out inside. I come up refreshed." When decisions are to be made, she begins by thinking things through. She turns things over in her mind, looking at things from a variety of angles, working things out inside. She listens to what other people say and adds that to her reflective data:

> I like to pass things by . . . particularly when I want to change the way we are doing things. You know, I lay the groundwork. Then I ask, how can we best do

this? . . . There are many avenues (of tapping other people's thoughts). If I just want to feel out something—whoever is in the office at the time—I just say, come on in and give me a feel for this; let me bounce this by you.

Pondered mutuality involves turning things over in one's mind, exploring options, pondering responses garnered through reciprocal talk, checking back with colleagues, cogitating on possible consequences. In a school setting this can involve coming prepared for a faculty meeting by thinking things out ahead of time while allowing for thinking together as a group:

Basically, where there is a problem or a decision that has to be made it is presented at the faculty meeting . . . I generally try to come up with some suggestions or ideas for solutions, and then its opened up for other contributions. Then we discuss, justifying one or the other, and through discussion we end up eliminating certain solutions. Sometimes variations will come up, and then we decide on a particular solution.

The process of pondered mutuality involves both internal and external action: reflection and reciprocity. Reflection *as action* is important to consider here, because reflection is often associated with passivity, or counterpoised with action and viewed as its opposite. In making decisions, these women principals described how they pondered, listened, spoke with others, then rethought or ruminated. They used all the mental skills required to organize and reorganize ideas. The pondering, or "thinking through toward solutions," provided groundwork for further interaction, which then cycled back into more ruminations. Such an infusion of the other into their own considerations may indeed help us understand the interactive intuitive characteristics often associated with women. These principals' reflection depended on meditation, intuition, observation, and communication. It is considered an action by virtue of its potential to affect change; change is observed in decisions made, in actions taken, and in choices proffered.

Donald Schon (1987) discusses the artistry involved in reflection. He begins with the premises that a core of artistry can be recognized in professionals, that artistry is an exercise of intelligence, a kind of knowing that is rigorous in its outcomes, and that one can learn about artistry by studying performance. Problem framing, implementation, and improvisation are elements of this artistry, which, he suggests are necessary to mediate the use of science and technique. Less clear in his discussion, however, is the issue of plurality that is inherent in pondered mutuality—the going back and forth between one's own reflections and the insights of the other. Yet Schon does indeed catch a powerful sense of mystery and magic involved in reflection, and in spite of its perspective of singularity he does much to expand our understanding of reflection-in-action.

Pondered mutuality involves reflecting, ruminating on ideas, keeping things in mind while accounting for the needs of the community. It assumes a recognition of both the inner world of the self and the community or context within which one exists as a person. Pondering is a form of reflection, a weighing of ideas in the mind, turning things around, thinking both critically and creatively. Pondered mutuality adds the dimension of the other to the thinking process and accounts for effect.

Collaborative Change

A fifth theme suggested by these women principals' approach to the principalship is that of collaborative change. After one principal's busy morning preceded by a long PTA meeting the night before she looked wearily at the new messages on her desk. Her voice and manner brightened visibly, however, when the phone rang and the caller apparently reminded her of the parent's willingness to fund a backboard for the playground which the student council had requested. She described the collaboration required to reach goals as well as the paradox of frustration and excitement that often accompanies the efforts:

> The student council made a formal written presentation to the PTA, with graphs and cost analysis and all (for the backboard). Sometimes you just have to go ahead even if the district won't support it. The district doesn't want to take work away from their maintenance people, on the one hand, but on the other hand, they don't get the job done. For example, we had a portable that had not been painted for twenty-two years! I worked and waited for two years to get it done by the district—and then I finally painted it myself with the children. I got into terrible trouble with the district, but the job was done! And that is what counts. You have to keep your eyes on the goal—getting things to work here for kids.

The student-principal-parent collaboration required to paint portables or mount backboards was only one illustration of change at this school. This school, like an increasing number of others, has a Child Study Team which collaborates in studying children's special needs. The process itself calls for the pooling of data and insights related to specific students in order to make recommendations for needed interventions or actions. It is by design a collaborative process, and it works best when the purpose of collaboration is to focus on the child's needs rather than the needs of some adults for some sort of philosophical or political triumph. This morning, however, the principal faced a troublesome situation. There was conflict between the resource specialist and the classroom teacher. The teacher bases her classroom-teaching strategies on an open-classroom concept and, according to the principal, is an excellent teacher who observes children's progress holistically. The specialist, on the other hand, takes a more rigid approach to learning, views children in terms of static grade levels, and puts heavy credence in understanding children primarily through test scores. The principal described her approach to the conflict:

> I try to talk to each teacher individually, try to be with them when they have a conference, try to be a mediator. Neither is up-front about the conflict. They continue to be polite with each other. I will say something like there is a real difference in philosophy here. I hope I can get them to deal with it openly some day.

During the meeting the conflict was hidden under the overlay of talk about test scores and what help the child most needed. The teacher expressed the fear of putting an overload of "help" on the child who was already seeing a tutor outside of school and would likely be more confused by the addition of other specialists, unless it was carefully coordinated. The group planned to meet with the mother the following week. The specialist wanted a longer meeting, the teacher a shorter one. The specialist saw the problem area as reading; the teachers thought the child needed specific help in mathematics. On almost every issue the two were at opposite poles. The principal's ability to mediate the situation was observable. She suggested that the specialist meet at 8:00 with the mother and go over the test scores and since the teacher was already familiar with these she could come in at 8:30 to complete the conference. This principal supported both teachers where she could, kept the group focused on the goal which was to find out what was best for the child, provided a win-win situation for the timing of the conference, and pondered her interest in getting these two together for a more rigorous conflict-resolving session at a later date. Collaboration, despite conflict, was essential if the child's best interests were to be served.

Collaboration marked the style of decision-making utilized at these schools. One principal described the process of building consensus while dealing with disagreements and frustration. A case in point was the overcrowding in the cafeteria. The district had started to phase out the school, and many parents had moved to other places to keep education going for their children. Later the district rescinded its decision, and the school grew rapidly, doubling in size in two years, while the cafeteria remained in the tiny portable.

> We had to devise ways to cope with that—students, teachers, cafeteria staff. The school nurse wrote a grant proposal and secured money for extra supervision, we altered our breakfast program to what the space could accommodate, we requested rearrangement of staff time so aides could work with the children at

high need times, we staggered class schedules. There were a number of ways we found together to work on the problem. There are still problems, and there always will be, but we have worked out many of them.

In this scenario the principal (1) set the tone by engaging key people in thinking about the issues involved as well as the benefits or constraints, (2) found people with vision who were strong and committed to making things happen, (3) kept the communication open and didn't hide anything, (4) took advantage of all existing school problem-solving structures, (5) thought things through, (6) looked with others for a solution or proposal, and (7) found ways to cope with the frustrations while working everything out. Collaboration was the thread running through the change process.

The women principals often used an informal collaborative approach when they wanted to pursue a new idea with the staff. One described her desire to encourage some team teaching so that teachers would be able to share their areas of expertise with the students. Her strategy was to toss out the idea in a faculty meeting with the comment that "if you like the idea, when you are ready, come talk with me about it." The suggestion was made in September. Before the winter recess the sixth-grade circuit had drawn up a rough draft and asked to talk with the principal to propose some departmentalization. The principal noted the fruitfulness of the collaborative approach which was born out in the effectiveness of their plans. Their enthusiasm would have been dampened by directives. This principal relies instead on offering suggestions and choices, giving out a lot of compliments and strokes, letting people know what her expectations are, engaging staff in planning, talking with them often. Obviously she has to deal with conflict and resistance from time to time and she tries to provide options: "if you don't want to participate, just think about the problem in another way, and develop an alternative within your own classroom."

Collaborative change is the art of defining common interests, common responsibilities, common problems and common solutions. It is also full participation in the development of those interests, the fulfillment of those responsibilities, and in problem-solving. These women principals chose a style which was collaborative by design and intent and they are convinced that it works. It is "co"-action which presumes some measure of cooperation, trust, mutuality, reciprocity, and interdependence. Action within this dimension is conjoint—a process of building consensus through participation and interaction. It requires a grammar of empowerment: the prepositions are non-hierarchical, that is power "with" instead of power "over" is the mode. Metaphors are connective rather than separatistic: building "bridges" instead of "walls" by asking for help and suggestions from others, expecting growth and change over time but not trying to "knit the whole sweater in one night."

Implications for A New Power Agenda

I draw the conclusion from my research that effective women principals use and talk about power in ways quite distinct from traditional power perspectives found in the literature of school administration and organizational theory. The "different voice" that emerges conspicuously from the data as women speak about their experiences as school leaders is one of connectedness and coactivity, of shared and expandable power, and of empowerment. The elements of this coactive empowerment are reciprocal talk, emotional energy, pondered mutuality, nurtured growth, and collaborative change. Effectiveness comes from the integrity of their power and leadership choices—choices not limited to women, yet developed through and validated by their experiences.

The vocabulary of *connectedness* symbolizes, perhaps most distinctly, the uniqueness of these women's perspective on power. Connectedness refers to the importance of relationships and the web of human interaction that permeates and enriches any personal or organizational endeavor. Connectedness is illustrated by caring, interdependence and the commitment to community.

Such a perspective is both circular and paradoxical. For example, a common phrase employed by the principals to describe schoolwide or individual improvement was "turning things around." Change was secured, not by commanding it and then spending energy picking up the pieces of resentment and broken relationships, but by nurturing growth over time, a cyclical activity of teaching/learning/acting. Their world is less an oppositional one, more a relational one, less linear, more circular or webbed.

The paradox lies in the association of power with "connectedness," rather than the traditional association of power with "autonomy." While autonomy is the primary mark of maturity in the patriarchal world, connectedness provides a vision of human community that embraces both the self and the other. Indeed, autonomy and community are not mutually exclusive concepts, for individuality and uniqueness can be valued in a connective community where equality, mutuality and reciprocity are present, and where separateness does not replace connectedness. Connectedness does, however, reject hierarchy in favor of an interactive web which balances autonomy and community.

Connectedness evidences itself in women's caring actions. These actions frequently involve choice or ethical decision-making. Gilligan (1982) has suggested a thematic distinction between the way men and women approach ethical decision-making. In her research she found two counterpoint themes: an ethic of justice and an ethic of caring. These represent different modes of thinking about relationships, and while not entirely gender specific, the ethic of caring is primarily traced through empirical observation of women, and through women's stories about their struggles in facing moral crises. In Gilligan's view this does not rule the ethic of justice out of women's experience, nor does it limit caring to women. Rather, the convergence of these themes in each sex is often seen in times of crisis and change. But an understanding of the ethic of caring developed out of women's experiences had been little explored until Gilligan's research opened up this area of study. The women in Gilligan's study perceive aggression as the fracture of human connection, while the activities of care are those which make the social world a safer community.

Historical Context

Early twentieth-century women leaders laid the groundwork for new understandings of power. Mary Parker Follett (1924) outlined a conceptualization of power that was intended for practical participatory strategizing in the business community. Follett, whose field was business economics, was a Bostonian who devoted her life to the study of how people treated each other. Her theoretical work included studies of human interaction, conflict resolution, and decision-making in organizations. In her theorizing Follett believed that people grew and changed by talking out conflicts and differences, searching for what each party really wanted. Once interests were identified, solutions could emerge requiring neither side to back down or compromise.

It is in Follett's work that we find the groundwork for a process of negotiation that discards the adversarial aspects of collective bargaining in favor of collaborative problem-solving. Such processes of negotiation do not rely on traditional notions of power as control or as the domination of decision-making. Follett (1924) views power as the central problem of social relations:

> our task is not to learn where to place power: it is how to develop power. . . . Genuine power can only be grown, it will slip away from every arbitrary hand that grasps it; for genuine power is not coercive control, but coactive control. Coercive power is the curse of the universe; coactive power, the enrichment and advancement of every human soul.

Power then cannot be limited to domination, for the basis of Follett's thinking is the concept of partnership—of coactivity. Coactive power is the capacity to make things happen effectively with, not over against, others. When two people decide on a course of action together and do that thing, neither has power over the other. Power is not a finite resource, but rather a renewable, or expandable resource. This kind of power—power with—is what democracy should mean in Follett's view. In drawing a distinction between "power over" and "power with," or coercive and coactive power, Follett moves away from the dyslogistic association of power and domination.

Follett makes a strong case for the development of collective ideas through a synergistic process. For her the object of a committee meeting is to create a common idea and the key is "that all together we may create a group idea, an idea which will be better than any of our ideas alone, moreover which will be better than all of our ideas added together." The idea, she suggests, is not produced by a process of addition, but by "the interpenetration of us all" (1923, 24). However quaint the language, Follett is interested in how people come to agreement, socially, politically. The implications of synergistic thinking in terms of understanding a power-with model of school administration are clear for working together in administrative cabinet meetings, faculty meetings, or parent-teacher association meetings where the achievement of a common educational vision in the context of pluralistic school communities depends on the identification of common interests and the development of jointly crafted concrete action.

Dorothy Emmet was among those influenced by the thinking of Follett, and her work foreshadows the redefinition project of contemporary feminists. Emmet's proposal (1954) is to set aside a singular definition of power and consider instead a range of meanings. If we want precision, Emmet contends, it is best sought "not by bastardizing certain members of the family (saying they 'are really not power'), but by trying to discover their idiosyncrasies in relation to the other terms with which they keep company in their several contexts." She develops a typology of power which broadens the range of meanings typically accorded to power, and praises the Follett distinction between power-over and power-with as illustrative of moving beyond the singularity and danger of power perceived primarily as domination.

Follett's theoretical work on the concept of power was both brief and unheralded, but Emmet acknowledges her debt to Follett and corroborates her vision by noting that power, defined as production of intended effects, would need to be distinguished as a generic term from domination which means achievement of intended effects through coercing other people. To produce intended effects without coercion requires definition of common interests, attention to socially valuable differences, and constructive problem-solving that focuses on a cooperatively achieved intention. Synthesizing the work of these two women it is possible to see ways to move beyond coercion to coactivity, and thus toward a redefinition of power and the development of a new power agenda.

While nineteenth-century "schoolmen" got credit for creating the American school system, while many women begged to teach as a part of their noble destiny and were hired when it was economically advantageous and the supply of men was short, while bureaucracies developed which stratified people by gender, what were women doing? How were they doing it? What were their own viewpoints about the female world? Were there no alternative discourses? Were there not challenges to the inherent sexual bias in the culture and the schools taking shape within that culture? Indeed there were. The work of one of the early feminists will be used to illustrate an alternative discourse present in the early twentieth century, and will suggest that hidden in the stories of some women principals of that time are some seeds for an alternative vision of school organization.

Charlotte Perkins Gilman was a serious critic of history and society, well known in the early twentieth century for her provocative study, *Women and Economics*. In 1911, the same year in which Frederick Taylor's book, *Scientific Management*, was published, Gilman's critique *The Man Made World or Our Androcentric Culture* appeared. She argued (1911, 22) that we have taken for granted since the dawn of civilization the notion that "mankind" referred to men and the world was theirs, while women were sharply delimited and seen as a sex, a subspecies:

> What we have all this time called "human nature" and deprecated, was in great part only male nature, and good enough in its place; that what we have called "masculine" and admired as such, was in large part human, and should be applied to both sexes; that what we have called "feminine" and condemned, was also largely human and applicable to both. Our androcentric culture is so shown to have been, and still to be, a masculine culture in excess, and therefore undesirable.

Gilman argues, as do many feminists, that the ideal is a human society, not a patriarchal masculine-dominated one, nor a matriarchal female-dominated substitution. But her writings also indicate a feminist methodology which requires full exploration of women's experience and perspective as a legitimate and essential prerequisite to human community. Such a viewpoint insists on both critique of culture and proposals for change.

Her discussion of education places women in participatory and responsible positions. She held the view that the origin of education is maternal: "the mother animal is seen to teach her young what she knows of life, its gains and losses; and, whether consciously done or not, this is education" (p. 143). Extending this to the human world, Gilman argued that the instruction of child by mother, and then extended by nursemaid, and by the "dame-school" (schools for little girls and boys run by women in their homes in colonial days), has been largely neglected in our "man-made" world where the dominant class views education as that which is organized in universities, colleges and public schools, and slowly filters downward. Gilman characterized the essential masculine attitude as one of opposition, of combat, of desire to overcome a competitor. The use of force is natural to the male, she contended, and he sees no necessity for enforcement other than by penalty. On the other hand, "the perfectly natural social instincts which lead to peaceful persuasion, to education, to an easy harmony of action, are contemptuously ranked as 'feminine,' or as 'philanthropic'—which is almost as bad." Gilman (1911, 183) argues that

> as a matter of fact the woman, the mother, is the first co-ordinator, legislator, administrator and executive. From the guarding and guidance of her cubs and kittens up to the longer, larger management of human youth, she is the first to consider group interests and correlate them. . . . As a father the male grows to share in these original feminine functions, and with us, fatherhood having become socialized while motherhood has not, he does the best he can, alone, to do the world's mother-work in his father way.

There are echoes of Gilman's argument in the research of Sally Helgesen (1990) whose diary studies of women managers suggest that these women feel their experience as mothers was beneficial:

> Increasingly, motherhood is being recognized as an excellent school for managers, demanding many of the same skills: organization, pacing, the balancing of conflicting claims, teaching, guiding, leading, monitoring, handling disturbances, imparting information.

The Relationship of Nurturance and Leadership

Gilman focused her attention on the educative aspects of motherhood, and extended educational responsibility also to nonmothers, that is, nursemaids, dame-school teachers, and fathers. She apparently did not see "the world's mother-work" as solely the work of women, but in an ideal situation, a shared human responsibility, learned from mothers, "to give to each child what is most needed, to teach all to their fullest capacity, to affectionately and efficiently develop the whole of them" (1911, 152). She was aware that many mothers did not see or take seriously the educative responsibility of mothering. She challenged her readers to consider the necessity of exploring the connections between mothering and education. To infer from Gilman's work a connection between nurturance and leadership is possible only thematically. She does not fully define mothering or mother-work, although the actions she describes imply nurturance, caring for the whole child, focusing on growth. The term "leadership" is not one she used, yet her arguments against an androcentric culture imply shared leadership as she describes "the change from the dominance of one sex to the equal power of the two."

Nonetheless, the theme connecting nurturance with educational leadership is compatible with Gilman's work and can be illustrated by nineteenth-century principals' stories as well. One principal from this period stressed the importance of knowing the "child life" of the school, and knowing the fears, hopes and aspirations of her staff. Here we see a caring affect, marked by relatedness and a responsiveness to the people with whom she worked. Another principal, in her successful efforts to connect home and school, took responsibility to teach nurturing skills to the mothers of her students.[5]

Strengths of The "Feminine"

Gilman characterizes the masculine world as one of opposition, combat, and competition. The feminine world is characterized, in her view, by connection, persuasion, and collaboration. In the classical sense the feminine is rooted in receptivity, relatedness, and responsiveness (Noddings 1983). All of the principals illustrate some attention to this human interrelatedness. Connection and collaboration appear to be important as well to the principals of Gilman's time: "we have understood one another"... "more than anything else (the children) enjoyed the trust that was placed upon them"... "mother-teacher collaboration (involves) 'the two greatest trainers of the child.' " Leadership is connective, persuasive, and collaborative.

Participation as Power

To the early feminists, participation in power was symbolized by the vote. To see participation in school governance as a resource of power is also possible in this view. Gilman's belief in the value of peaceful collective action as a form of problem-solving and Follett's commitment to the synergistic development of ideas can be illustrated by the student self-government committees organized by one early principal, and the parent action group organized by another. Shared responsibility empowers those who share it. To make schools livable places for the human family that inhabited them and to care for the health and welfare of the children, these principals apparently paid less attention to rigid hierarchical rules of governance than to the human needs which called for participatory problem-solving. They stood between school and community, caring for and involving both.

The school leaders and bureaucracy builders of the late nineteenth and early twentieth centuries likely did not envision or encourage principals with these characteristics. (See Tyack 1974.) The proponents of "scientific management" did not espouse warmth and caring, nurturance and trust, shared talk, ruminating over decisions together, and collaboration across levels of the organization. Hierarchy thrives on command and docility, "objectivity," control, layered decision-making, rules and directives. Bureaucracy, originally envisioned as promoting fairness, became, in effect, a fortressed framework for male-female inequality. Job discrimination by sex has pervaded public school management. The woman principal is caught within this paradox. She can choose to accept the hierarchical bureaucratic model with its patriarchal assumptions, and learn to "think like a man." Or she can plumb her own experiences and develop an effective style of her own, while running the risk of being stereotyped for doing things "just like a woman." There is, however, a caveat hidden in the juxtaposition of these two alternatives. In one sense, both alternatives are required for women in today's organizations. Understanding and learning to use traditional power structures within contemporary organizations, like schools, is necessary if one is to work for change from within. The danger, however, is co-optation. The more significant alternative is the one shaped by the questions "What difference will women make in terms of organizational leadership?" and "How will the organization and the power processes within it change because women participate in leadership?" But the danger is invisibility or intolerance, because women's ways of doing things are often perceived as not fitting the norm.

What would an organizational model look like, based on these elements of reconceptualized power. The dimensions of a theory of co-active empowerment can be used to project a symbolic institutional model of organizational leadership and administration in order to underline some initial comparisons between the coactive model and other organizational models which are familiar to us. The *androcentric* model is readily documented in contemporary bureaucratic history; the *mediative* model is suggested by Kerr (1964) for a university setting and may be useful for a transitional model of schooling; the *co-active* model grows most clearly out of women's experience and offers significant potential for the future as we develop interactive organizations along nonbureaucratic, nonhierarchical lines. Obviously this is an oversimplified framework for discussion, and does not give justice to a considerable overlap between the models. Nonetheless it is intended to illustrate what it could mean, both personally and structurally, to reconceptualize power within organizations.

Experience affirms that the processes of co-active empowerment are, in fact, workable. Effecting change, however, requires the identification of significant common interests, the careful building of consensus around the notion of collaborative change, and a commitment to the empowerment of principals, teachers, and parents at the school sites. Replacement of top-heavy hierarchical, bureaucratic structures of central administration, where they exist, would be essential. The school board, the superintendent, and

TABLE 21.1
Comparative Models

	Androcentric	Mediative	Co-active
Organizational structure	Hierarchical	Hierarchical	Webbed, interactive
Basic paradigm	Dominant/Subordinate	Mediator/Initiator	Collaborator
Action orientation	Controlling, commanding, acting over consent	Collegiality, seeking consent	Building of consensus through co-activity
Definition of power	Control *over*	Responsibility *toward*	Action *with*
Leadership style	Managing	Administering	Empowering
Power focus	Rule, hegemony, domination	Persuasion	Interdependence, participation, reciprocity
Key values	Authority, rank	Judgment, fortitude courage	Trust, caring, respect, connectedness

the central administration would have to be willing to take the risks associated with trying a new model of organization and invest emotional energy toward transformation of schooling. What could happen if district leadership chose to work within the coactive structural model is potentially encouraging. Perhaps, more than any other, the women principals of today's elementary schools will need to lead the way.

The person who stands at the intersection of school and community is the principal (Barth 1980). This research has focused on women's approaches to leadership and power at this particular intersection of American public life. For a number of years I have spent time immersing myself in the world of the female principal, ferreting out the history of the principalship with particular attention to women's participation, attempting to understand the complexities of the current context within which principals work, and trying to know and describe the way they approach the daily struggles of public school administration. I have come to appreciate and respect the interactive character of this role and the courageous audacity of the women who find in this role the possibility of empowering others. Now working in a church-related nonprofit organization, I find these perspectives on power equally relevant, and I continue to feel the urgency of the need to work together as women and men in revisioning and revoicing power for the sake of a just and peaceful global community.

I set out with the hope of enlarging the concept of power and redefining it from the perspective of women. It is too early to tell whether anything of the sort has been accomplished. What I did find was that the women I interviewed consistently defined power as the ability to get the job done, and then went on to describe their ways of working in nonhierarchical terms, evidencing no reliance on domination or coercion. In bureaucratic terms they saw themselves as having little power. What power they had they attributed to the process of meeting their goals for the sake of effective education for children and in working with teachers and parents at the school site, where they relied on their own skills in interpersonal relations and creativity. They used their emotional energies as resources of power, they nurtured growth, pondered decisions with others in mind, used talk as a tool of problem-solving, and worked collaboratively for change. They valued the concept of connectedness and risked the vulnerability of relating to others. The insights provided by the stories and strengths of these women school leaders offer the potential of enriching the texture of our life in community as we together, women and men, develop a new agenda of power inside and outside of school.

Notes

1. A typical text is Harry F. Wolcott (1973) The Man in the Principal's Office: An Ethnography. New York: Holt Rinehart and Winston. While women have served as principals for many years there has been no comparable ethnographic study of "Women in the Principal's Office". In William H. Roe & Thelbert L. Drake (1975) The Principalship, New York: Macmillan, all the pronouns used to refer to the principal are masculine, and Chapter 2 is entitled "The Principal—The Man and His Profession". Also notable is a radical decline in the number of women elementary principals in the U.S. during the 20th century—from a high of 55% in 1928 to a low of 11% in 1980—as indicated in Facing the Future: Education and Equity for Females and Males. (1980). Council of Chief State School Officers and National Association of State Boards of Education. Washington, D.C. This sharp downward progression of women in administration is hidden in a 'conspiracy of silence' or 'keeping Alice out and saying nothing about it,' according to Elizabeth Hansot and David Tyack in a policy paper for the Institute for Research on Educational Finance and Governance: "The Dream Deferred: A Golden Age for Women School Administrators." (May, 1981). Palo Alto: Stanford University.

2. Joyce McCarl Nielson, in Feminist Research Methods: Exemplary Readings in the Social Sciences, (1990) Boulder: Westview Press, argues that "the irreducible element in all feminist analysis is its focus on the distinctive experience of women—that is, seeing women rather than just men in center stage, as both subject matter of and creators of knowledge." So while women's experiences have frequently been hidden from view or considered a sub set of male experience, this research rec-

ognizes and names women's experiences, not in comparison to men, but within the integrity of their individual praxis.

3. See R. Kathleen Hurty, Women in the Principal's Office: Perspectives on Leadership and Power. University of California, Berkeley, Dissertation, Ph.D. (1985). Available through: University Microfilms, 300 N. Zeeb Road, Ann Arbor, MI 48106. My research was not intended as a comparative study between women and men in the principalship, but rather a contrast between the traditional understandings of leadership and power which is, in effect, the explication of men's experience, and women's experience which has been primarily hidden from view. The study, therefore, takes a preliminary and requisite step: naming the ways women use and talk about power out of their own experience as teachers, as principals, some as mothers, aunts, sisters, and as women. Without this naming, women would once more simply be compared to a male norm instead of making an authentic comparison between two identifiable modes of leadership and perspectives on power.

4. Influential in my thinking was the work of Mary Parker Follett. Her early exploration (1924) of the qualitative distinction between "power over" and "power with" became a fulcrum for her work on co-active power and to a certain extent symbolizes the direction of current challenges to power theory.

5. The stories about early principals in this section are from the field notes of an interviewer of "successful" principals whose findings are reported in the Seventh Yearbook (1928) pages 310–318, and in Pierce (1935) pages 124–125. For a fuller discussion of these stories see Hurty (1985).

Bibliography

Barth, R. S. (1980). *Run school run*. Cambridge, MA: Harvard University Press.

Bulletin of the Department of Elementary School Principals. (1928). *The Seventh Yearbook: The National Elementary Principal*, 7(3).

Cantor, D. W. and Bernay, T. (1992). *Women in power: The secrets of leadership*. Boston: Houghton Mifflin Company.

Chodorow, N. (1978). *The reproduction of mothering*. Berkeley: University of California Press.

Cohen, S. S. (1989). *Tender power: A revolutionary approach to work and intimacy*. Reading, MA: Addison-Wesley.

Dunlap, D.M. and Goldman, P. (1991). Rethinking power in schools. *Educational Administration Quarterly*, 27(1), 5–29.

Elstain, J. B. (1989). *Power trips and other journeys.* Madison: University of Wisconsin Press.

Emmett, D. (1954). The concept of power. *Proceedings of the Aristotelian Society,* 54, 1–26. Reprinted in J. R. Champlin (ed.), *Power.* New York: Atherton Press, 1971.

Ferguson, K. E. (1984). *The feminist case against bureaucracy.* Philadelphia: Temple University Press.

Follett, M. P. (1923). *The new state.* New York: Longmans, Green and Co.

———. (1924). *Creative experience.* New York: Longmans, Green and Co.

Gilligan, C. (1982). *In a different voice: Psychological theory and women's development.* Cambridge, MA: Harvard University Press.

Gilman, C. P. (1911). *The man-made world or our androcentric culture.* New York: Charlton.

Helgesen, S. (1990). *The female advantage: Women's ways of leadership.* New York: Doubleday.

Hochschild, A. (1983). *The managed heart: Commercialization of human feeling.* Berkeley, University of California Press.

Hurty, K. (1985). *Women in the principalship: Perspectives on leadership and power.* Dissertation, University of California, Berkeley.

Kanter, R. M. (1977). *Men and women of the corporation.* New York: Basic Books.

———. (1979). Power, leadership, and participatory management. *Theory into Practice,* 20(4), 219–24.

———. (1989). *When giants learn to dance: Mastering the challenges of strategy, management and careers in the 1990's.* New York: Simon & Schuster.

Kerr, C. (1964). *The uses of the university.* Cambridge, MA: Harvard University Press.

McCormick, T. (1993). Teacher Education programs. Unpublished paper.

Nielson, J. M. (1990). *Feminist research methods: Exemplary readings in the social sciences.* Boulder: Westview Press.

Noddings, N. (1984). *Caring.* Berkeley: University of California Press.

Pierce, P. R. (1935). *The origin and development of the public school principalship.* Chicago: University of Chicago Press.

Regan, H. (1995). Working together: A feminist construction of schooling. In D. Dunlap and P. Schmuck (eds.), *Women leading in education*. Albany: SUNY Press.

Rosener, J. (1990). Ways women lead. *Harvard Business Review*. 68(4) Nov.–Dec.

Ruddick, S. (1989). *Maternal thinking: Toward a politics of peace*. New York: Ballentine Books.

Schon, D. (1987). *Educating the reflective practitioner*. San Francisco: Jossey-Bass.

Schmuck, P. and Schmuck, R. (1990). Democratic participation in small-town schools. *Educational Researcher*, 19(8), 14–19.

Spender, D. (1980). *Man made language*. London: Routledge & Kegan Paul.

Tyack, D. (1974). *The one best system: A history of American urban education*. Cambridge, MA: Harvard University Press.

Tyack, D. and Hansot, E. (1982). *Managers of virtue: Public school leadership in America, 1820–1980*. New York: Basic Books.

Welch, S. D. (1990). *A feminist ethic of risk*. Minneapolis: Fortress Press.

TWENTY-TWO

In the Image of The Double Helix: A Reconstruction of Schooling

Helen B. Regan

The Double Helix: A Metaphor for School Organization

The double helix is a graceful shape. Two intertwined strands wind in parallel very much like the banisters of a spiral staircase. The double helix is the shape of the deoxyribonucleic acid molecule, known to most of us as DNA, the carrier of the genetic information which is the template for human life. In both its shape and function, the DNA double helix is a metaphor for a reconstruction of schooling.

Lakoff and Johnson (1980) have argued that metaphor is far more than a figurative device bringing vividness and style to our language. Rather they argue that metaphor is a central figure of language which shapes our understanding. "The essence of metaphor is understanding and experiencing one kind of thing in terms of another" (p. 5). They point out that a consequence of metaphor as a vehicle of constructing meaning in the world is not only illumination, but also obscurity. Viewed in this way, we can expect a new metaphor to lead us to new conceptualizations of aspects of schooling, and to uncover obscurities that are a function of familiar metaphors.

The prevailing metaphor for most organizations of the twentieth century, the pyramid, is also the prevailing metaphor of school organization. Wide at its bottom and narrow at its top, the pyramid symbolizes both the increase in and the diminishing opportunities for power, prestige, and reward characteristic of roles at the top of the hierarchy in contrast to roles at the bottom. Peggy McIntosh (1983), in her analysis of the pyramidal structure of organizations, has described a faultline that further divides the occupants of the top of the pyramid from those at the bottom.

Above the fault is the world that operates competitively in an either/or mode. Either people move up the pyramid and gain more wealth, power, and prestige, or they do not. The movement of those going up by definition prescribes failure for others because there is room for fewer and fewer as the pyramid narrows at the top. Because society projects this role onto them, mostly white males occupy this part of the pyramid, and the closer to the top, the more dominant their numbers.

Below the fault lies a whole different world, inhabited through role projection primarily by women, people of color, and low-status white males. Its organization is horizontal and collaborative; it is cyclical and repetitive. Most of daily life takes place here: doing the dishes, changing diapers, planting fields, teaching. These are tasks that must be done repetitively, cyclically. This is where caring and nurturing, relationship and community building happen. It is a both/and world.

As a high school principal with a doctorate in school administration, I was trained to operate successfully in the competitive, either/or world. I could and did act decisively, making tough choices between this possibility and that. I valued these qualities and was conscious of my use of them. But as a woman, I also had lived a life deeply rooted in the collaborative, both/and world below the fault. I used gifts of compassion and empathy daily to soothe students, encourage teachers, and console parents. Unlike my above-the-fault qualities, however, I did not value or acknowledge the contribution of my below-the-fault qualities to my success as a principal. It was not until a colleague, and friend, pointed them out to me that I even recognized them in my practice as a school administrator.

My friend had been in the audience when I had played the role of a candidate being interviewed for the superintendency as part of a conference for aspiring women administrators. Back at school the next day, she approached me tentatively, saying the person she had seen in that mock interview was tough all right, but she had none of the gentle, soothing qualities she had seen me use so effectively in many difficult situations in our school. Stunned though I was, I knew she was right. I had deliberately concealed a significant part of my skill because I believed it was unwanted, even viewed as a deficiency in the world of school administration.

My blindness to the worthiness of my below-the-fault qualities is quite understandable in retrospect. By virtue of their positions on the pyramid, the relative value of the either/or, competitive world above the fault, and the both/and, collaborative world below the fault is obvious. I had been taught, both directly and indirectly, to see only the world above the fault as important to school administration. The world below the fault, unnamed and devalued, simply did not exist in my consciousness as a factor in my practice as a school administrator despite the fact of its significance in my actual behavior. What I actually did in my work as school administrator is move easily back and forth across the faultline, using both sets of qualities as I needed them. For example, I organized a team building retreat for all department heads, but also acted swiftly and decisively to terminate the services of a staff member whom I believed was a danger to the students. I now see myself as having a wholeness, a totality of human experience and wisdom on which to draw as I did my job, that is inaccessible to people, generally men, who are restricted to life above the fault, and to people, generally women and people of color, who are restricted to life below the fault.

In my opinion, a fundamental structural flaw which is the source of much dysfunction in schools today is the hierarchical valuing of either/or and both/and qualities. Restructuring of schools requires abandonment of the hierarchical valuing of these two worlds. Rather, each world must be valued and cultivated for its own contributions. The double helix symbolizes this restructured world. Each strand represents a different facet of life as it was on the pyramid. One strand embodies life above the fault representing the necessity of choice; there are times when life is either/or. The other strand embodies life below the fault, representing collaboration; there are times when life is both/and. The hydrogen bonds linking the strands together in the DNA double helix represent the necessary and frequent passage from one mode of life to the other. The strands are intertwined, neither is above the other, because neither is more valuable than the other, and because it is not possible to live a fully human life on one strand alone.

The balance of this chapter describes a utopian model of what a reconstruction of schools in the image of the double helix might be like. The model explores the implications of the metaphor in four areas: (1) curriculum, teaching and learning, (2) decision-making, (3) assessment, supervision, and staff development, and (4) organization of space and time. It is an ideal, offered not in expectation that its faithful implementation is possible, or even desirable, but rather as a guide for making choices in the inevitably messy real world which is always demanding of compromise.

Because our society as currently constructed values the qualities of the either/or world, and devalues, even denies, the values of the both/and world, emphasis is placed on the both/and world, particularly from the perspective of women. Interested readers will have no trouble locating material on school administration, organization, and leadership from the perspective of the above-the-fault world, but little or nothing is available about school administration, organization or leadership from the perspective of the below-the-fault world. The pyramid, as the dominant metaphor, has rendered the world below the fault invisible. The double helix brings the both/and world to consciousness and signals it as a subject worthy of serious study. As it is, it's as if biologists have so far directed all their efforts to mapping the genes only one strand of DNA to the exclusion of the other. My intent is not to replace one omission with another, but rather to highlight that about which little is known, and to begin the complex task of synthesis.

The particular focus on women reflects my personal experience and knowledge. The entire story of the "both/and" world, however, will not be complete until the story is also told from the perspective of people of color.

Both/and Qualities

Their are five qualities represented by the both/and strand of the double helix which enrich schooling:

1. *Collaboration*—the ability to work in a group, eliciting contributions from and offering support to each member, creating a synergistic environment for everyone.
2. *Caring*—the development of an affinity for the world and people in it, translating moral commitment to action.
3. *Courage*—the capacity to move ahead into the unknown, testing new ideas in the world of practice, willingness to take risks.
4. *Intuition*—the ability to give equal weight to experience and abstraction, mind and heart.
5. *Vision*—the ability to formulate and express original ideas, persuading others to consider options in new and different ways.

The naming of these qualities evolved from the work of a group of women school administrators[1] joined together in the NorthEast Coalition of Educational Leaders.[2] With support and facilitation from Peggy McIntosh, the group met over a period of a year in 1986–87, struggling to identify the nature of their work as administrators which they knew from experience distinguished their practice from that of most other (male) administrators around them, and which was missing from the received wisdom of their graduate educations in administration. Since that time, Sally Helgeson has published *The Female Advantage*, which describes some of the same themes in the work of women in business. The work of both the NECEL group and

Helgeson are first steps in the project to recognize, name, value, and teach those qualities of the both/and world which enrich schooling.

Although this naming of the qualities of the both/and world as related to leadership originated in the experience of women, and in their analysis of that experience, it is important to remember that they are not qualities limited to women. Part of the power of the double helix as a symbol of a reconstruction of schooling lies in the hydrogen bonds that tie the two strands together. Passage from the world of one strand to the world of the other is possible and necessary; the qualities of each strand are essential to a complete understanding of schooling that draws on the totality of human experience.

At this point it is probably possible only for women and people of color to do the naming and the analysis of the qualities of the both/and world. Most white men see the world as constructed in pyramidal shape with the world below the fault essentially invisible and unexperienced and so they cannot talk about it or value it. There are exceptions, of course (see, for example, Wood 1991), and a long-term goal of reconstruction of schooling is to lead us all to see the world as constructed in the shape of the double helix so that each of us, female and male, of any race or ethnicity, moves with ease from one strand to the other.

So we will take the five both/and qualities of leadership as a staring point and examine each of the four areas of schooling: (1) curriculum, teaching, and learning, (2) decision-making, (3) assessment, supervision, and staff development, and (4) organization of space and time. We will find that use of the double helix, and the five qualities of the both/and world, as guides for envisioning how these four areas should be organized will lead us to select particular conceptualizations of these areas. In other words, thinking of schools from a both/and perspective will help us make either/or choices.

Implications of The Double Helix: Curriculum, Teaching, and Learning

Curriculum is the term we use to describe what should be the content of schooling. Choice is clearly required; deciding about a curriculum requires leaving some things out. How does the double helix guide us in making these choices of inclusion and exclusion?

Emily Style (1988) has suggested the metaphor of window and mirror as the description of the function of curriculum. "If the student is understood as occupying the dwelling of the self," she says, "education needs to enable the student to look through window frames in order to see the real-

411

ities of others and into mirrors in order to see her or his reality reflected," (p. 6). "Recent scholarship on women and minority men," she continues, "attests abundantly to the copious blind spots of the traditional curriculum. White males find, in the house of the curriculum, many mirrors to look in, and few windows which frame others' lives" (p.10). Style's metaphor captures the essence of the double helix; the either/or world of one strand, as we have noted, is predominantly the world of white male experience. Style notes that choices of inclusion and exclusion in curricula of traditionally constructed schools, reflecting the broken pyramid as they do, address only the world above the fault. Her advocacy of a multicultural curriculum which includes the experiences of all humanity is irrefutable from the perspective of the double helix. Each of us, regardless of gender, race or ethnicity, must find both windows and mirrors in the curriculum.

Another frame for analysis of the issue of curriculum resides within the concept of expertise. An expert is someone who knows more about a topic than others, enough to justify granting her the right to speak authoritatively about the topic, to be consulted about the topic by others. In a traditionally constructed school, the task at hand often reduces to the transfer of expertise through the teacher to the learner. What the experts know becomes what the learners should know. Expertise, however, traditionally defined, includes only the world above the fault of the broken pyramid, only one strand of the double helix, only knowledge as constructed predominantly by white males.

The question of expertise is further complicated by the role of the teacher. In traditionally constructed schools, often the teacher is not actually the expert, but rather a proxy for the expert. Her role is that of conduit, acting as the medium through which expertise is transferred to the learners. The actual expertise resides in textbooks, or district curriculum documents, or in standardized tests.

This situation is obviously hierarchical. Both learners and teachers are robbed of agency; neither actively makes choices about what to learn. In this case, the actual apex of the pyramid, the ultimate source of expertise, is anonymous—an unknown stable of textbook authors, an amorphous curriculum development committee, some poorly communicated set of standards devised somewhere else by somebody else with little personal meaning to particular learners and teachers. The consequences of this situation are well known—disinterested, unmotivated, even alienated learners, and technocratic teachers experiencing little joy in work deprived of most creativity.

Choices do need to be made, however. The world is an either/or place as well as a both/and place. Learners will be held accountable, both formally and informally to standards extending beyond the local situation.

What to teach cannot simply be a matter of whim on the part of learners and teachers. The curriculum must be *both* particular, personal and meaningful, *and* general, comprehensive, and abstract. In a reconstructed school, curriculum would be formed at a broad level through consideration of standards of the disciplines, expectations of the community, but also interpreted through consideration of the interests and experiences of the learners in particular classrooms.

The issue of balance between the particular, personal, and meaningful, and the general, comprehensive, and abstract leads us directly into questions of teaching and learning. Here again the experience of women is a rich source. A conceptualization of teaching from a both/and perspective, a feminist pedagogy, exists (see, for example, Culley and Portuges 1985). Essential to feminist teaching is respect for the experience of learners as text, and commitment to teaching as dialogue. Such a conceptualization of teaching contrasts sharply to teaching as transfer of expert knowledge, that is knowledge constructed from the perspective of only one segment of humanity, which forces teaching into a monologue where the teacher "professes" to passive students.

In the daily life of each classroom, these different conceptualizations of teaching have profound implications for teachers and learners. I am mindful of an elementary teacher teaching in a rural part of Connecticut who said to me once, while discussing the curricular decisions she makes, "At the beginning of the year, they voted that they lived on the Pacific Ocean so I knew I couldn't teach the tundra. I had to begin where they are." The tundra is officially in the fourth-grade curriculum of her district, but her valuing of her students' realities led her to ignore the prescription.

The significance of this teacher's decision can be appreciated further by considering conceptualizations of learning. Here again the double helix guides us to a choice. Just as recent scholarship has shed light on the limitations of the traditional curriculum, so too has recent scholarship shed light on the limitations of the traditional view of learning as filling an empty vessel, or receiving established wisdom. Catherine Fosnot (1989) views learning as an *act* in which learners construct personal meaning by connecting new information to structures of meaning already built within their minds. So it is that the tundra can become meaningful, and thus truly learned, only as learners can connect it to existing structures of meaning. In this teacher's judgment, for students living on the East Coast, but voting that they live near the Pacific Ocean, such connections are not yet possible.

A curriculum functioning as window and mirror is a caring approach to choice, valuing as it does the experience of all. Feminist pedagogy is a caring way of teaching, regarding teaching, as it does, as a dialogue in which the voice of each is important and listening to all is expected. A constructivist view of learning is a caring approach to learning, entailing as it does respect for personal meaning. Each of these three conceptualizations is collaborative; the classroom functions as a group in which the contribution of each is essential and learning is a synergistic process in which the materials each can draw upon to construct personal meaning are ever enlarged by the contributions of others. Learners serve at times as teachers, and teacher is at times a learner. Each of these conceptualizations draws upon intuition in addition to intellect, striking the balance between heart and mind, experience and abstraction. Each of these conceptualizations requires courage to implement because they are not understood within the world of pyramids. To those who know only the world of one strand of the double helix, such ideas may appear visionary to the point of impracticality; to those who know both worlds, they appear self-evident.

Expertise of the teacher drawing on these qualities of the both/and strand of the double helix becomes redefined as responsibility for the flow of dialogue in the classroom. Expertise becomes making the exquisite decisions about when to pursue what appear as tantalizing tangents and when to pursue the main idea relentlessly; about what topics will be most successful in assisting students to construct personal meanings about the world, and most successful in nurturing development of essential skills; about what materials to gather and sources to suggest. The teacher in such a classroom becomes the agent for hanging mirrors and opening windows.

Implications of The Double Helix: Decision-Making

Some decisions must be made every day such as the pedagogical decisions teachers make on the spot in deciding how to respond to a student comment, or whether or not the moment is propitious for introducing a brand new concept. Other decisions about the organization of a school and about the rules and norms governing the interactions of the people working within it are made deliberately removed from the exigencies of the moment. What guidance does the image of the double helix give us about who and how such organizational decisions should be made?

The message of the pyramid on this topic is so well known as to not need discussion. However, sometimes the daily norms within which we lead our lives slip below our consciousness. Any effort to examine these norms, much less change them, requires that they be explicitly laid out before us. So it is worthwhile stating that the superintendent sits at the apex of the pyramid above the principals and other middle managers who sit above the teachers who sit above the students. Power, prestige, information, and wealth reside in greatest quantity at the top and diminish rapidly with movement down the pyramid. This means the superintendent ultimately knows the most, has the ultimate authority and responsibility to decide, and gets the credit and blame for whatever goes right and wrong.

Examining just the flow of information immediately reveals the fundamental flaw in this structure. Superintendents do not always know the most; in some situations, they actually know the least. The pyramidal structure actually deprives them of information, prohibited as it is from flowing up the pyramid. The hydrogen bonds of the double helix tying one strand to the other suggest an entirely different information flow; rather than being limited to one way, information in a school reconstructed in the image of the double helix would flow freely in all directions. Access to information now limited to one role or another would improve the decision making of each.

The intertwined strands of the double helix suggest other changes in a reconstructed school as well. Decision-making becomes a collaborative process where role alone neither grants nor withholds authority and responsibility for decisions. The concept of shared decision-making, sometimes called teacher empowerment or school restructuring, has been widely discussed in the educational literature of the eighties (Conley et al. 1988). Under whatever name, the essential idea that decisions about the organization of a school are the right and responsibility of all mature members of that school is fundamental to the double helix.

In addition to its fundamental collaborative nature, shared decision making draws on other both/and qualities as well. In a reconstructed school, intuition is valued in the process of making decisions. Hard data and reason are not devalued; the essential difference in schools constructed in the image of the double helix is that intuition is not automatically dismissed as a tool for decision-making as it often is in pyramidal schools. From recent work on learning styles (McCarthy 1990), we know that some of us naturally and effectively make decisions using our reason while other equally as naturally and effectively make decisions using intuition. People speaking with the voice of intuition are sought and heeded in reconstructed schools, and when the occasion requires it, the different messages of reason and intellect are weighed equally, and a final choice is made based on grounds other than the source of the message.

Decisions made in a reconstructed school also reflect caring. The moral dimension of our lives in such a school assumes equal importance to the rational, technical side of our lives. Decisions are made because they are the most efficient and the most economical, but they are also made because they are right and compassionate. The conflict inevitable in such a complex approach is acknowledged and faced. Courage will be required at times to make the unpopular choice whichever it may be, and courage will be required at other times when it is necessary to acknowledge that a wrong choice was made. However, in a caring environment, the line between taking risks and failing at times, and incompetence, will be generously drawn; it will be safe to fail.

Implications of The Double Helix: Assessment, Supervision, and Staff Development

Assessment means making judgments about the quality of something. In schools, both learners and teachers are assessed. How does considering schools in the image of the double helix help us think about this complex and often controversial topic?

The only reasonable standard by which to judge the success of schools is the purpose for which they exist in the first place. Have students learned what we want them to learn, and are they able to do what they need to be able to do? Use of the overall purpose of schools as the standard by which to judge their performance requires that we know exactly what it is that we want students to learn and be able to do. This point leads us right back to the topic of curriculum. When considering that topic, we said that choices about what to teach must be made at a broad level extending beyond the local context, but also interpreted within the context of particular classrooms. The necessity of clarity about student outcomes becomes even more apparent as we consider them as the only reasonable standards for making judgments.

In schools constructed in the image of the double helix, expected student outcomes include knowledge, skills and attitudes characteristic of the both/and strand in addition to the either/or strand. Using the five qualities of the both/and strand as a lens to consider what this knowledge and these skills and attitudes might be is illuminating. Using this standard, we could judge ourselves successful only if we could demonstrate that the learners we have taught are caring persons who have developed an affinity for the world and people in it and have displayed the ability and the will to translate moral commitment into action. Our successful learners would have demonstrated the skill of working in groups contributing themselves, and eliciting and considering the contributions of others. Our successful learners would have demonstrated respect for the voice of intuition both by solving problems intuitively themselves, and by listening to the intuition of others, particularly if their own preferred learning style predominantly employs abstract reasoning. Our successful learners would have demonstrated courage by taking risks in the classroom, daring to be wrong on occasion. Our successful learners would have taken their first steps towards developing a personal vision of possibility by formulating and pursuing original ideas and encouraging classmates to join them in exploring the ramifications of their ideas.

Clarity of student outcomes is the first essential step for conducting an assessment of schooling. The second is choosing the method by which to make assessments. Traditionally we have done this by using a variety of standardized tests. Nationally normed achievement tests, state mastery tests, College Board tests are among the possibilities. All of these share the common feature of being decontextualized, multiple choice tests. They probably do give some indication of student mastery of the skills they are designed to measure, but mastery of such skills is only part of the story in schools constructed in the image of the double helix. Such tests obviously do not begin to assess the qualities of the both/and strand of the double helix. Valid assessments of these qualities must occur within their natural contexts; we must watch groups at work and take note of learners' responses to problems we pose and to problems that arise spontaneously in the flow of everyday classroom life. Both/and qualities are by their very nature cyclical, repetitive and embedded in the situation.

Once again, consideration of a topic in the image of the double helix guides us in making choices about an element of schooling. In this case, it is clear that current experimentation with performance assessment, or authentic assessment, is a development to be welcomed and supported.

The *Common Core of Learning*, published by the Connecticut State Department of Education (1987), is an example of a document specifying student outcomes broadly enough to leave room for the particular interpretation so essential to curriculum choices in schools constructed in the image of the double helix, but also specific enough to be useful in directing choices about how such assessments should be formulated. It organizes student outcomes into three areas: (1) attitudes and attributes, a section addressing many both/and qualities so often left out of statements of student outcomes; (2) understandings and applications, and (3) skills, two sections which specify traditional student outcomes, broadly stated. Cognizant that the familiar multiple-choice tests do not adequately address many student outcomes, the Connecticut State Department of Education is developing a series of performance assessments intended to produce a more complete picture of student learning.

Given that success in achieving student outcomes is the ultimate standard by which we judge the success of schooling, how then do we assess teachers?

In schools constructed in the image of the pyramid, teacher assessment, usually called teacher evaluation, reflects all the invidious hierarchical values of that metaphor. Evaluation is something done to teachers by persons above them on the pyramid who, by virtue of their position, have more knowledge and power than do teachers. As we have seen in the section on decision making, such assumptions embedded in the pyramidal organization of schools are not necessarily true, and furthermore, such an approach to teacher assessment denies the both/and quality of collaboration.

The standards by which such evaluation of teachers is done in traditional schools are generally descriptions of desired teacher inputs. Typical teacher evaluation systems reflect the results of the product-process research of the last twenty years or so. Generic lists of teacher behaviors found to be correlated to student achievement are used by observers to render judgments about the quality of teachers' performance. The use of such abstract, decontextualized standards is appropriate from the perspective of the either/or strand of the double helix, but, as always, when considering things from the perspective of both strands, this approach becomes only part of the story. How can teacher assessment be different in schools constructed in the image of the double helix?

The answer to this question leads back to the issue of expertise. Early in every teacher's career, and for a longer period in a few teachers' careers, there is little question that many people in a school know more about teaching than the novice. Also we know that novices need external standards by which to guide their decision-making while they are accumulating enough experience to create confidence in their own judgments about the situations before them. In these cases, judgments about a teacher's performance by another using external standards is necessary; it's also helpful when accompanied by specific suggestions.

Most teachers mature beyond this point and develop wise professional judgment grounded in both abstract knowledge about good teaching and the specifics of the particular classroom. Now the assumption of greater knowledge being a function of position on pyramid becomes especially dysfunctional. Persons higher up on the pyramid probably do not have more abstract knowledge about teaching than these mature teachers, and they definitely have less knowledge about the specifics of each classroom. Assessments of teachers conducted in the traditional way in these cases are practically useless. Furthermore, they are often demeaning and alienating to the teachers undergoing them, and even unsettling to some administrators who understand the falseness of them, but feel trapped by the expectations of the pyramid. Finally, they fail to focus on student outcomes, the only standard truly a measure of the success of schooling.

In schools constructed in the image of the double helix, for mature teachers, focus shifts from judgments of them to judgments by them. They are in the best position to conduct the complex, contextual assessments necessary for finding out if learners are successful, particularly when considering qualities of the both/and strand. The role of others in schools becomes

418

one of assisting them in addressing the issues raised by their assessments. And so we arrive at the topics of supervision and staff development.

For mature teachers making complex assessments of the learning of their students in all ways, the purposes of supervision and staff development become redefined. Rather than tools for fixing the deficiencies of teachers (often camouflaged as needs as in "needs assessment"), supervision and staff development in schools constructed in the image of the double helix become opportunities for collaborative problem solving. The problems are those of learners identified by teachers, and the topics are those collaboratively judged to be most useful for solving these problems (see Regan et al. 1992).

Implications of The Double Helix: Organization of Space and Time

Teachers work in rooms isolated from one another under schedules that prevent them from talking to one another. Any activity which takes them away from children is devalued. Such is the organization of space and time in schools constructed in the image of the pyramid. Because the value of collaboration is not understood in such schools, there is no reason to arrange space and time so that teachers may interact. Because the hierarchical value system of the pyramid mirrors the factory from which it emerged, teachers, the workers, remain on the line with the products, the students. The pyramidal model of organization does not contain any other conceptualization of the use of teachers' time.

In schools constructed in the image of the double helix, these arrangements of space and time must be drastically changed. Of the four qualities of the both/and strand of the double helix, it is the valuing of collaboration that most insistently requires redesign of this aspect of school functioning. The synergistic environment that results from collaboration is just as necessary for administrators and teachers as it is for learners. Teachers need access to the counsel of one another as they grapple with their enormous responsibility of leading each learner to success. Good ideas when added together total a sum greater than that of each idea standing alone. Administrators too need the counsel of teachers who also need the counsel of administrators. The planning needed to allocate resources, to design helpful staff development programs, to troubleshoot the unexpected, can occur most successfully when the knowledge and experience of everyone is pooled.

We have circled back to the topic of decision-making. Collaborative decision-making is seriously impeded by the traditional structure of schools, and we need to experiment with many new ways of organizing space and time. Once again, considering schooling in the image of the double helix leads us to make judgments about current ideas. Projects like the Coalition of Essential Schools, which allocates time in high school schedules into blocks, merit our encouragement and support. Smaller changes like the introduction of peer coaching into schools, or institution of common planning time characteristic of middle-school organization are also steps in the right direction. Perhaps the hiring of certified teachers as permanent substitutes who know the curriculum and children of each school could be used to enable teachers to leave their classrooms more frequently without the guilt of thinking that they have abandoned their only important responsibility to the hands of an unqualified person. However it is achieved, flexibility in arrangements of time and space, and a change in attitude which comes to value time away from students as essential to successful teaching as is time with them, are both fundamental to schools reconstructed in the image of the double helix.

Schools Reconstructed in The Image of the Double Helix

In an utopian world, the essential characteristics of schools reconstructed in the image of the double helix would be these:

1. The curriculum would be a broadly stated set of student outcomes including *both* elements of the canon of the either/or strand *and* new elements from the both/and strand of the double helix. This curriculum would be interpreted in specific classrooms to reflect the interests and experiences of the particular learners, serving as window and mirror for all.

2. Learning would be conceptualized as a construction of personal meaning by learners. Teachers would assist through use of a pedagogy which elicits the voice of each learner and draws on the experience of learners as text. Teacher expertise would be defined as ability to make instructional decisions that balance the general, comprehensive, and abstract aspects of the curriculum with the particular, personal, and meaningful.

3. Decisions about the organization of a school would be made collaboratively, drawing on the knowledge and experience of all roles, and seeking both the voices of intuition and reason.

4. Assessment would focus on student outcomes with understanding that complete assessment of the learnings of *both* the either/or strand *and* the both/and strand require both traditional objective, decontextualized measures as well as subjective, situated measures.

5. Assessment of teachers, with supervisory help, would be done of novice teachers, and those who are slow to develop professional judgment, using external standards.
6. For those teachers whose professional judgment has matured, the focus of assessment would shift from assessments of them to assessments of student learning by them.
7. Supervision and staff development would focus on issues raised by teachers as they consider the results of their assessments of student learning.
8. Space and time would be organized flexibly, enabling teachers to interact extensively with each other, and with administrators.

Schools organized with these characteristics would give formal expression to the both/and qualities of caring, collaboration, intuition, vision, and courage. They would draw on the totality of human experience, facilitating the movement of each person back and forth from one strand of the double helix to another. In and of themselves, they would be the enactment of a vision of how schools could be otherwise than they are.

Notes

1. Portions of this paper were previously published in the author's "Not for Women only: School Administration as a Feminist Activity," *Teachers College Record*, 91(4): 565–77.
2. The Group, entitled Future Directions: Reconceiving Women and Leadership, included Paulie Brading, Gwen Brooks, Cynthia Dubea, Carol Eaton, Vicki Hornus, Bethene LeMahieu. Eleanor McNamara, Helen Regan, and Susan Stevenson.
3. Northeast Coalition of Educational Leaders, 83 Boston Post Road, Subdury, MA. 01776.

Bibliography

Conley, S. C., Schmidle, T., and Shedd, J. B. (1988). Teacher preparation in the management of school systems. *Teachers College Record*, 90(2).

Connecticut State Department of Education. (1987). *Common core of learning*. Hartford: Connecticut State Department of Education.

Culley, M. and Portuges, C., (eds.). (1985). *Gendered styles: The dynamics of feminist teaching*. London: Routledge & Kegan Paul.

Fosnot, C. T. (1989). *Enquiring teachers enquiring learners: A constructivist approach to teaching.* New York: Teachers College Press.

Helgeson, S. (1990). *The female advantage: Women's ways of leadership.* New York: Doubleday.

Lakoff, G. and Johnson, M. L. (1980). *Metaphors we live by.* Chicago: University of Chicago Press.

McCarthy, B. (1990). *The 4MAT system.* Barrington, IL: Excel.

McIntosh, P. (1983). *Interactive phases of curriculum re-vision: A feminist perspective.* Working paper no. 124, Wellesley College Center for Research on Women.

Regan, H. B., Anctil, M., Dubea, C., Hofmann, J. M., and Vaillancourt, R. (1992). *TEACHER: A new definition and model for development and evaluation.* Philadelphia: RBS Publications.

Style, E. (1988). Curriculum as window and mirror. Listening for all voices: Gender balancing the school curriculum. Monograph, Oak Knoll School, Summit, NJ.

Wood C. (1991). Maternal teaching: Revolution of kindness. *Holistic Education Review,* 4(2).

TWENTY-THREE

Women Leading: An Agenda for A New Century

Diane M. Dunlap

Looking back over the studies and arguments presented in this volume, what lessons have we learned? What new questions are raised? What old questions still remain for future study?

We started with women as the center of inquiry, listening to their voices, looking at their leadership practices, learning from their ideas. The women we listened to, and talked with, are "insiders" in the sense that they are trying to be leaders inside society's education institutions. However, they also often proved to be "outsiders" in the sense that they were perceived as being different from the traditional leader, if by no other reason than by being female.

The women leaders studied in the different research projects reported in this volume found or created "safe havens" in work settings that were often perceived as nonsupportive. Some reported creating safe work settings where collaborative experimentation was the supported norm, and some reported "modulating their voices" to provide maximum leadership with minimal disruption where norms were not so supportive. Many reported a sense of pain, isolation, frustration, anger. They reported learning to understand the differences between spoken and enacted values. They were opportunists in taking advantage of found opportunities to improve practice as they saw it. They celebrate leadership, and decry our limited understandings of what might be possible if institutions and peers supported innovative change led by women who care for others and themselves as much as they are powerful in their actions.

Setting an Agenda

One of the goals of this volume has been to challenge ourselves to begin to form a practice, policy and research agenda for the new century soon upon us. Agenda setting, as Cobb and Elder (1972) persuasively argued, is a political act. Setting an agenda implies identifying and prioritizing issues to be addressed. Some issues are deemed more worthy by the agenda setters than others; some make it onto the agenda and others do not. Those who set the agenda are exercising power, in drawing people's attention to certain issues, in rank ordering the issues to be addressed, and in excluding other issues from discussion.

In this final chapter, I draw upon the work that has been written for this volume as well as on work that has appeared in other sources. I also draw from the many intense discussions among chapter authors and others who have met with us over the past four years. On behalf of the many women and men who have brought this volume to publication, I point to knowledge gained and questions raised by this research, and to questions still to be addressed.

Each action arena is focused on a few key questions:

1. *Practice.* How do women lead? What does leading feel like for the leader? Does being female make a difference? Should it? How should women lead? Is there such a thing as "women's leadership style?" Does leadership practice differ from site-to-site, and group-to-group? Does it vary over time? What does leading in an educational organization look and feel like? Based on these findings, what should we teach each other about leadership? What should we stop teaching about leadership? What does practice today tell us about women leaders for tomorrow?

2. *Politics and policy.* What are the politics of women leading in education? What is the impact on individuals? What are the implications for women who chose to lead policy and political changes? What political actions are called for by these findings? What policies should we work to maintain or change? How well are existing policies being implemented and evaluated? What new policies and politics will emerge in the future for women leaders in education?

3. *Research and theory.* Based on these findings, what should we be studying/theorizing about in relationship to women leading in education? Where do our current theories fail us? Where will we need new theories for tomorrow?

We used these questions to build the text itself. The chapters in this volume are concerned with discrepant knowledge about what it means today in Western societies to be female and a leader in education. We have included work that focuses on leadership practice, on policy development and the politics of change, and on theoretical exploration. We have included work that looks at individuals in schools and colleges, that reports on groups working together at particular sites, and on groups working in schools and colleges. In this chapter, I have also looked across the separate studies for themes that are so pervasive that they emerge as institutionalized norms across society boundaries. In this way, we have attempted to "triangulate" our separate understandings of the practices of women leading in education in order to build a more pervasive picture of current practice. Thus grounded in the voices of women leaders and the stories of their leadership, we can begin to explore and build an emergent practice, policy and research agenda for the new century.

Agenda Issue 1: Gender and Leadership in Education

Do we need to continue to study how women lead, how politics and policy affect their leadership, and how theory-building might contribute to an increased understanding of leadership potential? The studies and theories in this volume answer a resounding, "Yes!" Do we know what effects gender has on leadership? A not so resounding, "Yes, No, Maybe." For the first time in written history, women are in many formal and informal leadership roles throughout our educational organizations. They lead with individual differences in a societal context where there are still deep societal tensions between expectations of what it means to be a "good woman" and what it means to be a "good leader."

Begin with the voices of individual women leading in educational organizations. Women lead in many ways. Some report that being female makes a difference; some argue that it does not or should not. Some argue that any gender difference is positive; others argue that it is not entirely clear what the difference is, or could be, or should be. Questions about the role and magnitude of gender differences continues to be a matter of great and heated disagreement, and is played out in the daily lives of all men and women.

The larger issues that face women in education—and women in society as a whole—are often reduced in reality to a personal, daily struggle. (Coleman and Harris)

[T]here are some specific lessons we've learned that may apply to others. First, learning to live with ambiguity is a milestone on the way to maturity, especially through the uncharted paths of feminism and ethnicity. Second, sharing control, as we did, may be the only way to keep a vision alive. Finally, a crucial element of leadership is the ability to listen, guide, and follow. (Coleman and Harris)

When I was asked to be superintendent, only two Ojibwe people had been administrators before me. Both were men: one died and one was dismissed. The superintendency had been primarily the domain of white men and I was taking over the role from an ex-Marine whose administrative style seemed straight out of the Desert Storm ethos that permeated the country that year. (Ford Slack and Cornelius)

The voices of women leaders are diverse. They immediately belie any idea of "women" as a homogenous category. From Matthews' interviews, four distinct points of view emerged: activists, advocates, isolates, and individualists. Women Matthews categorized as "activists" cared passionately about issues of gender equity and actively supported efforts to correct the imbalance of women in educational administration. Women categorized as "advocates" supported women, joined advocacy organizations, and expressed the view that women bring unique strengths to school administration. Women Matthews categorized as "isolates" detached themselves from issues related to equity and most didn't believe that sex discrimination really existed. Last, women categorized as "individualists" believed the individual, male or female, took precedence over the group. They did not promote women nor did they believe in any kind of countermeasures to correct the sex imbalance in school leadership. Echoes of these categories emerge in many of the other studies reported in this text.

Moreover, Collay and LaMar document the pervasive persistence of the old feminized role of internal maintenance for the external (male) tasks of the world. Even the stereotypical notion of the woman leader as the collaborative connector stands at risk.

Relationships and feeling of connectedness, so important among women, changed when these women took leadership. Though many of their colleagues saw them as important figures in the school, others viewed these teachers as threats. Why does connectedness change when female teachers take leadership? Can female teachers maintain relationships with other women when they are in a power position? How can we redefine power and leadership in feminist terms? This is indeed fertile ground for further investigation. (Troen and Boles)

My early years as an elementary teacher were marked by little attention to the concept of power. I made the assumption, as did many of my colleagues, that I had little power and that there were "ways around the system" to get creative things done, when necessary. (Hurty)

[D]espite the predominance of women working in the field, and despite the affinity of the field to what has been socially considered as women's issues, men have been featured as the public figures, researchers, and theorists. Regardless of the reasons, explanations, and causes of this disproportionate representation of males in positions of influence and power, there has been little acknowledgement, discussion, or awareness of the facts of such a selective tradition. (Chaille)

This pattern of gender differentiation in teacher staff development was evident in all eight of our project schools. In the role of teacher, women and men had different teaching responsibilities and social tasks. The female teaching principal or lead teacher frequently had the greatest personal stake in improving professional development opportunities for teachers, while the male superintendent continued to represent outside interests, suffer under community pressure, and talk about budget concerns. (Collay and LaMar)

Yet, the ways in which the leadership of women is perceived seem of a kind. There are wildly different understandings of what leadership is, of what it could be, and of what it should be. Not all leaders must have charisma, nor is a charisma bypass required to enjoy collaboration. We learn from these studies that leadership does not always require followers, nor does it require possession of a formal leadership position. None of these women spent much time on the old acorns of managerial or Machiavellian truth (for example, "When in trouble, blame the victims, shoot the wounded, bury the dead, and then get to the next town quick.")

We tried to get those old man models out of our heads, and tried to help others do the same. We had a vision of compassion that was more process, I guess. Leadership meant striving to be open, humorous and compassionate. (Ford Slack and Cornelius)

If you are willing to sacrifice your time, are a people-person, are organized and consider yourself on a mission, you are ready for administration. If any of these are lacking, administration may not make you happy. . . . If you like a neat and tidy job, this is not for you. (Quoted in Edson)

There are disparieties in how women leaders are viewed by themselves and others. There is great energy, pain, frustration, anger reported.

427

It is possible to mediate confusion and conceptual anxiety with love and humor, but now I think that pain is the inevitable companion of finding new and better ways to lead in schools. (Ford Slack and Cornelius)

None of these women were given any formal preparation; the mentors assigned to them gave hit-and-miss assistance . . . all three women reported feelings of isolation and turned to teachers and old friends rather than face the complex challenges of the principalship alone. (Hart)

School administrators often feel isolated even though they are constantly interacting with others. (Pence)

Perhaps this (minimal contact once every few years) is a sad commentary on the loneliness of administrative roles in general, where even minimal contact takes on great importance. (Edson)

Leadership is seen as many different things. It varies from situation to situation, and from person to person. Leadership is evolving, emerging, watching for opportunities that one could not predict in advance. Like Coleman and Harris, often leadership is defined as making a way for others to lead after you. It is not one thing for all people in all situations. It is humanly created. We can change our understandings of what is possible.

Several pervasive themes raise the issue of individual reproduction of institutionalized societal norms, of resistance to automatic reproduction of norms, and of interpreting the societal as personal.

It came as a shock to realize I had become everything I said I would not. I had changed my appearance, monitored my thoughts so they remained politically in tune with my board's stated objectives, and become capable of convincing myself I had done none of this. From the board's point of view, I had become a promotable female—one who could be appointed at some future date to help satisfy the Ontario government directive of fifty per cent representation by females in administration by the year 2000 while at the same time not causing any loss of male power. (Worrall)

While faculty were observed mentoring international students who pursued research topics addressing such areas as occupational stratification, migration patterns or family studies in their country of origin, minority women students addressing similar topics in their communities in the United States reported disparaging comments from faculty and graduate students. (Romero and Storrs)

Although women principals face unique problems of identity and integration, they do not translate their personal experiences into professional actions to assure greater equality for students or employers. They take a personalized view of their experience; they see their experiences as individual, even idiosyncratic, and fail to comprehend the more fundamental concept of how gender serves as a segregating factor in the culture of educational institutions. (Schmuck and Schubert)

Agenda Issue 2: Schools and Colleges as Organizations

The voices of women leaders are always raised in organizational context. Here we can learn about our schools and colleges as organizations that, by their very structures, promote or denigrate leadership.

That's the kind of thing where it depends on who you know. Who you hook up with. What's around. I mean there's no formal way to do it at all. And its been a problem. I constantly hear, "Oh so and so is working on this project and that project," and I think, "God, that's really interesting. I would love to do that, but how did they find out about it?" And that's part of the informal process. (Quoted in Romero and Storrs)

Be prepared to work hard, accept knocks as challenges and know how to give and take. Success is possible, but you still operate in a man's world with an "old boy network" of advancement. (Quoted in Edson)

Self-definition for administrative women then entails not only who they are, but who they are against the backdrop of the bureaucratic worlds in which they live. They struggle to live in male-dominated worlds that often do not accept them and yet tempt them with the promise of inclusion. (Cooper)

The teachers we studied succeeded despite the structure of the schools in which they worked. Despite administrators who cautioned them or thought they were "cute," despite other teachers who questioned their right to take authority, and despite the bureaucratic structure which placed them in a low-power position, these teachers prevailed. (Troen and Boles)

The standardization and uniformity characteristic of bureaucratic organizations seem to discourage caring in teaching. (McCall)

Not only was the subject matter of race and ethnicity not treated seriously (in the Sociology Department), but nonwhite scholars were systematically ignored and berated. (Romero and Storrs)

Not a pretty picture. As stated in the opening chapter, while many positive images of strong leaders emerge from these chapters, they coexist with equally strong, negative images of the heavy price paid by strong leaders. Invisibility. Silence. Inequality. Oppression. Missing viewpoints and perspectives. Contradictions. These words describe reality for educational leaders who struggle to integrate new perspectives of gender, race, and class in organizations. Our education institutions may be the backbone of our democratic societies, but they are also all too often the conservers of unequal traditions and norms.

The agenda for schooling which emerges from the voices of these caring teachers and administrators is first, let our education organizations be good places for student learning. Second, let our schools and universities be good places for adults to work and learn as well. The schools of tomorrow will never be the learning communities we seek is they continue to be structured and managed in ways that produce inequality and inequity. Learning and equity can co-exist, but not in a democracy of emperors. Organizations do not have to look like monkey islands of dominance. Organizations are human creations; we can change them.

Agenda Issue 3: On Being Socially Incongruent

Perhaps the most powerful theme that permeates these studies is the curious balance drawn by women leaders and the organizations which employ them between maintaining/reproducing/resisting current norms and challenging/undermining/re-creating new ideas of educational practice. This is perhaps captured best by the woman superintendent in Bell's study who said "You see, if I weren't [a superintendent], I might be radical." She is alluding at once to her notions about changing the membership rules and, at the same time, to the conservative occupational context of which those rules are a part. Being a professional in her occupational context involves not openly challenging the rules, but constantly working to transform them without being so outrageous as to be ejected from the academy.

Here is creative social incongruence. Sometimes deliberate and conscious, sometimes intuitive and unidentified even in the midst of the open practice of "norm-bending." Measured conflict is the norm. If leadership is defined as taking a step away from the norm, and being a "good woman" is defined as staying within the norms, these women leaders challenge our notions of leadership and gender by their lives.

But what a fine line social incongruence draws! Just enough, but not too much. Too much gets one thrown out of the game. Just enough, but not too little. Too little is invisibility, and absence from any agenda for change.

And how this challenges our ideas about conflict! Here, acceptance of conflict is a basic norm for leadership. Conflict is not only not bad, but it is a given set of conditions which women leaders provoke, which demands protection of the leader and those around her, and which argues for dramatically increased understanding of conflict resolution skills. Creative social incongruence also implies that where conflict is not present, there is probably dominance at work.

Agenda Issue 4: On Not Being Alone, On Not Taking The Fall Alone

A fourth agenda issue for the future can be seen in the contrast of individual focus and individual remedy that emerges as one reads the pages of this text. So often, even these strong and individualistic women leaders see themselves as loners and not as examples of larger societal norms. Edson posed the question of why women continued to seek principalships at all in the face of all of the undeniable barriers outlined in the literature on principal practice. She found women at every stage of her longitudinal study determined to "push the limits," to be realistic about the obstacles facing them, and to know that their goals were not easily attainable. Many of these women were still reluctant to believe that discrimination exists and were likely to continue to look only at their own skills and credentials as the most important sufficient and necessary measure for leadership.

On the other hand, Scherr's study of women who chose not to aspire to superintendencies indicates that not all women walk with determination into overwhelming obstacles. Some chose not to be formal leaders, even when the opportunity was before them. What is interesting is that the women in both Edson's and Scherr's studies tend to view their choices as isolated and idiosyncratic. They also view the models of leadership that surround them as the only models available and the current organizational structures of their educational institutions as a "given."

Leigh, Diane, and Ellen in Hart's study also experienced socialization to their new assignments as an individual, idiosyncratic process. Schmuck and Schubert report that the women in their study do not translate their personal experiences into professional actions and argue that, because they see their experiences as idiosyncratic, they fail to comprehend the more fundamental concept of how gender serves as a segregating factor in the culture of educational institutions.

The pattern here is to interpret one's choices *only* in a personal context. What is amazing to me as I look at the many powerful leaders brought together in the pages of this volume, is that *even these most powerful women do not tend to see the broad patterns.* Individual leadership choice is personal, but it is also clearly social and organizational. To only see the personal is to emphasize loneliness and exclusion as a consequence of one's individual difference. To see the personal as also social and organizational is to open the possibilities of support and inclusion within a group.

431

Let us argue for group remedies for group problems. Acker describes a teachers workplace culture in primary schools where features of the organizational environment make it easier to manage in a collaborative, caring style. Valentine describes a woman-dominated work setting. Schmuck documents the power of advocacy organizations where revelation of one's experience can be shared and understood. Edson and Pence document the value of mentor relationships when they can bridge the sense of individual isolation, and Bell argues persuasively that ambivalence about gender can be a barrier to support to and from women colleagues. She notes that pressure to disaffiliate from other women comes from embedded sexism in the traditions of any occupation. Education is not excluded. Women leaders in education who yield to this pressure are vulnerable to an extraordinary sense of isolation and are inhibited from collective educational/political action for social change.

Transcendence may be moving from independent "get-ahead-ism" to group "get-ahead-ism." Leadership is always a political activity. Make it consciously so. Share that understanding, and you are not alone. Voices differ, but they can be joined in chorus instead of singing alone.

Agenda Issue 5: A Call for Action

Developing an agenda for future practice and research also means asking a series of questions about action. In the many conversations about our research and our professional lives that birthed this volume, we repeatedly touched upon three kinds of questions related to women leading in education—questions about educational practice, questions about political action, and questions about research and theory. We also recognized that, for any given question, there are multiple levels of action or intervention. The levels of action range from a level focused on individual experience, through group leadership within one site or across multiple sites, to organizational levels like districts and university systems, to the societal levels of national or international politics and institutionalized norms.

A question raised about women leading in education can be examined at any of these levels. It can be analyzed in the practice, policy, or theoretical action arenas. We used the combination of action arenas and levels of analysis to create this volume, and I return to it here to bring together some of the themes that emerge from the text.

Take gender, for example. At the individual level, each person can look at the action arena of (1) practice: What do I do with my day, where gender is an asset or barrier? Where is the best use of my time to extend my goals related to gender in my daily life? How can I improve my daily practice so that gender is an asset and not a barrier in reaching my practice goals? (2) politics and policy: Where do the politics of my setting interfere with my action goals on the basis of gender? Where can I work to change the politics or policies that directly affect my daily practice so that gender is not a barrier to my goal achievement? or (3) research and theory: What research do I need to do in my work setting so I better understand the interactions of gender with my goals? Where do theories need modified to better state the interactions of gender with my goals?

However, as extensive as these questions may be, they are not complete if the same kinds of questions are not asked at the level of (1) group/site: Who affects my daily practice on the basis of gender? How can I make those affects positive by changing policy or politics at my site? What data do I need to collect to understand better the interactions around gender at my site? (2) organization: How do my school or college attitudes about gender affect my daily practice? How can my organizational politics or policies be influenced to make gender affects positive for my daily practice? and (3) society. Using this framework to sort out goals and actions helps make sure that when an individual-level action is chosen, it is to resolve individual-level problems and not to resolve organizational-level problems. If society values about gender (our example) are a pervasive issue that affects all levels, then it is necessary and useful to think through what actions must go on at all levels to make individual-level actions sustainable.

Another way in which this framework is useful is in identifying gaps in knowledge. For example, in the first chapter, Gosetti and Rusch note that most current leadership theory is not very useful in predicting leadership behaviors of male or female leaders in the schools and colleges of tomorrow. Twelve subsequent chapters of this book make specific recommendations about improving training for leadership, and all of the chapters and studies provide new perspectives on leadership theory. Some of the specific recommendations are aimed at individuals and sites of practice; others are aimed at the organizational or societal level. Here are some pieces of new knowledge that partially fill the identified gap in leadership theory.

Hurty and Regan also present arguments for how new theory might be framed. Hurty uses individual experiences to reframe power theory; Regan uses a theoretical model based in the school site to argue for new theory formulation. Here are two more possible pieces of the framework. By identifying (*a*) what we know doesn't work, (*b*) what we know does work, and (*c*) using the framework of action arenas and levels of interaction, an agenda emerges for future practice and research on women leading in education.

Conclusion

Part of the core set of reasons for pursuing the studies and theoretical arguments in this volume is in answer to Noddings (1990) lament about the absence of feminist scholarship from educational administration as a field of study. It has been our intent to add the voices of many women leaders to our understanding of leadership in schools and universities. We have included studies from related but different nations, so our study will not be completely parochial. We have focused on issues of gender consciousness, but have tried to do so in ways that raise additional questions of the interaction of gender understandings with those of ethnicity, race, age, social class, national origin, and location, and other aspects of organizational and personal identity. We have focused on leadership, but have tried to regularly base the view of leadership in the classrooms and pedagogy that make educational organizations distinctive from other types of organizations. All of these objectives have been met, and add feminist scholarship to the field of educational administration.

Our view of the future also framed this volume. Our choices came from our understanding of the future(s) of education (and society) as unarguably more heterogeneous, more transforming, more unpredictable, and endlessly challenging. By the act of placing women leaders at the heart of the conversation, we argue for deliberate and continued examination of the old public and private domains of family and organization as they relate to men and women is schools and colleges. Old notions of separate, independent spheres of home and school already do not serve us well in today's intertwined realities, and will not carry the world successfully to a positively transformed future.

We argue for inclusion of these issues in any discussion of leadership in education: multiple aspects of gender and other social constructs which may impede the development of good education; caring, connectedness, and collaboration as part of the power that goes with leadership in any form; and thorough reexamination of the structures of our educational organizations wherever they limit leadership. The common theme that is woven throughout the volume is the deliberate, full-hearted development of learning communities that support learning and the learners. There is one destination. However, there are as many paths to that destination as there are successful leaders, small groups ready to form learning communities, and schools and universities ready to provide nurturing environments for learners in learning communities. This is the agenda for our new century—using all we know and can learn to cut ourselves a brand-new path to the learners of tomorrow.

Bibliography

Cobb, R. and C. Elder. (1972). *Participation in American politics: The dynamics of agenda-building.* Boston: Allyn and Bacon.

Noddings, N. (1990). Feminist critiques in the professions. In C. Cazden (ed.), *Review of Research in Education,* 16. Washington, DC: American Educational Research Association.

CONTRIBUTORS

Sandra Acker is Professor in the Department of Sociology in Education, the Ontario Institute for studies in Education, Toronto, Canada. She is the editor of *Teachers, Gender, and Careers* (Falmer Press, 1989) and the author of *Gendered Education: Sociological Reflections on Women, Teaching and Feminism* (Open University Press, 1994).

Colleen S. Bell is Associate Professor and Gordon B. Sanders Chair in Education at Hamline University in St. Paul, Minnesota. She is completing work with Susan Chase on a federally-funded study that focuses on women's experiences in the superintendency.

Katherine Boles is a visiting scholar at Harvard University. She was awarded a Spencer Post-Doctoral Fellowship in 1993 to study the development of the Learning/Teaching Collaborative, a teacher-initiated school restructuring project.

Christine Chaillé is Professor of Education at Portland State University in Portland, OR.

Willi Coleman is Associate Professor of Ethnic Studies at California Polytechnic State University, San Luis Obispo, CA. Her most recent publication is a 1993 essay in *Double stitch: Black women write about mothers and daughters,* P. Bell Scott et al (eds.).

Michelle Collay is Associate Professor of Education and Director of Graduate Education Programs at Hamline University, St. Paul, Minnesota. Her current research focuses on teacher empowerment and school-college collaboration.

Joanne Cooper is an Assistant Professor of Educational Administration at the University of Hawaii. Her most recent publications discuss the use of narrative in the study of school administration in the *International Journal of Qualitative Studies in Education* and organizational change in a community college in the *Review of Higher Education.*

Patricia Cornelius is Superintendent of the Bug-O-Nay-be-Shig School in northern Minnesota.

Diane M. Dunlap is Professor and Dean of the Graduate School at Hamline University, St. Paul, Minnesota. Her most recent publication is a chapter entitled, "Women in higher education administration in the USA" in Julia Evetts' (ed.) 1994 *Women and Careers.* (Longman)

Sakre Edson currently works part time in the nonprofit sector, while co-parenting four young children.

P. J. Ford Slack is Assistant Professor in Educational Leadership at the University of St. Thomas, St. Paul, Minnesota. Her research interests include the uses of drama, storytelling and narrative as qualitative research.

Patricia Harris is a buyer at California Polytechnic State University, San Obispo, CA. She is past Chair of the Advisory Board of the Center for Women and Ethnic Issues, and current Chair of the Cal Poly Staff Council.

Ann Weaver Hart is Professor of Educational Administration and Dean of the Graduate School at the University of Utah. Her book, *Principal Succession: Establishing Leadership in Schools,* was published in 1993 by SUNY Press.

Kathleen Hurty, a former public school principal, is an administrator with the National Council of Churches nurturing a nationwide network of ecumenical and interreligious organizations. She works with organizations in the process of transformation and with professionals and volunteers interested in exploring collaborative leadership.

Helen LaMar is Assistant Professor of Education at Minot State University, Minot, South Dakota.

Evelyn Nelson Matthews is Principal of Spencer Butte Middle School, Eugene Public Schools, in Eugene, OR.

Ava L. McCall is Assistant Professor in the Curriculum and Instruction Department at the University of Wisconsin Oshkosh, Oshkosh, Wisconsin. Her current research is studying students' responses to a multicultural, social reconstructionist social studies methods course as well as developing feminist pedagogy as a means of raising equity issues with students.

L. Jean Pence is Principal of Merlo Station High School and the Arts and Communication High School at C. E. Mason/Beaverton School District in Beaverton, OR. These campuses are 21st Century Schools that provide innovative learning environments for students.

Penny Poplin Gosetti is an Assistant Professor of Education at the University of Toledo, Ohio. Her current research focuses on issues of gender and privilege in private religious high schools.

Helen B. Regan is Associate Professor of Education at Connecticut College, New London, CT. She is currently working on a book about the contributions of women's experience to the conceptualization of school leadership.

Mary Romero is Associate Professor of Sociology at the University of Oregon. Her most recent publication is 1993's *Maid in the U.S.A.*

Edith A. Rusch is Assistant Professor in the Department of Educational Leadership at the University of Toledo, Toledo, OH. Her teaching and research focuses on democracy and schooling, diversity issues in leadership and organizational theory, and school restructuring.

Mary Woods Scherr is Assistant Professor of Education at the University of San Diego. Her research focuses on women as educational leaders and on issues of power and privilege.

Patricia A. Schmuck is Professor and Chair of the Department of Educational Administration at Lewis and Clark College, Portland, Oregon. She has authored books and articles about women in educational administration including, *Women Educators* and *Educational Policy & Management: Sex Differentials.*

Jane Schubert is Director of the Improving Educational Quality Project at the Institute for International Research, Arlington, VA.

Charol Shakeshaft is Professor of Education at Hofstra University NY and author of *Women in Educational Administration* (Sage, 1987, 1989).

Debbie Storrs is a doctoral candidate in the Department of Sociology at the University of Oregon where she is completing her dissertation on the topic of "mixed race". Her areas of interest include women of color in the U.S., the racialization of peoples and problems, and multicultural education.

Vivian Troen is a 4th grade teacher at the Edward Devotion School in Brookline, MA and project director of the Learning/Teaching Collaborative, a teacher-initiated school restructuring project. She is also on the faculty at Wheelock College, in Boston, MA.

Patricia A. Valentine is Professor of Nursing on the Faculty of Nursing at the University of Alberta, Canada, Edmonton, Alberta.

Alyson M. Worrall is a recent graduate of the Master of Education program at the Ontario Institute for Studies in Education, University of Toronto, Toronto, Ontario. She is a teacher and Department Head of Mathematics in a secondary school in Ontario, Canada.

INDEX

To the reader: Because this work is a collection of writings and studies by various authors, similar concepts may be discussed with differing terminology. The index subsumes synonymous terms from the text. Single references can be found in the bibliographic list at the end of each chapter. Chapters (Chap.) and notes (n.) are so indicated.